Reference Books Bulletin, 2002–2003

A compilation of evaluations September 2002 through August 2003

Prepared by the American Library Association Reference Books Bulletin Editorial Board

Edited by Mary Ellen Quinn
Compiled by Keir Graff

BOOKLIST Publications
Chicago 2004

Copyright 1996, 2004 by the American Library Association.

Permission to quote any review in full or in part must be obtained from the Office of Rights and Permissions of the American Library Association. Permission to quote a review in full will be granted only to the publisher of the work reviewed.

Library of Congress Catalog Card Number 73-159565

International Standard Book Number 0-8389-**8264-6**
International Standard Serial Number 8755-0962

Printed in the United States of America

Cover design by Jim Lange

Contents

- v   Preface
- vi   Reference Books Bulletin Editorial Board
- vii   Contributing Reviewers
- 1   Encyclopedia Update, 2002
- 6   Special Features
- 24   Reference on the Web

Reviews
- 37   Generalities
- 42   Philosophy, Psychology, Religion
- 44   Sociology, Anthropology, Political Science
- 51   Business, Economics, Resources
- 52   Law, Public Administration, Social Problems and Services
- 57   Education, Commerce, Customs
- 59   Language
- 61   Science
- 68   Medicine, Health, Technology, Management
- 73   Fine Arts, Decorative Arts, Music
- 75   Performing Arts, Recreation
- 80   Literature
- 89   Geography, Biography
- 94   History

Indexes
- 103   Subject Index
- 105   Title Index

Preface

The volume before you is the 35th annual compilation of reviews and other features as they appeared in *Reference Books Bulletin* from September 2002 through August 2003. It has been another great year for reference publishing. I believe that the quality of reference books continues to increase. The reviews from *Reference Books Bulletin* also point out instances where high standards may not have been met. In other words, reference and collection development librarians can continue to rely upon *Reference Books Bulletin* to assist them in making informed choices in this era of very tight budgets.

I would like to thank Mary Ellen Quinn, editor, and Keir Graff, editorial assistant, for their tireless efforts throughout the review process. And where would we be without the editorial board and contributing reviewers? I never cease to be amazed at the knowledge and dedication of our contributing reviewers. I would also like to thank the great folks at *Booklist* and ALA Publishing. Additionally, I would like to thank the University of Dayton for their continued support.

Jack O'Gorman,
Chair,
Reference Books Bulletin Editorial Board,
2003–2004

Reference Books Bulletin Editorial Board, 2002–2003

Jack O'Gorman, Reference Librarian, Roesch Library, University of Dayton, Dayton, Ohio, Chair.

Donald Altschiller, History Bibliographer, Mugar Library, Boston University, Boston, Massachusetts.

Barbara Bibel, Reference Librarian, Oakland Public Library, Oakland, California.

Christine Bulson, Adjunct Librarian, Milne Library, SUNY Oneonta, Oneonta, New York.

Susan Gardner, Reference/Instruction Librarian, Leavey Library, University of Southern California, Los Angeles, California.

Merle Jacob, Director of Library Collection Development, Chicago Public Library, Chicago, Illinois.

J. Sarah Paulk, Head Librarian, TTCPL, Tifton, Georgia.

Deborah Rollins, Head, Collection Services Department, Fogler Library, University of Maine, Orono, Maine.

Linda Loos Scarth, Reference Librarian, Busse Center Library, Mount Mercy College, Cedar Rapids, Iowa.

Cheryl Karp Ward, Penny Alumni Library, East Hartford High School, East Hartford, Connecticut.

Reference Books Bulletin Contributing Reviewers, 2002–2003

James D. Anderson, Professor, School of Communication, Information and Library Studies, Rutgers University, New Brunswick, New Jersey.

Susan Awe, Director, Business and Economics, Parish Memorial Library, University of New Mexico, Albuquerque, New Mexico.

John-Leonard Berg, Coordinator of Public Services, Karrmann Library, Platteville, Wisconsin.

Ken Black, Director of Teaching and Learning Technology, Dominican University, River Forest, Illinois.

Craig Bunch, Librarian, Coldspring-Oakhurst High School Library, Coldspring, Texas.

Nancy Cannon, Reference Librarian, Milne Library, SUNY Oneonta, Oneonta, New York.

Jerry Carbone, Director, Brooks Memorial Library, Brattleboro, Vermont.

Ann E. Cohen, Assistant Division Head, Information Center, Rochester Public Library, Rochester, New York.

Sharon E. Cohen, Boynton Beach, Florida.

Harold V. Cordry, Independent scholar, Baldwin, Kansas.

Charlotte Decker, Librarian, Children's Learning Center, Public Library of Cincinnati and Hamilton County, Cincinnati, Ohio.

Carole C. Deily, Reference Librarian, Plano Public Library System, Plano, Texas.

John Doherty, Librarian, Arts and Humanitied, Cline Library, Northern Arizona University, Flagstaff, Arizona.

Marie Ellis, Librarian IV Emeritus, University of Georgia Libraries, Athens, Georgia.

Stephen Fadel, Public Services Librarian, Everett Community College, Everett, Washington.

Lesley S. J. Farmer, Professor, CSU Long Beach, Long Beach, California.

Jack Forman, Public Services Librarian, San Diego Mesa College Library/LRC, San Diego, California.

Rochelle Glantz, Reviews Editor, Linworth Publishing, Santa Fe, New Mexico.

Susan Gooden, Librarian, Concord High School, Wilmington, Delaware.

Carol Sue Harless, Stone Mountain High School, Dekalb County School System, Stone Mountain, Georgia.

Nora Harris, Harris Indexing Service, Novato, California.

Dona Helmer, College Gate Elementary School, Anchorage, Alaska.

Robin Hoelle, Cynbrarian, Live Oaks Career Development Center, Mildford, Ohio.

Patricia M. Hogan, Administrative Librarian, Poplar Creek Public Library District, Streamwood, Illinois.

Jennifer L. Jack, Senior Librarian, U.S. News & World Report Library, Washington, D.C.

Jacqueline A. Jackson, Nelson Poynter Memorial Library, St. Petersburg, Florida.

Sally Sartain Jane, former Head of Adult Collection Development, Lee County Library System, Fort Myers, Florida.

Cynthia Jasper-Parisey, Upper School Library, Cincinnati Country Day School, Cincinnati, Ohio.

Sean Kinder, Humanities/Social Sciences Librarian, Helm Library, Western Kentucky University, Bowling Green, Kentucky.

Dan Kissane, Reference Librarian, Milne Library, SUNY Oneonta, Oneonta, New York.

Jeff Kosokoff, Head of Reference Services, Lamont Library, Harvard University, Cambridge, Massachusetts.

Marlene M. Kuhl, Catonsville Library, Catonsville, Maryland.

Abbie Vestal Landry, Head of Reference Division, Watson Library, Northwestern State University, Natchitoches, Louisiana.

Jan Lewis, Business Librarian, Joyner Library, East Carolina University, Greenville, North Carolina.

Art A. Lichtenstein, Director of Library, University of Central Arkansas, Conway, Arkansas.

Marilyn L. Long, Carmel Valley, California.

Kathleen M. McBroom, Resource Teacher for Library Media and Automation, Dearborn Public Schools, Dearborn, Michigan.

Christopher McConnell, Librarian, SUGEN, Inc., South San Francisco, California.

H. Robert Malinowsky, Manager of Collection Development and Reference, University of Illinois at Chicago Library, Chicago, Illinois.

Arthur S. Meyers, Library Director, Russell Library, Middletown, Connecticut.

Carolyn M. Mulac, Information Center, Chicago Public Library, Chicago, Illinois.

Clark Nall, Reference/Instruction Librarian, Joyner Library, East Carolina University, Greenville, North Carolina.

Kathryn C. O'Gorman, Director, Johnnie Mae Berry Library, Cincinnati State, Cincinnati, Ohio.

Maren C. Ostergard, Children's Librarian, Bellevue Regional Library, Bellevue, Washington.

Deborah Carter Peoples, Science Library Manager, Ohio Wesleyan University Libraries, Delaware, Ohio.

Margaret Power, Reference Services Coordinator, DePaul University Library, Chicago, Illinois.

James Rettig, University Librarian, Boatwright Memorial Library, University of Richmond, Richmond, Virginia.

Diana Donner Shonrock, Science Librarian/Family and Consumer Sciences Bibliographer, Parks Library, Iowa State University, Ames, Iowa.

Esther Sinofsky, Coordinating Field Librarian, Library Services, Los Angeles Unified School District, Los Angeles, California.

Mary Ellen Snodgrass, Independent Scholar, Hickory, North Carolina.

Kathleen Stipek, Adult Services Librarian, Alachua County Library District, Gainesville, Florida.

Stephen E. Stratton, Head, Collections and Technical Services, California State University, Channel Islands, Camarillo, California.

Martin D. Sugden, Reference Librarian, Florida/Genealogy Department, Jacksonville Public Library, Jacksonville, Florida.

Uri Toch, Corporate and Small Business Liaison, Schaumburg Township District Library, Schaumburg, Illinois.

Scottie Wallace, Managing Librarian, Downtown Reno Library, Washoe County Library System, Reno, Nevada.

Sarah Barbara Watstein, Associate University Librarian for Public Services, VCU Libraries, Virginia Commonwealth University, Richmond, Virginia.

Ann Welton, Grant Center for the Expressive Arts, Tacoma, Washington.

Christine A. Whittington, Director of Library Services, Greensboro College, Greensboro, North Carolina.

Carolyn N. Willis, Reference Librarian, Joyner Library, East Carolina University, Greenville, North Carolina.

Shauna Yusko, Children's Librarian, Bellevue Regional Library, Bellevue, Washington.

Encyclopedia Update, 2002

Compton's Encyclopedia — 1
Encyclopaedia Britannica — 1
Encyclopaedia Britannica Online — 1
Encyclopedia Americana — 2
Encyclopedia Americana Online — 2
Grolier Multimedia Encyclopedia Online — 3
The New Book of Knowledge — 3
The New Book of Knowledge Online — 3
New Standard Encyclopedia — 4
World Book Encyclopedia — 4
World Book Online — 4

This year's encyclopedia update includes two big print sets and their online counterparts—Encyclopedia Americana and Encyclopedia Britannica, scholarly tomes appropriate for the high-school level and up. Compton's Encyclopedia, Grolier Multimedia Online, New Standard Encyclopedia, World Book, and World Book Online are midsized encyclopedias aimed at the upper-elementary or middle-school level and up as well as at general readers. The New Book of Knowledge and The New Book of Knowledge Online cover the upper-elementary-school set. As in past years we gathered information for the update by sending questionnaires to the encyclopedia publishers, who provided helpful, detailed responses.

For purposes of comparison across similar encyclopedias, we chose to focus on one topic with numerous ramifications—September 11, 2001. Occurring rather late in the year, September 11 and its aftermath provided a case study in how the exigencies of the print format can affect an encyclopedia's currency. With earlier printings, *Encyclopedia Britannica* and *World Book* were caught a bit short, although both were able to add some relevant material. In the report it supplied to RBB, *World Book* stated that "the editors mounted a mammoth revision effort following the terrorist attacks on the United States," preparing two new articles and revising 13 others "in only a few days." Later deadlines allowed *Encyclopedia Americana*, *New Standard Encyclopedia*, and *Compton's Encyclopedia* more time to incorporate post–September 11 developments. *Americana*, *New Book of Knowledge*, and *New Standard* provide useful index entries that group together all content related to 9/11. Other topics that we checked were stem cells, space exploration, the euro, cancer, AIDS/HIV, and the name change from Bombay to Mumbai, plus a few more that caught our interest as we started to browse.

Librarians should be aware that *Encyclopaedia Britannica*, *Grolier Multimedia Encyclopedia*, and *World Book* are offered on CD-ROM, which RBB no longer reviews. Also not reviewed here are online versions of *Encarta* and *Funk & Wagnalls*. The online *Encarta* can be licensed, but libraries that are interested in *Encarta* would do better to purchase the multimedia-heavy CD-ROM or DVD-based versions, which offer access to *Encarta Online Deluxe*. *Funk & Wagnalls* is not available as a stand-alone but as part of *The World Almanac Reference Database*.

Online encyclopedias were last accessed on August 6, 2001. This year we replaced our usual recommendations statements with "pluses" and "minuses" that appear at the end of the review. As you will see, in some cases the "minuses" have more to do with the scope and purpose of the encyclopedia than with the actual content.

—*Susan Awe and Barbara Bibel*

Compton's Encyclopedia. 26v. 2002. Encyclopedia Britannica, $699 (0-944262-43-0).

Geared toward public and school libraries, *Compton's Encyclopedia* has a contemporary look and provides fairly current information at a basic level. It has retained the cumbersome "Fact Index," which functions as both an index and a supplement, with short articles and tables of sports champions, celebrity birthdays, and award winners in addition to index entries.

For 2002, Compton's has added 68 color images. Fourteen articles are new—*Hezbollah*, *International Campaign to Ban Land Mines*, and *Irritable bowel syndrome*, to name a few. *Biological and chemical terrorism* and *Euro*, among others, are new entries found only in the "Fact Index." Some 77 articles have been rewritten, including AIDS; *Bush, George W.*; *Terrorism*; and treatments of a number of U.S. states. *Israel* is out-of-date, ending with the 1999 election that made Ehud Barak prime minister. The article about the U.S. stops at the Clinton administration. Mumbai is still called Bombay, even in the "Fact Index." The article on Afghanistan is quite current, noting the appointment of Hamid Karzai as head of the interim government in December 2001, although the small map of Afghanistan is not very useful. The articles about U.S. states have data from the 2000 census, but city entries still use 1990 data. Articles on other countries have the latest available data. Both state and country articles have nice color graphs of population and economic trends, although monetary units have not been updated for European Union countries. The entry for cancer has good basic information about the biology, pathology, and causes of the disease. It mentions new experimental treatments such as hyperthermia and photodynamic laser therapy.

Pluses: Good color graphs of population and economic trends. Some current information.

Minuses: Many country articles are out-of-date. The practice of putting updated information into the "Fact Index" instead of incorporating it into main entries means that researchers have to look in two places, and more current information might be missed.

Encyclopaedia Britannica. 32v. 15th ed. 2002. Britannica, $1,295 (0-85229-787-4).

Encyclopaedia Britannica Online. [Internet database]. Britannica, pricing beginning at $495/year.

Encyclopaedia Britannica (EB) continues to be an authoritative resource. The articles are signed by more than 4,300 contributors and have extensive bibliographies. The latest printing retains the Micropaedia/Macropaedia/Propaedia structure: short articles for quick reference in the Micropaedia, in-depth treatment of broad topics in the Macropaedia, an "outline of knowledge" in the Propaedia. The articles on non-U.S. countries in the Macropaedia are extensive—*India* is 175 pages long. *Afghanistan* mentions the Taliban and the civil war, but it is not current. A note at the end of the article refers users to *Britannica Book of the Year* (which is given to first-time purchasers of the set) for the latest information. The events in the Middle East are well covered, with Ariel Sharon's election and the beginning of the Al-Aqsa Intifada mentioned in the entry on Israel. The articles on Islam and Judaism provide historical and spiritual context for the current conflict. Individual states are included in the article on the U.S. instead of having articles of their own. Stem cell research is covered in the Macropaedia articles on *Growth and development*, *Cancer*, and *Cells* and an article on *Bioethics* in the Micropaedia. An extensive article on the solar system covers each

Encyclopedias in Print

Name	Number of Volumes	Number of Entries	Number of Pages	Number of Illustrations	Percent of Illustrations in Full Color	Price
Americana	30	45,000	26,800	23,000	20	$1,049
Britannica	32	64,862	31,614	24,283	32	$1,295
Compton's	26	37,000	11,000	22,500	71	$699
New Book of Knowledge	21	9,243	10,576	27,850	93	$699
New Standard Encyclopedia	20	17,570	10,956	12,000	70	$575
World Book	22	17,000	14,196	27,500	80	$849

planet as well as space exploration and includes a detailed history of the U.S. space program. The events of September 11 are mentioned in the articles on hijacking, terrorism, and New York City. The latter has a color photograph of the World Trade Center towers in flames. There is a separate article on the World Trade Center with information about the 1993 and 2001 terrorist attacks.

The Macropaedia has 11 new articles, including *Baseball*, *Boxing*, *Feminism*, *Holocaust*, *Rock*, and *U.S. presidency*. Some of the 27 rewritten articles in the Macropaedia are *Broadcasting*, *Evolution*, *Human*, *Computers*, *Musical Forms and Genres*, *Israel*, *Sex*, *Occultism*, and *Sports*. A new map depicting indigenous skin color accompanies the article *Race*. The Micropaedia has 277 new and rewritten 166 entries. This printing also has 30 revised bibliographies and 38 new or replaced full-color insert plates, in addition to 142 new or revised drawings.

The latest version of *Britannica Online* offers content from *Britannica Student Encyclopedia* and *Britannica Book of the Year* as well as *Encyclopaedia Britannica*. *Britannica Student Encyclopedia* (formerly *Encyclopedia Britannica Intermediate*), intended for grades seven and up, is based on the *Compton's* database, and many of the articles are the same as or updated versions of those found in *Compton's Encyclopedia*. There are more than 8,500 articles in *Britannica Online* that do not appear in the print set, including entries for each U.S. county.

Britannica Online has a clean, uncluttered home page with a single search box. *Encyclopaedia Britannica*, *Britannica Student Encyclopedia*, Britannica Internet Guide, and Video and Media can be searched separately or in combination. Users may search with keywords, Boolean operators, and truncation. They may also browse alphabetically or by broad subject area. A spell-check option in the search engine will help them find what they need even if they are unsure of the correct letter combination.

A search for *Afghanistan* retrieves entries from *Encyclopaedia Britannica* and *Britannica Student Encyclopedia*, Web sites, magazine articles, and a video. Except for some magazine articles and Web sites, information is current through 2001. When we entered *September 11* as a search term, we retrieved numerous entries related to events on September 11 throughout history, but the only place we found reference to the events in 2001 was under the Magazines link. We had better luck with other search terms, such as *Taliban*, *terrorism*, and *World Trade Center*. Osama Bin Laden, Ariel Sharon, Yasir Arafat, and George W. Bush all have biographies current through 2001. The entry for the euro is a brief article with a graph of currency conversion rates for U.S. dollars and an illustration of the specifications for the official euro symbol; entries for the European Union countries still note old currency. New or rewritten articles published online in recent months include *European Union*, *Gaucho literature*, *Globalization*, *International Monetary Fund*, *Whaling*, and *World Trade Organization*.

The lack of a frequently updated current events feature means that *Britannica Online's* coverage sometimes lags. On the other hand, the combination of authoritative Britannica articles with other resources means that many topics are covered in depth. The entry on AIDS includes data about current drug treatment regimens, a map of Africa charting infection rates in various countries, a video, and very good Web links to sites such as the AIDS Research Institute at the University of California San Francisco. Information about stem cells is available in an array of encyclopedia entries, Web links, and magazine articles, along with several videos.

Britannica Online has a number of special features. The Workspace button on the menu bar allows users to mark articles and store them for research projects. The Spotlights feature offers articles with multimedia about popular topics such as dinosaurs, Shakespeare, and women in American history. Britannica Heritage has articles from previous editions by notable contributors as well as galleries of maps and images so that users can learn about the "changing nature of human knowledge." The World Atlas allows users to click on a part of the world to see regional maps or on index tabs to select political, physical, or economic maps. To see a map of an individual country, one must click on it to go to the article about the country and then click on the map. The Annals of American History Online is a collection of primary source material, including speeches, landmark court decisions, and essays, and requires a separate subscription. The *Britannica School Edition*, also a special subscription, includes the *Encyclopaedia Britannica*, *Britannica Student Encyclopedia*, and *Britannica Elementary Encyclopedia* (for grades four through six) as well as extra material for teachers to use in the classroom.

Pluses: The print version has in-depth, scholarly articles about major subject areas in the Macropaedia. The easy-to-search *Britannica Online* has authoritative information at several reading levels and an excellent selection of Web links.

Minuses: In print the Micropaedia/Macropaedia/Propaedia format is awkward and makes it harder for users to locate information quickly. *Britannica Online* is not as strong on current events as other online encyclopedias.

Encyclopedia Americana. 30v. 2002. Grolier. $1,049 (0-7172-0135-X).
Encyclopedia Americana Online. [Internet database]. Grolier, pricing from $415 in combination with other Grolier Online products. Visit [http://go.grolier.com] for free 30-day trial.

Encyclopedia Americana (EA), well known for thorough scholarly coverage since it was first published in 1829, had several new editorial programs for 2002—updating disease-related articles, expanding and updating coverage of scientific and technical institutions, and updating entries on Native American peoples—in addition to ongoing projects. Most of the changes occurred in the online edition. Of the 201 new entries, 39 were added to the print edition, among them *Allosaurus*; *Chirac, Jacques*; *Fox Quesada, Vicente*; *Mall*; and *Stem cell*. Thirteen print articles were replaced, including *Balthus*, *Nervous system*, and several entries related to insurance. A number of these new and rewritten articles had already been published in the online edition. Among the 95 print articles with major revisions are *Billy Budd*; *Chippewa*; *Elgin marbles*; *Killer* whale; Malnutrition; and Welty, Eudora. Other changes were made to reflect the 2000 U.S. census. More than 70 new photos, 60 of them in color, were added.

In the index under both September 11 attacks and terrorism, users will find citations to entries for bin Laden, Osama; Disasters; Hijacking; New York City; United States; and Bush, George Walker. With a revision deadline of mid-November 2001, it is too bad that the estimated number of people missing was not corrected from 5,000. Afghanistan includes the October 7, 2001, start of U.S. military action. There is no entry for the euro, and Italy is the only country article in which it is mentioned. Coverage of stem cell research and the controversies including President Bush's involvement is excellent. The handling of geographic name changes—such as Burma to Myanmar and Bombay to Mumbai—is uneven. Bombay's name was changed in 1995, which is about when Burma became Myanmar, but there's no mention of Mumbai in the article on Bombay, and it appears only in parentheses in the India article. Many bibliographies (for example, those for the entries Anthrax, Cooking, and Colorado) have no books added during the 1990s. And in general, as was mentioned last year, EA retains an overall drab appearance.

Encyclopedia Americana Online is well organized, well updated, and now easier to use. The attractive splash page, newly designed for the recently released version 3.0, leads the user to four modules: Browse, Americana Journal, Editors' Picks, and Profiles. Browse is an easy-to-use subject search that replaces the more cumbersome Topic Search, which has been relegated to the Advanced Search page. The expanded Americana Journal continues as EA Online's weekly update feature and is now searchable by keyword as well as by country. Editors' Picks, also updated weekly, contains essays on particular topics, and Profiles assembles 1,500 frequently consulted biographies, classified by subject. An atlas and dictionary are available via the GO frame, which simultaneously searches all Grolier databases to which a library subscribes.

EA Online's advantages over its print counterpart in terms of currency are significant. Here, the Anthrax and Colorado bibliographies have been revised (but users still find Bombay, not Mumbai, unless a full-text search is used). Afghanistan ends at the same point as the article in the print set—October 2001—but the online version has a more extensive bibliography and links to magazine articles and Americana Journal entries. Though there is still no entry for the euro, there is considerably more information than in the print set, especially in the Journal. Maps are a good size and readable and print quickly and easily. Most Web links are relevant and current. The fact that Article Search is the default is a drawback. A user who enters amphibian as a search term will get no hits, because the article title is Amphibia. A full-text search works better.

Searching for information related to September 11 is actually easier in the print edition. Online, Article Title search gives no results. On the other hand, doing a full-text search for September 11 retrieves almost 300 documents, with anything that seems related to the events of September 11, 2001, appearing far down on the list. A full-text search in Americana Journal works better.

EA Online has added thousands of current Web links plus new maps and illustrations. Among the several hundred new articles are Arzner, Dorothy; Horror literature; Northwest Coast Indians; Putin, Vladimir; Stem cell; and Unemployment insurance. The 48 replacement articles include Dime novels; Hitchcock, Alfred; Psychiatry; Shining Path; Social Security; and Water pollution. Several thousand articles were revised in the database, including biographies of astronomers, geologists, political and military leaders, and sports figures. For the new release, most of the articles now link directly to the OCLC WorldCat database. Another important enhancement to the new release is a text-only ADA-compliant version. Grolier hopes to make all of its online encyclopedias ADA compliant within two years.

Pluses: EA offers in-depth treatment of many topics and is especially strong in its coverage of North America—200 pages for Canada, almost 300 for the U.S. The new release of EA Online is a big leap in user-friendliness. Depending on a library's subscription package, several Grolier Online databases can be searched simultaneously.

Minuses: The print version has an uninviting appearance. Searching online often requires too many steps.

Grolier Multimedia Encyclopedia Online. [Internet database]. Grolier, pricing from $415 in combination with other Grolier Online databases. Visit [http://go.grolier.com] for free 30-day trial.

Designed for students in grades five and up, Grolier Multimedia Encyclopedia Online (GMEO) is user-friendly, current, and attractive. Seventy-five percent of the articles are signed, with affiliation or other identification of the author provided via a pop-up window. More than half the entries conclude with short, current bibliographies of print resources for further research; 1,800 of these were revised in 2001. Entries are also linked to Web sites and to full-text articles from general-and special-interest magazines. Articles tend to be shorter than those in comparable encyclopedias, reflecting the fact that GMEO often treats in separate entries topics that other encyclopedias would discuss in a broader context.

The encyclopedia can be searched by keyword or browsed by subject. Among more than 600 new articles are Biological warfare, Cousteau Society, Digital photography, Global warming, and Nutritional supplements. Additional new articles cover topics in Western music, Chinese philosophy, and film, to name a few areas. There is also a group of new articles related to the history and geography of Afghanistan. More than 100 articles have been rewritten or replaced, among them African American literature, Maori, and Supersymmetry. New multimedia shows seed germination, frog development, and other topics. The main Afghanistan article is current through June 2002. The article on September 11, 2001, is also current into June, with information on the beginnings of the joint U.S. Senate and House committee investigation on U.S. intelligence services.

The Research Starter feature now has more than 150 topics, many in the sciences. Brain Jam is the monthly feature highlighting a subject of current interest and often relates to the calendar month, such as National Parks Month in July. Timelines' new design consists of 24 main time line screens covering world history events from 4,000 B.C.E. to the present. GME News feature is updated weekly. An atlas and dictionary are available via the GO frame, which simultaneously searches all Grolier databases to which a library subscribes.

Pluses: An attractive, up-to-date resource. Depending on a library's subscription package, several Grolier Online databases can be searched simultaneously.

Minuses: Because this is a short-entry encyclopedia, users who want more detail will need to look elsewhere.

The New Book of Knowledge. 21v. 2002. Grolier, $699 (0-7172-0533-9).
The New Book of Knowledge Online. [Internet database]. Grolier, pricing from $415 in combination with other Grolier Online databases. Visit [http://go.grolier.com] for free 30-day trial.

Aimed at students in grades four through six, the New Book of Knowledge (NBK) provides balanced, appropriate, and engaging coverage of a wide range of topics. Encyclopedia entries are complemented by many appealing features, illustrations, and maps. For the 2002 edition, 32 completely new articles were added to the print set, among them Autism; Henson, Matthew; Hijacking; Homosexuality; and Putin, Vladimir. Thirty articles were rewritten, including Buddhism; Hawthorne, Nathaniel; Mental illness; Saudi Arabia; and Vectors of disease. Another 50 articles, including Bush, George W.; Girl Scouts; Nazism; Nigeria; and Terrorism, received major revisions. One hundred new color maps replaced existing ones, and new population density maps were commissioned for the 50 U.S. states, based on the 2000 census. New photographs, 32 black and white and 406 in color, were added so that approximately one-third of the space in NBK is now devoted to illustrations.

NBK added a helpful index entry, Terrorist attacks on the United States, which has references to several articles, including Defense, United States Department of; Hijacking; and Powell, Colin. A September 11–related paragraph has been added to Afghanistan, although there is nothing about the ensuing overthrow of the Taliban. Children using NBK for country assignments will not find up-to-date information about currency in some cases; though there is a reference to the euro in European Union, there is no entry for the euro, and individual European Union country articles have not been updated to reflect the change.

Each volume has its own index, and there is a comprehensive index volume for the set. Items such as pictures, maps, and diagrams are clearly identified in the index entries. Using the indexes is essential for finding some topics, such as toads. These are covered in the entries Frogs and toads, so children who go straight to the "T" volume won't find them. Contact lenses appears in the "L" volume instead of in "C," with no cross-reference from "C." Greater use of see references might help young readers find information more quickly and easily. All entries are signed, with a few words to identify the contributor; additionally, experts have reviewed some entries. Bibliographies appear in the "Home and School

Encyclopedias Online

Name	Number of Entries	Illustrations	Maps	Videos	Sounds	Web Links	Other Multimedia	Update Schedule	Base Annual Subscription Rate
Britannica Online	118,270	14,485	1,310	123	176	135,000		Biweekly	$495*
Encyclopedia Americana Online	45,000 plus 35,000 in Journal	4,750	1,000	4		151,000		Quarterly; Journal is updated weekly	$415†
Grolier Multimedia Encyclopedia Online	38,000	7,500	900	22	500	108,000	Panoramas, cutaways	Monthly; News is updated weekly	$415†
New Book of Knowledge Online	9,000	4,000	630	55	6	7,700		Quarterly; News is updated weekly	$415†
World Book Online	36,000	11,000	1,480	115	9,500	10,000	128 panoramas	Monthly (some features updated daily)	$395

* Total includes *Encyclopaedia Britannica*, *Britannica Student Encyclopedia*, and *Britannica Book of the Year*.
† Pricing is for a multiple package of Grolier Online databases; they are not available as individual subscriptions.

Reading and Study Guides," which accompanies the print set and is also available online. The bibliographies contain useful items, and students using the print set would be more likely to find them if they were attached to entries.

The entire NBK *Online* interface was redesigned in 2001. Articles in the online version may contain graphics, fact boxes, projects, and links to related NBK News stories (updated weekly), Web sites, articles in selected magazines, and further reading lists. Longer articles have tables of contents allowing users to easily access the sections they want. Features added in 2001 include the World History Time Line (a chronology) and Homework Help (how to research, study, and write), accessible from every screen; and Encyclopedia Spotlight (a monthly topic), Question of the Day (daily brain teaser), and Web Feat! (a fun-and-games approach to learning), accessible only from the main page. An atlas and dictionary are available via the GO frame, which simultaneously searches all Grolier databases to which a library subscribes.

A Subject Browse, Alphabetical Browse, and Advanced Search are available, in addition to a full-text Quick Search. A Quick Search for *September* 11 yielded a useful collection of 115 encyclopedia articles and NBK News stories; we liked being able to retrieve articles and updates in a single search.

Pluses: In both the print and online versions, NBK is well suited to younger encyclopedia users, an audience often overlooked by reference publishers. Depending on a library's subscription package, several Grolier Online databases can be searched simultaneously.

Minuses: NBK's target audience grows up quickly, so even elementary school libraries will need to have another encyclopedia on hand.

New Standard Encyclopedia. 20v. 2002. Ferguson, $575 (0-87392-106-2).

For 2002, Ferguson chose to improve the appearance of *New Standard Encyclopedia* (NSE) by using a paper that is whiter and with a greater opacity than used in previous editions. The set maintains its 20 volumes, updating or revising 60 bibliographies and 41 maps. There are more than 100 new four-color illustrations.

Entries are written by members of the encyclopedia editorial staff and vary from one or two sentences to 33 pages for *Africa*. The 29 new entries include *Al Qaeda*; *Bin Laden, Osama*; *Ebola fever*; *Enron Corporation*; *Euro* (currency information in relevant country articles was also revised to reflect this change); *Fibromyalgia*; *Fox, Vicente*, and *Giuliani, Rudolph*. Approximately 12 articles, including *Chemical-biological warfare*, *Pakistan*, and *Terrorism*, were extensively revised. September 11 is listed in the index and is covered by mentions in 10 different articles, including *Airline*; *Bush, George Walker*; *New York City*; and *Pentagon*. The revised entry on *Afghanistan* is current thorough November 2001 and the fall of the Taliban, but the small map is not very useful. U.S. 2000 census data were used to update all city, state, and other entries, where relevant. An important change to this edition is the "Fact Boxes," providing basic information for eight countries, among them Afghanistan and Brazil, with more planned. Also new are name changes for major cities in India (for example, Bombay to *Mumbai*, and Calcutta to *Kolkata*). *See* references help users with the transitions. Bibliographies following some entries list only two or three books. Sixty were updated in 2001, but often (as in *New Mexico* and the *Netherlands*) references are nearly 10 years old. Many articles are very brief, and often the longer ones do not offer as much detail as comparable articles in other midsized encyclopedias.

Last year we noted in our review of NSE that the article on Australia barely mentioned the Australian aborigines: "It is disturbing to see a paragraph under the heading 'The People' that begins with 'From the time of its settlement in the late 18th century' and focuses on 'British stock' and European immigrants." For 2002, the same paragraph begins "The Australian aborigines, or Koori, are the earliest known inhabitants of Australia."

Pluses: New Standard's price makes it an affordable choice for libraries wanting to offer a supplemental encyclopedia on a limited budget.

Minuses: On many topics New Standard offers less extensive information than comparable encyclopedias, and it has less visual appeal.

World Book Encyclopedia. 22v. 2002. World Book, $849 (0-7166-0102-8).

World Book Online. [Internet database]. World Book, pricing from $395. Visit [http://www.worldbookonline.com] for free 30-day trial.

World Book continues to be a first choice for libraries, schools, and homes. It is up-to-date, accessible, easy to use, and well illustrated. One hundred new articles have been added to this edition. They include *Code talkers, DVD, Nasdaq,* and *Herbal medicine.* Kobe Bryant, Al Pacino, Shel Silverstein, and Kenneth Starr are some of the individuals covered in new biographical entries. Among 139 extensively revised or rewritten articles are *Camera, Classical music, Geology, Internet, New Zealand, Red Cross,* and *Zionism.* About 300 illustrations are additions or replacements, and more than 190 maps were added or changed. More than 200 bibliographies were revised. There is a special supplementary volume that covers the 2000 U.S. census in depth, in addition to the census article within the set.

Although the article on Afghanistan is current only through the Taliban takeover in the late 1990s, events of September 11 are included in two new entries—*Bin Laden, Osama* and *World Trade Center*—and in revisions to *Hijacking, New York, Terrorism, United States,* and more. The article on stem cells is the only one we found that gives a full explanation of what they are and discusses the ethical questions about research. Fact boxes for relevant European countries have been revised to reflect that their currency is the euro. Entries reflecting international events, such as those for countries in the Middle East, are up-to-date and detailed, with accurate maps. The article on cancer discusses current U.S. statistics for the various types of cancer and current research as well as the causes and treatment of the disease. The index is easy to use and detailed, including page numbers for illustrations and maps. The research guide is useful for students who need help organizing a project.

The newest version of *World Book Online* has a clean, uncluttered look on its home page. The encyclopedia contains the complete text of the print edition and the *World Book Dictionary* as well as 6,000 articles created for the electronic version (including entries for all U.S. senators, national parks and monuments, major universities, and literary works and films) and 13,000 Back in Time articles from *World Book* annuals. Users may enter terms in a search box, browse by broad subject area or media type, or use the basic or advanced keyword search functions. The advanced search mode allows Boolean operators, limits (article text, title word, Atlas, media type, Back in Time, or Special Reports), and truncation. In addition to articles, search results show hits in media and other features, making it easy to capture all related elements in a single search. The search *Afghanistan,* for example, finds 93 articles, 12 tables, 12 pictures, 1 audio clip, and so on.

Articles added the past year or so include teams of the National Football League; major films (*Chinatown, Of Mice and Men, Oklahoma!*); current news topics (*Ecstasy; Enron Corporation; Homeland Security, Office of*); and biographies (Hamid Karzai, Anna Kournikova, Marcia Muller, Pervez Musharraf). *Atheism, Evolution,* and *Petrochemicals* are among the revised articles. The article on Afghanistan is current into June 2002 and the meeting of the loyal jirga. This can be supplemented by several articles added to the Behind the Headlines feature in later months. There is an article on the euro with pictures of the coins and bills, and the "Money" section of Facts in Brief for the 12 nations that have adopted the euro has been updated. The events of September 11 have their own entry, and a number of entries have been updated with reference to these events (although not all of them are retrieved in the *September 11* search). Articles are enhanced by links to Special Reports, which provides background on current events, and Back in Time, which allows users to see articles in earlier *World Book* editions. For example, a student writing a report on Israel has access to the 1948 article about the formation of the state.

From the home page, the researcher can access several features. Today in History is a daily listing of past events. Feature of the Month highlights an important event that occurred during that month: in August, the topic was hurricanes. Behind the Headlines summarizes important news stories. Several additional databases are available from WB Online. Surf the Ages, which replaces Surf the Millennium, assembles related articles and Web sites from different historical periods. Users may visit ancient Egypt or a medieval physician working during a plague epidemic. The More Resources box leads to tools for parents, teachers, and students. These tools include articles on how to do research and prepare written and oral presentations, ideas for teachers involving the use of the encyclopedia in class projects, and projects for parents and children. What's New offers information on recent updates. There is also a link to *World Book Research Libraries,* which offers eight extensive collections of primary sources in broad subject areas (science, literature, history, etc.) and requires a separate subscription.

WB Online is very current. Features such as Behind the Headlines are revised daily, and new and revised articles and media are added monthly. Web links are validated on a continuous basis. The new site design is easier to navigate, and it makes all of the features available from anywhere in the site. Articles download faster, too.

Pluses: High-quality, accurate, current information delivered in attractive print and online packages.

Minuses: Because World Book is a general encyclopedia, users who need more depth on some subjects will have to use other sources.

Special Features

Atlas and Dictionary Update, 2003 — 6
Business Trailblazers — 7
Canadian Reference Sources — 8
Core Collection: Physics — 9
Core Collection: Poetry — 10
E-book Roundup — 10
Just the Facts: A Look at Almanacs — 11
Lives of Champions — 12
Reference Books in Spanish for Adolescents and Adults — 12
Reference Sources on Beer — 13
Reference Sources on Wine — 14
Top 10 Science Reference Sources — 15
Twenty Best Bets for Student Researchers — 15
Working Women — 16
Works in Progress: Defining a Dictionary — 17
Another Look At . . .
    Bartlett's Familiar Quotations — 18
    Biography Resource Center — 19
Focus Reviews
    New Catholic Encyclopedia — 19
    Encyclopedia of New Media — 19
    Encyclopedia of Aging — 20
    Encyclopedia of Food and Culture — 20
    McGraw-Hill Encyclopedia of Science & Technology — 21
    Grzimek's Animal Life Encyclopedia — 21
    Encyclopedia of the Enlightenment — 21
    Encyclopedia of Modern Asia — 22
    Dictionary of American History — 22
    Encyclopedia of American History — 22

Atlas and Dictionary Update, 2003

In our May 15, 2002, issue we presented a roundup of current editions of world atlases and English-language dictionaries, and we intend to update that roundup each year. Listed here are new titles and editions that have appeared between April 1, 2002, and March 31, 2003. Some of the reviews are printed here for the first time; others are excerpts of reviews previously published in RBB. You can find our complete list of atlases and dictionaries under Special Lists and Features on the *Booklist* Web site at [http://www.ala.org/booklist].

We took a comprehensive look at children's dictionaries in our October 15, 2000, issue. This year, we are adding new and revised children's dictionaries to the annual print roundup, and we will let you know when the complete and updated list of children's dictionaries is available online.

Atlases

Atlas of the World. 10th ed. 2002. 448p. Oxford, $85 (0-19-521919-8).

Oxford advertises that its *Atlas of the World* is updated annually, and in some instances this is true. Some of the statistical information in the thematic section is new, and a page in the agriculture section updates a map regarding the "Crisis in Africa" with reference to the recent drought. A page of lists of countries and their population includes 2001 estimates. The company asserts that there is a "brand new . . . Gazetteer of Nations," but the text appears to be identical to the ninth edition except for the elimination of part of the information on Djibouti so that East Timor, a new country in May 2002, will fit in. Some of the statistics in the gazetteer have changed, and there are a few new country flags. The page in the introduction entitled "World: Regions in the News" has changed—Afghanistan and Colombia are added and Caucasus and India are removed.

The maps appear to be similar to those in the ninth edition with the addition of national parks and nature reserves around the world. There are a few revisions. The New York City map indicates the former site of the World Trade Center. This and other city maps are still in a separate section with a separate index.

Libraries owning the eighth or ninth edition of Oxford should wait for the eleventh edition in 2004 for changes in the world that may occur this year. Public, academic, and high-school libraries without a recent Oxford atlas may want to consider the tenth.

Hammond World Atlas. 4th ed. 2002. 408p. Hammond, $75 (0-8437-1836-6).

The fourth edition of the *Hammond World Atlas* is really a new edition from the "Mapmakers of the 21st Century." Changes from the third edition, published in 2000, include a "Thematic Section" that has a broader scope with different titles; e.g., "Languages" becomes "Global Linguistic Diversity." The double-page spreads in this section have fewer atlas features and look more like encyclopedia articles. Thin colored lines lead readers from words in the text to photos, but sometimes the lines are difficult to follow. The population page in the earlier edition had a world map with a point of light for every 50,000 people, maps showing annual rate of population increase and density, and graphs of other population information. In the fourth edition the population page has three graphs, a small table with growth projections by continent, and text with illustrative photographs but no maps.

Hammond's new "Satellite Photo Section" contains 48 pages of beautiful photography illustrating subjects such as environmental problems (a carpet of algae off the Adriatic coast), settlement patterns (Venice and New York), and volcanism (Mount St. Helens). The photographs have an accompanying explanation paragraph; unfortunately, Mount St. Helens is identified as being in Oregon. The name of satellite or imaging process, ground resolution, exposure altitude, and date of the image are also included.

The most important part of the atlas, the "Map Section," contains 180 maps in a similar arrangement to the previous edition. The physical maps are from actual digital elevation data using new colors. The map paper is shiny, which is a change from earlier editions. There are new maps—one of Alaska almost fills a page, and Hawaii is a quarter of a page. Maps of cities and metropolitan areas are either inset maps or grouped together on a few pages. The New York City map has been updated since 9/11. There is no city map of Baghdad. The statistical tables are revised, with some cities declining in population. These tables are easy to read, with dots connecting the city to the statistic. The index supposedly still has 110,000 entries. The Canadian territory Nunavut has been dropped from the index, and Nunapitchuk, Alaska, appears to have taken its place. Unlike Oxford's *Atlas of the World* (see above), Hammond lacks detailed country information, and there are no flags.

The fourth edition of the *Hammond World Atlas* is recommended as a first purchase among medium-sized atlases for academic, public, and high-school libraries. It is a complete revision with new material, and, most importantly, the maps are fantastic.

National Geographic Family Reference Atlas of the World. 2002. 351p. National Geographic, $65 (0-7922-6930-6).

This atlas is a smaller version of the standard *National Geographic Atlas of the World* (National Geographic, 1999). There are both political and physical maps of the continents and the oceans. The colors are outstanding on the smaller regional political maps so there is no confusion as to borders. The book lays flat on all pages, meaning no lost letters or features in the binding margin.

On each regional map page are also information boxes that give brief data and flag pictures for all nations and territories. Inset maps of all major island nations and territories are also provided. Accompanying thematic maps show population density, land use, and weather averages for the regions. World maps with information on the economy, crops, mining, Internet connectivity, and many other topics are presented with text to explain their significance. U.S. maps are given more pages than the rest of the world, so students will find locating U.S. features relatively easy.

The back matter of the atlas contains a useful gazetteer to locate features and places, a glossary of geographic terms as well as a glossary of non-English geographic terms used in the maps, and world city population tables. The atlas also contains several maps of the solar system that place the earth in the solar system and galaxy for a clear understanding of just where we live. One interesting map delineated the oceans and seas of the world, so students won't have to guess where the Andaman Sea or Bay of Fundy are located. Geographic comparison tables will also assist students in comparing the continents and the features of the planet easily.

Altogether, a great package that should be high on the list of titles for school and public libraries that are seeking a solid atlas that won't break the budget this year.

Dictionaries

Shorter Oxford English Dictionary. 2v. 5th ed. 2002. 3,750p. index. Oxford, $150 (0-19-860575-7).

Like the previous edition, this "abridgement" of Oxford's flagship OED "sets out the main meanings and semantic developments of words current at any time between 1700 and the present day." It has "more than one-third of the coverage of the OED" and more than half a million definitions, with 83,500 illustrative quotations from 7,000 authors. Some 3,500 new words have been added. The most welcome change to this edition is that the text is much easier on the eyes than in the fourth edition. [RBB Ja 1 & 15 03].

Dictionaries for K–12

American Heritage High School Dictionary. 4th ed. 2002. 1,664p. Houghton Mifflin, $25 (0-618-17388-9).

Houghton Mifflin fills the gap between its *American Heritage Student Dictionary* (rev. ed., 1998) for grades six through nine and its *American Heritage College Dictionary* (4th ed., 2002) with this sanitized version of the latter, containing everything except the vulgarisms and offensive terms. The introduction has been written specifically for high-school students.

The McGraw-Hill Children's Dictionary. 2003. 830p. McGraw-Hill, $24.95 (1-57768-298-X).

This new addition to the world of children's dictionaries is targeted at students in elementary through middle school. The more than 30,000 entries are easy to read. "Word History," "Homophone Note," and "Synonyms" boxes give extra information about some words. Frequent small photographs and drawings (one to two per page on average) illustrate some definitions and add to the appealing look. [RBB N 1 02]

Scholastic Children's Dictionary. 2002. 648p. Scholastic, $17.95 (0-439-36563-5).

Designed for students ages 8 through 12, this dictionary updates one published in 1996. Because the pronunciation guide uses letter sounds instead of symbols and entries are clearly laid out, it may be easier for readers at the younger end of the age range than similar dictionaries. There is excellent use of detailed labeled illustrations. Definitions include homophones and sample sentences; highlighted boxes provide information about prefixes, suffixes, synonyms, and word histories. Almost 200 terms have been added to the word list, among them *browser, cell phone,* DVD, *Internet, rap,* and SUV. The updated reference section includes 2000 population figures and the 1996 and 2000 presidential elections.

—*Mary Ellen Quinn*

Business Trailblazers

Business biography often seems designed to inspire as well as inform, and these three reference sources are no exception. Although there is some overlap (Oprah, for example, is found in all three), each volume has a different focus, and each contains entries for people not covered in the others.

A to Z of American Women Business Leaders and Entrepreneurs. By Victoria Sherrow. 2002. 252p. bibliogs. illus. index. Facts On File, $44 (0-8160-4556-9). 338.

This reference work describes about 140 representative women who made names for themselves as business leaders over the history of the U.S. The author tried to provide a wide variety of women, crossing decades, ethnicities, and types of businesses. She also looked for women who overcame significant obstacles and were "firsts" for various reasons (e.g., female bank president, million-dollar-company founder). In addition, she also chose women who have been subjects of significant writing. Included are business celebrities such as Jenny Craig, Lydia Pinkham, and Oprah Winfrey as well as less-well-known leaders such as stenographer Mary Foot Seymour and colonial farm owner Susanna Wright.

Entries are arranged in alphabetical order. Each one-to two-page article begins with the woman's major accomplishments, then traces her life, and ends with a short list of additional reading. The reader gets a taste of each personality but will not derive all the information needed for in-depth research. About 10 percent of the articles include black-and-white images of the subjects. The treatment is generally benign, so controversies such as Tootsie Roll president Ellen Gordon's move of her factory to Canada are not covered.

The volume ends with a bibliography of recommended sources on the

Special Features

topic, a list of articles sorted by career field, a chronological list, and an index. A list by ethnicity would have been useful. The business fields tend to cluster around traditional female interests: appearance, family products, communications. However, manufacturing (including aviation and technology), construction, and shipping are also represented.

Providing an accessible introduction to U. S. businesswomen, this resource should find a broad audience in high-school, academic, and public libraries.

American Inventors, Entrepreneurs, & Business Visionaries. By Charles W. Carey Jr. 2002. 410p. bibliogs. illus. index. Facts On File, $65 (0-8160-4559-3). 338.092.

More than 280 individuals from the seventeenth through twentieth centuries who helped change the American economy are profiled here. The author tried to select "people from all categories of American life," including those who made significant contributions yet were never famous as well as superstars. Some well-known names are here: Wally Amos, Dale Carnegie, Conrad Hilton. But how many people recognize Henry Morrison Flagler, who was instrumental in the development of Florida, or Ida Rosenthal, cofounder of the Maidenform Brassiere Company? Though a number founded or led flourishing business enterprises, others, such as George Washington Carver, Philo Farnsworth ("the father of television"), and Nikola Tesla, inventor of the alternating-current electric motor, were failures on the business side.

Each entry provides birth date (and death date where applicable), followed by a page or two on the person's life and innovations, and concludes with a brief further reading list. A general bibliography, subject indexes that arrange entries by invention or business type and by year of birth, and a general index complete the volume.

This volume is worthy of inclusion in reference collections of public, academic, and high-school libraries. Its content is wide-ranging and its entries provide interesting reading.

100 Most Popular Business Leaders for Young Adults: Biographical Sketches and Professional Paths. By Rochelle Logan and Julie Halverstadt. 2002. 419p. bibliogs. illus. index. Libraries Unlimited, $60 (1-56308-799-5). 338.092.

With the publicity regarding corruption in several important companies and the downturn of American companies' stock values, this book may appear to be a victim of bad timing. Yet it provides positive examples of individuals who combined vision and hard work to create a product or service that filled a need and made a profit. The authors explain in their preface that their book is designed to provide inspiration as well as education about becoming a corporate leader. Of the 100 leaders, only two, Steve Case and Martha Stewart, have been in the news recently for their questionable business transactions.

Although the book profiles people with diverse backgrounds, the majority of entries are for white males, reflecting the business reality. The authors have focused upon businesses that should be of interest to teens. Therefore, many of the CEOs are in fields such as computer technology, entertainment, food, or fashion. Some of them, such as Walt Disney, George Eastman, and Henry Ford, established companies that are the backbone of the American economy or changed American life. Others, such as Paul Newman and Oprah Winfrey, have made their names as celebrities as well as captains of industry. The articles are arranged alphabetically, and many include a photo. An inspirational phrase or quote and a categorization of the subject's expertise begin each article. Length varies, but the emphasis of each article is upon the professional career, not the personal life. A chronology, brief bibliography, and philosophical quote conclude the entry. Some Web sites are included.

This volume can be used not only as a biographical reference tool but as inspiration for young entrepreneurs. It should find a home in high-school and public libraries.

—*Mary Ellen Quinn*

Canadian Reference Sources

Like their counterparts in the U.S., Canadian librarians have a standard reference tool kit. The following English-language resources were chosen with undergraduates and general readers in mind.

Books

Associations Canada, 2003: The Directory of Associations in Canada. 24th ed. 2003. 1,822p. Micromedia ProQuest, $325 (1-895021-97-9).

This directory contains detailed information on Canada's not-for-profit sector, including business and trade associations, consumer groups, registered charities, and special interest groups.

Canada, 2002. By Wayne C. Thompson. 18th ed. 2002. 176p. Stryker-Post, paper, $13.50 (1-887985-40-9).

A comprehensive guide to Canada, written by an American, which discusses Canada's culture, people, geography, history, political system, foreign policy, defense policy, and economy.

Canada Year Book, 2001. Ed. by Nathalie Turcotte. 2001. 563p. DIANE, $75 (0-7567-1416-8).

This work contains information about Canada's people, environment, and economy. It includes current statistics, articles, maps, and photographs.

Canadian Almanac & Directory, 2003: Over 50,000 Facts and Figures about Canada. 156th ed. 2002. 1,500p. Micromedia ProQuest, $275 (1-895021-93-6).

Claiming to be "Canada's best-selling national sourcebook since 1847," this volume contains a wealth of information, including national statistics, national awards and honors, color portraits of prime ministers, and color photographs of flags and emblems. In addition, there are detailed addresses and contact names for Canadian banks, universities, libraries, and other organizations.

The Canadian Encyclopedia: Complete, Unabridged, Expanded, Updated Year 2000 Edition. By James H. Marsh. 1999. 2,640p. McClelland & Stewart/Tundra, $64.95 (0-7710-2099-6).

Described as "an indispensable reference tool for all things Canadian," this volume contains 10,000 articles written "from the Canadian point of view." Special features include maps and comparative statistics of Canada's major cities. Entries cover many features of Canadian culture, history, sports, and politics and quintessential Canadian interests and personalities such as hockey, the beaver, and Celine Dion.

The Canadian Oxford Dictionary. By Katherine Barber. 2001. 1,710p. Oxford, $45 (0-19-541731-3).

An award-winning dictionary containing 130,000 entries, including 2,000 "distinctly Canadian words and meanings." The dictionary specifies Canadian pronunciation and spelling of terms. It also has a reference component with entries on place-names, people, and historical events.

Canadian Trade Index, 2003. 2v. Macrae's Bluebook, $190 (0-9731565-7-0).

Detailed information on more than 29,000 Canadian manufacturers, exporters, distributors, and service companies, with data on more than 25,000 products and services.

Canadian Who's Who, 2003. 28th ed. Ed. by Elizabeth Lumley. 2003. 1,400p. Univ. of Toronto, $185 (0-8020-8865-1).

An authoritative work containing biographical information on more than 15,000 prominent Canadians representing a wide spectrum of society, including academics, businesspeople, politicians, athletes, artists, and others.

Dictionary of Canadian Biography: Volume 14. By Ramsay Cook and others. 1998. 2,280p. Univ. of Toronto, $100 (0-8020-3476-4).

This 14-volume series contains biographies of notable individuals who contributed to the history of Canada and died between 1000 and 1920. Volume 14 covers 1911 to 1920.

Encyclopedia of Literature in Canada. Ed. by W. H. New. 2002. 1,000p. Univ. of Toronto, $75 (0-8020-0761-9).

The diversity of Canadian literature is evident in this volume that examines English, French, native, and multicultural works. Also included are articles on authors, literary and social issues, and significant Canadian historical and cultural events.

Historical Atlas of Canada: Canada's History Illustrated with Original Maps. By Derek Hayes. 2002. 272p. Univ. of Washington, $60 (0-295-98277-2).

One thousand years of Canadian history are explored in more than 420 original maps, which the author claims are "essentially all the historically significant maps of the country." Includes Norse voyages, French and British explorations, native maps, early maps of Canadian cities, and maps related to significant historical events.

The Oxford Companion to Canadian Literature. 2d ed. By Eugene Benson and William Toye. 1997. 1,199p. Oxford, $65 (0-19-541167-6).

The second edition (the first was published in 1983) includes updated entries and 300 additional articles. Covers writers, poets, historians, philosophers, genres, critical surveys, publishers, books, and more.

Who's Who in Canadian Business, 2003. 23d ed. Ed. by Gillian Holmes. 2002. 1,100p. Univ. of Toronto, $179.95 (0-8020-8870-8).

Biographical and contact information for more than 5,400 Canadian business leaders.

Who's Who of Canadian Women, 1999–2000. 9th ed. Ed. by Gillian Holmes. 1999. 1,169p. Univ. of Toronto, $129.95 (0-9209-6655-1).

A collection of biographical information on more than 3,700 "powerful and innovative" Canadian women.

Databases

Canadian Business and Current Affairs (CBCA) Reference. 1982–2003. [Online database]. Micromedia ProQuest, contact for pricing [http://il.proquest.com/products/pt-product-cbca.shtml].

CBCA *Reference* indexes 650 active periodicals, including more than 200 Canadian periodicals. Coverage includes daily news, business, science, the arts, law, and medicine. The database contains full-text articles from more than 200 periodicals.

Canadian Periodical Index (CPI.Q). 2002. Gale, $595 (0-7876-6496-0). **CPI.Q.** [Online database]. Gale, pricing from $1,546 [http://www.gale.com].

CPI.Q indexes more than 400 Canadian (French-and-English-language) and international periodicals. It contains full-text articles from more than 160 periodicals, including full text of selected sections of the *Globe and Mail*, Canada's national newspaper. Coverage consists of news, arts and humanities, business, social sciences, and health sciences.

CANSIM II: Statistics Canada's Socio-Economic Database. [Online database]. Statistics Canada, pricing from $500 [http://www.statcan.ca].

This online database provides Canadian socioeconomic statistics on a broad range of topics, including agriculture, education, population and demography, trade, and others.

—*Michelle Hendley*

Core Collection: Physics

I once saw a physics major wearing a T-shirt that said "Physics Is Phun." With a solid core collection, physics can be fun for librarians and library patrons. For this core collection, my standard was a midsize public or academic library, with or without a physics program. Titles recommended are in print as of October 2002.

Books

Buildings Blocks of Matter: Supplement to the Macmillan Encyclopedia of Physics. 2003. 500p. Macmillan, $130 (0-02-865703-9).

This supplement to the *Macmillan Encyclopedia of Physics* (1996) updates recent physics developments for an encyclopedia that is not currently in print. To keep their collections up-to-date, libraries should consider purchasing the supplement if they have the encyclopedia.

CRC Handbook of Chemistry and Physics, 2002–2003. 83d ed. Ed. by David R Lide. 2002. 2,664p. CRC, $139.95 (0-8493-0483-0).

CRC H*andbook of Chemistry and Physics* is the best handbook for physical constants, formulas, and other data. A must-have for both small and large libraries.

Encyclopedia of Physical Science and Technology. 18v. 3d ed. Ed. by Robert A. Meyers. 2002. 15,453p. Academic, $3,750 (0-12-227410-5).
McGraw-Hill Encyclopedia of Science & Technology. 20v. 9th ed. 2002. 15,600p. McGraw-Hill, $2,495 (0-07-913665-6).

Libraries that serve larger communities or universities that support physics programs should consider the *Encyclopedia of Physical Science and Technology*. Midsize public libraries and colleges without a physics major would be sufficiently supported by the ninth edition of the *McGraw-Hill Encyclopedia of Science & Technology*. Libraries with the 1987 or 1992 edition of the *Encyclopedia of Physical Science and Technology* should consider updating it if their budgets can bear the cost. The *McGraw-Hill Encyclopedia of Science & Technology* covers broader scientific topics, and the *Encyclopedia of Physical Science and Technology* has more physics-specific information. For example, the former has 2 pages on quantum theory, and the latter has 22 pages on the topic.

McGraw-Hill Dictionary of Physics. 2d ed. By Sybil P. Parker. 1997. 498p. McGraw-Hill, paper, $24.95 (0-07-052429-7).
The Penguin Dictionary of Physics. 3d ed. By John Cullerne and John Daintith. 2001. 592p. Penguin Putnam, paper, $17 (0-14-051459-7).

Reference collections should have a recent physics dictionary. Both the *McGraw-Hill Dictionary of Physics* and *The Penguin Dictionary of Physics* are solid choices. *McGraw-Hill* defines 9,200 terms, usually with a sentence or two. The definition indicates the discipline that the term is used in, such as acoustics, optics, or nuclear physics, but does not include cross-references. The Penguin dictionary covers 4,500 terms with one-or two-paragraph definitions. Cross-references are indicated in all-capital letters. Because both dictionaries are low cost, libraries could buy both, but either dictionary will suffice.

Physically Speaking: A Dictionary of Quotations on Physics and Astronomy. By Carl C. Gaither and Alma E. Cavazos-Gaither. 1997. 367p. Institute of Physics, $29.99 (0-7503-0470-7).

This entertaining book offers quotations on physics and astronomical topics. Arranged topically under headings such as *Force*, *Time*, and *X-ray*, it includes quotes by such notable figures as Einstein, Schrodinger, and chief engineer Scotty from *Star Trek*. Includes a subject-by-author index and an author-by-subject index.

Web Sites

Physics information is well represented on the Internet. Physicists have led in the development of the Internet and in the inclusion of valuable content. Below are some recommended physics sites.

American Association of Physics Teachers. [http://www.aapt.org/].
This is the Web site for a professional society of teachers of physics, in both colleges and high schools.

American Institute of Physics. [http://www.aip.org/].
This site includes a career bulletin board where you can post a question to a practicing physicist, job listings, and links to other sites.

American Physical Society. [http://www.aps.org/].
Presents information about the society, its products, and services, with links to other sites.

Physics: An Annotated List of Key Resources on the Internet. [http://www.ala.org/acrl/resmar00.html].
Provides comprehensive physics information. The Association of College and Research Libraries sponsors this site.

PhysicsWeb. [http://www.physicsweb.org/].
One of the largest collections of physics related links, from the Institute of Physics.

—*Jack O'Gorman*

Special Features

Core Collection: Poetry

Reference works that focus exclusively on poetry may seem a luxury for many libraries, especially because poetry is covered so thoroughly within more general literature sources. We offer this list of core resources for libraries that can afford to invest in a few poetry-only reference tools. Most of the titles are appropriate for collections serving general readers and students at the high-school level and up. Depending on their needs, some libraries will want to add works that have more of a research emphasis or provide greater diversity. It is also a good idea to have a few poetry anthologies, such as An Anthology of Modern American Poetry (Oxford, 1999) and The Top 500 Poems (Columbia, 1992), on the reference shelves.

The field of poetry reference has several attractive online options, and these are noted below.

The Columbia Granger's Index to Poetry in Anthologies. 12th ed. 2002. 2,400p. Columbia Univ., $295 (0-231-12448-1).

Even if you have no other poetry titles in your reference collection, you need this one, a reference classic that indexes approximately 400 anthologies. For around twice the cost (depending on number of users), the online version adds additional indexes and some biographies and commentaries; offers multiple search options; and, best of all, provides full text for more than 30,000 poems, thereby lessening the frustration of not being able to put a poem in your patron's hand because you don't own all the anthologies to which Granger's refers.

A bigger but comparably priced poetry database is Roth's PoemFinder, which indexes more than 800,000 poems with full text for approximately 100,000, around 10,000 of them still under copyright. K–12 schools can opt for the curriculum-based version, World's Greatest Poetry. Because they all provide biographical and analytical information as well as poetry citations and text, any of these databases could constitute a smaller library's entire poetry reference collection.

Contemporary Poets. 7th ed. 2000. 1,443p. St. James, $190 (1-55862-349-3).

A decent literature reference collection will provide adequate, albeit scattered coverage of poets, so a biographical source devoted to poets is not an absolute necessity. However, there is a lot to be said for the convenience of finding almost 800 poets in a single volume, and this authoritative source is one of the few "poets only" guides around. For fuller chronological coverage, some libraries hang onto older editions. An attractive alternative or add-on for libraries serving high-schoolers is World Poets (Scribner, 2000), which treats 110 most-studied poets from all eras. For libraries needing more breadth and depth, Gale's Dictionary of Literary Biography series has a number of volumes on poets.

Critical Survey of Poetry. 8v. 2d rev. ed. Ed. by Philip K. Jason. 2002. 5,029p. Salem, $475 (1-58765-071-1).2d ed. Salem, $475.
Masterplots 2: Poetry Series. 8v. Ed. by Philip K. Jason. 2002. Salem, $475 (1-58765-037-1).

While Critical Survey examines poetry at the author level, Masterplots 2: Poetry Series provides explication of more than 1,300 poems. Both revisions will be available online in the fall of 2003 as part of MagillOnAuthors and MagillOnLiterature, respectively, and Salem offers both databases as a discounted package. Salem's three-volume Notable Poets (1998) covers 110 poets and is an option for smaller libraries that can't afford or don't have space for Critical Survey of Poetry.

Encyclopedia of American Poetry: The Nineteenth Century. Ed. by Eric L. Haralson. 2001. 536p. Fitzroy Dearborn, $100 (1-57958-008-4).
Encyclopedia of American Poetry: The Twentieth Century. Ed. by Eric L. Haralson. 2001. 846p. Fitzroy Dearborn, $125 (1-57958-240-0).

Encyclopedia of American Poetry: The Nineteenth Century was published as a companion to the Library of America's anthology American Poetry: The Nineteenth Century. It covers many poets that are not found in other reference sources, in addition to poets who are well known, and also has entries for types of poetry. Encyclopedia of American Poetry: The Twentieth Century has entries for landmark poems as well as poets, movements, styles, and more. Though on the scholarly side, these are the only reference works that offer their particular geographic and chronological focus, and larger libraries should have them.

The New Princeton Encyclopedia of Poetry and Poetic. Ed. by Alex Preminger and T. V. F. Brogan. 1993. 1,434p. Princeton Univ., paper, $45 (0-691-02123-6).

This scholarly volume is the standard source for information on the history and criticism of poetry and poetic technique and theory. A smaller version, The New Princeton Handbook of Poetic Terms, has 200 entries for terms that are "most common in literary study."

Poetry Criticism. 1990–. Gale, $135/vol.

Entries in this ongoing title, which is making its way toward 50 volumes, provide biographical sketches, author portraits, primary bibliographies, annotated full text, and excerpted criticism. A cumulative index is published separately. Poetry Criticism is available online as part of Gale's Literature Resource Center. Another ongoing (but so far much smaller) resource from Gale, the curriculum-oriented Poetry for Students, analyzes poems most studied at the high-school and undergraduate levels.

Poet's Market, 2003. Ed. by Nancy Breen and Vanessa Lyman. 2002. 572p. Writer's Digest, $24.99 (1-582-97124-2).

For poets who want to get their work into print, this guide describes more than 1,800 opportunities, including book publishers, small presses, journals, magazines, and chapbook publishers.

—Mary Ellen Quinn

E-book Roundup

Some innovations begin with false starts, like Betamax as a video format. I think that e-books, in general, have overcome their false starts and have viability as reference sources.

I look forward to the day when e-books have a common interface, making them as easy to access as the printed reference books on library shelves, regardless of publisher. Inclusion of e-book records in the online catalog is an important issue for the success of e-books, as catalogs will serve as gateways to the e-books. Many libraries will have their access to e-books supplied via consortia, so consortia will also be of critical importance to the format's success.

Because libraries will negotiate prices for e-books individually or with their consortia, this survey does not discuss costs. But even libraries that cannot afford to spend a dime on e-books have access to the many electronic texts available on the Web. Project Gutenberg [http://www.Gutenberg.net/] is the granddaddy of e-books—and it is free. It publishes public domain titles in a plain-vanilla ASCII format. According to the Project Gutenberg Web site it contains 6,267 e-books. Titles are in either .txt or .zip format. There are a few reference books on this site, such as the 1911 edition of Roget's Thesaurus. The interface is intentionally simple, simultaneous users are allowed, and printing is easy.

Librarians have an increasing number of e-book options to consider. Some are collections of titles from one publisher, from a variety of publishers, or on a specific topic. Some, like netLibrary, are e-book management systems. Here is a sampling of different models in the developing world of e-books.

ABC-CLIO. [http://www.abc-clio.com].

ABC-CLIO provides e-book versions of all its titles, available individually or as collections. ABC-CLIO e-books offer unlimited simultaneous access from any browser, and special readers are not needed. They also include OPAC-ready MARC records, a hosting option, and special print and e-book pricing.

Circumstances of a library's access to ABC-CLIO may vary. For example, my library has access to the ABC-CLIO e-books via the OhioLINK consortium and via netLibrary. The OhioLINK implementation is not restricted by the number of simultaneous users, and the interface is simpler. Larger screen size and no frames make the content easier to read. However, the netLibrary interface is easier to navigate, so there are trade-offs.

Baker and Taylor. [http://www.btol.com/].

Library wholesaler Baker and Taylor is expanding its role to include hosting and distribution of e-books with a product called ED, which stands for eContent Delivery. It includes the online catalog records and the management, acquisition, and delivery of e-books. Some 5,000 e-books in Adobe PDF format from leading publishers are available. ED e-books will be integrated into B&T's existing collection development and purchasing tools.

books24x7. [http://books24x7.com].

Libraries tired of spending large chunks of their book budget on computer books could benefit from this product. With a nice interface allowing simultaneous users, and easy printing, books24x7 is a good example of a well-constructed e-book site. It offers 3,000 information technology and business books, with 20 to 50 new titles added each week. Digital reference materials come from Macmillan, O'Reilly, Osborne/McGraw-Hill, Que, Sams, and other publishers.

ebrary. [http://www.ebrary.com/].

Partnerships are an important development for ebrary. For example, Adobe, R. R. Bowker, and Blackwell's Book Services have partnered with them. Ebrary has also introduced aggregated collection databases in business, computers, engineering, humanities, life and physical sciences, and social sciences. The ebrary interface is easy-to-use, providing simultaneous multiuser access. As discussed in RBB's June 1 and 15, 2002, issue, printing and copying limitations have been imposed, and some publishers don't allow 100 percent of the content to be viewed. Overall content is good, with more than 150 publishers participating. There is a PDF-based reader that libraries can download.

netLibrary. [http://www.netlibrary.com/].

The partnerships between netLibrary, an OCLC subsidiary, and Adobe, Gale [http://www.gale.com/libraries/e-books/], ABC-CLIO, H. W. Wilson, and other publishers are exciting developments for reference use of e-books. The publisher-created limitations mentioned in the February 1, 2001, RBB review of netLibrary are still in place. For example, within a consortium, only one reader may check out a title at a time. The netLibrary interface is user-friendly, but the text is displayed in a small window. There is an e-book reader from netLibrary, and a few of the netLibrary titles are available via Adobe's e-book reader. Printing or copying and pasting material from netLibrary is clear and easy to do. NetLibrary's new reference center, netLibrary for kids, and the vault of library career resources are examples of new developments.

OverDrive. [http://www.overdrive.com].

Retail distributor OverDrive has entered the library market with Digital Library Reserve, designed to help libraries create their own e-book collections for offline use. OverDrive's server hosts more than 30,000 e-books from 400 publishers, including Oxford and Greenwood. Printing must be enabled by the publisher, as must text-to-speech options. OverDrive recently partnered with Fictionwise [http://www.fictionwise.com], the e-book retailer, to provide digital lending for small and independent libraries.

Oxford Reference Online. [http://www.oxfordreference.com/].

As stated in RBB June 1 and 15, 2002, "Given Oxford's reputation for high-quality reference materials, and the ease of use, convenient features, and reasonable cost of its new database, libraries should certainly take a look." As of February 19, 2003, there were 125 Oxford titles available online. My library has incorporated these titles into our Web subject guides, and they are getting heavy use by our faculty, staff, and students. The interface is solidly designed and easy-to-use. Simultaneous use and printing are not difficult.

Safari Books Online. [http://www.safaribooksonline.com/].

O'Reilly Publishing and Pearson Technology Group have created Safari Books Online. Safari focuses on providing information technology e-books to enterprises and individuals. Publishers include O'Reilly, Addison-Wesley, Que, Peachpit, and Cisco Press. Users can cut and paste code and make online notes. This vendor includes good coverage of tech topics such as Linux, Java, and XML.

xreferplus. [http//www.xreferplus.com/].

Xreferplus specializes in reference books, many with a British focus. According to their Web site, xreferplus has 100 titles from 23 publishers in their core reference collection. The site includes unlimited remote access and unlimited concurrent usage, and it requires no additional software. The site includes many cross-references and an attractive interface. Printing is a snap, and entries include a guide for citing that entry.

—Jack O'Gorman

Just the Facts: A Look at Almanacs

Encyclopaedia Britannica Almanac, 2003. 2002. 1,184p. Encyclopaedia Britannica, $19.95 (0-85229-833-1); paper, $10.95 (0-85229-923-0).

The New York Times Almanac, 2003. By John W. Wright. 2002. 998p. Penguin, paper, $11.95 (0-14-200169-4).

Time Almanac, 2003: With Information Please. Ed. by Borgia Brunner. 2002. 1,039p. Time, $31.95 (1-929049-87-0); paper, $10.99 (1-929049-95-1).

The World Almanac and Book of Facts, 2003. By Ken Park. 2002. 1,002p. World Almanac Educational, $31.95 (0-88687-883-7); paper, $11.95 (0-88687-882-9).

Almanacs have long been a staple of the library's ready-reference shelf. This year the traditional almanac field of three (*The New York Times Almanac*, *Time Almanac* [formerly *Information Please*], and *The World Almanac and Book of Facts*) is joined by *Encyclopaedia Britannica Almanac*.

The World Almanac and Book of Facts is the grande dame, with a first publication in 1868 and published annually since 1886. *Time Almanac* began as the *Information Please Almanac* in 1947 with a title change in 1999 when the company, now part of the Family Education Network, teamed with Time, Inc., publishers of *Time* magazine, to produce a "new" almanac. The origin of this almanac was a radio show, "Information, Please," that aired from 1938 to 1952, where listeners tried to stump panelists. The title now is *Time Almanac: With Information Please*, reflecting the participating publishers. *The New York Times Almanac* evolved from the *Universal Almanac*, which began publication in 1990 and was discontinued in 1997. The editor, John Wright, who owned the rights to the content, convinced the newspaper to join with him to publish another "new" almanac.

Publishers say the Internet age has not diminished the popularity of almanacs in print form. World now sells more than one million volumes annually. And reference librarians still consider the print version of an almanac a favorite source for concise, current, quick information.

It is interesting to compare the basic contents of almanacs. For an eternity (or so it seemed) the index of *World* was in the front. This year it is at the end of the volume! The *Time* index was in the back until 1987, when it was moved to the front, where it remains. Both of the other almanacs have the index at the end. All four have some type of table of contents in the front. *Time*'s is a keyword and section index. A block of color pictures reflecting the events of the previous year appears in all of the almanacs except *The New York Times*. A variety of colored maps are in all of the volumes, and country flags are in all except *The New York Times*. The arrangement of topics is similar at least in the front, with all of the almanacs starting with news of the year, top ten news stories, or late-breaking news. Although all the almanacs have the year 2003 in the title, the usual cut off date is late October. *The New York Times* and *Time* include results of the 2002 elections, and these two and *World* include Nobel recipients for 2002. However, *Britannica* includes events only through June 2002.

Britannica and *World* have the best selection of recommended Web sites arranged by broad subjects. *Britannica* and *The New York Times* have a list of airlines by on-time performance. Each almanac has a section on the countries of the world, with all giving the percentage of Arabs in Lebanon as 95 percent except *Britannica*, which gives a figure of 93 percent from 1996. *Britannica* is the only almanac that does not have a section on major cities in the U.S. *Time* is the only one that lists population percentages by sex (48.1 percent of the population in Boston is men). Two of the almanacs (*Britannica* and *Time*) use 2000 population figures for the U.S.; the other two use 2001 estimates. Only *The New York Times* does not include a section on inventions. A list of U.S. colleges and universities is considered a necessary inclusion by this reviewer but is found only in *Time* and *World*. The *Time* list is less useful because the colleges are only listed by state.

What are the pluses and minuses for each almanac? *Britannica* capitalizes on its publisher's reputation and has a number of "greats" chosen by the editors—authors, inventions, Web sites, films, orchestras, and the most influential leaders of all times. There are also a number of "Did You Know " boxes, including the facts that windshield wipers and laser printers were invented by women. In addition to colored maps of areas of the world, a locator map accompanies each country description. Essays similar to what can be found in an encyclopedia treat lighthouses, several diseases, and a number of other topics. The minus for this almanac is the relative lack of currency.

The New York Times is the least attractive almanac, with narrow margins, thin paper, and lots of text. There are excerpts from articles from the newspaper in some sections ("Times in Focus") and seven pages of statistics on immigration in the U.S. *Time* has some unique features, such as "Seventy-five Years of Great People" —*Time* magazine's persons of the year. Association with the magazine is stressed in other ways, with an introduction to each topic written by a *Time* reporter. There is a crossword puzzle guide with lists of words by number of letters, Old Testament names, etc.

The World Almanac certainly has name recognition and has sold more than 80 million copies since 1868. In the last five years "Quick Quiz" and "It's a Fact" boxes have been added, and there are annual special features—"The Elderly" and seven fact-filled pages on all aspects of terrorism can be found in this year's edition. Trivia still abounds, with statistics on vehicle miles per licensed driver by state, a transplant waiting list by type of organ, the harness horse of the year from 1947 to 2001, and the components of the Dow Jones Averages as of last fall.

The price, size, and number of pages for each almanac are about equal, so which is best? Of course all reviewers (see any online bookstore) have their personal preferences based on their interests, eyesight, etc., but this reviewer-librarian still chooses *The World Almanac and Book of Facts* as number one in terms of coverage, currency, and usability, with *Time Almanac* providing serious competition.

—Christine Bulson

Lives of Champions

As high-profile achievers and role models, sports figures are popular choices for biographical research. The following is a list of sports biography titles for the school and public library reference shelf. Because so many of the people covered in these sources are still alive, information goes out-of-date quickly, so we have limited our list to titles that are very recent or, in the case of the series from Omnigraphics and UXL, ongoing. We have also generally confined ourselves to works that cover a variety of sports.

Athletes and Coaches of Summer. 2000. 544p. Macmillan, $80 (0-02-865493-5).

Athletes and Coaches of Winter. 2000. 516p. Macmillan, $80 (0-02-865523-0).

These titles are part of the Macmillan Profiles series aimed at middle- and high-school students. The summer volume profiles 193 athletes who excel in sports such as auto and horse racing, baseball, golf, soccer, and tennis; the winter volume covers 159 stars of football, figure skating, ice hockey, and men's basketball, among other activities.

Biographical Dictionary of American Sports: Baseball. 3v. Rev. ed. Ed. by David L. Porter. 2000. 1,865p. Greenwood, $295 (0-313-29884-X).

The first edition of this title was one of four companion dictionaries published in the late 1980s; other volumes covered football, basketball and other "indoor sports," and "outdoor sports" (skiing, soccer, tennis, and so on). Supplemental volumes treating all the sports were published in 1992 and 1995. *Baseball* is the first of the dictionaries to appear in a revised version. It profiles 1,450 individuals, 477 of them new, in entries generally between 300 and 600 words long. Appendixes list players by place of birth and major position played as well as managers, executives, umpires, Hall of Famers, and Negro League and Girls League players.

Biography Today: Sports Series. Omnigraphics. (ea. vol. 200p., $39).
- **Volume 1.** 1997. (0-7808-0069-9).
- **Volume 2.** 1998. (0-7808-0261-6).
- **Volume 3.** 1999. (0-7808-0365-5).
- **Volume 4.** 2000. (0-7808-0416-3).
- **Volume 5.** 2000. (0-7808-0417-1).
- **Volume 6.** 2001. (0-7808-0463-5).
- **Volume 7.** 2002. (0-7808-0511-9).
- **Volume 8.** 2002. (0-7808-0637-9).

One or two volumes, each covering between 10 and 15 athletes, are added every year to this series designed for ages 9 and up. Profiles are easy to read and include bibliographic references and, in most cases, an address of where to write for more information. There are general, birthplace, and birthday indexes as well as a cumulative index for the series in each volume.

Great Athletes. 8v. Rev. ed. 2002. Salem, $475 (1-58765-007-X).

This revision of the 20-volume *The Twentieth Century: Great Athletes* (1992) and its 3-volume supplement (1994) adds more than 200 athletes (for a total of 1,058) and updates nearly 600 of the original entries. The 1,000-word profiles are written to be accessible to middle-and high-school students. Each entry includes a list of references. Indexing is by sport, country, and name.

Sports Stars. UXL. (ea. vol. $95).
- **Series 1.** 2v. 1994. 622p. (0-8103-9859-1).
- **Series 2.** 2v. 1996. 574p. (0-7876-0867-X).
- **Series 3.** 1997. 342p. (0-7876-1749-0).
- **Series 4.** 1998. 370p. (0-7876-2784-4).
- **Series 5.** 1999. 348p. (0-7876-3683-5).

The first volume in this series for middle-schoolers surveys 80 professional and amateur athletes, and each succeeding volume adds around 30 more. Profiles of athletes in earlier volumes are brought up-to-date in later ones. Entries average seven pages in length and include athletes' addresses and lists of sources. Photos and sidebars add interest, and indexing is cumulative.

—Mary Ellen Quinn

Reference Books in Spanish for Adolescents and Adults

Atlases

Atlas culturales del mundo. By John Baines and others. 2v. 2002. Ediciones Folio, v.1: Cultura y sociedad del antiguo Egipto (Atlas of Ancient Egypt), 115p. (84-413-1682-1); v.2: El Islam: Revelación e historia (Atlas of the Islamic World since 1500), 140p. (84-413-1683-X); set, $89.95 (84-413-1681-3).

Gr. 9–adult. These exquisitely designed atlases include excellent color maps, charts, photographs, and drawings as well as informative chronological charts, glossaries, bibliographies, and indexes. *Cultura y sociedad del antiguo Egipto* provides a comprehensive yet accessible panorama of the culture and society of ancient Egypt. *El Islam: Revelación e historia* offers an overview of Islamic history, values, culture, and perspectives. Students of history will not be disappointed.

Atlas del antiguo Egipto. (Atlas of Ancient Egypt). Tr. by Pilar Careaga Castrillo. 2001. 215p. Alianza Editorial, $79.95 (84-206-4475-7).

Gr. 9–adult. Through wonderful color photos, drawings and charts, and an accessible text, this attractive, large-format volume presents the history, religion, economy, art, science, and daily life of the people of ancient Egypt. A glossary and an index add to the value of this historical atlas, originally published in 2001 by Istituto Geográfico de Agostini, Novara, Italy.

Dictionaries

The American Heritage Spanish Dictionary, Spanish/English, Inglés/Español. 2d ed. 2001. 1,103p. Houghton Mifflin, $26 (0-618-12770-4).

Gr. 9–adult. With an emphasis on American English and Latin American Spanish, the second edition of this bilingual dictionary includes new technological, scientific, and business terms. Speakers of all the Americas will appreciate the different meanings of more than 120,000 words, presented in an easy-to-understand design. Notes on grammar usage are a plus.

The Concise American Heritage Spanish Dictionary. 2d ed. 2001. 616p. Houghton Mifflin, $14 (0-618-11769-5).

Gr. 9–adult. Similar in design to (but a bit more compact than) *The American Heritage Spanish Dictionary*, this bilingual dictionary includes more than 70,000 words and phrases. The emphasis on American English and Latin American Spanish as well as the informative guides and tables will assist students of either language.

Diccionario Akal del español colloquial. (Akal Dictionary of Colloquial Spanish). By Alicia Ramos and Ana Serradilla. 2000. 384p. Ediciones Akal, $29.95 (84-460-1449-1).

Gr. 8–adult. Designed for Spanish learners, this well-designed dictionary includes more than 1,400 idiomatic and colloquial Spanish expressions, definitions, usage guidance, and English equivalents. The authors made special efforts to incorporate commonly used idioms from Spain. Despite a few regionalisms, Spanish speakers from the Americas will recognize most expressions, including vulgarisms that are widely used in the Spanish-speaking world. Useful English- and Spanish-language indexes and suggested activities complement this innovative lexicon.

Diccionario de historia y política del siglo XX. (Dictionary of History and Politics of the Twentieth Century). 2001. 741p. Tecnos/Grupo Anaya, $22.95 (84-309-3703-X).

Gr. 9–adult. More than 1,500 alphabetical entries highlight the most important concepts, institutions, and individuals of the twentieth century in fields such as history, politics, human geography, and socioeconomics. From *Abacha, Sani* (president of Nigeria), to *Zulú*, students will find basic information and explanations about the movements and events that shaped the 1900s. Despite the lack of maps and photographs, the dictionary format is accessible and easy to use.

Diccionario ingles. (English Dictionary). Rev. ed. 2001. 528p. Houghton Mifflin, paper, $13 (0-618-14271-1).

Gr. 9–adult. Especially designed for native Spanish-speaking students of English, this English dictionary provides English and Spanish definitions in a side-by-side format. The two-column format—which includes sample sentences, idioms, and phrases in both languages—makes it easier for English-language learners to understand English definitions as they review the Spanish words. A pronunciation guide and spelling table further assist students.

Diccionario de la lengua española. (Dictionary of the Spanish Language). 2v. By Real Academia Española. 2001. Editorial Espasa-Calpe, $54.95 (84-239-6814-6).

Gr. 9–adult. Now in its twenty-second edition, the lexicographic bible of the Spanish-speaking world is available in two manageable volumes. With more than 11,000 new entries and 28,000 words from the Americas, this new edition incorporates both Peninsular and Latin American usages, adding immensely to the value and usefulness of this prestigious dictionary. Despite the small, difficult-to-read font, serious students of the Spanish language should have access to this universally accepted arbiter of the lexical and semantic peculiarities of the language of more than 300 million Spanish speakers worldwide.

Diccionario de sinónimos y antónimos del español actual. (Dictionary of Synonyms and Antonyms of Current Spanish). 2001. 1,024p. Ediciones SM, $12.95 (84-348-8140-3).

Gr. 8–adult. Spanish speakers—especially from the Americas—will welcome this comprehensive dictionary of synonyms and antonyms. Many expressions are characteristic of current Spanish from both sides of the Atlantic or foreign acquisitions not yet accepted by the Spanish Royal Academy. Colloquialisms, vulgarisms, and national or regional variants are clearly labeled. This dictionary will assist all Spanish speakers (and Spanish learners), whether they are searching for sophisticated vocabulary or youthful slang.

Lema: Diccionario de la lengua española. (Lema: Dictionary of the Spanish Language). 2001. 1,896p. SPES Editorial, $19 (84-8332-213-7).

Gr. 9–adult. The purpose of this dictionary is to explain necessary and common Spanish vocabulary for contemporary users. The editors have given special care to ensure word meanings reflect current usage. With almost 100,000 entries, *Lema* includes clear definitions identified as to level of usage, illustrative examples to help clarify meaning, idiomatic expressions, etymologies following the entry word, and useful charts alongside the definition explaining basic grammar rules. The easy-to-read typography and design add to its value. One caveat: most examples consider only usage in Spain.

Distributors

Bilingual Publications, 270 Lafayette St., Ste. 705, New York, NY 10012
Lectorum Publications, 111 Eighth Ave., Ste. 804, New York, NY 10011-5201

—Isabel Schon

Reference Sources on Beer

Ancient Egyptians used to say the mouth of a perfectly happy man (or woman) is filled with beer. Now, the mind of a perfectly happy beer drinker can be filled with knowledge about that beer!

Beer and beer resources come in many varieties. Listed here are books and Web sites with a focus on beer from around the world. There are three well-known authors in the beer world, Michael Jackson, Brian Glover, and Stephen Beaumont. Each author has several books on beer, brewing, and other malts and ales. Their most current or comprehensive books are highlighted. Web sites were last accessed on February 4, 2003.

Books

The Running Press Pocket Guide to Beer: The Connoisseur's Companion to More Than 2,000 Beers of the World. 7th ed. By Michael Jackson. 2000. 208p. Running Press, $12.95 (0-7624-0885-5).

The worldly traveler's guide to beer, pubs, and breweries discusses and rates beers from around the globe. The history, culture, and geography of each region or country are discussed along with the beer. Each beer is rated with up to five stars and is compared only to other beers in the region. A lengthy introduction includes a beer glossary and summation of what makes a great beer. The index includes both beers and breweries.

Other books by Michael Jackson include *Michael Jackson's Beer Companion: The World's Great Beer Styles, Gastronomy and Traditions* (Running Press, o.p.), *Michael Jackson's Great Beer Guide: The World's 500 Best Beers* (DK, 2000), and *Ultimate Beer* (DK, 1998).

Premium Beer Drinker's Guide. By Stephen Beaumont. 2000. 224p. Firefly, $24.95 (1-55209-510-X).

Beaumont defines premium beers as "the special-occasion drink for everyday people." Naturally, this guide includes only premium beers, ones that according to Beaumont "stimulate your senses and challenge your perceptions and, above all else, make a bold statement in your glass." Arrangement is by type of beer—wheats, hops, bocks, darks. Ratings for price, freshness/durability, and availability are noted along with extensive notes on the beer and brewery. Beers are recommended to accompany barbecue, spicy foods, desserts, cigars, and seasons of the year. Other books by Beaumont are *Taste for Beer* (DIANE, 1999) and *The Great Canadian Beer Guide*. (McArthur, 2001).

The World Encyclopedia of Beer. By Brian Glover. 2001. 256p. Lorenz Books, $29.95 (0-7548-0933-1).

This book makes you thirsty just looking at it. It is both a written and pictorial history of beer and the brewing process as well as a guide to beers from around the world. It does not rate beers; rather, it provides a brief description of beers from a particular region or country, their alcohol content, and flavors or ingredients that give each beer a unique taste. Vibrant color photographs depicting beer bottles and cans; malts, barley, and hops; and the history and culture of beer add flavor to each page. Glover is also the author of *The Beer Companion: An Essential Guide to Classic Beers from Around the World* and *The Complete Guide to Beer*, both published by Lorenz in 1999 but now out-of-print.

Special Features

Web Sites

The Beer Hunter. [http://www.beerhunter.com/].
If you want one expert opinion on good beer, then try this site. Sponsored by *RealBeer.com* (see below), it is the official site of Michael Jackson, known in the beer world as "the Beer Hunter." Jackson discusses different beer styles, offers personal beer tasting notes and ratings, and provides a Q and A on beer. Much of the content on the site is reproduced from Jackson's books, which you may purchase via the site. Unique features include reviews of beer events and postcards—all of course with Jackson's name on them.

The Beer Info Source. [http://beerinfo.com/].
This is a homegrown index of beer-related resources, compliments of Webmaster John Locke. The design is simple and outdated, but there is no advertising. The links are updated weekly and focus on beer alone, no cigars or food. The Beer Info Source supports and encourages the responsible enjoyment of alcoholic beverages. It provides a large collection of resources for those planning to open a brewpub, tavern, or bar. Books, legal information, brewer's calculations, and formulas can be found in the more than 1,000 links to the WWW Virtual Library page on beer and brewing.

BeerAdvocate.com. [http://www.beeradvocate.com/].
"There are no beer experts, just beer drinkers with opinions" is the slogan of this Web site, which has been around since 1996. A cozy hangout for the less knowledgeable beer connoisseurs, containing beer reviews from both the site owners, Jason Alstrom and Todd Alstrom, as well as everyday beer drinkers, this site is self-funded, with no advertising, so the reviews are honest and opinionated. A beer forum is on tap for lively discussions with other beer lovers.

RealBeer.com: The Beer Portal. [http://www.realbeer.com/].
"The beer portal" is an accurate description of this sleek, consumer-focused Web site. Don't let the advertisements deter, as the content is rich with hundreds of links to beer-related Web sites, online books and publications, and beer headlines from around the world. For travelers, a worldwide database of bars and taverns, brewpubs, breweries, festivals, beer tastings, and tours awaits. *RealBeer* is a great source for "Beer of the Month" club information.

—Sue Polanka

Reference Sources on Wine

People have been enjoying wine since ancient times. Wine plays an important role in religious rituals, and it adds to the pleasure of a fine meal. Recent medical research shows that moderate, regular consumption of wine is good for one's health. Despite the current economic slump, wine sales remain stable. It is not surprising that people who want to learn more about wine come to the library to find information. Even small libraries with limited budgets can afford a few basic resources. An encyclopedia and a book covering the basics of tasting, storage, and service will answer the majority of questions. Those requiring greater depth should add an atlas and some regional guides. Tasting Wine [http://www.tasting-wine.com/] and Wine Lovers Page [http://www.wine-lovers-page.com/] are good supplemental Web sites.

Encyclopedias

Christie's World Encyclopedia of Champagne and Sparkling Wine. By Tom Stevenson. 1998. 335p. Wine Appreciation Guild, $50 (1-891267-06-X).
Explains the history and production methods of champagnes and sparkling wines, covering the grape varieties, regions, and vintages and offering picks of the best.

The Global Encyclopedia of Wine. By Rebecca Chapa and Peter Forrestal. 2001. 912p. Wine Appreciation Guild, $75 (1-891267-38-8).
Provides international coverage and local detail about every wine-growing country, enhanced with beautiful color photographs.

Larousse Encyclopedia of Wine. 2d ed. Ed. by Christopher Foulkes. 2001. 624p. Larousse, $45 (2-03-585013-4).
An excellent general source that includes information on choosing, keeping, serving, and tasting wine as well as pairing wine and food. It covers the wines of the world with maps, including lesser-known wine regions in China, Japan, and India.

The New Sotheby's Wine Encyclopedia: A Comprehensive Reference Guide to the Wines of the World. 3d ed. By Tom Stevenson. 2001. 600p. DK, $50 (0-7894-8039-5).
This source covers the basics of wine making and tasting as well as the wines of Europe, North and South America, the Levant (Turkey, Israel), Australia, and New Zealand. The author gives his choices of the best wines in each area.

Oxford Companion to Wine. 2d ed. Ed. by Jancis Robinson. 1999. 819p. Oxford, $65 (0-19-866236-X).
This second edition has more than 500 new and 1,500 revised entries providing comprehensive coverage of all aspects of wine making, a historical perspective on wine and wine drinking, and delightful articles on the literature of wine and wine in English literature. It also covers new wine regions not found in other sources, such as Bhutan, Ethiopia, and Korea.

Oz Clarke's Encyclopedia of Grapes: A Comprehensive Guide to Varieties and Flavors. By Oz Clarke and Margaret Rand. 2001. 320p. Harcourt, $40 (0-15-100714-4).
Two award-winning wine writers have produced a resource about the basic raw material. They explain viticulture, give a history of the vine, and provide A–Z articles on each kind of wine grape and the types of wine made with it.

Wine. By Andre Domine. 2001. 928p. Konemann, $49.95 (3-8290-4856-4).
This lavishly illustrated encyclopedia has entries for all of the wine-producing countries and regions of the world, with choices of the best wines. The wines receive ratings from one to three stars. An appendix has a glossary, designations of origins, and vintage charts.

Atlases

Hachette Atlas of French Wines & Vineyards. 2d ed. Ed. by Pascal Ribereau-Gayon. 2000. 300p. Hachette, $50 (1-84202-069-2).
Explores the history of French wines and analyzes the wine production in each region. It also explains the French appellation system.

Oz Clarke's New Wine Atlas: Wines & Wine Regions of the World. By Oz Clarke. 2002. 336p. Harcourt, $60 (0-15-100913-9).
This unique atlas explains the importance of the vineyard for wine making, discussing the role of the soil, climate, and water in production. In addition to maps of the world's wine regions, there are 75 unique hand-painted panoramic maps of vineyard areas.

Regional Guides

An Encyclopedia of the Wines and Domaines of France. By Clive Coates. 2000. 608p. Univ. of California, $42 (0-520-22093-5).
Coates, a British Master of Wine, spent 35 years traveling around the French vineyards. He provides in-depth coverage of all the French wine regions with maps, the French wine laws and appellations, and wine ratings (one to three stars).

The Oxford Companion to the Wines of North America. Ed. by Bruce Cass. 2000. 301p. Oxford, $45 (0-19-860114-X).
The more than 1,400 wineries in North America produce some of the world's finest wines. This volume has essays by wine experts and wine makers about trends and demographics, quality, the wine media, distribution, organic wines, and genetics in addition to A–Z entries about terminology, vineyards, and wineries.

General Texts

Exploring Wine: The Culinary Institute of America's Complete Guide to Wines of the World. 2d ed. By Steven Kolpan and others. 2001. 820p. Wiley, $60 (0-471-35295-0).
The wine educators from the Culinary Institute of America cover wine

tasting, wine making, and the wines of the world. They provide information about health and pairing wine with food and offer detailed coverage of service, storage, and purchasing, including buying wine at auctions.

Windows on the World Complete Wine Course, 2003 edition. By Kevin Zraly. 2002. 208p. Sterling, $24.95 (1-4027-0090-3).

This annual volume provides a good explanation of wine basics: tasting, wine regions, buying, storing, and serving. It also has a glossary, pronunciation guide, and recommendations.

The Wine Bible. By Karen MacNeil. 2001. 910p. Workman, paper, $19.95 (1-56305-434-5).

This excellent practical guide by the director of the wine program at the Culinary Institute of America has comprehensive coverage of the world's wines in plain English. It looks at the major wine regions, placing the wines within each region's history, culture, and cuisine. This is a good source for circulating collections and for libraries with small budgets.

—*Barbara Bibel*

Top 10 Science Reference Sources

The sciences being a hot area in reference publishing now, we had lots of candidates for our first "top 10" science list—so many, in fact, that we have limited ourselves to items that are classed in the 500s of the Dewey decimal system. Titles were selected based on reviews that appeared in RBB from the December 1, 2001, to the November 15, 2002, issues.

Encyclopedia of Evolution. Ed. by Mark Pagel. 2002. 1,205p. Oxford, $325 (0-19-512200-3).

This outstanding encyclopedia brings together 365 articles written for users with varying backgrounds. No other recent encyclopedia provides comparable authoritative in-depth coverage of biological evolution.

Encyclopedia of Prehistory. By David Lambert. 2002. 400p. Facts On File, $50.50 (0-8160-4547-X).

The diagrams and charts are especially valuable in this guide to how the planet was formed and how animals, plants, and other organisms evolved. An excellent choice for school and public libraries, although younger students might find it a challenge.

Encyclopedia of Weather and Climate. 2v. By Michael Allaby. 2002. 672p. Facts On File, $150 (0-8160-4071-0).

Covering approximately 3,000 terms in meteorology and climatology, this book stands out as a basic, accessible reference for the high-school level and up.

International Wildlife Encyclopedia. 22v. 3d ed. 2002. 3,168p. Marshall Cavendish, $499.95 (0-7614-7266-5).

This updated and revised edition covers all forms of world wildlife—insects, fish, amphibians, reptiles, birds, and mammals. The combination of familiar and uncommon species, extensive color illustrations, and informative text makes it particularly suited to school and public libraries.

Magill's Encyclopedia of Science: Animal Life. 4v. 2d ed. Ed. by Carl Hoagstrom. 2002. Salem, $435 (1-58765-019-3).

The 1991 *Magill's Survey of Science: Life Science* and its 1998 supplement have been updated and refocused from general life science to a discussion of nonhumans from the kingdom *Animalia*, with an emphasis on animals in nature.

Mathematics. 4v. Ed. by Barry Max Brandenberger. 2002. Macmillan, $375 (0-02-865561-3).

A refreshing cross-disciplinary approach characterizes a work that is designed to give users a view of how mathematics functions in everyday life. Its emphasis on clarity makes it a good choice for students from the middle-school all the way to the undergraduate level.

Oxford Companion to the Earth. Ed. by Paul L. Hancock and Brian J. Skinner. 2001. 1,174p. Oxford, $75 (0-19-854039-6).

Another discipline-specific overview from this publisher, covering climatology, geology, geophysics, oceanography, paleontology, and other earth sciences. Although language is somewhat technical, care has been taken to make concepts accessible.

Rain Forests of the World. 11v. 2002. 670p. Marshall Cavendish, $329.95 (0-7614-7241-1).

In a set intended for readers in grades four through eight, eye-catching illustrations help convey information about the plants, animals, people, and microorganisms that populate tropical and temperate rain forests.

UXL Science Encyclopedia. 2v. 2d ed. 2001. Ed. by Ron Nagel. 2,048p. UXL, $350 (0-7876-5432-9).

With many new or revised entries in its updated edition, this basic encyclopedia remains a solid choice for middle-and junior-high-school students. The addition of color illustrations provides visual punch.

World Atlas of Coral Reefs. By Mark D. Spalding and others. 2001. 424p. University of California, $45 (0-520-23255-0).

This unique atlas, written by a team of experts with support from a variety of organizations, summarizes our present knowledge of the geographic distribution and conservation status of coral reefs. It should be of interest to anyone seeking definitive information on one of the most beautiful, biologically diverse ecosystems on the planet.

—*Mary Ellen Quinn*

Twenty Best Bets for Student Researchers

For the new school year, we took another look at titles we reviewed in the past 12 months that are designed for students from the elementary-through high-school levels. Here are our top choices for school and public libraries.

Africa: An Encyclopedia for Students. 4v. Ed. by John Middleton. 2002. Scribner, $375 (0-684-80650-9).

The highly regarded *Encyclopedia of Africa South of the Sahara*, published in 1997, has been adapted and updated for high-school students. This version has about 450 entries on countries, regions, geographic features, cultural groups, personalities, and other topics. [Je 1 & 15 02].

America the Beautiful. [Internet database]. 2001. Grolier, pricing from $209 in combination with other Grolier databases. [http://www.go.grolier.com].

Although the online version of the venerable state series found in most K–12 and public libraries has impressive statistics—1,000 articles; 2,700 photographs; 400 maps, many of them interactive; 1,000 Internet links; 550 profiles; 115 games and puzzles; 60 time lines; and 400 places to visit—it is the site's user-friendliness, clean look, and well-planned arrangement that will draw users. [RBB F 15 02].

Animal Sciences. 4v. Ed. by Allan B. Cobb. 2002. Macmillan, $375 (0-02-865556-7).

This set, like others in the Macmillan Science Library, is designed to accommodate middle-school students through college undergraduates. The work contains approximately 300 clearly written entries on a variety of topics relating to animal science. [RBB Je 1 & 15 02].

Biology. 4v. Ed. by Richard Robinson. 2002. Macmillan, $375 (0-02-865551-6).

Another title in the Macmillan Science Library. This set provides 432 signed entries on a broad range of topics pertaining to biology, including basic concepts, history of the science, related fields, and issues, as well as topics of special interest to young adults. [RBB Je 1 & 15 02].

Complete American Presidents Sourcebook. 5v. By Roger Matuz. 2001. 1,632p. UXL, $199 (0-7876-4837-X).

Report writers in grades five through ten are the audience for this survey of U.S. presidents. Each entry provides a general overview of the president's term(s) in office, his life before and after the presidency, and significant issues and events that he faced. This information is followed by a profile of the First Lady and at least one primary source that highlights the president's agenda. [RBB N 1 01].

Constitutional Amendments: From Freedom of Speech to Flag Burning. 3v. By Tom Pendergast and others. 2001. 528p. UXL, $130 (0-7876-4865-5).

There are numerous reference sources on the U.S. Constitution, but few are designed to be accessible to middle-schoolers. Each amendment gets a chapter that includes historical background, details about the drafting and ratification processes, a summary of significant court cases, and a discussion of how the amendment has affected Americans in their everyday lives. [RBB S 15 01].

Dangerous Planet: The Science of Natural Disasters. 3v. By Phillis Engelbert. 2001. 446p. UXL, $130 (0-7876-2848-4).

Avalanches, earthquakes, floods, and wildfires are among the 16 natural disasters explored for the benefit of young adults. Each chapter is divided into sections that tell of one or two major disasters in history, explain the scientific nature and short-and long-term consequences of each type of disaster, and discuss how humans can cause and prevent the disaster or mitigate its effects. [RBB D 1 01].

Endangered Animals. 10v. Ed. by Penelope Mathias. 2002. Grolier, $409 (0-7172-5584-0).

Information on more than 400 extinct or threatened animals is nicely organized and packaged for the elementary-and middle-school levels. Entries are arranged alphabetically and include at least one large color photo or artistic rendering. A number of rare and obscure animals are included, and the selection of species is representative of the various causes of endangerment. [RBB Mr 1 02].

The Environment Encyclopedia. 11v. Ed. by Ruth A. Eblen and William R. Eblen. 2001. 1,547p. Marshall Cavendish, $459.95 (0-7614-7182-0).

An update and repackaging of the Houghton Mifflin *Encyclopedia of the Environment* (1994), which was among the first resources to focus on the human and social aspects of environmental issues. The editors selected and updated or commissioned 400 articles, arranged alphabetically over a broad range of topics and incorporating many more illustrations and photographs. The layout and presentation are most suitable for middle-school through senior-high-school students. [RBB O 15 01].

Exploring Earth and Space Science. Ed. by Peter Mavrikis. 11v. 2002. 880p. Marshall Cavendish, $329.95 (0-7614-7219-3).

Entries explain major concepts and people involved in the fields of chemistry, earth science, physics, space science, and environment. There are color photos, diagrams, and charts illustrating most concepts. The set is appropriate for upper-elementary-and middle-school students. [RBB F 1 02].

Makers of Science. 5v. Ed. by Derek Gjertsen and Michael Allaby. 2002. Oxford, $140 (0-19-521680-6).

Middle-and high-school students will enjoy using this set, which takes a slightly different approach to ordinary biographical information on scientists by incorporating the political and social settings as well as the scientific achievements of more than 40 European and U.S. scientists. Recommended as an attractive supplement to other, more comprehensive science biography resources. [RBB Je 1 & 15 02].

Mathematics. 4v. Ed. by Barry Max Brandenberger Jr. 2002. Macmillan, $375 (0-02-865561-3).

Taking a refreshing, cross-disciplinary approach, this work for the junior-high level and up gives users a view of how mathematics functions "in everyday life, as well as its role as a tool for measurement, data analysis, and technological development." [RBB Jl 01].

Medieval World. 10v. Ed. by Sally MacEachern. 2001. Grolier, $345 (0-7172-5520-4).

Among the several reference sets on the Middle Ages designed for middle-and high-school students, this one stands out for its use of full color throughout. Some 226 alphabetically arranged articles introduce readers to important people, places, events, concepts, and customs of the period. [RBB F 1 02].

Physics Matters! 10v. By John O. E. Clark. 2001. Grolier, $309 (0-7172-5509-3).

Here is a reference source that aims to make a complex topic accessible to grades five through ten. The striking illustrations and color photographs help explain how the concepts discussed in the text apply to life situations. [RBB O 1 01].

Rain Forests of the World. 11v. 2002. 670p. Marshall Cavendish, $329.95 (0-7614-7254-1).

A nice introduction for readers in grades four through eight, with information about the vast array of plants, animals, people, and microorganisms that dwell in tropical and temperate rain forests as well as issues such as conservation, deforestation, and tourism. Entries are enhanced by maps, illustrations, and vivid color photographs. [RBB Ap 15 02].

The Revolutionary War. 10v. By James R. Arnold and Roberta Wiener. 2002. Grolier, $269 (0-7172-5553-0).

For elementary-and middle-school students studying the American Revolution, information is arranged in a chronological sequence from the events leading up to the war, through the years of fighting, to the founding of the new nation. Each volume is highly illustrated with pictures of significant people and places as well as maps. [RBB Ap 1 02].

Schirmer Encyclopedia of Art. 4v. By Ann Landi. 2002. Schirmer, $345 (0-02-865414-5).

Author Landi writes that this introductory work for students in middle school through high school responds to increased interest in the visual arts and in visual culture in general. There are 300 biographies of artists and 100 topical articles that cover eras, movements, and genres. [RBB Ap 15 01].

Shakespeare's World and Work. 3v. Ed. by John F. Andrews. 2001. 750p. Scribner, $295 (0-684-80629-0).

Scribner's scholarly *William Shakespeare: His World, His Work, and His Influence* (1985) has been retooled into an attractive resource for junior-and senior-high-school students. More than 250 A–Z entries shed light on Shakespeare's plays, characters, and themes as well as life and times. [RBB S 1 01].

The Supreme Court of the United States: A Student Companion. 2d. ed. By John J. Patrick. 2001. 398p. Oxford, $45 (0-19-515008-2).

Information related to many aspects of the Supreme Court, including its structure, history, origins, development, composition, functions, duties, and objectives, is packaged for students ages 12 and up. In this second edition, content has been expanded and updated to reflect recent rulings and to describe the current status and significance of certain controversial topics, such as abortion and affirmative action. [RBB Je 1 & 15 02].

UXL Encyclopedia of Science. 10v. 2d ed. Ed. by Ron Nagel. 2002. 2,048p. UXL, $350 (0-7876-5432-9).

With more than 600 entries—approximately 50 new and 100 updated—the latest edition of a title first published in 1998 and geared toward middle-school and junior-high-school students provides information on topics in the study of physical, earth, and life sciences as well as the fields of technology, engineering, mathematics, environmental science, and psychology. [RBB F 15 02].

—*Mary Ellen Quinn*

Working Women

The "working woman" is nothing new, but for years women's contributions outside the domestic sphere were largely ignored in reference literature. One of the by-products of the women's movement has been a proliferation of research on women with respect to their occupations. Now that the index to Gale's Women in World History (1999–2002) has finally been published, the researcher can look in the "Occupation/Experience Index" to find groupings of women who were abolitionists, consumers' advocates, countesses, ophthalmic surgeons, nuns, or vaudeville performers. Similarly, the "Index by Occupations and Realms of Renown" in American National Biography (Oxford, 1999) offers agriculturists, choreographers and dance instructors, educational reform advocates, and Quakers, to name just a few categories—although here, one has to take the extra step of sorting the women from the men. Another alternative is offered by the growing number of resources that take an activity-specific approach. Here is a selection of other recent biographical tools profiling women at work.

A to Z of American Women in Sports. By Paula Edelson. 2002. 278p. Facts On File, $44 (0-8160-4565-8).

A look at more than 150 women who have had a significant impact in sports, including some who are not athletes in the traditional sense but made their contributions in coaching, refereeing, and being the "first" in their fields.

A to Z of American Women Writers. By Carol Kort. 2000. 274p. Facts On File, $40 (0-8160-3727-2).

Here are profiles of 150 women from the seventeenth century to the present who have had a significant influence on American writing, representing diversity of style, genre, ethnicity, and subject matter as well as time period and region in which they lived and worked.

A to Z of Women in the Performing Arts. By Liz Sonneborn. 2002. 264p. Facts On File, $44 (0-8160-4398-1).

This compendium of biographies of 150 American female performers packs a wealth of data into compact form. Choice of entries is multicultural and multinational.

American Women in Technology: An Encyclopedia. By Linda Zierdt-Warshaw and others. 2000. 384p. ABC-CLIO, $75 (1-57607-072-7).

More than 300 women, as well as technology disciplines, associations, laboratories, agencies, awards, and related topics, are the subjects of entries in this volume.

American Women Writers, 1900–1945: A Bio-Bibliographical and Critical Sourcebook. Ed. by Laurie Champion. 2000. 407p. Greenwood, $95 (0-313-30943-4).

This book profiles 58 American women writers who published their significant works between 1900 and 1945. The biographical information is brief and includes the most basic details, while the overview of the major works and themes is quite substantive and will be very useful for research.

Biographical Dictionary of Congressional Women. By Karen Foerstel. 1999. 300p. Greenwood, $65 (0-313-30290-1).

A good overview of the role the 200 women who have made it to Congress have played and of the political trends that have made their presence there noteworthy.

A Biographical Dictionary of Women Healers: Midwives, Nurses, and Physicians. By Laurie Scrivener and J. Suzanne Barnes. 2002. Greenwood, $74.95 (1-57356-219-X)

Among the more honored female health workers—Clara Barton, Margaret Sanger, Faye Wattleton—this book's 240 entries also elevate the undervalued.

The Biographical Dictionary of Women in Science: Pioneering Lives from Ancient Times to the Mid-20th Century. 2v. Ed. by Marilyn Ogilvie and Joy Harvey. 2000. Routledge, $195 (0-415-92038-8).

Contains biographies of approximately 2,500 women in science around the globe, from antiquity to modern times. This title is more wide-ranging than others in the field, with excellent indexing and reference lists that have scholarly appeal.

Encyclopedia of Women Social Reformers. 2v. By Helen Rappaport. 2001. 888p. ABC-CLIO, $185 (1-57607-101-4).

This encyclopedia includes more than 400 reformers from the French Revolution until the present, from 64 countries. The author takes a very liberal view of *reformer*, encompassing writers and philanthropists.

From Suffrage to the Senate: An Encyclopedia of American Women in Politics. 2v. By Suzanne O'Dea Schenken. 1999. 800p. ABC-CLIO, $125 (0-87436-960-6).

More than 675 entries cover women, actions, events, and organizations that have impacted women's lives through policies and politics.

Historical Encyclopedia of American Women Entrepreneurs. By Jeanette M. Oppedisano. 2000. 283p. Greenwood, $79.50 (0-318-30647-8).

Biographies of 120 women from 1776 to the present illustrate how, no matter how diverse their origins, all were similar in that they faced obstacles, took risks, and beat the odds.

International Encyclopedia of Women and Sports. 3v. Ed. by Karen Christensen and others. 2001. 1,428p. Macmillan, $350 (0-02-864954-0).

With the growth of interest in women's sports, this compendium helps bring together a variety of information covering individuals, sports, and related issues. There are 150 articles, half of them devoted to sports by country or region.

International Women in Science: A Biographical Dictionary to 1950. Ed. by Catherine M. C. Haines and Helen M. Stevens. 2001. 383p. ABC-CLIO, $75 (1-57607-090-5).

The focus here is on British women, although the book does include women from Europe, South Africa, China, Japan, Australia, India, and New Zealand among its 400 entries.

Nineteenth Century British Women Writers: A Bio-Bibliographical and Critical Sourcebook. Ed. by Abigail Burnham Bloom. 2000. 456p. Greenwood, $95 (0-313-30439-4).

Covers the full gamut of literary genres. Both prominent and lesser known, but not obscure, authors of the period are featured among the 93 writers profiled.

Notable Women Scientists. Ed. by Pamela Proffitt. 1999. 668p. Gale, $105 (0-7876-3900-1).

Profiles 485 women from antiquity to the present and from around the world who have made an important contribution in a wide range of scientific disciplines.

Women Rulers throughout the Ages: An Illustrated Guide. By Guida M. Jackson. 1999. 471p. ABC-CLIO, $75 (1-57607-091-3).

This biographical dictionary builds on an original work, *Women Who Ruled*, which was published a decade ago. It revises past entries and adds more than 200 new ones for coverage of 504 women.

—*Mary Ellen Quinn*

Works in Progress: Defining a Dictionary

"Language is difficult to put into words," warns John Morse with a guarded, sparkly cheer. "That motto is often heard hereabouts," he adds. Maybe the motto helps to explain the quiet at Merriam-Webster, Inc., where Morse is president and publisher. Perhaps because language won't submit easily to the tongue or the will, words loll inaudibly for now on Merriam-Webster galley proof sheets. They sequester themselves among filed citation cards. And they trickle discreetly from one editor to another on a drab February morning in Springfield, Massachusetts.

In the earsplitting peace of the dictionary office, the editors have their hands full. For after 19 months of toil, a staff of 60 has reached the final stages of editing the eleventh edition of *Merriam-Webster's Collegiate Dictionary* for publication in July 2003. Since the first edition appeared in 1898, the *Collegiate* has sold more than 55 million copies. The second-best-selling English-language hardcover book in history, it is runner-up to the Bible. Obviously, this dictionary absorbs and rewards care.

So, how do they make a dictionary?

The word *definition* has been defined by lexicographical historian Herbert C. Morton as follows: "A definition is a snapshot of a word at rest," he opines. The current Merriam-Webster in-house company manual for professional definers soberly remarks: "Definitions are to define the meanings of words. In general, once they have done that, they are to stop." As Morse explains it, a dictionary should include words already verifiably intrinsic to the culture for which the dictionary is intended and should define them with a fastidiously concise clarity. But, of course, there is more to it.

The eleventh *Collegiate* refines the definitions of words included in the tenth while also adding and defining 10,000 new words and senses. "A new sense of the word *cookie* is just as important to us as defining *dweeb* for the first time," insists Morse. Ten main editors scrutinize every definition, ushering each word through 12 stages of editorial review before the process concludes; a word's revision cycle may persist for as long as eight months. None of the 12 stages could be called rote or pro forma, not even the final reading and approval bestowed. Big changes can overtake a definition at the last minute.

Consider the case of the irksome polysyllable *postmodern*. Originally, the M-W definition ran to almost 200 words. By February, it consists of barely 70. "I was one of the people who struggled with that," Morse recalls with a sigh. Conspicuously scuttled in the revision were full-scale assessments of both postmodern architecture and literature as subtopics. The adjective may continue anyhow to puzzle some of us. However, a lot can be said for entering and exiting the definition without having to inhale more than twice.

Squeezing the wordage from definitions is nothing new for definers. "Dictionaries have always been fairly disciplined creations, going back at least to the time of Dr. Johnson," Morse says. Not that he always likes to squeeze his words; in fact, the eleventh has expanded the tenth by 64 pages. Still the publisher complains, "I wish the eleventh could hold 2,000 pages, so we could tell all the stories we know how to tell." When needled about just what stories he means, Morse replies, "*The New Collegiate Dictionary* is a kind of glossary of American life."

Do tell, let's say, of *tattletale gray*. Once included in the *Collegiate* and now evicted, this color was best known in its heyday as "a light gray used in a 1950s advertising campaign for a brand of laundry soap," remembers Morse with enthusiasm. "If you didn't use the soap, white shirts would come out a *tattletale gray*. So people began using the phrase simply as a color, without the negative overtones." For the color fancier, *tattletale gray* might well givevim to a neglected spot on the spectrum in 2003. Now can it, if Merriam-Webster won't officially define it?

Probably not. But since the dictionary only describes current usage as it is, and does not seek to prescribe future usage, the definer cannot carry a torch for bygone lingo, no matter how luscious or seemingly needed.

A consolation: our big American mouths keep coming up with unforeseen mutterings, that Morseian glossary. Consult the eleventh edition and you'll find *oy*, *buckytube*, *McJob*, and *mockumentary*, all new to the Collegiate Dictionary; also, *shock jock*, *psyops*, *gut check*, *lookism*, and *tankini*. Moreover, in the great beyond of the M-W Web site [http://www.Merriam-Webster.com], new words scramble in each day, contributed by a vast and growing readership. (For example, *srop*, submitted stealthily by the surnameless "Brian" of New Jersey, means "to halt.") Since opening the Web site in 1996, Morse and his colleagues have been able to inspect and serve the habits of dictionary users with a confident, unprecedented intimacy. The eleventh *Collegiate* is their first print edition to benefit directly from such privileged oversight.

Before the Web, the company would typically field 1,000 letters from readers in a year. At present, users send M-W 1,000 e-mails every month, offering comments on company products—and just asking questions about whatever words happen to bewilder or beguile. The company can observe which words are most frequently looked up online at any given time, for instance. (After 9/11, the most popular were *surreal* and *succumb*. When Princess Diana died, the words of choice included *paparazzi* and *cortege*.) Online customer response can lead the editorial staff to make adjustments in revisions of print dictionaries.

For that reason and others, Morse has found his print and electronic products complementary, not competitive. In fact, M-W's Web products have helped to promote the print product. Online users often make print purchases only after enjoying initial Web contact. "Many of our users tell us that they use both online and print dictionaries—typically online at work and print at home—and they assure us that they continue to buy our print products." Accordingly, the eleventh *Collegiate* will be packaged and sold together with a CD-Rom and a Web dictionary-access kit.

Despite the hubbub of business novelty, let's not leave the words behind. Among the 165,000 entries in the eleventh is a new one, *migraineur*, that somehow rivets me ("an individual who experiences migraines," reads the definition). This word has a yen, I feel, for two others not at home in the eleventh but safely archived online: the verb *quon* (contributed by "Lindsay" of Arlington, Virginia, and meaning "to let loose and relax") and the noun *ninawaggalie* (coined by "Elise," address unknown, to signify "a crunchy vegetable that is colorless!!!" [sic]).

The writer, like the professional definer, must weigh and measure, savor and squeeze. And so I do this with those three: "The *migraineur*, chewing her *ninawaggalies*, told herself, 'Go *quon*!'"

—Molly McQuade

Another look at . . . :

Bartlett's Familiar Quotations

Bartlett's Familiar Quotations. 17th ed. Ed. by Justin Kaplan. 2002. 1,431p. indexes. Little, Brown, $50 (0-316-08460-3). 808.88.

According to his entry in *American National Biography*, "ask John Bartlett" was once a common answer to questions in the environs of Harvard College. Bartlett went to work in a Cambridge, Massachusetts, bookstore when he was 16, and "his copious memory and love of books soon had university faculty and students using him as a ready reference tool." His notebook of common phrases and quotations eventually became *A Collection of Familiar Quotations*, which he had privately printed in 1855. By the time he died in 1905, the collection had gone through nine editions. Almost 100 years and eight editions later, people still ask John Bartlett when they are seeking the source of a common phrase or hoping to dress up a speech with a pithy saying.

The seventeenth edition of *Bartlett's* has 25,000 quotations from 2,500 authors. It follows in the path of its predecessors by adhering to certain traditions yet also strives to remain relevant and up-to-date. Bartlett's original collection relied heavily on literary sources, such as the Bible and Shakespeare, and these, as current editor Kaplan tells us in his preface, "are still major components." Structurally, arrangement is still chronological and access is abetted by an index of authors and a very detailed keyword index. But for this edition, hundreds of "purely mechanical, nonsubstantive cross-reference and footnotes" have been eliminated, and full citations are used in place of the often-confusing *Ibid*. And Bartlett's continues to widen its net beyond canonical sources, casting about for material from culture both high and low. New among the quoted are Maya Angelou, George W. Bush, Bill Clinton, Princess Diana, Rudy Giuliani, Frank McCourt, Robert McNamara, and Jerry Seinfeld. Selections from Charles Darwin, Bob Dylan, and Virginia Woolf, among others, have been expanded. Some authors, such as popular eighteenth-century English writer Anna Laetitia Barbauld, have been excised, although cutting has not been as deep for this edition as it was for the sixteenth, also edited by Kaplan.

There are hundreds of other quotation books from which to choose. Among those that are comparable in size to *Bartlett's*, *The Oxford Dictionary of Quotations* (5th ed., 1999) is arranged alphabetically by author, and *Random House Webster's Quotationary* (1999) is arranged by subject. In addition to these general anthologies, there are books of quotations by women and by African Americans; books of humorous or religions quotations; and books for quotations about movies or sports (for a rundown of some recent examples, see "Other People's Words: Recent Quotation Books," in our July 2002 issue). Strictly speaking, the new *Bartlett's* may not be a necessary purchase for libraries that have the sixteenth edition and a good array of other fairly current titles. But because it is one of the handful of reference staples that patrons are likely to ask for by name, no self-respecting library should be without it.

—Mary Ellen Quinn

Biography Resource Center

Biography Resource Center: Version 2.0. [Internet database]. 2002. Gale, pricing from $3,823 [http://www.gale.com/]. (Last accessed September 16, 2002).

Biography Resource Center (BRC) originally appeared in 1999 (we reviewed it in our November 1, 1999, issue), and a new version is now out. The interface of BRC 2.0 will look familiar to subscribers to other Gale products such as Literature Resource Center and History Resource Center. The number of reference sources in the BRC database has grown from 50 to 83, and the number of magazines and journals with full-text articles has increased from 232 to 250. Not surprisingly, the number of individuals included has also increased. If libraries choose the option of adding the Complete Marquis Who's Who database, they have access to an additional one million biographies, many of which are not included in the basic product.

The ways to search remain essentially the same. There are now two kinds of Name Search: Name Contains and Start of Last Name. Name Contains is the default, although Start of Last Name might be a better choice because it generally results in a cleaner search. Custom Search, where searches may be done by occupation, nationality, birth and death date and place, and gender, has been renamed Biographical Facts Search. Full Text Search has been replaced by Advanced Search, where full-text searches can be limited by source or magazine date. A new way to limit the search is by image, although this link is buried at the bottom of the Biographical Facts Search and hard to find. There are currently more than 20,000 portraitsrom 'N Sync to Russian politician Gennadi Zyuganov. Through this search one may also find a photo of a very young Alan Greenspan!

As before, documents are grouped by category of resource, such as Thumbnail Biographies and Magazine Articles. Links to Web sites are a new feature here. With a click on a link, a box appears with a disclaimer from the vendor and the option of closing the box or viewing the site. As might be expected, some links are dead and others do not work. Tabs make it easy to move from one category to another. In our earlier review, we commented that BRC had no Next option that would allow the user to move from one document to the next one in the same category. It is now possible to go from one document to the next without returning to the documents list. Citations to entries from Contemporary Authors are still misleading. They are cited as "Contemporary Authors . . . 2002," but many of the Contemporary Authors essays are from earlier dates.

Some entries include a link to recent updates, but updating is spotty. When we last looked, the most recent update for Pete Sampras was dated September 9, 2002, while those for President Bush and Colin Powell were done in July.

There is no question that this is an amazing resource. Biographies in Spotlight On (a feature on the home page) illustrate the breadth of the database—Elvis Costello, Winston Churchill, Ken Griffey Jr., Tom Hanks, Joan of Arc, Shannon Lucid, Amadeu Mozart. As with all Gale products, BRC is not inexpensive; however, librarians and patrons of high-school, academic and public libraries will find that it's the right place to begin research on an individual.

—Christine Bulson

Focus Reviews

★**New Catholic Encyclopedia.** 14v. 2d ed. 2002. bibliogs. illus. index. maps. Gale, $1,195 (0-7876-4004-2). 282.

New Catholic Encyclopedia (NCE) was first published in 1967 as an update to the Catholic Encyclopedia, which first appeared in 1907. Four supplements to NCE have been published over the intervening years, the latest in 1995. Not simply an encyclopedia of Catholicism, although it certainly addresses Catholic doctrine and the history of the church, NCE "includes information about persons, institutions, cultural phenomena, religions, philosophies, and social movements that have affected the Catholic Church from within and without."

Entries are alphabetically arranged, signed by the scholar(s) who wrote or revised them, and augmented with excellent supplemental bibliographies, which have been updated for this second edition. Each volume begins with a color plate, and there are black-and-white illustrations and see references throughout. The index volume plays a critical role because users likely will not know that cloning, for example, is discussed in the entry Human genome.

Use of the 1967 edition in concert with the supplemental volumes was unwieldy, so integration was certainly in order. This second edition "updates and incorporates the many articles from the 1967 edition and its supplements . . . and adds hundreds of new entries." But 18 volumes are now 14, so clearly some editing has taken place. Entries have been shortened. The discussion of the hymn Stabat Mater has been cut in half, reflecting changes in its liturgical use today. Some entries are gone entirely, such as the excellent article on Black theology in one of the supplements. Brief mention is made of the movement and its leading exponent, James Cone, in the second edition's entry African American Catholics in the United States (history of). New to this edition is an entry for Womanist theology, a type of theological reflection grounded in the experience of African American women. Some entries have been expanded to include more current information. The article on Afghanistan, the Catholic Church in now mentions the Taliban, al-Qaeda, and U.S. military action there over the past year or so. Others aren't as complete. The entry for Stein, Edith (Teresa Benedicta of the Cross), St. fails to mention the controversy surrounding the 1998 canonization of the Jewish-born Carmelite nun who died in Auschwitz and the resulting strain on Catholic-Jewish relations. Finally, some entries have been practically rewritten. Homosexuality is no longer equated with narcissism or thought of as a disorder. Homosexuals are no longer called inverts or deviates.

The second edition of New Catholic Encyclopedia is less a revision of an earlier version than a new work entirely. Multivolume encyclopedias serve as a snapshot in time of current thinking on a variety of issues. By including, excluding, abbreviating, or enhancing entries, the editors are expressing what they believe to be of importance vis-a-vis the Catholic Church at the start of a new millennium. In addition to matters Christian in general and Roman Catholic in particular, this second edition offers Catholic thought on more universal subjects such as democracy, justice, and the self. For this reason alone, academic, public, and many high-school libraries should acquire it.

—Christopher McConnell

Encyclopedia of New Media: An Essential Reference to Communication and Technology. Ed. by Steve Jones. 2002. 532p. bibliogs. illus. indexes. Sage, $125 (0-7619-2382-9). 302.23.

The introduction to this work starts with "What is new media? There is no single answer to be given." One is left with the feeling that new media is whatever the editor (a professor of communications at the University of Illinois at Chicago, president and founder of the Association of Internet Researchers, and coeditor of the journal New Media & Society) deemed appropriate, which is hardly surprising given that this is still an emerging field.

It is safe to say there is something for everyone within the just over 250 entries, which typically run from 500 words to about 2,500 (for Internet and Multimedia). There are the Internet-related terms one would expect to find (ARPANET, World Wide Web), but there are also entries for artists (Nam June Paik) and musicians (Brian Eno) as well as for specific works (The Soul of a New Machine). Many of the entries are biographical, including those, such as Steve Case and Bill Gates, who will be familiar to general readers, and those, such as feminist historian Donna J. Haraway and software engineer Pattie Maes, who may not. A work of this nature will inevitably cause some to question what should or should not have been covered. For example, the latest file-stealing service du jour (KaZaA) has but one page reference in the index (referring to the article Napster) and is not mentioned at all where it would more appropriately appear, in the entry Peer-to-peer. In addition to a name index, a general index concludes the volume, helping, for example, to steer a user with initials in mind (ISPs) to the right spot (Internet service providers). A topical list divided into 12 categories is at the beginning of the work.

All entries conclude with useful bibliographies, which, not surprisingly, feature a large number of Web citations. One expects some dead links for such entries, and this was indeed the case for a few randomly checked, though there were not very many, and only one typo was spotted within these links. Somewhat puzzling is the lack of Web addresses in spots where they would be expected. Most notable in this regard is the entry *The New Hacker's Dictionary*, which opens by stating it is "available online as well as in book form" but fails to cite a single Web entry in its bibliography. Both it and the entry for *The New Hacker's Dictionary*'s current author, Eric Raymond, completely overlook a page of links to Raymond's writings at [http://catb.org/~esr/writings].

Can this information be found on the Web? Of course—but only after wading through hundreds of hits and likely not in as clear and concise form as what appears here. Although some explanations may get a bit too technical for a computer novice, most will be understandable for the interested layperson. Recommended for all academic and public libraries that don't mind the fact that many entries will be dated very quickly.

—Ken Black

Encyclopedia of Aging. 4v. Ed. by David J. Ekerdt. 2002. 1,591p. bibliogs. illus. index. Macmillan, $495 (0-02-865472-2). 305.26.

The great increase in the scholarly study of aging is attributable to both demographic increases and the growth in clinical and social services to the aging population. Correspondingly, we see an increase in the number of reference works published in an area that is of high interest popularly, academically, and professionally. In more than 400 entries, this encyclopedia aims "to present advanced ideas about aging at an accessible level." The editor in chief, Ekerdt, a professor of sociology and gerontology at the University of Kansas, and six other editors worked with the many contributors (also more than 400), both scholars and practitioners from the U.S. and abroad.

Topics represent the range of information in gerontology, covering biological, medical, psychological, and sociological topics as well as social and public policy issues. Articles range from very specific, for example, *Congregate housing* or *Fluid balance*, to more general essays, such as *Bereavement* or *Visual arts and aging*. About one-third to one-half of the articles focus on biological, medical, or psychological aspects of aging. There are also good treatments of social policy—a history of Social Security, articles on adult protective services, housing options, etc. Many of the articles are broken into segments. *Cellular aging* has a general overview article, then four more-specific ones dealing with such issues as cell death or DNA. *Long-term care* and *Retirement* are similarly broken into segments. This is a useful approach when the audience may vary in levels of familiarity with the topics.

Most of the emphasis is on the U.S., with some attention given to other countries and cultures and comparisons between cultures. Several articles fall in the topic group of aging around the world—entries on China and Japan, three to four pages on Western Europe or South Asia. The cross-cultural articles are not comprehensive enough to make this work international in scope. The whole of sub-Saharan Africa, for example, is dealt with in one fairly brief article.

The signed articles are presented alphabetically. In the fore matter there are alphabetical lists of the articles by both title and author (the first of which has several articles listed out of alphabetical sequence near the beginning). A very useful feature follows: lists of articles grouped by specific topic areas, for example, "Cognition," "End of Life Issues," and "Work." Each article also has cross-references to related articles and a bibliography; however, some of the authors have cited research in the body in the briefest style (e.g., "Jones, 1984") and have not included those references in the bibliography. A very detailed index allows access to the wealth of factual information in the entries despite the omission of references to some topics one would expect, for example, respite care and use of restraints. But, on the whole, the coverage of both general topics and very specific information is impressive. Many well-produced illustrations and diagrams accompany the text in an exceptionally attractive product

There is no dearth of reference publishing in this area. Many consumer-oriented titles that deal with specifics of health or retirement are available in print, as are some more-encyclopedic popular works such as *The Encyclopedia of Health and Aging: The Complete Guide to Health and Well-Being in Your Later Years* (rev. ed., Key Porter, 2001) and *The Encyclopedia of Aging and the Elderly* (Facts On File, 1992). The new edition of the one-volume *The Graying of America: An Encyclopedia of Aging, Health, Mind, and Behavior* (2d ed., Univ. of Illinois, 2001) is suitable for general readers and undergraduates. The two works that are the most comparable in scope are the new edition of George Maddox's *The Encyclopedia of Aging: A Comprehensive Resource in Gerontology and Geriatrics* (3d ed., Springer, 2001) and James Birren's *Encyclopedia of Gerontology: Age, Aging, and the Aged* (Academic, 1996). The Birren work, although older now, is still in print, and its review in RBB noted that it "is a comprehensive source that offers a multidisciplinary overview of all aspects of aging." Written for professionals, it is accessible to educated lay readers. The Maddox work, now in its third edition, is also a broad look at aging, with articles ranging from general interest to very specialized topics. Its style, heavily referenced with research, may be less accessible to the general reader, even the educated lay reader whom Ekerdt also has in mind.

On the whole, this new encyclopedic treatment is an outstanding choice for academic libraries serving both professional programs and other courses of study as well as being suitable for larger public libraries. It balances the task of presenting advanced information in an accessible fashion extremely well.

—Margaret Power

★**Encyclopedia of Food and Culture.** 3v. Ed. by Solomon H. Katz. 2002. appendix. bibliogs. illus. index. maps. Scribner, $395 (0-684-80568-5). 394.1.

The *Journal of Social History* recently published "Review Essay: Food and History" (fall 2002) by John C. Super. The author highlighted two significant resources in the study of food, *The Cambridge World History of Food* (2000) and *The Oxford Companion to Food* (1999). The *Encyclopedia of Food and Culture* should certainly be an addition to future essays. Edited by an anthropologist with assistance from a culinary historian, this new set complements the Oxford and Cambridge offerings.

As the title implies, the encyclopedia discusses food in its relation to society. The 600 articles, arranged alphabetically, cover everything from the significance of Betty Crocker to bioactive food components. Chronological scope encompasses the Paleolithic origins of hunting and current trends such as comfort food and fusion cuisine. Length of the signed articles ranges from less than a page for most biographies (*Birdseye, Clarence; Escoffier, Georges-Auguste*) to more than 10 pages for *Dairy products* and *Sensation and the senses*. Some topics, among them *Beer, France,* and *Fruit*, are examined in series of subentries. *See also* references and current bibliographies are at the end of each entry, with some bibliographies containing Web sites. Interspersed throughout the text are boxes and sidebars on subjects such as genetically modified organisms, a controversial topic that is treated impartially. A box adjacent to the entry on Julia Child provides three quotations by Child. The best one is this advice: "No matter what happens in the kitchen, never apologize." The volumes also include tables with statistical information; for example, production, imports, and exports of butter by country.

In addition to the set's 550 black-and-white photos and 50 maps, each volume has a section of color plates, an eclectic mix illustrating relationships between culture and food. A plate in volume 1 offers a detail of a Spanish still-life painting containing biscuits, a page from a Belgium biscuit catalog, and a photograph of a bread vendor in Central Asia. Interesting textual links between culture and food include a discussion of the problem of litter in the U.S. because of fast-food restaurants and the elevation of the chef, making "going to restaurants a combination of high theater and spectator sport."

The contributors are listed in the appendix with affiliation and the articles they wrote. They include a number of U.S. academics but also Alan Davidson, the editor of *The Oxford Companion to Food*; the famous Paris bread baker, Lionel Poilane, who died last fall; Chef Fritz Blank of Deux Cheminees in Philadelphia; and cookbook author Elisabeth Lambert Ortiz. The appendix also has "Dietary Reference Intakes" and a "Systematic Outline of Contents," which is a good finding tool. The index is comprehensive, indexing minor names such as Marjorie Hendrick and the Watergate Inn, which are mentioned in the entry *United States: Middle Atlantic*.

Criticisms are few. A general bibliography would have been useful because sometimes books mentioned in articles are not cited in the accompanying bibliographies. The ice cream entry says nothing about the great variety of flavors that are now in existence. The cookbook article fails to mention the effect of Erma Rombauer's *Joy of Cooking* on women in the twentieth century.

Although this is an expensive resource, it is well worth the money. Recommended for all academic and public libraries that have patrons interested in food and culture.

—*Christine Bulson*

McGraw-Hill Encyclopedia of Science & Technology. 20v. 9th ed. 2002. bibliogs. illus. indexes. maps. McGraw-Hill, $2,495 (0-07-913665-6). 503.

It has been 5 years since the publication of the eighth edition of this internationally known encyclopedia and 42 years since the first edition. For students, the general public, and researchers, the *McGraw-Hill Encyclopedia of Science & Technology* has become the most-used general encyclopedia covering science and engineering technology. From its first edition in 1960, its goal has been to provide information that was understandable and authoritative for the general public, secondary school students, undergraduates, and researchers. The principal purpose is stated in the preface: "To provide the widest possible range of articles that will be understandable and useful to any person of modest technical training who wants to obtain information outside his particular field of specialization." It has maintained this goal through the years, with no other science encyclopedia targeting such a wide range of readers.

There are still 20 volumes, printed in double-column format, with good use of white space, excellent illustrations, bibliographies, and a detailed analytical index. The ninth edition contains 7,100 signed articles written by more than 5,000 authors from universities, industry, and government agencies, including 30 Nobel Prize winners. Each article begins with a definition and concise overview of the topic, followed by a discussion, and ends, in most cases, with a brief bibliography. Within the articles there are some 62,000 cross-references to related articles, providing the reader the widest possible access to all related topics. The index volume contains a list of all contributors with their affiliations and the titles of each articles that he or she has written.

Of particular use are the 15 subject study guides that provide a program of study and reference that can be used by educators in secondary schools and colleges. These guides permit an individual to become informed on a particular topic. The topical index is a useful tool that groups the 7,100 articles under 87 major subject categories. Finally, the analytical index provides access to all of the information included in the 19 volumes of text. The color of the line drawings has changed from a lavender tone to a turquoise tone. The color illustrations are the same and excellent. However, the black-and-white photographs were in many cases better and crisper in the eighth edition. The binding should hold up to extreme use.

Though editors state that the encyclopedia has been extensively revised and new entries have been added, the total number of articles is the same as reported in the eighth edition. There is no indication which articles were dropped and which are new. With an encyclopedia covering such a wide range of topics, one cannot expect all articles to be completely rewritten. However, one would expect articles on topics of great interest to the general public to have some revision. The entry for *Acquired immune deficiency syndrome* (AIDS) has had no revision, even though great advances have been made in the treatment of the disease, and there is no bibliography. In spot-checking other articles, it appears that revisions are minimal. Some articles have had one or two new additions to the bibliography. There has been some expansion on material relating to the human genome, biotechnology, neuroscience, and forensic science. When the total number of articles remains the same, it makes one wonder what was dropped to add the six new entries covering forensic science.

All in all, this is still a highly recommended encyclopedia for general information on science and technology. It is not intended to be the last stop for the latest information on current "hot topics." For libraries on a limited budget, the ninth edition may not be necessary if the eighth edition is owned, especially if a good collection of up-to-date, specialized encyclopedias and dictionaries has been purchased.

—*H. Robert Malinowsky*

★**Grzimek's Animal Life Encyclopedia:** v.8–11: Birds. 4v. 2d ed. Ed. by Donna Olendorf and others. 2002. bibliogs. glossary. illus. index. maps. Gale, $375 (0-7876-6571-1). 590.

It has been 30 years since the U.S. publication of the original 13-volume *Grzimek's Animal Life Encyclopedia* (1972–1975). Bernhard Grzimek served as director of the Frankfurt Zoo for more than 30 years and was also very active in the preservation of animal species in the wild as well as in captivity. In contrast to older works on animals, his encyclopedia, which was first published in Germany in 1967, was more concerned with animal behavior and conservation than with mere descriptions of appearance and habitat. In 1990 McGraw-Hill published a substantial revision of the four volumes of *Grzimek's* that dealt with mammals. Not only was the text of *Grzimek's Encyclopedia of Mammals* greatly updated but the set was graced with 3,000 color photographs that were created using new techniques for underwater, night, and action shots. The original 13-volume *Grzimek's*, meanwhile, went out of print. Since 1990 there has been a significant increase in reference materials on animals, in part because of a growing awareness of biodiversity and conservation. But even with this bounty, librarians have been waiting for a new edition of *Grzimek's*. Gale has stepped into the breach with a completely revised, 17-volume *Grzimek's Animal Life Encyclopedia*, of which the four volumes dealing with birds are the first to appear. Additional volumes will be released over the year.

Like its parent set, the new edition of *Grzimek's* adheres to a taxonomic arrangement. Following a set of essays on topics such as bird song and migration, material is arranged by class, then by order, then by family. For each family, entries are headed with summary data on details such as size and numbers of genera and species. Following this are standardized sections on evolution, physical characteristics, distribution, habitat, behavior, diet, reproduction, conservation status, and significance to humans. Entries conclude with species accounts that list key facts on selected species and further resources. Distribution maps, approximately 480 color photographs depicting birds in natural settings, and more than 1,300 very attractive illustrations of featured species accompany the text. One slight disappointment is the photographs, which are nice enough but nothing special, especially compared to those in *Grzimek's Encyclopedia of Mammals*. Each volume winds up with the same back matter: a bibliography, a list of bird-related organizations, a list of contributors to the first edition of *Grzimek's* (some of whom also contributed to the second), a glossary of bird terms, an "Aves Species List," and an index to all four bird volumes.

Reviews of the first edition of *Grzimek's Animal Life Encyclopedia* and of the revised mammal volumes often contained caveats about access. Unless one is familiar with zoological classification, it is not easy to navigate through a taxonomical arrangement, and the indexing did not always help. There are similar frustrations in the new edition. For students, in particular, libraries can offer other, more accessible options for animal research, with entries for individual species arranged A–Z and written in less technical language. Now that we have so many more choices, is there still a place for *Grzimek's* on the reference shelves? The answer is yes, especially for larger public and academic libraries. In its second edition, *Grzimek's* may no longer be just about the only animal life encyclopedia around, but when it is completed, it will certainly be the most comprehensive.

—*Mary Ellen Quinn*

★**Encyclopedia of the Enlightenment.** 4v. Ed. by Alan Charles Kors. 2003. 1,900p. bibliogs. illus. index. maps. Oxford, $495 (0-19-510430-7). 940.2.

As Kors' preface observes, the Enlightenment is "a set of tendencies and developments of European culture from the 1670s to the early nineteenth century (including in the American outposts of that culture)." An encyclopedia that attempts to cover such a span of time and most of western Europe and America is faced with a daunting task. Fortunately, the more than 400 contributors from around the world are up to it, producing a work that will be of use to anyone interested in virtually any topic from this time period.

The alphabetically arranged set of just under 700 entries (counting the many subentries, such as the separately authored articles "An Overview" and "Philosophical Legacy" under the main entry *Colonialism*) has articles running from about a page or so (*Defoe, Daniel*; *Latrobe, Benjamin*) to more than 14 pages (*Republicanism*). Topics include overviews of cities or countries (*Milan*, *Spain*) as well as of more general topics such as *Moral philosophy*, *Opera*, or *Technology*. Fully half of the entries are biographical, covering people from all disciplines and countries. Among them are several contemporary figures, such as historians Peter Gay and Jurgen Habermas. One of the longest entries (at more than 12 pages) is the historiographical *Enlightenment studies*, which describes the conflicts engendered by and the diverse constructions applied to the concept of the Enlightenment over the past 300 years. The encyclopedia itself reflects this diversity by presenting, as the preface states, "a wide range of general and particular contexts, schools of thought, and interpretations." For example, the article *Sexuality* concludes by noting that "[the Marquis de] Sade's writing marks an important turn, showing pornography as political because it focuses on subjugating women, and as erotic because that subjugation is the source of arousal and sexual performance." On the other hand, the contributors for the entry *Pornography* state "we believe that Sade was a bad man and a boring writer who deserved his incarceration."

The encyclopedia is augmented by more than 200 illustrations (primarily reproductions of engravings or other art), six maps, a topical outline of articles at the beginning of the set, and a superb index at the end. All articles conclude with cross-references to other entries and a bibliography that typically lists primary works, important scholarly works regardless of language, and the most useful studies in English. Many bibliographies include brief annotations.

This is the third work published recently that bears the same title. Facts On File's *Encyclopedia of the Enlightenment* (1996) is a one-volume resource intended for a more general audience. The two-volume *Encyclopedia of the Enlightenment* edited by Michel Delon (Fitzroy Dearborn, 2001) is a translation of a work originally published in 1997 in France, featuring just over 350 entries from more than 200 contributors, although there are no biographical entries. The recent publication date of the Fitzroy Dearborn set at a price ($285) just over half that of the Oxford could give many libraries pause before deciding to add the latter to their collections. Academic institutions offering programs in Enlightenment studies could not go wrong with both sets, but Oxford has an edge in that it is not as centered on France. The inclusion of biographical entries likewise gives Oxford an advantage in any larger public or academic libraries that have a need for material in this area.

—*Ken Black*

★**Encyclopedia of Modern Asia.** 6v. Ed. by David Levinson and Karen Christensen. 2002. bibliogs. illus. index. maps. Scribner, $695 (0-684-80617-7). 950.

The goal of the editors was to make this hefty set "the standard reference work on Asia," intended not only for scholars and students but for a broader audience of "journalists, tourists, government officials, writers, teachers, and the general reading public." More than 2,600 accessible entries ranging from 200 to 4,000 words from hundreds of contributors have achieved a further editorial goal of expressing the diversity of modern Asia from a variety of Asian perspectives while also indicating Western viewpoints. The focus is on twentieth-century Asia and on earlier people and events whose impact is still felt. Thus, there are entries on Basho, the seventeenth-century Japanese poet, and on Confucius (as well as separate entries on Confucianism in China, Japan, and Korea).

The editors define Asia as extending from Japan in the east to Turkey in the west, and from Kazakhstan in the north to Indonesia in the south. Thirty-three nations are covered in depth, while other regions and countries that might have received greater coverage are treated in less depth: the Caucasus, Siberia, Australia, Lebanon, Syria, Jordan, Israel, and the Arabian peninsula nations. The editors note extensive treatment of the latter five in Macmillan's *Encyclopedia of the Modern Middle East* (1996) as well as in other works. Some countries, such as Australia, were felt to be culturally and politically closer to Europe.

Among the subjects of entries are countries, cities, regions, natural features, religions, social issues, languages, people, events, customs, and grown and manufactured products. Primary coverage of countries and regions is broken down into consecutive entries. Bangladesh, to take one example, is treated in a four-page profile, followed by entries on its economic system, education system, history, and political system and on the Bangladesh Nationalist Party, Bangladesh-India, and Bangladesh-Pakistan relations. The numerous entries on regional relations and, in many cases, relations with the U.S. are a valuable feature of the encyclopedia. For a nation like China, there are hundreds of relevant entries scattered throughout the set. These can be located using the "Reader's Guide," a table of contents organized first by five major subregions of Asia, then by topic, then by country. Under the topic "Arts, Literature, and Recreation" alone are almost 80 entries for China, among them *Ang Lee*, *Architecture—China*, *Beijing Opera*, *Birds and birdcages*, *Ginseng*, *Hungry Ghost Festival*, and *Lacquerware*. Repeated at the front of every volume, the "Reader's Guide" is a useful finding aid.

Each entry is followed by a list for further reading. Supplementing the entries are some 1,300 black-and-white illustrations, sidebars, and tables; 90 maps; regional and topical outlines; and, in volume 6, a 230-page index. Sidebars add an interesting mix of content, including excerpts from primary source documents such as literary or religious texts, preambles to national constitutions, and travelers' accounts. Cross-references between entries are infrequent. Coverage is up-to-date enough to cover the post-Taliban government in Afghanistan. One misses more extensive coverage of Russia, covering as it does northern Asia from Europe to the Pacific, though there is nearly a page of index entries under the heading *Russia*.

The only resource providing such comprehensive and diverse treatment of the topic, *Encyclopedia of Modern Asia* is highly recommended for academic and public libraries. Its accessible style makes it worth considering for high-school libraries as well.

—*Robert Craig Bunch*

★**Dictionary of American History.** 10v. 3d ed. Ed. by Stanley L. Kutler. 2002. bibliogs. illus. index. maps. Scribner, $995 (0-684-80533-2). 973.

★**Encyclopedia of American History.** 11v. Ed. by Peter C. Mancall and Gary B. Nash. 2003. bibliogs. illus. indexes. maps. Facts On File, $935 (0-8160-4371-X). 973.

For 60 years the *Dictionary of American History* (DAH) has been the unrivaled source of choice for information about the history of the U.S. from its precolonial days on. Today it has an apparent rival in the *Encyclopedia of American History* (EAH). Both reflect recent trends in the ways in which American history is studied, taught, and interpreted.

For the DAH this means shedding the vestiges of the political and military emphases of its 1940 first edition and thoroughly incorporating analytical filters such as race, gender, ethnicity, and class in making sense of the American story. It also means a more synthetic approach. While retaining its alphabetical organization running from the first volume through the eighth, this edition has reduced the number of entries from more than 7,100 to 4,434. DAH continues to eschew biographical entries in deference to other plentiful sources of biographies of contributors to American history (in fact, DAH was originally intended to be used in conjunction with the publisher's *Dictionary of American Biography*, which has been continued as *The Scribner Encyclopedia of American Lives*). However, it has helpfully introduced maps and illustrations as well as an "archival" volume. This supplement consists of maps accompanied by commentary depicting American territory from around 1550 to 1855, the Civil War era, and lower Manhattan from 1675 to September 12, 2001. The bulk of the supplementary volume presents transcriptions of primary documents. These range in topic and time from Powhatan's 1607 plea for peace to John Smith to the nativist American Party platform of 1856 to an excerpt from Upton Sinclair's *The Jungle* to Stokely Carmichael's Black Power speech of 1966 to Al Gore's December 2000 concession speech. *See* references link the primary documents to entries in the dictionary proper and vice versa.

In the dictionary itself readers will find the same sort of informative articles they have come to expect, including articles on topics they now assume will be covered. These include an eyes-wide-open treatment of college athletics, the lobbying power of the AARP, the Clinton impeachment, sexually transmitted diseases, and the 9/11 attack and its aftermath. Even brief entries, such as the one on home-shopping networks, conclude with an up-to-date bibliography and *see also* references to related articles. An extensive alphabetical index offers access to these riches. A complementary access tool, a guide to eras of American history, correlates relevant chapters in several very recent textbooks with lists of articles in the dictionary.

This approach by era, secondary in the DAH, forms the foundation of the EAH. Each volume reflects one of the eras in *The National Standards for United States History, Revised Edition*, used to organize the history curriculum. Thus, the set's applicability as a complement to classroom instruction is self-evident. Each volume, organized A–Z, covers in approximately 3,500 entries the key events, people, and trends that gave an era its distinctions and that influenced the eras to come.

The first volume, treating "Beginnings to 1607," provides rich context for the era of voyages of discovery. It depicts the Europe emerging from feudalism and religious wars, energized by science and curiosity and motivated by trade, as well as the cultures of the native peoples of the Americas, ill-prepared for their clash with outsiders. So it is that an encyclopedia of American history accommodates articles on Michelangelo and Leonardo da Vinci as well as Columbus and Elizabeth I. The back-of-the-book chronology (a feature of every volume) gives this context temporal structure. Every volume also includes transcriptions of primary documents (more selectively than the DAH) and a volume-specific index.

Befitting a reference tool designed to strengthen the high-school curriculum, EAH includes maps and other illustrations. Because it, unlike DAH, has biographical entries, many of the illustrations are portraits.

The potential drawback of the organization by era is fragmentation of broad topics such as education, religion, literature, race, and labor. These and others receive their due through an era-specific article in each volume (with the usual exception of the scene-setting volume 1). Information about specific topics treated in a dedicated article in just one volume (e.g., *Ford Motor Corporation*, *Lewis and Clark expedition*, *Harvard College*, *Haymarket riot*) may appear in other volumes as well. As in the DAH, entries in the set's comprehensive index knit these disparate discussions together. Also as in DAH, EAH's signed articles conclude with bibliographic references.

Each set has unique strengths. So, which to have? Ideally, both! But if it can be but one, libraries should consider their clientele's needs. Academic libraries confined to one option should go with the DAH. High-school libraries should go with EAH, and their librarians should capitalize on its value as a tool designed to support the curriculum. Public libraries need to consider whether users are most likely to be high-school students (in which case EAH) or college students and college-educated adults (in which case DAH). Libraries cannot go wrong with either of these reference distillations of centuries of American history.

—James Rettig

Reference on the Web

Ancient Rome in Cyberspacce - 24
Advertisements Are Forever - 25
Back and to the Right - 25
Bits and Bytes of Poetry - 25
Clay Tablets Go Digital - 26
Cocktails in Cyberspace - 26
Computer History - 27
D'oh! Springfield on the Web - 28
Floods, Fire, Famine—and Worse - 28
Graphic Novels - 29
Islam - 30
More Sites on Sleuths: Chicago Crime - 31
Nazi Germany - 31
Oh Canada!—Desktop Reference - 32
The Other Football - 33
Painters & Prices - 33
The Quick and the Dead - 34
Scouting for SF - 34
Wikepedia - 35
Women in Sports - 35

Advertisements Are Forever

Much as we hate to admit it, most of us love advertising. The clever new commercials crafted for the Super Bowl telecast often provide more excitement than the action on the field; Internet users forward those clever European Ikea commercials that have been deemed too racy for domestic distribution; and phenomena like the Spanglish-speaking Taco Bell Chihuahua have the potential to make an impact not only on eating habits but also on pet ownership. In fact, with most TV programs throwing away the script to explore unfocused (if still tampered-with) "reality," commercials may be one of the last places viewers can still see a tight, well-crafted comedic vignette.

Of course, most of us still get Howard Beale–angry ("I'm mad as hell and I'm not going to take this anymore!") about the *frequency* of advertising, but that's another matter. What's undeniable is that people buy fashion magazines for the pretty models in the ads, they hate missing the trailers for movies, and they have learned to live with the radio commercials that are edging songs off the airwaves. I found quite a few.

And now a word from a bunch of sponsors. (All sites last visited April 3, 2003.)

Advertising Age: The Advertising Century. [http://adage.com/century/timeline/timeline_top.html].

The online counterpart to an *Advertising Age* special issue, this list of top 10s and 100s kicks off with a quote from Marshall McLuhan: "Historians and archaeologists will one day discover that the ads of our time are the richest and most faithful daily reflections any society ever made of its whole range of activities." Even more than art? Well, probably. At any rate, these arbitrary lists of the best ad jingles, slogans, icons, campaigns, and creators are informative and entertaining.

HarpWeek Presents . . . 19th Century Advertising: A Taste of the Advertisements Found in the Pages of *Harper's Weekly*, 1857–1872. [http://advertising.harpweek.com/AdvertisingHome.htm].

This site, privately funded by a history enthusiast, offers a small but interesting selection of old *Harper's Weekly* ads. It's with grim timeliness that they reproduce an 1862 ad for "The Soldiers' Bullet Proof Vest."

The History of Advertising Trust Archive: Picture Gallery. [http://www.hatads.org.uk/library.htm].

For interesting comparisons between U.S. and U.K. advertising history, users can visit the "Picture Gallery" of the HAT Archive. A small sample of the more than two million archived items, this illustrated, annotated time line indicates the Brit ad industry was, as we might guess, a bit staid in comparison to its Yankee counterpart.

Rare Book, Manuscript, and Special Collections Library: Duke University. [http://scriptorium.lib.duke.edu/].

There are three interesting sections here. The first, "Medicine and Madison Avenue," presents images and information on about 600 health-related ads first printed between 1911 and 1958. They are browsable by category (with divisions like "Over-the-Counter Drugs" and "Personal and Oral Hygiene") and searchable, and a time line from the 1840s through 1997 helps put the material in context. A 1947 print ad for Barbasol Lotion Deodorant shows a woman leaning away from her date and reminds us that "you can't be a wolf with 'Athletic Aroma.'"

Another section, "Emergence of Advertising in America: 1850–1920," is much larger, with more than 9,000 images. There are 11 browsing categories (from "Advertising Ephemera" to "Tobacco Advertising"), several means of searching, and a time line. Those who feel the preservation of advertising is like putting litter under museum glass should be interested in seeing the hype that existed even in 1860. And, on a sobering note, it is absolutely important to the historical record to preserve ads such as "Valuable Gang of Young Negroes," from 1840 New Orleans. Also of note are four late-nineteenth-century scrapbooks; it was a hobby for young women to make collages out of colorful ads.

"Ad*Access" focuses on a later period, 1911 through 1955, and print ads (newspaper and magazine) in five subject areas: radio, TV, transportation, beauty and hygiene, and World War II. The arrangement is similar to the first two sections, and the images are probably more interesting to modern users: After all, who can resist the inherent hilarity of advertising writers trying to discuss "woman's oldest hygienic problem"? It's a far cry from the current TV commercials that use animations to demonstrate absorbency.

The reproduction quality is very good for all three databases, though the navigation could be more graceful.

So go ahead and visit these sites—you deserve a break today.

—*Keir Graff*

Ancient Rome in Cyberspace

History Link 101. [http://www.historylink101.com/ancient_rome.htm]. (Last accessed October 14, 2002).

There is, predictably, a wealth of sites on ancient Rome, I found few that functioned as easily searchable general references. One that did catch my eye as being useful to a wide number of people is the Ancient Rome section of History Link 101. History Link 101 is primarily designed for (and used by) world history students in grade 12 and under, but much of the material is also appropriate for older users who are not expert in the area.

History Link 101 is a good-sized portal, with links to other Web sites categorized by subject. Some of the links are themselves portals, so it's easy to start wandering down ever-more-winding roads. Because, on the Web, all roads do not lead to Rome, remember to bookmark the home page before you set out. In general, I found most links to be both active and well selected. Ancient Rome is divided into the same six categories as all History Link subject areas: art, biographies, daily life, maps, pictures, and research. Each site receives ratings from one to five (worst to best) in "Visual" (clarity and number of images) and "Content" (amount and depth of material). These ratings tend to be high, so they're not as useful as they might be.

Roman Daily Life covers recipes, clothing, the military, games, coins, funerals, Roman numerals (with a handy conversion engine), technology, and the role of women. Roman Art links to many collections of photographs of architecture and art, some small but several (such as Maecenas, with more than 2,000 photographs by Leo C. Curran) quite extensive. Roman Pictures leads to many more images and seems somewhat redundant as a separate category but focuses more on larger pictures of Rome and Roman ruins. Roman Maps is extremely useful, encompassing everything from simple maps of the city to historical and interactive maps and to a University of Virginia site (Aquae Urbis Romae: The Waters of the City of Rome) that is "a cartographic history of 2,800 years of water infrastructure and urban development in Rome." The last even includes QuickTime flyover animations. Roman Biography needs development, with only 10 biographies of, mostly, the usual suspects (Cleopatra, Constantine, Julius Caesar, and others). Finally, Roman Research offers a variety of pages with more in-depth information, some in the form of long essays on subjects from mythology to daily life. Also, a number of public-domain original texts and translations (Virgil's *Aeneid*, Tacitus' *Histories*) are shown. Some of the items in this catchall category might have been easier to find if placed under other headings (for example, why not put Daily Life links under Roman Daily Life on the main page?).

Although History Link 101 has much to offer, better organization would make it easier to navigate. Fortunately, as this issue went to press, a search function had just been added, which should help users jump to the information they're looking for. Students and interested amateurs alike will find a good deal of useful information here.

—*Keir Graff*

Back and to the Right

AARC: The Assassination Archives and Research Center. [http://www.aarclibrary.org/]. (Site last visited on November 5, 2002).

Although the Web sees the publication of many bizarre conspiracy theories—and the murky circumstances surrounding the murder of our thirty-fifth president are certainly one of the most popular jumping-off points—what sets AARC apart is its reliance on source material. You won't find rambling screeds about government robots who control the weather here; what you will find are more than 35,000 pages of reports, transcripts, and other documents that relate to the chilling events of November 22, 1963.

The Public Library section will be of most use to most users and contains complete or partial records of findings by the Warren Commission, the Garrison Investigation, the House Select Committee on Assassinations (HSCA), and the Assassinations Records Review Board as well as select documents from the FBI, the CIA, other agencies and commissions, and the holdings of the LBJ Library. The pages are scanned, not transcribed, so you are essentially viewing them in their original context (they are also viewable in Portable Document Format with applications like Adobe Acrobat). The Research Annex, a planned subscription service, will offer even more documents but is not yet viable.

For the JFK researcher (to call someone an "assassination buff" seems somehow inappropriate), there is a terrific amount of information here; even for the casual conspiracy theorist, it makes surprisingly engrossing browsing. For example, if you know that Oliver Stone's film JFK was based on New Orleans District Attorney Jim Garrison's trial of shady character Clay Shaw, you can examine a wealth of trial transcripts yourself to see what the film's real-life counterparts said or were said to have done.

The major problem with this site is that there is no overriding search function; thus, if you are interested in finding references to David Ferrie, one of the most unusual figures with ties to the assassination, there is no way to search for his name. Although the site has a clean layout, and sidebars provide overviews of each group of information, users must rely on tables of contents and occasional indexes within the material itself—as if using a printed document—rather than take advantage of their computer's ability to search text. (Perhaps it's the fact that the pages are scanned as images, rather than text, that creates this limitation.) The huge documents are often broken down by date or by subject to some degree—if you scan down the HSCA Final Assassinations Report, you'll find links to conclusions like "Lee Harvey Oswald owned the rifle that was used to fire the shots . . . " Still, the need to visually find nuggets of information dramatically slows access to this trove of information. The Catalog section of the site offers a number of CD-ROMs for sale and says that they are searchable; because they contain much information that is available on the site, it's possible that this represents a conspiracy to earn a few dollars from researchers who need to target specific facts.

Whether you believe these documents ultimately back the "single-shooter" findings of official investigative bodies like the Warren Commission, or whether you believe they point to a chilling conspiracy and cover-up, is up to you.

—*Keir Graff*

Bits and Bytes of Poetry

The technowizards who are turning life upside down for most of us must have heard George Pope Morris' long-ago cry, "Woodman, spare that tree!" Instead of hewing down towering oaks and pulping them to print books of poetry, it's now possible to publish poems without paper at all. To read them, all you have to do is step up to a library computer terminal, outwit the search engine, and wait an eye blink while your request shoots from your local area network up to the local Internet service provider, where it's bumped along until it reaches the server hosting the poem in question; coded as long strings of 1s and 0s, the poem is routed through the lines with the least traffic until it reaches your computer, where the microprocessor assembles the binary gobbledygook into standard text and sends it to your monitor where electron beams are fired at a phosphor-coated piece of glass so you can read it.

Of course, considering most of the former librarians I work with, you'll probably print it out anyway.

In keeping with our Spotlight on Poetry, here are some useful poetry Web sites. (All sites last accessed February 14, 2003.)

The Atlantic Online: Poetry Pages. [http://www.theatlantic.com/unbound/poetry/poetpage.htm].

Most online poetry collections focus on the classics; fans of brand-new poems should visit this section of The Atlantic Online. Select poems from new and recent issues are reprinted, usually with audio of the author reading—although the recording quality is often inferior. There are also essays, interviews, and their "Audible Anthology" of readings, with poems dating back a half-dozen years.

Bartleby.com: Verse. [http://www.bartleby.com/verse/].

Though bordered with ads and therefore not as pure seeming as the many university efforts, this site has size on its side and offers thousands of poems by hundreds of authors, with the complete text of many influential (and copyright-free) anthologies and primary works. A pull-down menu features shortcuts to a dozen influential scribes, from Dickinson to Yeats, but scroll down the main page for the full selection. This site's navigation bars are not intuitively organized, but at least it's searchable. A major flaw: T. S. Eliot's famous poem, "The Love Song of J. Alfred Prufrock," is viewable with Internet Explorer but not Netscape Navigator.

The Internet Poetry Archive. [http://www.ibiblio.org/ipa/].

Sponsored by the University of North Carolina Press and the North Carolina Arts Council, this site features seven contemporary poets so far: Seamus Heaney, Yusef Komunyakaa, Phillip Levine, Czeslaw Milosz, Robert Pinsky, Margaret Walker, and Richard Wilbur. However, by including quality audio clips of the authors reading their poems, the Internet Poetry Archive recognizes the importance of not just reading poetry silently but hearing it aloud. Having the chance to see a photo of the poets and to hear them read their own work (sometimes with an introduction) is invaluable. Several poems are not reproduced in text, but all entries have a select bibliography, most have a biography, and some feature audio panel discussions about the poet's work. On Wilbur's page, links to the bibliography and biography were broken. An excellent example of what the Internet is capable of when Web sites are used not to indiscriminately inundate us with information but to use their multimedia capabilities selectively.

Magic Island Poetry Database: World Poetry. [http://www.lingshidao.com/waiwen/index.htm].

On the home page, Webmaster "Magic Stone" states his aim "to impart to you joy and surprise through the magic of poetry." Clearly an "Information Wants to Be Free" proponent, Magic Stone admits to swiping any poem he can, wherever he can get it—legality be damned. The result is a fascinating hodgepodge of more than 13,000 poems from around the world, from Persian to Portuguese. Most are in English, but some are untranslated. Formats vary, too; some are readable with a mouse click, while others are compressed files that must be downloaded to be read (although they unzip themselves). If you, too, believe that poetry wants to be free, you'll find this site a refreshing anecdote to the Anglocentric bent of most poetry Web sites. If you speak Chinese, visit [http://www.poesy.tk/] for a truly staggering number of classical and modern Chinese poems plus a great many foreign poems translated into Chinese. (You'll need Chinese characters installed on your computer.) Use Internet Explorer rather than Netscape Navigator for Magic Island Poetry Database.

—*Keir Graff*

Clay Tablets Go Digital

The looting of the National Museum in Baghdad may not have been as extensive as first feared, but it brought home a disturbing fact: the treasures of the past are never truly safe. We tend to assume that documents and artifacts will be permanently available to posterity once they've been set behind glass or stored in a climate-controlled vault. But even the most diligent care can be eclipsed in an instant by catastrophe, whether natural or political in origin.

Surprisingly, it may be the Web that offers our best hope of preserving these relics. Paper and stone may feel more substantial than electronic bits and bytes, but paper crumbles and stone can be stolen. Web sites mirrored at institutions on multiple continents should be safe from everything short of a global electromagnetic pulse—and in that case, we're going to have bigger problems to worry about.

Scholars are busy protecting troves of knowledge from the depredations of looters and bombs. Scrolling with a mouse may not be the same thing as holding a clay cuneiform tablet in our hands, but there are consolations: it's cheaper than a ticket to the cradle of civilization, and we can all see the tablet at the same time. (All sites last visited May 19, 2003.)

CDLI: Cuneiform Digital Library Initiative. [http://www.cdli.ucla.edu/index.html].

Clay tablets from ancient Mesopotamia are the earliest surviving written documents. The cuneiform (wedge-shaped) characters record everything from creation myths to recipes to receipts. About 120,000 tablets are scattered around the world, and approximately 60,000 have been posted online by the CDLI, thanks to "an international group of Assyriologists, museum curators and historians of science." Entries consist of photos or drawings of the tablet (definition is excellent, and they may be enlarged considerably), transliteration of the text, and provenance information. The Education section has such useful features as a who's who of cuneiform studies, bibliographical tools, history of third-and fourth-millennium Mesopotamia (from the Late Uruk period to UR III), and articles about the cuneiform writing system, Sumerian grammar, and Mesopotamian medicine. The war notwithstanding, the work is urgent: according to a recent Associated Press article, "Thousands [of tablets] are plundered each year in Iraq and dumped on the world antiquities market," where they can easily end up in private hands.

Duke Papyrus Archive. [http://scriptorium.lib.duke.edu/papyrus/texts/homepage.html].

More than 1,400 ancient Egyptian papyri are browseable by topic (including the type and original location of the document) and language (including Arabic, Coptic, Hieratic, and others). Some are fragmentary, some are very complete, but most are pictured in quality photos. Most works are not translated but described with content summaries (such as "the final scene of a comedy about the preparation of a giant fish for dinner"). Additional sections offer general information about papyrus, writing in Egypt under Greek and Roman rule, and the history and future of papyrology. An interesting fact: many papyri have been salvaged from the cartonnage of Egyptian mummies—they were pulled from recycling bins in administrative offices, layered on the linen-wrapped corpse, and covered in plaster.

The Electronic Text Corpus of Sumerian Literature. [http://www-etcsl.orient.ox.ac.uk/].

It's still a far cry from *The Nanny Diaries*, but in comparison to the other sites covered here, the Electronic Text Corpus of Sumerian Literature is more accessible to the casually interested user, featuring "over 400 literary works composed in the Sumerian language in ancient Mesopotamia during the late third and early second millennia B.C." These include narratives (such as my favorite, "Gilgamesh and the Bull of Heaven"), myths, poetry, letters, hymns, proverbs, and more. Some are fragmentary, but others are complete enough to offer real insight to ancient communication and storytelling. This site does not include images.

ETANA: Electronic Tools and Ancient Near Eastern Archives. [http://www.etana.org/coretexts.shtml].

Ironically, many books *about* the world's earliest texts can be hard to find, having themselves fallen out of print. The "most useful" of these are being gathered, scanned, and posted online, where they are also searchable. Another portion of the site, Abzu, helps users search materials related to the study of the ancient Near East, whether books available through ETANA, unaffiliated Web sites, transcripts of presentations, or articles.

—*Keir Graff*

Cocktails in Cyberspace

If intelligent beings were visiting our planet (or even living here) and wanted to learn something about us, they might very well employ the World Wide Web. Because they would have mastered interstellar travel, our hottest technology would look a bit quaint to them, but perhaps, when they tired of abducting and interrogating trailer-park dwellers in Nevada, they might find it a useful way of learning about our priorities.

Were they to type *world peace* into Yahoo! and click "Search," they'd be returned 485,000 hits, which would indicate that humans are quite keen on this topic—until they searched *drinking* and got 6,770,000 hits. Being superadvanced life-forms, they'd realize that the act of drinking includes apple juice as much as gin and juice, so perhaps they'd refine the search to *alcohol*. As they scrambled up the ramp to their saucer, they'd probably think that with an interest level of 7,780,000 hits, it's a marvel we haven't drunkenly bombed ourselves into oblivion.

That's not very sound science, but there are a huge number of drinks-related sites out there. Most preach either the fun (drinking games!) or dangers (you'll kill yourself!) of imbibing fermented and distilled beverages, but fortunately, some of them are addressed to sensible folks who like a sociable toot now and again. I'll focus strictly on cocktails here.

Bar-None Drink Recipes. [http://www.barnonedrinks.com/].
This site strikes a nice balance between content and aesthetics. Drinks recipes are indexed by category and searchable with Boolean terms. The Bartending Tips page has truly useful sections: a dictionary of drinks-related terms, tips for equipping and stocking your bar, a reference section that includes a metric conversion chart, and explanations of various bartending techniques. New sections for articles and reviews don't have many entries yet. Bar-None also has a copious drinking-games section (should the taste and effect of alcohol be too boring for you), different forums that allow users to exchange information, and a shareware version of BarBack, a handy recipe program that not only tells you what you can make with what you've got on hand but tells you what to buy to make the drinks you like.

The Designated Drinker. [http://www.designateddrinker.com/].
Because I'm rumored to be the author of this site, you'll have to take it with a coarse grain of salt when I tell you the "Top Tipples" list is truly definitive. This isn't really reference, but if you're lacking strong opinion in matters of drink, you'll find plenty here.

iDrink.com. [http://www.idrink.com/indexnew.htm].
The corporate counterpart to Webtender (see below), iDrink is flashier but allows the same option of searching cocktails according to what you've got at home. On our visit, however, the "Recipe Name Search" didn't work—the search button simply cleared the field rather than fetching information. Content is fairly unimpressive, and judging from the top-10 drink recipes, the target audience of this Canadian site is younger drinkers who want a fast, sugary buzz. Festooned with ads (including really annoying strobing banners), iDrink allows you to create a user profile and also sells memberships (which, for $19.95, include a "free" T-shirt). Overall, iDrink . . . not.

The Webtender: An On-Line Bartender. [http://www.webtender.com/].
What this site lacks in visual panache, it makes up for in data and accessibility. Users can browse drinks by name, category, alcohol, ingredient, or even the glass it's served in. Ingredients are browsable by name, type, and alcohol. Searching is sophisticated, allowing users to locate a name or ingredient(s) using key words, exact phrases, or syntax (e.g., if you know you like bourbon, sweet vermouth, and orange juice but hate gin, type *+bourbon +sweet vermouth +orange juice –gin*—and, incidentally, you prefer Manhattans to Bronxes). Even better, you can tell the Webtender what you've got in your bar and ask it to tell you what drinks your selection allows. Statistics allow you to see what other users have looked for (sadly, Jell-O shots are the most requested, along with a lot of other fuel for collegiate bacchanals) or to see what's in the database (5,788 alcoholic drinks from 3,824 contributors). With most reference sites, accuracy is always a question; however, cocktail recipes, like the English language, belong to the people and have evolved from the sacred (the martini) to the profane (the, ahem, Screaming Orgasm), so some might say there are no wrong answers. Other useful portions of the site include a brief bartender's handbook, a site index (some listings, like drinking newsgroups, are only shown here), and a forum. Click "About the Webtender" and you'll learn a truly interesting tidbit: the Webtender is a 28-year-old Norwegian named Pal Loberg who doesn't drink much but does enjoy working with databases. Just as well—writing code and drinking cocktails just don't mix.

—*Keir Graff*

Computer History

We tend to think of history as bygone eras of high collars and quaint manners and of museums as dusty warehouses of petrified lore. It's surprising to learn that computers, despite their recent arrival on the stage of human events, have energetic cadres of historians cataloging their every development, from the first tentative beep to the latest retort via artificial intelligence. What does make sense is that many computer museums show their exhibits in cyberspace. (Sites last visited on October 17, 2002.)

Computer History Museum. [http://www.computerhistory.org].
Established in 1996, this Silicon Valley nonprofit claims to have "one of the largest collections of computer-related artifacts, documents, film, and photographs in the world." It's not all online, but much useful information is. One of the best features, a time line of computer history, covers the years 1945 to 1990 and is searchable by year or topic; handy links at the end of each entry allow the user to select "More this topic" to sort results even more specifically. The two full online exhibits are "A History of the Internet, 1962–1992" and "Microprocessor Evolution, 1971–1996." The first uses text and images in a time-line format to provide an engaging overview, while the second, essentially a flowchart, will appeal more to technology wonks. Although the collections encompass Artifacts, Documentation, Ephemera, and Media (Audio/Digital/Film/Photo/Video), only the first category is searchable on the site. When the full collection is digitized, it will be a valuable resource for researchers. An online exhibit of 10 collection highlights includes wonderfully goofy audio samples of a "musical" IBM 1403 printer. Also useful is a document archive with full-text files of landmark works and manuals (including a pamphlet on Walter Hart's 1892 "Equationor," an early calculator). Although the layout is clean and the site easily navigable, the search function, powered by Google, failed to unearth several key items on the site, and the site is not fully Netscape compatible.

Computer Museum of America. [http://www.computer-museum.org/].
Founded way back in the dark ages—1983—this San Diego institution has a modest Web presence, including a Computer Hall of Fame (recent inductees include Nolan Bushnell, Michael Dell, and Steve Jobs); a newsletter called the *Circuit*; and an online exhibit hall. Three full exhibits—"The Computer Comes Home: A History of Personal Computing," "The Computer Photography of Arthur Lavine," and "IBM Speakers Slide Show"—provide a variety of perspectives in a slide-show format, which creates a nice simulation of walking along the walls of a real-life museum. Twenty-five stand-alone items are pictured and described in one or two paragraphs. So, if you've been dying to get a look at an actual RCA COSMAC ELF (a hobbyist computer kit from the early 1980s), here's your chance. Information is easy to find, and the search function, although also powered by Google, seemed to find material within the site with more ease than the search function of the Computer History Museum.

DigiBarn Computer Museum. [http://www.digibarn.com/].
Billed as a "'memory palace' for the nerd-inclined," this sprawling, good-humored site is the Internet outgrowth of the year-old DigiBarn. Located in an actual barn (with pigs) in the Santa Cruz Mountains of California, the burgeoning collection is a tribute to the "'cambrian explosion' of personal computing that ignited in 1975." The collection is roughly organized into Prehistoric Computers (including a 1920s Comptometer); Historic Systems (not housed at DigiBarn but extensively photo documented, including MacIntosh logic board #5, from 1983); Print Documentation (ads, brochures, magazines, books, articles, diagrams, manuals, newsletters, comics, product packaging, posters, and T-shirts); Video and Audio Documentation (including a video tour); Computer Game Systems; Software (including images of the installation and boot-up sequence of Windows 1.0); Graphs and Trees (including "a re-visiting and revising [of] the famous Bushy Tree diagram of the lineage of visual interactive computing systems"); Parts; Songs; Jokes; and Just Weird Stuff (including a tennis shoe computer pedometer). These entries are idiosyncratic; many simply consist of a photo, while others are surprisingly robust, with multiple photos, information, and links. This is really a fun site; however, because the physical space encourages hands-on interaction and is in such a unique setting, this may be the museum that calls not for a cyberjourney but for a road trip.

These are only a fraction of the destinations you'll find if you type "computer museum" into a search engine. It seems people just love using computers—to learn about computers.

—*Keir Graff*

D'oh! Springfield on the Web

How much information on TV shows is available on the Web? The answer might be an equation expressed as the total number of cable channels multiplied by the number of times a teenager uses the remote to change channels on the weekend. Whether the episode lists, trivia storehouses, chat rooms, and virtual worlds are preteen fan pages or official, network-sanctioned sites, when TV watchers want to share their love of shows, they move from the one-way conduit of the boob tube to the more interactive realms of cyberspace.

What's the reference tie-in? Well, for better or for worse, TV shows are the popular literature of our times, and just as British readers once followed the adventures of Pip in Dickens' *Great Expectations* from week to week, today's library patrons may want to know where they can find out who Tony Soprano had whacked in the second season. Obsessive fans of various shows tend to deal in fact, too, whether stumping each other with trivia or fetishizing the imaginary worlds they visit each week from the comfort of their couches.

There are so many sites, we might say visiting them is a journey of Homeric proportion—Homer Simpson, that is. In the sitcom spirit, and to provide an example of what is out there for just one show (I'm not even going to start with *The X-Files*), let's take a journey to . . . 742 Evergreen Terrace, Springfield, U.S.A.

Last Exit to Springfield. 1997–2002. [http://www.lardlad.com/].

Created and maintained by Adam Wolf, an 18-year-old in Adelaide, Australia, this remarkably designed site boasts biographies of the Simpson family and the primary real-life voice talent behind them; an episode guide with paragraph-long summaries; 2,588 MP3 quotes from shows; games; and more. The site is searchable, with an engine powered by Google. Perhaps the most interesting thing here, however, is a feature called FOX Update, in which Wolf discusses the network's attempts to shut down *Simpsons* fan sites for unauthorized use of images and audio. Wolf argues that most of these sites earn their operators no money while providing FOX with free advertising for its premier show. This section was originally created in 2000, and although it's hard to tell what is currently happening in this controversy, scuttlebutt on the Web indicates that there used to be many more *Simpsons* fan sites. Many other unauthorized sites for TV shows exist in this semilegal limbo—it's hard for creators to resist the urge to include actual material from the shows—but *The Simpsons'* popularity makes it the best example.

New Springfield. [http://www.newspringfield.com/].

Though New Springfield (apparently seceded from Olde Springfield) is chock-full of *Simpsons* news items, images, sound files, games, screen savers, trivia, comic strips—even a *Simpsons* discography—it's not searchable and of little use for reference purposes, even our lighthearted ones. The episode guide merely links to the official *Simpsons* site.

The Simpsons Archive. [http://www.snpp.com/].

Whether this site makes you shake your head in awe or sad disbelief depends on whether you're a fan of *The Simpsons*. Maintained by members of the alt.tv.simpsons newsgroup, there are more details here than there are sprinkles in a donut factory. On the front page, links lead to FAQs, Guides & Lists; Upcoming Episodes; Episode Guide (focusing more on trivia); Episode Capsules (with synopses); Miscellaneous (including articles, interviews, and even academic papers); Simpsons-L (a newsgroup); Web Links; and About the Archive. Also on the splash page, The Springfield Times links to *Simpsons*-related news in real life. The search function is powerful. I can never remember the name of the baby with one eyebrow, little Maggie's nemesis, but by typing *baby with one eyebrow* into the search box, I'm led to the Maggie File, where I learn that his name is Gerald. The information on Maggie alone is astounding, especially given her relatively minor role: which actors have voiced her sounds, what she wears, significant events in her life, distinguishing characteristics (including a list of times she's fallen). There's also an attempt to answer the question "Is Maggie a genius?"

It's hard to even summarize the vast content of this site, as each main link on the splash page subdivides into an elaborate subcategory, and each page beyond that is packed with a wealth of information. Even the episode guides—which could just summarize the action—include overlooked trivia, references to movies, references to previous episodes, things you'll note if you freeze the frame, continuity goofs, reviews—Lisa's sax solo in the opening credits is even transcribed.

Hyperbole is dangerous, but I'd be shocked if you had a question about *The Simpsons* you couldn't answer here, probably within a few minutes. Thanks to the search engine, a vaguely remembered line of dialogue or episode plot can be pinned down promptly.

The Simpsons.com. [http://www.thesimpsons.com/].

Though it invites users in with silly animation and a fun, interactive map of Springfield, the official site is skimpy on content. Find the Hall of Records and you'll be able to peruse bios of both the real-life people who create the show and their animated counterparts. The episode guide is comprehensive, but the synopses don't improve on *TV Guide* any. As Chief Wiggum might say, "Okay, folks. Show's over, nothing to see here."

The Simpsons Sourcebook: The Golden Years: A Tribute to Seasons 1–10. [http://www.frinky.com/].

Can we already be nostalgic for the good old days of a show that's been airing 13 years? Apparently, the answer is yes. This is a well-designed, fun, and interactive site for fans, though not nearly the trove of information that the Simpsons Archive is. They have the standard FAQs and bios, an episode guide (with user reviews), plus a message board, chat room, games, contests, fan scripts, and more. But the most "useful" information falls under the Multimedia link: Framegrabs (video captures), Scans & Grabpics (various stand-alone images that should appeal greatly to preteens), and KBBL Radio (MP3 files of songs from the show). If Kirk van Houten singing "Can I Borrow a Feeling?" doesn't put a smile on your face, you might need a visit from Dr. Hibbert. This site is not searchable.

These five sites are among the most trafficked, but the list goes on and on like . . . a really long-going-on thing. D'oh!

—*Keir Graff*

Floods, Fire, Famine—and Worse

Catastrophes and cataclysms enthrall us in complicated ways. Naturally, we fear them and we feel concern for the victims. But we also find them exhilarating—how else can we explain what's happened to the ten o'clock news?

It shouldn't be much of a surprise that tracking disasters on the Web is pretty easy. Whether we want to learn where things are dangerous today, or how best to duck, the information is just a few mouse clicks away. (All sites last viewed September 17, 2002.)

Disaster! Finder. [http://disasterfinder.gsfc.nasa.gov/].

This "search service" is a project of the NASA Solid Earth and Natural Hazards Program and functions primarily as a portal to a wide variety of Web sites, mostly government or university affiliated. Categories include Disaster Management, Disciplines, General, Organizations, Systems, and Type. Clicking on a category brings up a page with further, annotated divisions: under General, Conferences and Workshops lists 14 conferences, workshops, and meetings that focus on disaster-related topics. Under Type, there are groupings from Animals (with a link to the Novato, California-based Marin Humane Society's "Barnyard Animal Rescue Plan") to War (with an old-but-active link to a CNN list of Kosovo sites), with everything from Comets and Asteroids to Forestry in between. Highly searchable—both the site itself and the Natural Disaster Reference Database—although the basic search function won't work in Netscape Navigator (try Internet Explorer).

Earth Watch. [http://www.disasterrelief.org/EarthWatch/].

Graphically pleasing and simple to navigate, Earth Watch is a section of Disaster Relief, a Web site that is a joint venture between the American Red Cross, CNN Interactive, and IBM. A map of the globe is marked with up to thirteen unlucky icons representing problems from transportation disasters to pestilence. Clicking on an icon brings up a short news item about the event in question. Links in a left-hand navigation bar include Forum, Get Help, Give Help, Links, All Stories, and Library. The links page is useful, if not as extensive as some of the government sites, while the library offers unique features like a disaster dictionary and a disaster IQ test. The "Forum" link was broken during our test.

Federal Emergency Management Agency. [http://www.fema.gov/].

As you might expect from a federal agency, this is a massive site. A convenient, omnipresent tool bar along the top allows users to easily find a wealth of information on different aspects of disaster: fact sheets on reducing risk for and surviving everything from earthquakes to extreme heat, statistics about presidentially declared disasters, lists of this year's disasters to date, training resources, emergency contacts, press releases (recent and archived), and a history of the agency itself. Other resources of interest that have links on the home page include a highly searchable photo library with often-artistic images that put a human face on events; Storm Watch and Current Weather, with links to National Weather Service maps, video, and Doppler radar; and Active Disasters, a pull-down menu with information on counties that have recently been designated for FEMA assistance. Terrorist threats are assessed, too, with the "Current Nationwide Threat Level" displayed. When last viewed, links to articles about 9/11 efforts and terrorism preparedness dotted the home page.

ReliefWeb. [http://www.reliefweb.int/w/rwb.nsf].

A project of the United Nations Office for the Coordination of Humanitarian Affairs, this site (like FEMA) focuses on human response to catastrophe. Headlines link to articles and press releases about recent floods, fire, and famine—and what is being done to help the victims. MapCentre links to a surprising variety of maps, divisible by country and emergency and subdivisible by type, source, or keyword. Links for Complex Emergencies and Natural Disasters provide information on aid efforts to awful events around the globe. Although this site is obviously not the best source for weather or hard news, many entries provide snapshots of far-away scenarios that we may have missed in our morning newspapers. For instance, in a press release dated September 4, we learn that "470 people died in the floods and landslides triggered by heavy monsoon rains beginning in mid-July in Nepal. The disaster has affected 47 of the country's 75 districts and left 32,000 people homeless." Furthermore, we learn, this is more or less an annual occurrence as hundreds in the Himalayan kingdom die each year during monsoon season. Although fairly searchable, ReliefWeb is best if you are looking for current events worldwide or in a specific country. Design is not eye-friendly (long lists aren't broken up well), and you may fall into acronym soup.

One very interesting resource falls under Early Warning: a list of approximately 40 Web sites, from Famine Early Warning System Network [http://www.fews.net/] to Minorities at Risk [http://www.cidcm.umd.edu/inscr/mar/], that have a mission of helping people get the drop on all manner of crises, both sudden and slow moving.

U.S. Department of State. [http://www.state.gov/].

While this government resource deals primarily with unrest caused by political matters, the site does treat "Crisis Awareness and Preparedness" with a vast array of links, many to FEMA, covering dangers from heat waves to tsunamis; Travel Warnings give updates on threats of violence or disease to U.S. citizens traveling abroad. Both these parts of the site and Emergencies Abroad have a great many resources for victims of disasters, whether it's a list of doctors and hospitals in Burkina Faso or papers on helping children deal with grief. There are some broken or outdated links throughout the site.

Of Visual Interest

Discovery Channel Hurricane Cam. [http://dsc.discovery.com/cams/hurricane.html].

During hurricane season (June through November), storm buffs may want to watch the refreshed-hourly satellite images for the distinctive swirl that means a hurricane is forming out over the Atlantic.

Worldwide Earthquake Information. [http://www.seismo.usbr.gov/seismo/curWorld.html].

We may only read about major earthquakes several times a year, but the earth is rumbling almost all the time. This interesting site takes its information from the National Earthquake Information Service and presents it in a simple manner: recent quakes (over five on the Richter scale) are shown as magenta dots on a world map. Clicking on the dot reveals date, time, location, and magnitude of the temblor; the map itself is color-coded to reveal historical quake data. On a trivial note, the map makes attractive and conversation-enhancing desktop wallpaper.

—*Keir Graff*

Graphic Novels

What exactly is a graphic novel? Are the words simply a euphemism for *comic book*? In a society that races to replace any term that has a whiff of the lowly with a high-flown alternative (*sanitation engineer* for *garbageman*, for instance), it's easy to assume this is the case. However, after a decades-long evolution, drawn stories told frame by frame with inked dialogue have come a long way from pulpy superhero tales that sold for a nickel.

In a very basic sense, a comic is still what it used to be, a slim thing on flimsy paper that's usually published at regular intervals and often has ongoing story elements. A graphic novel, like a regular novel, is a stand-alone story that is published as a book. It's easy to get confused, though, because some people will still use *comics* for the whole genre or *graphic novel* for any comic-style work that's handsomely published, even if it's just a collection of superhero stories. And although *comic* is fine with some folks, for others it's an insulting implication that they like to curl up with a copy of *Archie*.

How to handle the terminology? I've developed a simple system that will avoid offending even the most condescending comic-book cognoscenti: if it's clearly for children, such as *Casper the Friendly Ghost*, use *comic book* with confidence; for anything else, use *graphic novel*. You may receive a smug correction, explaining why Daniel Clowes' *8-Ball* is a comic but his *Ghost World* is a graphic novel—aficionados are a notoriously detail-oriented lot—but you won't have erred by telling a fan his favorite form is just kid stuff.

And what the heck are *manga*? Japanese comics, noted for characters with big hair and big eyes. In their home country they have fans of all ages—and both genders. Though the story sensibility is very different, manga art has been infiltrating American pop culture for some time. Even if you think you're not familiar with it, you probably have seen some examples already (think Pokemon).

Following are some sites that will help you avoid getting ink on your face. (All sites last visited December 16, 2002.)

Overviews

Comic Books for Young Adults: A Guide for Librarians. Ed. by Michael R. Lavin. [http://ublib.buffalo.edu/lml/comics/pages/].

Librarian Lavin presents, in clear outline format, an argument that comic books belong in libraries; an explanation of formats; collection development issues; guides to publishers and genres; recommended comics and graphic novels; and an *extremely* extensive bibliography of related resources.

The Librarian's Guide to Anime and Manga. By Gilles Poitras. [http://www.koyagi.com/Libguide.html].

Treating both *manga* (Japanese comics) and *anime* (Japanese animation, often derived from *manga*), this librarian and author of *The Anime Companion: What's Japanese in Japanese Animation?* (1999) explains what they are; discusses issues of violence, nudity, and sexual content; analyzes emerging trends; recommends Internet resources and books; and offers many annotated buying recommendations. A truly useful tool in navigating this foreign world.

Recommended Graphic Novels for Public Libraries. Ed. by Steve Raiteri. [http://my.voyager.net/~sraiteri/graphicnovels.htm].

Raiteri, a librarian at Greene County Public Library in Xenia, Ohio, has been an avid fan for 25 years and is the graphic novel buyer for his system. This list consists of the best titles out of 850 he's bought, appropriate for ages 10 to 16, and includes ISBN and price. Subdivisions include various superheroes (you know the difference between DC and Marvel, don't you?), science fiction and fantasy, comedy, and *manga*.

Raiteri's brief but knowledgeable annotations will be a help to many librarians, and rank beginners will benefit from Suggested Opening Collection: 30 Selections. This site presents all its information in three pages (with the largest portion on the first page) and is not indexed or searchable, although you can easily remedy that by hitting ctrl+f to use your browser's search capability.

Reviews

Artbomb.net: A Graphic Novel Explosion. By Warren Ellis and Peter Aaron Rose. [http://www.artbomb.net/home.jsp].

With a mission of "broadening the appeal of diverse comic books and graphic novels," this site, by writer Ellis and Internet producer Rose, is well on its way. In this recommend-only publication, reviewed titles are listed alphabetically and by a detailed genre breakdown. Reviews are lively, and the site is well designed. If that's not enough, it offers news, interviews, and even a few comics for your reading pleasure.

The Comics Get Serious: Graphic Novel Reviews and Other Stuff. By D. Aviva Rothschild. [http://www.rationalmagic.com/Comics/Comics.html].

The author of *Graphic Novels: A Bibliographic Guide to Book-Length Comics* (1995) offers thorough, highly opinionated reviews of roughly 150 works, which are organized by title, subject, kid-friendliness, and best-worst status. Rothschild has been on indefinite hiatus since March, however.

No Flying, No Tights: A Website Reviewing Graphic Novels for Teens. By Robin Brenner. [http://leep.lis.uiuc.edu/publish/rebrennr/304LE/gn/index.html].

Brenner, the brains behind this intelligently written, visually pleasing site, is a 25-year-old library technician in Lexington, Massachusetts. Graphic novel reviews are divided into eight genres (including science fiction, nonfiction, realism, and, yes, superheroes) and also indexed by creator, title, and publisher. Core lists, news, and links complete the package. Reviews aren't nearly as detailed as in The Comics Get Serious (see above), but Brenner's sensibility and book choices seem right on.

Free Samples

Want to view graphic novels online? While some contain elements of sound or animation—and perhaps await yet another genre name—the lineage is clear. Purists may object, since graphic novels involve readers by making them turn pages, while electronic versions allow them to sit back. Still, it's interesting to watch evolution in action.

Electric Sheep Comix. [http://www.e-sheep.com/main.shtml].

Free views of graphic novel–styled works by Patrick Farley, on mature subjects and in a variety of styles: *Apocamon* retells the Book of Revelation as *manga* (be warned of strong irreverence); *Barracuda: The Scotty Zaccharine Story* is an insider jab at the decline of dot-com San Francisco; and *The Spiders* offers an imaginative telling of the Afghan-U.S. conflict. Includes convenient (and often tongue-in-cheek) content warnings.

Fantagraphics Books. [http://www.fantagraphics.com/comics/comics.html].

Fantagraphics, "publisher of the world's greatest cartoonists," offers a rotating crop of work by promising young artists. As of this writing, Alex Fellows' B*lank Slate* provided an acutely observed portrait of a grief-stricken young man and his father.

My Obsession with Chess. By Scott McCloud. [http://www.scottmccloud.com/comics/chess/chess.html].

Comic guru McCloud's site includes many experiments with form that take advantage of computers' capabilities and that would not normally fit the graphic novel designation. This fine piece of memoir, however, does. (For a very interesting exploration of the possible online future of graphic novels, see his *I Can't Stop Thinking!* [http://www.scottmccloud.com/comics/icst/index.html].)

—*Keir Graff*

Islam

Although world events have tightened the focus on countries where Islam is the primary religion, its teachings and sects are poorly understood by many Westerners, for whom belief is synonymous with extremism. With an estimated one billion followers, Islam—like Christianity—has many interpretations, and library users may well wish to better acquaint themselves with this topic. As ever, the intelligent browser uses the Web for reference with a keen eye as to who is writing the material; certainly with religious Web sites, most information is propagated by believers. All sites were last visited August 19, 2002 (or Jumada Al-Thani 11, 1423 on the Islamic lunar calendar).

About.com. [http://islam.about.com/blintroa.htm?PM=ss12_islam].

Useful as a jumping-off point for further research, the Introduction to Islam section defines *Islam*, *Muslim*, and *Allah*; gives some statistics on Muslims; and provides brief essays about the beliefs and teachings of Islam and the daily lives of its believers. Not purely objective—it is written from a Muslim point of view—it nonetheless provides an overview without being dogmatic. Links provide more information and resources treating the Qur'an, Islamic clothing, and September 11 and the notion of *jihad*. On another part of the Web site, under the subheading Agnosticism/Atheism, About.com guide Austin Cline presents an Index of Islamic Sects [http://atheism.about.com/library/FAQs/islam/blfaq_islam_sects.htm?terms=islamic+sects]. With succinct explanations of groups like Sunni, Shi'a, and Wahhabi, this is an invaluable quick reference for researchers searching for meaning behind the headlines.

AllExperts.com. [http://www.allexperts.com/getExpert.asp?Category=947].

This is an intriguing resource. Volunteer "experts" will answer specific questions within three days, via e-mail. Although the level of expertise varies, it's hard to think of a more targeted search engine. Experts are listed by name and availability, and a "View Profile" link connects users to a biography, some quotes, and user ratings of the expert—these last utilize a format similar to Ebay, where "customers" (in this case, question askers) rate the "seller" (the expert) on knowledge, clarity of response, timeliness, and politeness. A little "shopping" and the curious can receive a personalized response from a practicing Muslim. In our test, in response to a question about dietary requirements, volunteer Abdai provided a four-paragraph answer within 24 hours. Though his response (which cited biblical verse) was far from a dispassionate encyclopedia entry, it was concise, direct, and perhaps offered greater insight into the mind of a Muslim than would a resource vetted by a cadre of tenured theologians.

IslamiCity. 1995–2002. [http://islamicity.com/education/]

The "Education Center" of this massive Muslim Web site provides many tools useful for both non-Muslims who seek a greater understanding of Islam and practicing Muslims looking for study aids. Features include Understanding Islam, a brief FAQ ; Culture and Arts, covering a broad selection of Islamic arts and architecture, calligraphy, culture, history, and mosques; History, spanning the birth of Muhammad in 570 C.E. through the 1970s; Islam and Science, a glossary of Islamic terms—many with pronunciation guides or audio examples; and iEducation, links to Islamic schools and articles about teaching and learning Arabic. Another fascinating resource is the Holy Quran Center [http://islamicity.com/mosque/quran/]. Users can search the Qur'an by topic or phonetic query, listen to recitations while viewing translations or Arabic script, or read one of more than 20 translations in languages from Albanian to Urdu. This site can be slow and occasionally buggy (on our last visit, the Back button of the browser didn't always work), but the wealth of information makes it a worthwhile destination.

Virtual Religion Index: Islamic Studies. 1997–2002. Rutgers University Religion Department [http://religion.rutgers.edu/vri/islam.html].

This Web portal, compiled by the Rutgers University Religion Department, provides briefly annotated links to roughly 50 Web pages, sites, and other portals. Headings include General Resources, Muhammad—The Prophet, The Quran, Hadith (Oral Tradition), Shari'ah (Law), Shi'a, Sufis, and Modern Movements. The links lead to articles, bibliographies, electronic publications, essays, glossaries, speeches, and translated texts that will be most useful to students and serious researchers. But allowing scholars to screen the selections has its advantages—a sample annotation, for Islamic Texts & Resources Meta Page, warns: "Many links obsolete. Needs up-dating."

—*Keir Graff*

More Sites on Sleuths: Chicago Crime

In the past, our Sites on Sleuths series has focused on fictitious mysteries and the authors who create them. This year we tried doing something a little different by reviewing sites that examine actual, historical whodunits from the Windy City. As it turns out, most of them have been turned into fiction.

Click2Flicks: Chicago: The Story behind the Movie. [http://www.click2flicks.com/chicago/chicago_ch1.htm].

Chicago journalism has been a fertile field for enduring fact-to-fiction tales. The Leopold and Loeb case (see below) spawned books and movies. Ben Hecht and Charles MacArthur drew on their real-life journalistic experiences to write the play *The Front Page*, which has endured both on stage and through several film versions (most notably in 1940 as *His Girl Friday*). Not surprisingly, the fictional versions tend to examine the role the media plays in the perception—and outcome—of the events they cover.

Chicago, winner of Best Picture at this year's Academy Awards, has similarly interesting origins. The singing story of two dolls who use stints on "Murderess Row" to further their careers draws on two real-life killings—and, like *The Front Page*, was once a play. A young *Chicago Tribune* reporter named Maurine Watkins reported on Beulah Annan, a flapper who played a jazz record after shooting her lover, and Belva Gaertner, a cabaret singer who shot her married boyfriend. Both women were acquitted amid a hailstorm of publicity, and Watkins went on to write the successful play *Chicago* based on their stories. Bob Fosse turned the play into a musical in 1975; his stage musical provided the template for the new film version.

Carole Bos, author of this hyperlinked article, tells the story succinctly and claims to have been at pains to use original source material whenever possible. She also does a credible job of putting real-life events in context while explaining the development of the entertainments they became.

History & Hauntings.com: Home of Ghosts of the Prairie and the American Ghost Society: The Murder Castle of H. H. Holmes. [http://www.prairieghosts.com/holmes.html].

Erik Larson is getting a lot of attention for *The Devil in the White City* [BKL F 15 03], his account of the man he calls "the first urban American serial killer." In 1886, Herman W. Mudgett, alias Dr. H. H. Holmes, moved to the Englewood neighborhood of Chicago and built a hotel that was literally a deathtrap, designed to help him catch and kill the naive young women he lured with promises of work during the Columbian Exposition (or World's Fair) of 1893.

Larson hasn't made his findings available on the Web, but another, lesser-known writer has. In a four-chapter excerpt from his book *Haunted Chicago* (Whitechapel, 2003), Troy Taylor offers a history of Holmes from a slightly different perspective: Taylor is a prolific author, ghost hunter, and the president of the American Ghost Society. But despite Taylor's interest in the paranormal, the first three chapters simply offer a chronology of this bizarre tale, with the barest mention of rumored hauntings. The fourth chapter covers Holmes' trial and execution, then explores a possible "Holmes Curse" afflicting those responsible for the killer's capture and conviction. Although the writing isn't stellar, it is full of detail, and even the last passage sticks mostly to the facts, not spectral speculation.

infoplease.com: All the Knowledge You Need: The St. Valentine's Day Massacre. [http://www.infoplease.com/spot/valmassacre1.html].
about.com: Organized Crime: St. Valentine's Day Massacre. [http://organizedcrime.about.com/library/weekly/aa021403a.htm].

The St. Valentine's Day Massacre, in which Al Capone's hitmen knocked off a considerable number of Bugs Moran's gang in a North Side garage, is possibly the most famous event in gangster history. For Chicagoans, the 1929 event produced what seems to be a 100-year hangover, as even today we're greeted with mimed machine guns and "rat-tat-tat" sounds when traveling abroad. The murders and the milieu that spawned them are responsible for cultural fallout including bus tours, pizza chains, Halloween costumes, dinner theater—so much silliness that it's easy to forget how gory this crime really was.

There are many sites with a St. Valentine's Day Massacre recap, most of them badly in need of editorial guidance, but we recommend sticking to infoplease for their succinct outline. For more detail, plus a cheesy prefatory polemic, visit about.com.

Jazz Age Chicago: Urban Leisure from 1893 to 1934: The Leopold and Loeb Case of 1924. [http://www.suba.com/~scottn/explore/scrapbks/leo_loeb/leo_loeb.htm].
Leopoldandloeb.com. [http://www.leopoldandloeb.com].

The first, fascinating site is written by Scott Newman, a Ph.D. candidate at Loyola University in Chicago. Although he focuses not on crime but on the cultural life of the city during the first third of the last century, his article on the Leopold and Loeb case of 1924 is an important stop for anyone needing an overview. The defendants, two wealthy students at the University of Chicago, kidnapped and murdered 14-year-old Bobby Franks because they wanted to commit the perfect crime. As Newman states, the details of the case aren't quite as interesting as the public's response: the notion that two privileged brainiacs could so coolly dispatch a neighborhood kid struck a blow to the cherished self-image of the middle class.

Newman offers a hyperlinked essay interpreting the crime; period newspaper articles, maps, photographs, and a bibliography of suggested online resources (including Meyer Levin's 1956 novel version, *Compulsion*). The essay may contain a little too much academic jargon for some readers, but the ideas are interesting. For other users, the contemporary newspaper accounts may be the highlight—after all, it was the reporters who helped break the case.

Leopoldandloeb.com offers less interpretation but a much more detailed re-creation of the killing. Author Marianne Rackliffe has done extensive research, and though her prose falters a bit when she tries to bring readers into the moment, the wealth of detail ultimately wins out. A telling quote from Nathan Leopold, vis-a-vis his interest in the life of Christ: "The idea of nailing somebody to something was very appealing to me."

—*Keir Graff*

Nazi Germany

The Web can be like a conceptual conundrum proposed by M. C. Escher: a single Web page is like a room, from which it's possible to walk directly into any of the billions of other rooms on the Internet (see *Small Pieces Loosely Joined* [Perseus, 2002] for a lively discussion of this concept). This connectedness can be helpful and efficient (allowing us to surf links to related sites); humorously apt (when we accidentally type *nerd* instead of *nerf*); or disconcertingly inappropriate (such as a horse lover stumbling upon a pornographic site for those who, um, love horses).

Certain research themes make this especially clear. There are perfectly valid reasons for researching child pornography or Nazi Germany, but search engines aren't good at discerning user intent: type *Nazi* into Google, and the first Web page to appear is the home page of the American Nazi Party. We may grudgingly support even Nazis' right to free speech, but we don't want to learn about the Holocaust from them.

Here are several sites to help users find historical data, not hate speech.

German Propaganda Archive. [http://www.calvin.edu/academic/cas/gpa/].

Propaganda was essential to the Nazi machine; examining it may help us understand how so many people accepted an abhorrent regime. Communications professor Randall Bytwerk, of Calvin College, has collected a great many translated speeches, flyers, pamphlets, posters, cartoons, essays—even propaganda *for* propagandists. Many of the speeches seem more boring than bloodthirsty, bringing Hannah Arendt's immortal (or glib, depending on your viewpoint) phrase, "the banality of evil," to mind.

The History Place: Nazi Germany/World War II. [http://www.historyplace.com/index.html].

This commercial site has lengthy articles about Hitler ("The Rise of Hitler" and "The Triumph of Hitler"); biographies of Adolf Eichmann, Rudolf Hess, and Reinhard Heydrich (hopefully, more will be forthcoming); an article about the Hitler Youth (five chapters); a photo-essay on Auschwitz today; and time lines treating both World War II in general and the Holocaust in particular. The time lines are useful as they contain photos and even a few audio clips (such as Hitler speaking) that will help make events come alive for students.

The quality of the writing is average (and occasionally jokey: "It is hard to imagine tens of thousands of Germans shouting 'Heil Schicklgruber!' instead of 'Heil Hitler!'"), but its simplicity makes it appropriate for middle-to high-school students. Blinking banner ads and sometimes slow loading times can be annoying.

A Teacher's Guide to the Holocaust. [http://fcit.coedu.usf.edu/holocaust/default.htm].

This substantial site groups its materials into time lines (such as *The Ghettos* [1939–1941] or *Aftermath* [1945–2000]); examinations of roles played by different groups (victims, perpetrators, bystanders, and more); and examples and analysis of art of the period. This last section is particularly interesting and offers examples of both Nazi-approved art and the art of their victims.

Web links, term definitions, audio pronunciations of terms, and images are woven into the text. A teachers' resources section includes even more tools: bibliographies, documents, a glossary, maps, photo galleries, movies, music, panoramas, and more. Student Activities contains lesson plans for elementary-, middle-, and high-school students.

Wikipedia: Nazi Germany. [http://www.wikipedia.org/wiki/Nazi_germany].

Not everyone will trust an open-content encyclopedia, given its potential for mischievous misuse; conversely, some will trust it more than a traditionally published work, reasoning that the greater the number of editors, the better the vetting process. Furthermore, mistakes can be corrected instantly.

Wikipedia's *Nazi Germany* entry provides a user-friendly look at this wretched historical period. An overview and chronology are followed by outlines of Third Reich military, police, and political organizations; biographies of key figures (from military leaders to refugees); a glossary of related terms (from A*nschluss* to *Zeppelin*); and links to related articles. The entire entry is extensively hyperlinked—it's possible, with two mouse clicks, to find oneself reading about Los Angeles' 1943 zoot-suit riots.

—*Keir Graff*

Oh Canada!—Desktop Reference

One of the pleasures of many Canadian Web sites is the clean and consistent presentation across the wealth of government resources. The government of Canada's Web site regulations require a "common look and feel" for ease of navigation. This dedication to usability is carried into the academic and business sector as well. The following selection of a variety of basic reference sites is provided to entice all users of the World Wide Web to look north. These are just examples; there are many more wonderful sites to visit and use. All sites were last accessed on April 1, 2003.

Official Government Sites

Agriculture and Agri-Food Canada Online. [http://www.agr.gc.ca/]
The point of contact for information on agriculture, the environment, rural life, etc.

Citizenship and Immigration Canada. [http://www.cic.gc.ca/].
The source of information about immigrating, studying, working, visiting, etc. A related site is the Canada Customs and Revenue Agency [http://www.ccra-adrc.gc.ca/]. The wait times table for crossing the U.S.-Canadian border at points of entry is useful.

Environment Canada: The Green Lane. [http://www.ec.gc.ca/].
The source for information on the environment and the weather. The Green Lane includes a link to EnviroZine [http://www.ec.gc.ca/envirozine/english/home_e.cfm], an online environmental magazine.

Government of Canada. [http://canada.gc.ca/].
This gateway to the many agencies is easy to browse, navigate, and search. While sporting the common look and feel, it, like the related pages, has its own subtle distinctions.

Health Canada. [http://www.hc-sc.gc.ca/].
Links to healthy living, disease, health protection, and related information. There is a special section related to SARS (severe acute respiratory syndrome).

Library and Archives of Canada. [http://www.nlc-bnc.ca/].
This site is fun to explore with its many online exhibits of living memory, places, people, etc. Among the research services are a variety of genealogical sources.

National Archives of Canada. [http://www.archives.ca/02/0201_e.html].
One could spend a quiet afternoon browsing the collections or do a careful search guided by excellent onscreen tips. The "Census of the Northwest Provinces, 1906" [http://www.archives.ca/02/020153_e.html] is an example of the materials found.

National Research Council Canada. [http://www.nrc-cnrc.gc.ca/].
Provides assistance in the development of research in "biotechnology, information and communications technologies, measurement standards, molecular sciences, aerospace, manufacturing, construction, ocean engineering and others." One of its services is the Canada Institute for Scientific and Technical Information (CISTI) [http://cisti-icist.nrc-cnrc.gc.ca/]. Document delivery is an important part of CISTI's function.

Natural Resources Canada. [http://www.nrcan-rncan.gc.ca/inter/index.html].
Here is everything from information for exporters to climate to disaster information and much more in its site index. The Atlas of Canada [http://atlas.gc.ca/site/english/index.html] is a marvelous collection of online maps of physical, social, and environmental information.

Statistics Canada. [http://www.statcan.ca/].
Provides statistics "that help Canadians better understand their country—its population, resources, economy, society and culture." The data are extensive, easily navigated, and fast loading. One interesting report is the "Profile of Languages in Canada."

Other Useful Sites

Athletics Canada [http://www.athleticscanada.com/] is the source for information on events, athletes, officials, Paralympic programs, etc. The media links are a bit out of date, but the other links to many kinds of information appear to be very useful.

Canada 411 [http://www.canada411.ca/] is the online telephone directory.

Canada Newswire [http://www.newswire.ca/htmindex/etoday.html] offers up-to-date news about financial dealings and business activities affecting Canadian companies.

Canadian Civil Engineering History & Heritage [http://collections.ic.gc.ca/civileng/eng/] is a digital archive of photographs and textual information about the engineers and engineering historic sites plus links to other significant sites.

Canadian Initiative on Digital Libraries [http://www.nlc-bnc.ca/cidl/] serves as a gateway to information about creating digital collections and to a variety of libraries with collections.

The Children's Literature Web Guide [http://www.ucalgary.ca/~dkbrown/] is one of the oldest and best maintained educational sites on the Web. It is the starting place for education students, teachers, parents, and all others to locate Web sites on authors, books, storytelling, etc.

Churchill Northern Studies Centre [http://mail.churchillmb.net/~cnsc/] has been conducting subarctic research since 1976. The site includes information on research, learning vacations, educational programs, and materials.

The Globe and Mail [http://www.globeandmail.com/], like most major newspapers, has an online presence. Check here for one of the views from north of the border.

Google Canada [http://www.google.ca/] offers searching in either French or English. One can search the world or limit to Canadian sites.

Images Canada [http://www.imagescanada.ca/] "provides access to the thousands of images held on the Web sites of participating Canadian cultural institutions." A search for *wildflowers* in the site search engine retrieved 592 images.

Maclean's [http://www.macleans.ca/] is the one Canadian magazine U.S. residents are likely to know. Selected articles are provided online, including an archive of special topics.

National Post [http://www.nationalpost.com/home/] is a widely read, sometimes controversial newspaper. It has even been called an alternative newspaper in spite of its wide circulation. Online, it is part of Canada.com [http://www.canada.com], which offers versions of the newspaper tailored to different Canadian cities.

—Linda Loos Scarth

The Other Football

With springtime rolling in, reference librarians may start seeing terrified parents who have been drafted to coach soccer. Maybe they're discombobulated after learning (from a six-year-old child, no less) the game the rest of the world calls *football* is played not by 300-pound powerhouses who can hospitalize a player with a legal hit but by average-sized athletes recruited for their agility. Perhaps they're impressed by the concept of a sport with no timeouts yet incredulous that games can end in nil-nil draws. Or possibly, still grieving Oakland's Super Bowl spanking, the insult has been compounded when a son or daughter has announced a desire to play not Pop Warner Football but soccer.

These folks need help if they're going to figure out what *offside* means in this sport, not to mention *indirect free kick* and *red card*. Fortunately, there's a wealth of information available on the Web—and, unlike in soccer, you can use your hands to get to the action. (All sites last accessed January 17, 2003.)

AYSO: Rules, Policies, Guidelines. [http://www.soccer.org/gen/docs/rules.html].
The American Youth Soccer Organization (AYSO) regulates the game for youngsters. This useful page has downloads for rules and regulations, national bylaws and regional guidelines, and the player/parent handbook. There are guidelines for playing with different age groups and smaller-than-usual teams (that's the number of players, not the size). AYSO is an "everybody plays" organization, so win-hungry coaches may wish to look for another sanctioning body (perhaps the I Live through My Kids Organization).

FIFA: Laws of the Game, 2002. [http://www.fifa.com/refs/laws_E.html].
FIFA (Federation Internationale de Football Association) is the worldwide governing body of soccer at the professional level. Although many rules won't apply to kids who are four feet tall (e.g., they won't be playing on a field 120 meters long), coaches may appreciate authoritative explanations of difficult-to-grasp concepts like *offside*.

National Federation of State High School Associations: Soccer. [http://www.nfhs.org/rules-soccer.htm].
Here you'll find information on rules as they've been adapted for high-school players and coaches. Sections include rulebook revisions, interpretations (offering help with gray areas like "Are religious head wraps or long skirts legal for play in soccer?"), official soccer signals (with a slow-loading page of photographic examples), and a field diagram with instructions for the scorer and other relevant personnel. While a complete rule book is not posted, a hard copy is available for a fee.

National Soccer Coaches Association of America: Coaching Tips. [http://www.nscaa.com/tips/index.html].
Twenty-five short articles cover different aspects of coaching, from "The Effective Assistant Coach" to "Introduction to Nutrition and Soccer Performance." Good for those moving beyond the basics.

Soccer Glossary. [http://www.firstbasesports.com/soccer_glossary.html].
Selected from the book *Soccer Made Simple: A Spectator's Guide* (First Base Sports, 1994), this list of 200-plus terms covers everything from *advantage rule* ("A clause in the rules that directs the referee to refrain from stopping play for a foul if a stoppage would benefit the team that committed the violation") to *zone* (a type of defense).

SoccerHelp: Youth Soccer Coaching. [http://www.soccerhelp.com/].
Sections include topics, rules, skills, and drills. An alphabetical listing allows unfamiliar terms to be located fairly quickly. And common conundrums are linked to guidelines by phrase from the first page, from "How to Teach Dribbling" to "Should You Push Up When You Attack?" Many coaching aids are available only on the subscription part of the site (pricing starts at $15.95 for 45 days), but there is much free material here.

—Keir Graff

Painters & Prices

AskART: "The Artists Bluebook": Extensive Information about 28,000 American Artists. [http://www.askart.com/]. (Last accessed January 6, 2003.)

This privately held corporation has two goals: to create and maintain the most complete database of American artists in the world and to assist "a democratic system in which art can be transacted in a global marketplace made efficient and fair by accessible knowledge." The corporation claims its site draws collectors and dealers, curators and educators, and, naturally, scholars. Given the breadth of information here, that may well be the case, although AskART serves them all (except perhaps the dealers) more as a general reference than an in-depth resource for a few.

The splash page features an artist search, by either name (last or first and last) or alphabetical browsing. Artists from the 1600s to the present day are included. John Singleton Copley (Colonial American portraitist who moved to England in 1774 to take up history painting) and Keith Haring (1980s and 1990s graffiti-cartoon artist) are equally accessible by last name–only search. Each artist's summary page lists birth and death dates, the state they're most affiliated with, and a quick stylistic ID. There is also information under the headings Books on this Artist, The Periodicals, The Biography & Bulletins, Artwork for Sale/Art Wanted, Dealers for This Artist, Exhibits for This Artist, Museums for This Artist, and The Images. These links are only active if AskART has the corresponding material available.

A somewhat redundant table of contents lists Current Exhibits, # Museums Holding, Biography, Active Bulletins, # Books, # Periodicals, Image Gallery, # Auction Records, Graphs, and Record Price. Users who sign up for free Artist Alert Updates will receive e-mails when artist records are updated. Most of the information comes from records that AskART has been developing since the early 1970s (when it was the quest of now-deceased founder Roger Dunbier), although in true Internet reference fashion, users may submit new material and corrections.

This may be the easiest way of attaining the size and comprehensiveness hoped for, especially in the case of little-known or overlooked artists. A biography of Arlene Hooker Fay, a Montana artist who enjoyed success in the Pacific Northwest with her paintings of Indians, was submitted on her death by an acquaintance. Also in true Internet fashion, it is not simply a dry biography; those looking up Fay will also be able to read tributes from friends and family that have been added to the entry.

The size of each entry varies with the fame of the subject. A major painter like Edward Hopper receives a lengthy biography, a stunning list of museums that hold his work, nearly 100 images available to pay users, and literally hundreds of bibliographical references, while the relatively unknown Indiana artist Floyd D. Hopper (no relation) has a three-sentence summary, eight images, and a four-item bibliography. Still, without slighting the Hoosier artist, that may be plenty of information for most.

Other sections accessible from the front page include a Museum Directory, searchable by name and/or city (or, by leaving the search fields blank, it is possible to call up the entire list ranked by state or name); Dealers (searchable much the same way, although full listings take some time to load); Auction Houses (shorter, complete list only); and Professional Associations (likewise). Directory listings include brief genre descriptions (e.g., the Edwin A. Ulrich Museum of Art at Wichita State University specializes in "outdoor sculpture"), addresses, phone numbers, e-mail, and Web sites when applicable. Another useful splash-page function is the ART Travel Directory, which sorts museums and art dealers by destination. A search for *New York City* with a 10-mile radius around the city retrieved 168 results; *Santa Fe* (after offering a choice between 8 different Santa Fe's) offered a more manageable 44 possibilities. Also useful is the extensive glossary, searchable not by keyword but by letter. A sample definition is *inimage*: "A surrealist technique that is the opposite of collage: rather than pieces being glued together to make a composite image, pieces are cut away from an existing picture to make an image."

Under the heading Categories of Interest, links select groupings of interest to various browsers: Highest Auction Prices, Hudson River School, Notable Sculptors, Notable Women, California Artists, and many more. As these include short essays treating the history of each genre or movement, they can be especially useful to students or enthusiasts.

Although most of AskART's content is free, some features are only available (or fully available) for a membership fee of $19.50 per month. Most importantly, subscribers have full access to art images, sometimes hundreds of paintings (versus a maximum of five for nonpaying users). Other fee features include graphical analysis of each artist's sales and auction records.

Overall, AskART is a very promising site, easy to navigate, well designed (although it could cut down on visual clutter), and fairly fast. If it continues to grow, it could become a very important Web reference, despite its twin mission of education and commerce.

—*Keir Graff*

The Quick and the Dead

Sometimes we have legitimate reasons for searching out the cold, hard biographical data on famous folks—although more often than not we're just wondering which newsmaker shares our birthday (incidentally, in my case it's televangelist Jim Bakker). Or maybe we just want to engage in the timeless sport of age guessing. Matters can be complicated, however, when we realize we're not sure whether the person we're thinking of is even still alive. What follows is an analysis of sites that help you find out when people were born and whether they're alive—and, if they've passed from this world to the next, where you can find their mortal remains. (All sites last accessed on August 29, 2002.)

Anybirthday.com. [http://www.anybirthday.com/].

This simple site claims to have more than 135 million birthdays, although it's certainly missing a lot of people I know. It's also not the best source for celebrity birthdays—a search for Frank Sinatra yields 25 results sorted by zip code, and even if you know to look for Francis Albert Sinatra (the singer's birth name), you're out of luck: zero results. But the simple search (for best results, use first name, last name, and zip code) may well allow you to track down the birthday of a friend or coworker—then request an e-mail reminder one week before the special day. If you're worried about the privacy implications of this site (which claims to get its data from public records), a quick "Opt Out" procedure allows you to remove your own record from the database.

Biography.com. [http://www.biography.com/].

This vast, highly commercial site, an outgrowth of the TV show *Biography*, claims to have 25,000 of "the Web's best bios," and it very well may. It's certainly a useful resource for quick access to biographical data on well-known (and fairly well known) people. Using the BioSearch feature on the splash page to search Arthur Ashe, we learn at the beginning of his 17-paragraph bio that the groundbreaking tennis player was born July 10, 1943, and at the end that he died (of pneumonia related to AIDS, contracted during a blood transfusion) February 6, 1993. Also on the splash page is a quick search that, with a few mouse clicks, allows you to find out which celebrities were born on a particular day. Although seemingly hundreds of other sites offer this feature—most focus more on movie stars, singers, and athletes—Biography.com certainly includes them but features Isaac Asimov, not Cuba Gooding Jr., as its top pick for January 2. This site seems quite slow when accessed via Netscape Communicator—even lurching to a halt—but works quite well with Internet Explorer.

Dead or Alive? [http://www.dead-or-alive.org/dead.nsf].

Some celebrities occupy a murky netherworld of near fame; we find ourselves wondering, "Is so-and-so still alive?" After all, recent deaths may not have made it into standard references yet, and we may have just plain missed others. As of last viewing, this site reported 6,023 records of famous and semifamous people "who have died 'recently' or might plausibly be dead. For living people, 'might plausibly be dead' means that they have reached a certain age or, in some cases, been out of the limelight so long that a reasonable person might conclude they could have passed away." Searchable more than a dozen ways, from "Died on This Date" to "People Alive over 85," the site takes a frank approach to the problems of accuracy and lists the last update for each record. For instance, we learn that, as of August 29, 2002, Jack Palance was still with us, although Josh Ryan Evans (the tiny actor who played Timmy on the soap *Passions*), was not (his death on August 5 being updated on August 10).

Find a Grave. [http://www.findagrave.com/].

Once we've ascertained someone is no longer with us, we may wish to find out where he or she is buried, either to pay our respects or just to sate our curiosity. This site has grown in recent years from one man's quirky vision into a massive database, with most of the records and corrections contributed by users. Divided into "Famous Graves" and just "Graves" (i.e., people like you and me), Find a Grave offers a number of different searches, although the more information the user has, the better (accuracy is also key: architect Ludwig Mies van der Rohe, buried in Chicago's Graceland Cemetery, won't come up if you try *van der Rohe* for the last name). Searching by location of the grave also offers interesting browsing. Records often contain plot location, photos (of the deceased and/or his or her tombstone), bios, and tributes from fans. Hyperlinks and different categories allow you to sift information in a surprising number of ways (want to find out how many celebrities have had their ashes scattered at sea?). Some bios of famous people are terse (*Capone, Al:* "Gangster"), while those of near unknowns are comprehensive (see that of mystery writer *Keeler, Harry Stephen*), so it is a somewhat unpredictable resource. But, that's life—and death.

—*Keir Graff*

Scouting for SF

Speculative fiction has presented us with many fantastic scenarios, from sentient microorganisms to technologically advanced civilizations that died out before our own solar system cooled. In recent years, the line between fact and fiction seems to be drawn more finely:

a 1950s sf novel depicting a global computer system that allowed people in Minnesota to instantly blip messages to Micronesia would clearly have been a flight of fancy; living in a world where the Internet exists, we quibble with authors who simply overestimate its power (too often, the Internet seems an electronic catchall that allows anyone with a dial-up account to locate any document ever created anywhere).

For our Spotlight on SF/Fantasy, it seemed appropriate to see whether sf authors and publishers are embracing some of our most advanced technology to showcase their work. After all, you'd think the people who dream of electric sheep would be among the first to make their work part of the electronic nerve system that's rapidly connecting everyone in the world. Turns out, that's not quite the case . . . yet. (All sites last visited March 3, 2003.)

Baen Free Library. [http://www.baen.com/library/].

There are a lot of sites for fan fiction and amateur authors, a few that anthologize previously published SF short stories from established writers, and several places where longer, public-domain works are available. Many publishers offer sample chapters or excerpts from the books they sell. The Web site of Baen Books, however, is one of the only places where writers who also get paid for their work willingly post book-length works for free. Eric Flint, "First Librarian," makes a great case for this approach in his essay "Introducing the Baen Free Library"; he also puts his money where his mouth is by posting six of his own books. Most titles are available as HTML zip files; MS Reader, Palm, or Rocket zips; or RTF zips.

It's interesting to examine this brave new experiment in context with recent shifts in the music industry; because file sharing seems unstoppable, more and more artists are offering their songs for free, hoping to find fans who will support them through ticket sales, merchandise, and, yes, buying CDs. Publishing seems less at risk from file sharing, because there's a lot more aesthetic difference between a paperback and a computer file than there is between a CD track and an MP3. Nonetheless, Baen's approach is similar, as it hopes its Web experiment will amount to a global version of lending a recommended book to a friend. Word of mouth, as Flint points out, is the best way to build a writer's audience.

Free Speculative Fiction Online. [http://www.freesfonline.de/].

This portal, recently updated by creator Richard Cissee, links to novellas, novelettes, and short stories that have been published elsewhere online, primarily on the Web versions of *Asimov's*, *Analog*, and *F & SF*. These are mostly recent stories, but Cissee notes that he refuses to link to pirated SF. Hugo and Nebula Award–winning and –nominated stories are indicated. The splash page lists more recent additions; browse by author and many more stories are accessible, including those by well-known authors such as Brian Aldiss, J. G. Ballard, Philip Jose-Farmer, Larry Niven, and Roger Zelazny.

Project Gutenberg: Fine Literature Digitally Re-Published. [http://www.gutenberg.net/].

Because most free Web publishing relies on finding works that are in the public domain (generally speaking, printed before 1923), most SF works are naturally ruled out. However, a simple search for *science fiction* returns 35 seminal works by authors such as Edgar Rice Burroughs, Jules Verne, and H. G. Wells. I was delighted to find *A Journey in Other Worlds: A Romance of the Future* (1894), by fur-trading heir and hotelier John Jacob Astor, which gets off to a great start: three adventurers—Dr. Cortlandt, President Bearwarden, and Ayrault—manipulating "silk-covered glass handles" as they steer their craft *Callisto* through the clouds of Jupiter. One of Astor's own voyages didn't go nearly as well—he went down with the *Titanic*!

SciFi.com: Sci Fiction. [http://www.scifi.com/scifiction/].

One of the only sites to sport a really futuristic look, the Web site of the SciFi channel posts new stories every week or two, both original and classic. The archive is not searchable, but scrolling reveals well over 100 stories between the two categories.

Clearly, free SF publishing online remains in its infancy. Many readers, however, may be like me and simply prefer to read their tales of intergalactic adventure the old-fashioned way—in a yellowing paperback.

—*Keir Graff*

Wikepedia

Wikipedia. [http://www.wikipedia.com]. (Last accessed August 1, 2002)

In last year's Encyclopedia Update we checked on the progress of N*upedia* [http://www.nupedia.com], the "open content" Web-based encyclopedia. This time around we look at *Wikipedia*, a "complementary encyclopedia project" that we found as a link from the N*upedia* home page. N*upedia* editor-in-chief Larry Sanger is one of *Wikipedia*'s founders.

What is *Wikipedia*? For starters it's an online encyclopedia, something like N*upedia*, but different, in that you, or anyone else, can not only contribute an article but can make changes to anyone else's article. A *Wiki*, it seems, is—well, we're still not sure, but it's just one of many new-to-us terms we encountered on the site, along with *flame-wars*, *slash-dotted*, and more. The approach is the opposite of N*upedia*'s, which has good content but gets bogged down in its peer review process. At *Wikipedia* anything gets posted, good or bad, and then, the theory goes, is corrected, expanded, refined, and fashioned into a real encyclopedia article as more people interact with it.

Wikipedia started in January 2001 and already has more than 35,000 articles. Searching is rudimentary, and quality varies tremendously. There are long, detailed articles on game theory and Alexander the Great along with entries for every character on *The Simpsons*. Information on Afghanistan ranges from a lengthy survey of the nation's history, with a fairly extensive list of references, to an entry on the military that merely lists a few statistics and cites no sources. New pages added on August 1 include the brief but adequate *Broccoli*, *Prairie*, and *Social realism* and the incomprehensible ("KM [short for *Katten Mickelin*] is a deity within Kmism"). There are policies about using copyrighted material and maintaining a neutral point of view, but there is no overall editorial plan. At this early stage, *Wikipedia* is more about the process than about someone looking for an article on space exploration or the Civil War.

What about authority and reliability and all the other things we've been taught to look for in an encyclopedia? We were prepared to hate *Wikipedia*, but were disarmed when we got to the section "Wikipedia: Our Replies to Our Critics," which answered all these questions and more. The Wikipedians admit that coverage is limited and unbalanced, that a lot of the articles are mediocre, that content is vulnerable to partisans and cranks. But though they do plan to institute a review process whereby some articles will be frozen as the "approved" versions (even as the revision process continues), they believe that their process of continuous editing means that articles can only improve. Bad content will be edited out, and good content will rise to the top, like cream: "As further edits accumulate, the quality of the article moves asymptotically towards perfection, and likewise the quality of the encyclopedia as a whole." Maybe. We'll keep an open mind.

—*Mary Ellen Quinn*

Women in Sports

This year marks the thirtieth anniversary of Title IX of the Educational Amendments of 1972, which mandates equal opportunity for women in federally funded education, including athletic programs. In honor of this landmark legislation, we went online to scout for some sites related to women in sports. Like so much else on the Web, coverage of women in sports is a hit-or-miss affair, with many links of limited value and many others moribund or sadly out-of-date. But we did find a handful of sites that have useful reference content and can supplement the several good print titles on the topic, including Encyclopedia of Women and Sports (ABC-CLIO, 1996) and International Encyclopedia of Women in Sports (Macmillan, 2001).

All-American Girls' Professional Baseball League. 1999. [http://www.aagpbl.org].

There is a lot of information here about the All-American Girls' Professional Baseball League, which was formed in 1943 and folded in 1954. Pages include a league history, complete team rosters, photographs, articles (some written especially for the site by a professor of history), a chronological listing of all the teams, and a smattering of player biographies.

History of Women in Sports Timeline. [http://www.northnet.org/stlawrenceaauw/timeline.htm].

The St. Lawrence County Branch of the American Association of University Women has compiled this extensive chronology, which is arranged in parts, from "to 1899" to 2002. The earliest recorded event occurs in 776 B.C.E., when the first Olympics were held in Greece. Women were excluded, so they organized their own Games of Hera. Among the 2002 events that are listed are several milestones—boxing promoter Aileen Eaton's induction into the International Boxing Hall of Fame (the first woman to be so honored) and Caroline Hamilton's and Ann Daniels' trek to the North Pole, which made them the first all-female team to journey to both the North and South Poles. Detracting somewhat from the site are the facts that no sources are provided and no dates are given other than the years for the achievements that are chronicled.

Women and Girls in Sports. [http://www.feminist.org/sports/sports.asp].

This page of the Feminist Majority Foundation Web site provides news on the latest challenges to Title IX. It also links to various features, including "Empowering Women in Sports," a very detailed report on Title IX's first two decades. Another thorough examination of Title IX can be found at *Gender Equity in Sports* [http://bailiwick.lib.uiowa.edu/ge/], although this project of the University of Iowa's Women's Athletics Department does not appear to have been updated since May 2000.

—Mary Ellen Quinn

Reviews

Generalities

Mysterious Creatures: A Guide to Cryptozoology. 2v. By George M. Eberhart. 2002. 722p. bibliogs. illus. indexes. ABC-CLIO, $185 (1-57607-283-5). 001.944.

Big Foot, mermaids, and the Loch Ness Monster are familiar to most readers, but hundreds of other equally strange creatures have been logged in this work for the high-school level and up. Some of these creatures, or cryptids, are real, some extinct, some legendary, some hallucinatory.

The purpose of the work is to seriously study cryptids as distribution anomalies, unknown variations of known species, survivors thought to be extinct, mythical animals, paranormal creatures with animal-like characteristics, and hoaxes. More than 1,085 unknown animals are covered in field-guide format, some with pictures or drawings. Most articles include an etymology of the name, scientific name if available, variant names, physical description, behavior, habitat, significant sightings, present status, and possible explanations, such as misidentification of a known species or survival of an extinct species. The articles end with lists of chronologically arranged sources, many of them primary materials, and include both print and Internet resources. There are also entries for 40 major cryptid categories such as birds and sea monsters; these entries have useful cross-references to entries on specific creatures. Following the A–Z entries are lists of 431 species discovered or rediscovered since 1900 (such as the thylacine, a canid marsupial of Australia believed to be extinct since 1936 but seen by reliable witnesses up to the present time) and freshwater bodies in which unknown animals have been reported. A geographical index and a "Cryptid Index" close the set.

This reference work is more scientific and comprehensive than *Cryptozoology A* (Fireside, 1999) and will be an asset to public, school, and academic libraries where patrons are interested in cryptozoology. It is useful as a biological guide, a folklore reference, and a study of paranormal creatures.

Computer Sciences. 4v. Ed. by Roger R. Flynn. 2002. 1,196p. glossary. illus. index. Macmillan, $325 (0-02-865566-4). 004.

Here is an attractive, readable set designed to present the history of computers and reflect on their purpose, use, and impact today. Nearly 300 entries are organized into four volumes, usually with black-and-white illustrations, photos, or charts. Signed entries are two to four pages long and often include sidebars, definitions for terms or concepts, *see also* references, and bibliographies with a handful of current sources, many of them online. University professors are among the contributors. Repeated at the beginning of each volume are the preface, tables of measurements, time lines, and table of contents. Each volume concludes with the same glossary and topic outline and a volume index, with a cumulative index at the end of volume 4.

Volume 1 (*Foundations: Ideas and People*) covers history; volume 2 (*Software and Hardware*), the nuts and bolts of the technology; volume 3 (*Social Applications*), how computers affect our everyday lives; and volume 4 (*Electronic Universe*), the networked society. Organization within each volume is alphabetical. Some representative subjects covered in volume 1 include *Babbage, Charles*; IBM *Corporation*; and *Transistors*. In volume 2 we learn about *Client/server technology*, *Game controllers*, and *Touch screens*; in volume 3, about *Airline reservations*, *Educational software*, and *Spreadsheets*; and in volume 4, *Cookies*, *Global positioning systems*, and *Political applications*. Several articles are current enough to include the 9/11 attacks and October 2001 anthrax letters.

There are so many interrelated topics that dividing them by volume is confusing to a user. *Chemistry* and *Electronic campus* are in volume 4, but *Distance learning* and *Physics* are in volume 3. *Assistive computer technology for persons with disabilities* is in volume 4, although it could be considered a social application. *Art* and *Music composition* are placed in different volumes. The topic outline lists entry headings under broad topics and might be helpful in providing an overview, but it gives no indication of the volumes in which the entries can be found.

For academic libraries, the standard *Encyclopedia of Computer Science* (4th ed., Grove, 2000) will probably be adequate, even though this field changes so rapidly. High-school and public libraries where there is emphasis on technology may want to add this set for its detailed coverage of people, concepts, and applications.

Encyclopedia of Computer Science and Technology. By Harry Henderson. 2003. 450p. appendixes. bibliogs. illus. index. Facts On File, $82.50 (0-8160-4373-6). 004.

This encyclopedia focuses on computers and issues related to computers. More than 400 entries, arranged alphabetically, provide information on hardware, software, computer languages, operating systems, applications, the Internet, key individuals, and social issues such as the digital divide. With a limited number of entries, topic selection appears based on popularity. For example, Microsoft Windows gets a three-page main entry, while the Macintosh operating system is only mentioned within articles related to Macintosh (e.g., *Jobs, Steven Paul*).

Articles average about a page in length. The longest, *History of computing*, stretches to just over four pages. All articles have a list of further readings, usually two to eight items, often including Web sites. Citations for books and articles are current, with several from 2002.

Articles on various computer languages might be too technical for the novice computer user. For example, the article on C++ provides sample code. On the other hand, articles on hardware seem tailored for the beginner. *Mouse* traces the development of the mouse, includes a diagram of a mechanical mouse, and has statements such as "Activating a button is called *clicking*." As a result, both beginners and more experienced computer users should find this resource helpful.

The 167 black-and-white illustrations include charts, drawings, flowcharts, photographs, and screen shots. Four appendixes include a list of bibliographic guides (both print and Web based) to the computer field, a chronology of computing, important awards, and computer-related organizations. The encyclopedia also offers a listing of entries by general category in the front and a keyword index in the back.

The strength of this resource is its currency. It makes a nice supplement to older works such as the *Encyclopedia of Computers and Computer History* (Fitzroy Dearborn, 2001), the *Encyclopedia of Computer Science* (4th ed., Grove's Dictionaries, 2000), and the *World of Computer Science* (Gale, 2002). Recommended for high-school, public, and academic libraries.

ARBAonline. [Internet database]. 2002. Libraries Unlimited, pricing from $150 [http://www.ARBAonline.com]. (Last accessed Dec. 2, 2002).

American Reference Books Annual (ARBA) has been in print since 1970. There is now an online version covering the years 1997–2002. The obvious advantage of ARBA *Online* is currency. The ARBA annual volumes usually appear in April or May with reviews of sources published in the previous year. ARBA *Online* presently contains more than 10,000 reviews with 1,700 to 1,800 being added each year, or 150 to 200 reviews added each month. ARBA is attempting to provide more reviews of Web sites and databases. The publishers plan that in time the database will be as comprehensive for Web sites as for print resources. To accomplish this, a call for additional reviewers is prominently displayed on the Web site.

The interface for the database offers basic and advance search options to search by keyword, title (not author), subject, and publisher. For the basic search, the exact words or phrase and all or any of the words are also options. This may give surprising results. For example, a search for *Britannica Concise Encyclopedia* with the parameters of exact phrase and all words results in no exact match but more than 1,200 titles that contain at least one of the search words. Searches by subject are difficult if the exact ARBA heading is unknown. To find reviews of world atlases, the heading "Geography and Travel Guides-Geography-General Works-

Atlases-International" is required. A title search is a more efficient way to find the correct subject heading.

The format of the online reviews is similar to the print volumes except the ISBN and the price appear at the end of the review, not in the citation. They are ranked by relevancy, but there is no description of the basis for relevancy. Citations may be sorted by author, publisher, year, title, or subject. Reviewers continue to be credited at the end of the review and may be searched by keyword, exact phrase, and all words, but there is no comprehensive list of reviewers, which print volumes include.

As with any reference source produced both in print and online, there still are advantages to the print source. The useful table of contents, with topics subdivided and even sub-subdivided, is not replicated online. Since the price of ARBA Online begins at $150 with no limit on simultaneous users and the most recent print volume (2002) is $120, the online version may be the logical choice for many libraries.

The Europe of 1500–1815 on Film and Television: A Worldwide Filmography of Over 2550 Works, 1895 through 2000. By Michael Klossner. 2002. 512p. bibliog. indexes. McFarland, $85 (0-7864-1223-2). 016.79143.

This specialized filmography encompasses a variety of formats, including but not limited to shorts, animation, television series, silent films, miniseries, epics, and war films. According to the author (a librarian and film reviewer), the volume complements such works as Gary A. Smith's *Epic Films: Casts, Credits, and Commentary on Over 250 Historical Spectacle Movies* (McFarland, 1991), which covers films on the ancient world, and Kevin J. Harty's *The Reel Middle Ages: American, Western and Eastern European, Middle Eastern, and Asian films about Medieval Europe* (McFarland, 1999). The coverage here begins in 1500, the cutoff date for Harty's book. Most of the films were produced in Europe or the U.S.

Each entry (arranged in alphabetical order) contains the title, alternate title, date, length, director, whether the film is black and white or color, cast (in order of appearance, with character name), nationality, producer and production company, literary source, cinematographer, score composer, a brief synopsis or description with critical commentary (20 words to several paragraphs), and one other filmographic source. Works based on Shakespeare's plays are omitted; however, productions based on his life are included. Opera and ballet films are omitted, but musical comedies and operettas are included. Fairy tales are not included, but several films based on folklore are listed. The bibliography includes titles to assist readers in "finding information on other historical films and TV and to demonstrate that scholarly and fan interest in historical films is increasing." Name and subject indexes complete the volume.

The Europe of 1500–1815 on Film and Television is recommended for large public libraries and academic libraries that support a film studies curriculum.

The Oryx Holocaust Sourcebook. By William R. Fernekes. 2002. 397p. appendix. indexes. Greenwood, $55.95 (1-57356-295-5). 016.94053.

This book brings together hundreds of resources in the burgeoning area of Holocaust material, saving the researcher much time and effort scouring bibliographies and Web sites. Seventeen chapters cover, among other items, general reference works, narrative histories, fiction, books for children and young adults, periodicals, Internet resources, sound recordings, and information on organizations, museums, and memorials. The focus is on Holocaust-related materials in English published since 1990 and currently available.

Each chapter includes a general overview of the materials, followed by annotated citations. Many of these annotations are quite extensive, noting organization of the material and describing the editorial importance of the work. The annotations, which are especially full for the text material, make this sourcebook far more valuable than a general bibliography. Another strength of the book is the multidimensional nature of the sources noted. One can find annotations on materials that are not often reviewed, including photographic archives and art of the Holocaust, which will be helpful to teachers and others putting together curriculum to reach a wide variety of students. There are three indexes, listing authors and performers, titles, and subjects. The subject index could use more detail; as it is, it limits one's ability to pull together works on the same subject covered in different media.

The Holocaust is part of the curriculum in primary and secondary schools, and there has also been a strong interest in Holocaust studies at the college level. *The Oryx Holocaust Sourcebook* is unique in its focus and coverage and should find a strong audience with teachers and researchers.

Outsider, Self Taught, and Folk Art Annotated Bibliography: Publications and Films of the 20th Century. By Betty-Carol Sellen with Cynthia J. Johanson. 2002. 348p. index. McFarland, $49.95 (0-7864-1056-6). 016.7450973.

This bibliography complements Sellen and Johanson's earlier publication, *Self Taught, Outsider, and Folk Art: A Guide to American Artists, Locations, and Resources* (Rev. ed., McFarland, 2000). While the earlier book includes a listing of galleries and other venues, organizations, educational opportunities, and biographies of artists, this bibliography contains annotated entries for books and exhibition catalogs, periodical and newspaper articles, and films and video.

A description on the back of the book (but not included in the introduction and therefore lost if the book is bound) states that "outsider art (self-taught art, folk art) is made up of paintings, drawings, sculptures, assemblages, and idiosyncratic gardens and other outdoor constructions created by people who have had little or no formal training in art and who produce (or at least began by producing) art without regard to mainstream recognition or the marketplace." The fact that the outsider artists are not usually self-promoting makes information about them particularly difficult to find and often of regional or local interest.

The bibliography of more than 3,600 items from the twentieth century (through 1999) and predominately about art and artists in the U.S., is divided into four parts according to publication type ("Books and Exhibition Catalogs," "Periodical Articles," "Newspaper Articles," and "Films and Videos"). Each section includes an introduction characterizing the material in that medium and explaining criteria for inclusion and procedures for listing material. All books and exhibition catalogs were either in print or available in the Library of Congress, the National Museum of American Art, or the Museum of American Folk Art. Most articles are from periodicals "that specialize in folk, self-taught, and outsider art" and were identified using art and periodical indexes and, especially, recommendations from collectors, gallery staff, and other experts. Newspapers are from collectors' and galleries' clipping files and print and electronic bibliographies. The authors note that film and videos are especially difficult to identify, verify, and locate and include annotations from other sources if they could not view them personally.

Entries provide standard bibliographic components, and each is annotated. Sellen and Johanson intend their annotations to be "descriptive rather than evaluative," but they are also pithy, straightforward, and a delight to read. An index leads readers to entries for individual artists and some subjects.

Outsider, Self Taught, and Folk Art Annotated Bibliography is highly recommended for academic, art, and museum libraries. There is no other bibliography as comprehensive or up-to-date. Libraries that do not also own Sellen and Johanson's *Self Taught, Outsider, and Folk Art: A Guide to American Artists, Locations, and Resources* should consider purchasing both books because they complement each another.

Reference Guide to Science Fiction, Fantasy and Horror. 2d ed. By Michael Burgess and Lisa R. Bartle. 2002. 605p. indexes. Libraries Unlimited, $75 (1-56308-548-8). 016.8093.

Designed to "provide the librarian, researcher, and fan with a path through the labyrinthine maze of amateur and professional reference materials in the related fields of science fiction, fantasy, and horror," this volume updates one published in 1992. The book is divided into 32 sections (up from 29 in the first edition), including "Encyclopedias and Dictionaries," "Magazine and Anthology Indexes," "Subject Bibliographies," "Character Dictionaries and Author Cyclopedias," and "Film and Television Catalogs." Each section begins with a scope note explaining what is included and why. Complete bibliographic citations are followed by literate and readable annotations that vary from a brief note to three or four lengthy paragraphs. The annotations consist of description and succinct analysis of the strengths and weaknesses of each item. As the authors point out in their introduction, 150 of the 705 entries are new to this edition, and many more have been revised.

One of the new sections, "Major On-Line Resources," is a particularly valuable examination of 20 Web sites, ranging from *Science Fiction and Fantasy Research Database* ("Five stars for this extraordinarily useful site") to the Ultimate Science Fiction Web Site ("This hodge-podge site has clearly grown way beyond the control of its manager"). The final section, "Core Collections," lists titles that would be appropriate for the reference collections of academic, public, and personal libraries. The ambitious institutional collections are subdivided by size and type of library—for example, there are different lists for large city systems, medium-sized county and city libraries, and small public and county libraries (which would work for high-school libraries, too). Separate author, title, and subject indexes complete the work.

RBB called the first edition of *Reference Guide to Science Fiction, Fantasy and Horror* "one of the best and most complete works to be published on the three popular genres of science fiction, fantasy, and horror," and this is no less true of the second. Because the three genres that are covered have only increased in popularity, most public and academic libraries will want this title on their shelves. Libraries that bought the first edition will certainly want to update.

The Social Sciences: A Cross-Disciplinary Guide to Selected Sources. 3d ed. Ed. by Nancy L. Herron. 2002. 494p. bibliogs. indexes. Libraries Unlimited, $75 (1-56308-985-8); paper, $60 (1-56308-882-7). 016.3.

This is a collection of bibliographic essays written or updated by 12 subject specialist librarians, all but two of whom are at Penn State University. After an opening chapter for general social science sources, each chapter treats one of the traditional social science disciplines: political science, economics, business, history, law, anthropology, sociology, education, psychology, geography, and communication. The subtitle, *A Cross-Disciplinary Guide to Selected Sources*, implies special attention to newer cross-or interdisciplinary fields, such as women's studies, gender studies, and queer (or lesbian-gay) studies, but these areas are completely ignored—they don't even make the subject index. Areas studies, by now well-established cross-disciplinary social science areas, do receive limited attention (six pages, according to the subject index).

Each chapter opens with an essay about the nature of the discipline and its information sources. The various sections devoted to types of sources begin with brief overviews. Unfortunately, source citations do not include an indication of extent (pagination or number of volumes), but they are followed by descriptive annotations and means of electronic access if that is available. The volume concludes with indexes for authors (both personal and corporate), titles, and subjects. The subject index is largely a rearrangement of the table of contents.

Any reference guide reaching its third edition is well on its way to becoming an established tool for librarians, scholars, and students. This useful tool is recommended for academic and large public libraries.

Thematic Guide to American Poetry. By Allan Burns. 2002. 309p. bibliogs. indexes. Greenwood, $54.95 (0-313-31462-4). 016.811009.

The latest addition to the Greenwood series of thematic guides to literature for students features 21 narrative essays on such broad themes in American poetry as "Art and Beauty," "Family Relations," "Loss," and "War." The essays are arranged alphabetically, and each begins with a theme-related quotation followed by a chronologically arranged discussion of how the theme is treated differently across individual poems. On average, chapters are 12 pages long and discuss 12 individual poems. Each chapter concludes with a list of anthologies in which each poem appears (abbreviations correspond closely with *Columbia Granger's Index to Poetry in Anthologies*). Brief biographical sketches of all the poets covered appear in the back of the volume along with a further reading list and an index.

The aim of the guide is to "help students better understand what poems are saying, specifically against the wider backdrop of American poetic traditions." The narratives for each poem are pithy and clear, discussing only generally how the poem portrays the theme under discussion. Although author Burns, an English professor, tends to favor some of the same poets (250 poems are represented, but only 86 poets), the only criteria for inclusion is high-quality poetry of the U.S. that is readily available in standard anthologies. The limited space in a single volume necessarily requires somewhat arbitrary exclusiveness, but the poems that are chosen are well explicated. In essays that allude to poems discussed in other chapters, a referential note is made.

Currently, although plenty of explication is available for individual landmark poems, guides that discuss American poems through broad-based thematic essays are scarce. Indexes like *Columbia Granger's* only have very literal subject indexing and cannot be solely relied upon.

Thematic Guide to American Poetry provides a valuable outlet for students or teachers looking for poems on a given theme and is recommended for high-school, academic, and public libraries.

The Horn Book Guide Online. [Online database]. 2002. Greenwood, $150–$300 [http://www.hornbookguide.com/]. (Last accessed September 13, 2002).

The Horn Book Guide, a semiannual compilation of children's literature reviews from the publisher of the highly regarded bimonthly *Horn Book Magazine*, is now available as a subscription database containing more than 40,000 reviews from 1989 to 2001. *The Horn Book Guide* evaluates new fiction and nonfiction for readers from preschool to young adult. Books are rated from one (outstanding) to six (unacceptable), and single-paragraph annotations are specific in their praise and criticism of elements such as plot, dialogue, theme, illustration, characters, and accuracy. The database adds the advantage of various search options and the ability to instantly retrieve reviews and to create lists of materials for the library or classroom. It is updated twice a year, following the publication of the print issue.

The database may be searched by keyword (which searches for terms in the title, review, and subject fields), author or other contributor, title, series, publisher, rating, and grade level. Advanced Search adds options such as subject, genre (for entries published after 1997), year the review was published, and ISBN. Several kinds of browse searches are available: Recent Reviews, Authors A–Z, Illustrators A–Z, Subjects A–Z, and Newbery Winners. Under Recent Reviews, fiction titles from the latest issue of *The Horn Book Guide* are arranged by age group, and nonfiction is sorted by general Dewey decimal system categories. The Subject list is quite detailed; *Animals—Piranhas*; *Jelly beans*; *Journalists—Women*; *Ride, Sally*; *Walt Disney Company*; and *Weather–Clouds* are just a few examples of the headings that are used. Newbery award winners are displayed in reverse chronological order. Searches bring up full records (author, title, pagination, publisher, date, ISBN, genre, grade level, rating, review, and subjects) instead of lists of results. Authors' names are hyperlinked to entries for other books by the same author. An icon indicates books that have a one or two rating. Titles or full records can be saved to a list for printing.

Combining desirable content with flexible searching, *The Horn Book Guide Online* will prove very valuable in school and public libraries for curriculum use and readers' advisory as well as collection development. Academic libraries supporting teacher education programs should also consider it.

Strictly Science Fiction: A Guide to Reading Interests. By Diana Tixier Herald and Bonnie Kunzel. 2002. 297p. bibliogs. indexes. Libraries Unlimited, $55 (1-56308-893-2). 028.

A new entry in the Genreflecting Advisory Series, *Strictly Science Fiction* deals with a genre about which many librarians feel insecure. Beginning with Mary Wollstonecraft Shelley's *Frankenstein*, the authors describe more than 900 titles that are "currently in print or likely to be in library collections." Herald and Kunzel believe that science fiction cannot be divided into neat subgenres, so they take a "dominant features" approach. Titles are grouped into chapters that represent not only subgenres ("Action Adventure") but also themes ("Us and Them"), formats ("Short Stories"), and readership ("The Golden Age of Science Fiction Is—Twelve"). Extensive cross-referencing helps in cases where a book is covered in more than one chapter.

Most title entries are annotated, although the only bibliographic data that is supplied is author, title, and date. Icons identify award winners, classics, books that have film versions, and selections that can be recommended to young adults. The final chapter, "Resources for Librarians and Readers," is a detailed survey of journals, Web sites, reference sources, and more. An appendix lists award winners and "bests." The volume concludes with an author/title index, a subject index, and a character index.

Like other volumes in the extremely useful series, this title will not only serve as a readers' advisory and collection development tool but will also educate librarians. Recommended for public and high-school libraries.

The Essential Desk Reference. 2002. 815p. index. Oxford, $30 (0-19-512873-7). 031.02.

Filled with factoids covering every conceivable subject area, *The Essential Desk Reference* combines the attributes of an almanac, directory, specialized dictionary, encyclopedia, and more. A table of contents facilitates browsing; the book is separated into the broad categories of "World," "United States," "The Sciences," "Arts and Leisure," "Prizes and Awards," and "Work and Home." An alphabetical index allows a user to conduct more precise searches.

The scope of the content in this single volume is overwhelming. Within the "World" category one can locate lists of the world's largest islands, highest mountains, and longest rivers. There are chronologies of dynasties and monarchies; overviews of 172 nations' geography, people, governments, and economy; a good deal of data on the United Nations; and several pages of information regarding religion (who knew that grocers had a patron saint?). The book dedicates a fairly substantial section to the U.S., and it is here that one can locate lists of lobbyist groups, presidential election results from 1789 to 2000, the texts of the Declaration of Independence and the Constitution, brief descriptions of landmark Supreme Court cases, and more. The "Arts and Leisure" category takes up about a quarter of the book and provides the user with unending trivia in the form of lists: major authors, artists, orchestras, musicians, ballets, actors, and museums, among others. "Work and Home" includes helpful tips on personal finance and home safety, lists of area and international dialing codes, postal rates, measurement and temperature conversions, and English-language usage and style. There is even a page on Morse code, closely followed by the Braille alphabet!

The sources used to compile the various lists and tables are provided. If the information used was taken from a Web site, the page's address is given. It is important to note that much of the data can be gleaned from other print and Internet sources and that other one-volume compendia are available—notably the *New York Public Library Desk Reference* (3d ed., Macmillan, 1998) and the *Cambridge Factfinder* (4th ed., Cambridge, 2000), not to mention the perennial favorite, *World Almanac and Book of Facts*. *The Essential Desk Reference* is appropriately priced and is recommended for libraries that need another current, one-stop resource.

Britannica Online School Edition. 2002. [Online database]. Britannica, $545 [http://eb.com]. (Last accessed September 6, 2002).

Britannica Online School Edition provides articles and resources geared toward K–12 settings. Specifically, Britannica has gathered the following sources: *Encyclopaedia Britannica* (geared to high-schoolers), *Britannica Student Encyclopedia* (geared to middle-schoolers), *Britannica Elementary Encyclopedia*, *Britannica Internet Guide*, and video and media (photos and audio clips). Altogether, these five databases offer 118,000 articles, 22,000 images, and 2,000 video clips. Also available are *Merriam-Webster's Dictionary and Thesaurus*.

The splash page offers a keyword search in one or more of the five databases (the Merriam-Webster's components require separate searches), with all five as the default, or an Alphabetical Browse, Timelines, or World Atlas search in a selected encyclopedia. It should be noted that the search engine is somewhat limited; Boolean operators are the only advanced search option. When a keyword search is conducted across more than one encyclopedia, results are organized by resource. A separate list of entries is displayed for each source, and the first sentence or phrase of each entry is included to aid the reader in selecting relevant articles. Articles from "several dozen" magazines are an additional option offered on the results page. The reading level of each source is always clearly noted, but the fact that students have access to content from all of them is an advantage. The *Britannica Student Encyclopedia* article on mathematician John Nash has more detail than the one in *Encyclopaedia Britannica*, but only the *Encyclopaedia Britannica* article includes links to additional content, such as yearbook entries.

In the World Atlas the student can explore a variety of thematic maps, continent by continent. There is also an alphabetical list of countries that links to articles in *Encyclopaedia Britannica* or *Britannica Student Encyclopedia*, depending on which was selected. In Time Lines, short entries are arranged under topics such as "Architecture," "Religion," and "Women." In some cases, these entries are linked to encyclopedia articles.

The sidebar offers access to Video Browse, yearbook articles, and Spotlights, which are special collections of material on such topics as dinosaurs and the Normandy invasion and will be familiar to *Britannica Online* subscribers. There are also "interactive study guides" for students, organized into separate activities for K–5 and 6–12, and resources for teachers to incorporate into the curriculum. We found some cases where users may encounter difficulties, depending on their systems. For example, users working in Netscape might not be able to open Timelines.

With *Britannica Online School Edition*, Britannica offers an ambitious mix of encyclopedia information and value-added services. Much of the same content and many of the same features are available through *Britannica Online*, the major difference being the addition of *Britannica Elementary Encyclopedia* as well as special student and teacher resources. Libraries should take a look at both sites and decide which one best meets their needs.

The Columbia Guide to Digital Publishing. [Online database]. Columbia Univ., pricing from $295 [http://www.digitalpublishingguide.com/]. (Last accessed February 26, 2003).
The Columbia Guide to Digital Publishing. Ed. by William Kasdorf. 2003. 750p. Columbia Univ., $65 (0-213-12498-8); paper, $34.95 (0-213-12499-6).

Edited by William Kasdorf, president of the Society for Scholarly Publishing, this guide—available in both print and electronic formats—bills itself as the only comprehensive reference work on all aspects of digital-era publishing. Its intended audience ranges from those in the publishing industry to printers, agents, rights managers, and librarians. In 15 chapters, each by a different contributor or contributors, the book begins with "Introduction to Publishing in Today's Digital Era" and then looks at markup languages (with emphasis on XML); how to organize, edit, and link content; how to convert and upgrade textual data; composition, design, and accessibility issues; content management; e-books; archiving; digital rights management; and other topics. Contributors include George Alexander, executive editor of *The Seybold Report*; Frederick Bowes III, president of Electronic Publishing Associates; and Heather Malloy, digital archive manager at John Wiley & Sons.

The online version has a clean, simple layout with no fancy graphics to detract from the screen. In keeping with current Web design, it features a horizontal format with tabs across the top of the page, together with a box for entering a term to be searched and a link to an advanced search page. In advanced mode, searches can be limited by content category (such as text or bibliography) and by chapter.

Tabs provide access to Table of Contents, Glossary, Bibliography, Name Index, and General Index. Anyone may access these, but only subscribers may view the actual chapters. The Table of Contents can be viewed in a collapsed or expanded format, much like folders on a hard drive. Chapters may also be expanded for a brief synopsis and view of all the headings and subheading. For subscribers, the headings link directly to the chapter, with the chapter displayed in the right frame and the navigational display in the left. The Glossary may be searched by letter; for example, D includes terms such as DVD, *DocuTech*, and *dial-up*. The Bibliography cites Web sites as well as books and articles, and citations are linked to relevant chapters. The Name Index, unique to the online version, allows searches for proper names ranging from AAP and Adobe to Macromedia and Steve Wozniak. The General Index mirrors the one in the print version. A "My Guide" feature acts as a customizable folder for saving chapters, glossary terms, bibliographic citations, and the like, for a specific search. A subscription is needed to access this feature. In addition to institutional subscriptions, individual subscriptions are available on a daily, monthly, and annual basis ($6.95/$29.95/$99.95, respectively).

The guide provides an excellent technical overview of the constantly evolving world of electronic publishing. Updates and hyperlinks add value to the online version, which is well organized and easy-to-use. Considering the topic, the decision to offer an online version makes sense. However, unless a library has a special interest in the topic of digital publishing, the print version will probably meet most needs.

World Press Encyclopedia: A Survey of Press Systems Worldwide. 2v. Ed. by Amanda C. Quick. 2002. 1,285p. appendixes. bibliogs. illus. index. maps. Gale, $295 (0-7876-5582-1). 070.

Twenty-one years after publication of the first edition, this completely revised work contains articles on the press and media in 232 countries and territories. Arranged alphabetically by country, entries generally cover the history of the Fourth Estate, press laws, economic framework, censorship, attitudes toward foreign media, a chronology of significant recent events, and a bibliography. Several entries are illustrated with black-and-white graphs depicting Internet use, top-circulation newspapers, and the number of personal computers; basic country data are also included. Three appendixes provide comparative statistical rankings (newspaper circulation, television stations, radio sets, etc.); annotated listing of news associations and organizations; and a collection of regional maps. A unified author-subject index provides easy access to the contents of both volumes.

Compiled by 80 contributors, the individual essays vary greatly in quality and length (200–30,000 words). For some smaller and less developed nations, such as Belize and Benin, the essays are quite short. Essays for countries where the press is strictly regulated, such as Cambodia, can also be skimpy. Two additional appendixes would have been helpful: a listing of the Web sites for major newspapers and a general bibliography listing guides, directories, and handbooks to the world press.

World Press Encyclopedia is an excellent reference source providing concise information for material currently dispersed in numerous print and Web sources. Especially valuable is the bibliography at the end of each entry. The Ghana essay, for example, cites a wide variety of sources from American media publications to Ghanaian newspapers. Useful for students, scholars, and those seeking quick information, this unique source is recommended for public and academic libraries.

The Facts On File Dictionary of Proverbs: Meanings and Origins of More Than 1,500 Popular Sayings. By Martin H. Manser. 2002. 440p. bibliog. indexes. Facts On File, $45 (0-8160-4607-7). 082.

This attractive and useful resource book focuses on commonly used expressions in the English language and in English literature. There is no attempt to be culturally inclusive. Each entry is arranged alphabetically on a two-column page. The boldface proverb precedes a concisely written definition and factually documented origin of the saying. *There's no rose without a thorn* typifies the basic structure of each entry: namely, definition, example of use, origins, variant expressions, cross-references, and proverbs with similar or opposite meanings. Each entry varies in length according to available source material and popularity of expression.

The editorial consistency is rare and a credit to the skillful selection and editing techniques of Manser, who also compiled *The Facts On File Dictionary of Foreign Words and Phrases* [RBB Ag 02], among other works. An index of key words and an index of themes complete this valuable addition to the Facts On File Library of Language and Literature, which is recommended for public and academic libraries. Libraries looking for a more comprehensive guide can turn to Wolfgang Mieder's *A Dictionary of American Proverbs* (Oxford, 1991), with approximately 15,000 entries, while those who want representation of other cultures should consider the *Cassell Dictionary of Proverbs* (1998) or *Multicultural Dictionary of Proverbs* (McFarland, 1997).

Exploring Animal Rights and Animal Welfare. 4v. 2002. 512p. bibliogs. glossaries. illus. indexes. Greenwood, $128 (0-313-32245-7). 179.3.

Designed for middle-schoolers, this series examines the ways animals are treated or mistreated by humans in volumes titled *Using Animals for Food*, *Using Animals in Research*, *Using Animals for Entertainment*, and *Using Animals for Clothing*. The volumes use the same arrangement: an introductory chapter in which a general overview or history as well as all sides of the issue are spelled out; 10 chapters discussing all aspects of the topic; and a final chapter presenting all sides of the various arguments related to the topic. A glossary, bibliography, and index provide reference aid. In addition to a handful of books, each volume's bibliography includes Web sites. Some, such as the sites for the ASCPA, the Humane Society of the U.S., and PETA are found in all four volumes. There is no comprehensive index.

The text is easy to read and comprehend and delivers information in an unbiased manner. Boxes appear throughout the books, enhancing the text with additional facts or definitions. Some boxes appear at the end of a section and pose questions for the reader to ponder. There are illustrations of animals in many situations, including experimentation. All of the photographs are black and white. Although colored photos are not essential to the topic, students are more responsive to colorful illustrations. The set would be useful for research papers or as a resource for debate topics and is recommended for school and public libraries.

Consulta. [Online database]. Gale and Oceano Grupo Editorial, pricing from $3,750 [http://trials.galegroup.com/consulta/]. (Last accessed February 24, 2003).

Gale and Oceano Grupo Editorial, a respected Spanish publisher, have collaborated to produce a database similar to Gale's English-language online resource centers. It includes more than 100 Oceano reference titles, over 60 journals, 1,600 primary source documents, 6,200 images, and 10,500 chronology records. Among the materials included are *Medicinas alternativas* (*The Gale Encyclopedia of Alternative Medicine*), *Gran enciclopedia interactiva Oceano* (*Oceano Great Interactive Encyclopedia*), *Manual Merck de informacion medica para el hogar* (*The Merck Home Medical Information Manual*), and *Grandes personajes* (*Great Figures*). Periodicals include the Spanish edition of *Americas*, *Personal Computing* (Mexico), *National Geographic en Espanol*, and *Siempre!* The Web links offered by subject group are reliable sources in both Spanish and English.

The home page (*Inicio*) has a search box (*Buscar*) and a series of icons on the tool bar that link to Help, Web sites, and the library's catalog. Users may enter terms in the box or click on one of the various search options. The options are Busqueda simple (basic search), Busqueda avanzada (advanced search), Biografias (biographies), Galleria (images), Cronologia (chronologies), and Diccionarios (dictionaries). The advanced search employs the Boolean operators *y* (and), *o* (or), and *no* (not). It also allows users to limit by publication date, title words, full-text keywords, and author. The dictionaries provide full Spanish definitions as well as synonyms and antonyms in addition to Spanish/English, Spanish/French, and Spanish/German translations.

Search results organized by type: Referencias (reference sources), Revistas (periodicals), and Fuentes Primarias (primary sources), with tabs that allow the user to move from one type to another.

A series of searches on a variety of topics brought mixed results. To find a biography of Pablo Casals, entering the terms *Casals*, *Pablo* in the biography screen with and without the various qualifiers (nationality, gender, profession, etc.) produced no hits. Users must know his Catalan name, Pau, to find information. A search using *Casals*, *Pablo* in the general search box did produce eight citations. Biographies of people in the news, such as Ariel Sharon, Yasser Arafat, and George W. Bush, are available, but those of cultural significance tend to be Spanish rather than Hispanic or Latin American. Information on HIV/AIDS is available using the terms SIDA or *sindrome de immunodeficiencia adquirida*. There are plenty of references, but the related subject links offered are *erotismo* (which got no results when we clicked on it) and *pornografia*, and, for some reason, a text of Sor Juana de la Cruz appears as a primary source.

Finding overview articles about countries is difficult. Entering country names—*Mexico*, *Estados Unidos* (United States), *Francia* (France)—brings up long lists of entries that are supposedly ranked by relevance, but none are overview articles. Even using the advanced mode, there are no overviews. The Mexico search brought up articles on biodiversity, geography, various historical eras, etc., but no general overview. There are no maps available in the database.

Consulta is an ambitious endeavor that is off to a good start. With a more precise search engine and more material dealing with Latin America, it will be an excellent resource. Libraries serving Spanish speakers will want to consider *Consulta*, but they should also have a general encyclopedia such as Grolier's *Nueva Enciclopedia Cumbre en Linea* for efficient access to country overviews with maps.

The Times Digital Archive. [Internet database]. 2002. Gale, pricing from $5,400 [http://www.gale.com/Times/]. (Last accessed September 13, 2002).

Over the next 18 to 20 months, Gale is posting a dream of a database, the *London Times* from 1785 to 1985. This is the full-text archive, including not only newspaper articles but also advertising and classified ads, editorials, birth and death notices, book reviews, crossword puzzles, letters to the editor, and the Court Page, which details the activities of the royals. The entire *Times* data package, which is currently limited to issues from 1936 to 1949, will gradually increase in size with monthly additions to the archive, which Gale projects will be completed in late 2003.

The Infotrac search engine offers options—Relevance searching, Keyword searching, Browse by Date, and Advanced Search—that suit a variety of research needs. While a Keyword search will look for every mention of a search term, Relevance searching "retrieves records based on the extent to which the search terms are entered." We found it tricky to use without referring to Help. Keyword and Relevance searches can look for terms in the entire article content or be restricted to title, citation, and abstract. Further limits include date, section (Advertising, Business, Editorial and Commentary, Features, News, People, Picture Gallery), and articles with illustrations. In Advanced Search these categories can be refined again. For example, Business can be limited to "Business and Finance," "Shipping News," or "Stock Exchange Tables." For those who want to see an issue of the *Times* for any particular day, selecting Browse by Date brings up a clickable calendar.

Result sets are displayed in the History section at the bottom of the page. Keyword matches are listed chronologically from oldest to newest, while Relevance matches are ranked. The user clicks on a results set to view citations, each of which is accompanied by a thumbnail of the page on which the article appears, showing its position. Additional information includes title and subtitle, date, page and column, issue, and number of words per article. Users can view an image of the clipped article, an image of the page on which the article appears, or a PDF (portable document format) version of the page. A pink box highlights the search term each time it appears in text. Viewers can increase the size of an article to 133, 200, or 400 percent to enhance PDF presentation, which can be murky in its original cramped point size. Telescoping is especially valuable for accessing maps, charts, crossword puzzles, and detailed press photos, which appear to best advantage at 200 percent. There are several options for printing, e-mailing, and otherwise retrieving a document. Links direct the user to additional articles on the same page or in the issue of the paper.

This is a sophisticated database, requiring some patience and skill to use. The finished archive will have enormous potential as a research tool and suit the needs of large public and academic libraries as well as historians, journalists, and educators. The major drawback is slow loading, but this can be forgiven when the user is rewarded by such valuable content.

Philosophy, Psychology, Religion

Magill's Encyclopedia of Social Science: Psychology. 4v. Ed. by Nancy A. Piotrowski. 2003. 1,810p. bibliogs. glossary. illus. index. Salem, $385 (1-58765-130-0). 150.

This update and major revision of the *Survey of Social Science: Psychology Series* (1993) is a change in style as well as name. Not only are there fewer volumes (four rather than six), but the content has been made more accessible to the general reader and high-school or lower-division college student. Instead of standardized style and organization, the new edition varies the presentation as the editor and contributors felt appropriate for the content. There are 177 new entries, and 103 have been revised. The remaining 162 appeared in the original.

Each volume has a complete list of entries, which vary from one to eight pages in length. There is also a categorized list of entries under 66 broader subjects (such as "Emotion," "Psychopathology," "Sleep"). Each entry begins with a statement of the type of psychology and the fields of study into which the information falls. All essays in the 1993 version had standard subheadings, but many of these have been reformatted, with subheadings tailored to fit the topic. There may be a short summary statement and a list of key concepts, as appropriate. Each entry is accompanied by a short annotated bibliography of "Sources for Further Study." These are followed by *see also* recommendations.

Volume 4 includes a lengthy detailed index to the set. It also has a 25-page glossary and an annotated bibliography divided into categories. This is followed by a Web site directory of associations, academic informational sites, mental health and self-help organizations, and other psychologically related sites. Of special interest is the "Mediagraphy" of films and television programs dealing with psychiatric or psychological issues. "Organization and Support Groups" is a directory of North American and international services, associations, foundations, and societies. An 11-page summary of pharmaceuticals used for depression, anxiety, and other disorders includes brief commentary, generic and trade names, dosages, and side effects. One-paragraph biographies of 60 prominent psychologists (some of whom are also the subjects of encyclopedia entries) appear in the "Biographical List of Psychologists." The supplementary information section is topped off by a list of references to notable court cases from 1843 to 2002 involving psychological issues.

Much has happened in the last 10 years, both in psychology and in people's information expectations, making the revision worth considering for libraries catering to an interested lay public, high-school students, and beginning college students. It also appears to be a useful ready-reference tool for librarians.

Psychology. 6v. 2002. bibliog. glossary. illus. index. Grolier, $379 (0-7172-5662-6). 150.

Color photographs and specially commissioned artworks accompany the chapters in this attractive and highly useful reference set that covers the entire spectrum of psychology. Designed primarily for high-school students and young adults, the volumes focus on broad topics such as "History of Psychology," "Developmental Psychology," and "Social Psychology." Each volume has its own contents list at the beginning and a set glossary and index at the back. The "Resources" section, which is repeated in each volume, offers lists of Web sites and related reference works. Additional value is provided by color-coded fact boxes featuring information (important dates, terms, works, people, etc.) related to the subject discussed. Individual chapters are consistently well designed; no detail is too small—notable features include succinct introductions, pull quotes, embedded cross-references, and picture captions.

The chapter on "Physical Therapies" (in volume 6, *Abnormal Psychology*), which examines ways in which the body is treated to relieve symptoms of mental disorders, mirrors others in the set in that it is comprehensive in scope, chock-full of information in a variety of formats (narrative, text boxes, photographs, etc.), highly readable, and a useful jumping-off point for students seeking to acquaint themselves with its subject. Here, readers will find information on anxiolytics, antidepressants, antipsychotic drugs, mood-stabilizing drugs, physical interventions, psychosurgery, choosing treatment, and choice of treatment. Here too readers will find an illustration showing how selective neurotransmitter reuptake works; fact boxes on antidepressant side effects, technology and dopamine, licensing drugs, and psychiatry and human rights, among other topics; photographs of, for example, a patient prepared for electroconvulsive therapy, the covers of self-help booklets published by the National Institute of Mental Health, and a pack of 20 mg capsules of Prozac; and examples of psychotic art produced by patients hospitalized for schizophrenia. A "Connections" box at the end of the chapter refers readers to other relevant chapters in the set.

This is the set to which high-school students would turn while attempting to understand psychology, and it is recommended for reference collections in high-school libraries and young adult departments of medium-sized and large public libraries. It may well have use for general audiences; as such it will be welcome in the adult departments of medium-sized and large public libraries with ample collections in psychology. College undergraduates would be better served by *The Gale Encyclopedia of Psychology* (Gale, 1996). High-school and public libraries that already own the Gale work will find that *Psychology* is written for a different audience and that it is a timely addition to their reference collections.

American Religious Leaders. By Timothy L. Hall. 2003. 430p. bibliogs. glossary. illus. index. Facts On File, $65 (0-8160-4534-8). 200.

Part of Facts On File's American Biographies series, *American Religious Leaders* traces the lives of 270 individuals who shaped the spiritual consciousness of our nation. The names selected for this informative work include universally recognized icons like Billy Graham, Abraham Heschel, and Martin Luther King Jr., but infamous characters like Jim Jones and David Koresh are also given a fair and impartial treatment. A balanced choice of subjects representing all major religious groups as well as names emanating from more secular milieus gives a sense of completeness to the volume.

Each entry is carefully written and researched by Hall, professor at the University of Mississippi Law School, who is responsible for another Facts On File title called *Supreme Court Justices: A Biographical Dictionary* (2001). The uniform biographies are about one page in length and arranged alphabetically, giving vital dates and religious affiliation followed by a chronological review of the subject's life and memorable contributions. A bibliography concludes each entry. It should be noted that this biographical series treats both the living and the dead. Some 60 black-and-white photographs and a useful glossary add to the appeal of the work.

Recommended for the general reader seeking biographical information on prominent religious figures.

The Great Popes through History: An Encyclopedia. 2v. Ed. by Frank J. Coppa. 2002. 593p. bibliogs. illus. index. Greenwood, $125 (0-313-29533-6). 282.

The Great Popes through History is a thoroughly researched set providing biographical material on 46 selected popes as well as a substantial bibliography. The entire 2000-year history of the papacy is divided into five eras: early, medieval, Renaissance and Reformation, early modern, and modern. Each historical section is edited by an eminently qualified scholar who introduces his or her period with an overview that addresses the political and religious milieu influencing the papacy in general and the representative popes specifically. The individual entries, about nine per section, are written by an international group of specialists representing various disciplines and institutional affiliations. The sections close with extensive bibliographic notes.

Entries average about eight pages in length, and each includes an illustration and a bibliography. The selection of popes resulted from a rigorous consultation process based on their contributions to church and society. A short list of names includes St. Peter, St. Leo the Great, St. Gregory I, Innocent III, Pius IX, and John Paul II. A chronology of all popes and an index add much to this work.

The Great Popes through History complements Routledge's *The Papacy: An Encyclopedia* (2002), which covers every pope through history as well as various related topics. Libraries supporting a strong interest or aiming for comprehensive coverage will want to add it to their collections. It might also be considered by academic and public libraries that want something on the topic but don't need Routledge's exhaustive treatment. Another choice for smaller collections is *Encyclopedia of the Vatican and Papacy* (Greenwood, 1999), also edited by Coppa.

Pilgrimage: From the Ganges to Graceland: An Encyclopedia. 2v. By Linda Kay Davidson and David M. Gitlitz. 2002. 769p. appendixes. bibliogs. illus. index. maps. ABC-CLIO, $280 (1-57607-004-2). 291.3.

This splendid encyclopedia is a delight to read and pleasing to view. The authors begin with an introduction warranting special note; in less than 10 pages, the reader receives a comprehensive overview of the history, nature, and purpose of the pilgrimage, cutting across cultures and particular faith traditions. Pilgrimage is defined here as "a journey to a special place, in which both the journey and the destination have spiritual significance for the journeyer."

The 600-plus alphabetically arranged encyclopedia is more representative than exhaustive, giving "greatest emphasis to pilgrimage sites with the widest range and inclusiveness and the longest duration." Examples include Gettysburg, Graceland, Lenin's Tomb, Lourdes, Masada, and Mecca. Major religious traditions, among them Buddhism, Eastern Orthodoxy, Hinduism, Jainism, Judaism, Native American religions, Protestantism, and Roman Catholicism, are treated in respect to the role of pilgrimage. There are also entries for people, concepts, and other topics important to pilgrimage; for example, *Apparitions*; *Indulgences*; *Peron, Eva Duarte de*. Ranging in length from a paragraph or two to several pages, entries are generally thorough and uniformly well written, with good documentation (including Web addresses when appropriate). A few maps are added for reader convenience. The text is frequently enlivened with the anecdotal details of actual pilgrim experiences and frequent illustrations which adds a nice balance to the encyclopedia format. See and see also references assist the reader through the variety of subjects. Two helpful sections complete this absorbing work: a listing of pilgrimage sites by country and religion, plus 40 pages of historic and contemporary bibliography. Highly recommended for academic and larger public libraries.

★**Religions of the World:** A Comprehensive Encyclopedia of Beliefs and Practices. 4v. Ed. by J. Gordon Melton and Martin Baumann. 2002. 1,507p. bibliogs. illus. index. maps. ABC-CLIO, $385 (1-57607-223-1). 291.

With religion playing an important role in front-page news, questions about various faiths are common at the reference desk. This new encyclopedia, the work of more than 200 international scholars, will be very helpful because it takes a different approach to the subject. Many traditional encyclopedias of religion focus on a single faith, like Catholicism or Judaism. Others, like Mircea Eliade's *Encyclopedia of Religion* (Macmillan, 1995), take a comparative approach to topics such as myth, sacred texts, rituals, deities, and so on. *Religions of the World* surveys "the present religious situation around the world as the twenty-first century begins." An introductory statistical section offers tables showing the status of religions in the world population as a whole and on each continent.

The encyclopedia's 1,200 alphabetical entries offer three kinds of material. A series of core essays cover 16 religious traditions. These include not only the various Christian, Jewish, Islamic, and Buddhist denominations but also Jainism, Shintoism, Zoroastrianism, Sikhism/SantMat, ethnoreligions (that is, indigenous, traditional religions), New Age religions, and unbelief, which, despite its criticism of religion, often functions like one. These essays discuss the history of each tradition, looking at how and why each developed rather than at doctrines and practices.

In addition to the entries covering the main traditions, there are entries for the 276 recognized nations and territories of the world. These have statistical tables and maps as well as a discussion of the active religions. Approximately 1,000 entries cover the various religious bodies. Many of these, such as *Reconstructionist Judaism* and *Shi'a Islam*, are part of larger religious groups. Others, such as *Falun Gong* and *Al Qaeda*, have political significance. This is the only source that covers the full spectrum of the world's religions, from *Muslim Brotherhood* and *Roman Catholic Church* to *African Apostolic Church of Johane Marange*, *British Israelism*, and *Lao Buddhist Sangha*. It includes *Goddess spirituality*, *UFO religions*, *Vodou*, and small sects, such as *Disciples of Mother Meera*. Each entry discusses the group's origin, history, and organization. There is also information about ecumenical contacts and the present status of the group and a mailing address and Web site. Each entry has a brief bibliography. Indexing is adequate, although we found several errors.

With comprehensive coverage and an innovative approach to the study of religion, *Religions of the World* is an excellent addition to public and academic library reference collections. It supplies the pieces missing from traditional encyclopedias of religion.

★**The New Encyclopedia of Judaism.** Ed. by Geoffrey Wigoder. 2002. 854p. bibliog. glossary. illus. index. New York Univ., $99.95 (0-8147-9388-6). 296.

The New Encyclopedia of Judaism is a revised and expanded second edition of *The Encyclopedia of Judaism* (Macmillan, 1989). Recognizing that Judaism is not just a systematic presentation of beliefs or the codification of abstract theological thought, the volume presents a very intimate portrait of this tradition, including liturgical, ethnic, and secular elements.

Entries are alphabetically arranged and written by scholars, though unsigned. Biographical entries are limited to those who have contributed to the development of Judaism and include biblical figures, philosophers and theologians, and leaders of movements within Judaism. There are good survey articles for *Conservative Judaism*, *Orthodoxy*, and *Reform Judaism*. Other entries cover the books of the Hebrew Bible. Although theological positions on such topics as *Creation*, *Principles of faith*, and *Redemption* are presented, emphasis is placed on ritual aspects of Judaism. In the entry *Sabbath*, the three daily services (i.e., morning, afternoon, and evening), along with special services such as festivals and memorials, are described, with details regarding the differences among Hasidic, Sephardi, and Ashkenazi Jews. The entry for *Responses, liturgical* includes a table of principal responses used in public worship. Other entries describe Judaism's position on social issues such as *Abortion*, *Capital punishment*, *Divorce*, and *Homosexuality*. In addition to black-and-white illustrations, groups of color plates are interspersed throughout the volume, depicting illuminated manuscripts, synagogues, Torah scroll shields, and works of art.

What is new in this revised edition? In addition to some 1,200 revised entries, the treatment of early Jewish literature is enhanced with entries for all the books of the Apocrypha (e.g., *Tobit, Book of*) and some pseudepigraphical works (e.g., I *Enoch*). Greater attention is given to women in Judaism. There is a new entry for *Feminism* to complement the entry for *Women*. The only female biblical judge, *Deborah*, now has her own entry, having been included formerly in the entry for the Book of Judges. The contemporary movement *Zionism* (*Return to Zion* in the first edition) is covered in more depth, with entries for some of its notable exponents (e.g., Golda Meir and David Ben-Gurion). Finally, although entries include no reading lists, this new edition concludes with an annotated bibliography.

Another single-volume reference work for Judaism is *The Oxford Dictionary of the Jewish Religion* (1997), which is more comprehensive in scope and scholarly in nature. But the two really can't be compared. *The New Encyclopedia of Judaism* is intended as as a "resource for both Jewish families and those interested in learning more about the religion." The content, accessible yet authoritative, makes this reference work appropriate for both public and academic library collections.

Sociology, Anthropology, Political Science

Distinguished Native American Spiritual Practitioners. By Troy R. Johnson. 2002. 293p. appendixes. bibliogs. illus. index. Greenwood, $69.95 (1-57356-358-7). 299.

Although there is increased interest in Native American religious practices, there are relatively few new reference books on the topic. Johnson, California State University–Long Beach associate professor of American Indian studies, provides a basic reference tool on the lives of 100 contemporary and historical Native spiritual leaders. Each of the 100 lengthy (1,000 to 2,000 word) entries begins with a "quick summary heading" listing the individual's full name at birth (with variants), birth and death data, education, and leadership title. Entries conclude with a three-to nine-item bibliography for further reading and research. Wherever possible, a Web site and a black-and-white photograph are included.

Subjects include Aiowantha (Hiawatha), Charles Eastman, Quanah Parker, Susan La Flesche Picotte, Pretty-Shield, Kateri Tekakwitha, and White Buffalo Calf Woman. Some were educated as medical practitioners; others were cultural heroes recognized by their nation as prophets or healers. There are two appendixes. One lists "Native American Spiritual Practitioners and Healers by Birth Date" (year), and the second lists them by nation or group. The lengthy bibliography includes three double-columned pages of Web sites.

The introduction does not explain how the main entry names were selected. In some cases, the entry heading reflects the subject's birth name (as in the case of the person commonly known as Hiawatha, whose entry is under *Aiowantha*). In other cases the entry appears under the commonly recognized name (for example, *Sitting Bull*). *See* entries help resolve most difficulties. Other drawbacks include guide words being listed only on odd-numbered pages and no guide to pronunciation.

Even with its minor shortcomings this work is helpful, especially in locating biographical information on healers of the nineteenth and twentieth centuries. There is some overlap with *Encyclopedia of Native American Religions: An Introduction* (rev. ed., Facts On File, 2000), which offers discussions of spiritual traditions as well as biographical information on Christian missionaries like Marcus Whitman. Teamed together these two works will provide good coverage. This moderately priced reference work will be most useful in public and college libraries where there is a local or curricular need for information on Native American religious practices.

Handbook of Egyptian Mythology. By Geraldine Pinch. 2002. 257p. appendix. bibliogs. illus. index. ABC-CLIO, $55 (1-57607-242-8). 299.

Students at the high-school level and above who are doing research on Egyptian mythology will find this volume interesting and helpful. The first chapter discusses the nature of myths and the history of Egypt from the predynastic to the postpharaonic period. The second goes through several myth complexes and cycles and their variations. The third chapter, "Deities, Themes, and Concepts, " is an alphabetical listing of well over 100 topics and is the meat of the book. Articles range in length from a single line to several pages. All have *see also* references, and most cite both secondary and primary sources. Entries are readable and note where particular deities absorbed characteristics of others during historical periods. The inconsistencies of Egyptian mythology are noted, as in the variations of the Osiris stories. The frankly sexual nature of many of Egypt's creation myths is not glossed over, nor are the coupling habits of the gods.

A final chapter is an annotated list of print and nonprint resources on Egyptian myth, some of which may be found in many larger public and academic libraries. A few novels influenced by Egyptian myth are also listed and annotated, including Norman Mailer's *Ancient Evenings* and Elizabeth Peters' *The Snake, the Crocodile, and the Dog*. A few videos are reviewed, and several Web sites and CD-ROMs are listed. Pinch's annotations are clear and informative and not without a certain dry humor.

A very helpful glossary defines Egyptian words and other terms that are commonly used in Egyptology. The appendix listing primary sources would be of most use to college students beginning to study Egyptian mythology or Egyptology. This volume is recommended for medium-sized and large public libraries and academic libraries with lower-division mythology and Egyptology classes. It joins others of the publisher's Handbooks of World Mythology, including *Handbook of Mesoamerican Mythology* (2002) and *Handbook of Norse Mythology* (2001).

Sociology, Anthropology, Political Science

Dictionary of the Social Sciences. Ed. by Craig Calhoun. 2002. 563p. bibliog. Oxford, $75 (0-19-512371-9). 300.

Social science language has become an essential feature of literary studies and the humanities and is increasingly becoming part of the lexicon of the popular media. Today it is difficult to read a newspaper or hear or see the news on the radio or television without encountering terms like *civil society*, *paradigm*, *real income*, or *welfare economics*. Designed for students and nonspecialists, the *Dictionary of the Social Sciences* serves to orient readers to the concepts, theories, methodologies, schools of thought, and individuals that define classic and contemporary scholarship in the social sciences. Offering jargon-free definitions of key terms across a wide spectrum of separate, but interconnected, disciplines, the dictionary features more than 1,500 entries ranging in length from 50 to 500 words and covers the vocabularies of anthropology, cultural studies, economics, human geography, political science, sociology, and numerous other important fields within this arena. A lengthy bibliography concludes the volume. *See* references at the end of the entries provide added value.

Despite its ambitious scope, readers are advised that the social sciences are not covered equally in this volume. A careful reading of the preface sheds light on the guidelines that influenced entry selection. For example, law is not included, and history and psychology are treated more selectively than economics, politics, and sociology. The dictionary succeeds because it is a carefully written and researched work, but some readers will need to supplement their use of it with additional and more specialized dictionaries.

The last decade has seen the publication of several works that provide coverage of the social sciences in a convenient one-volume format. Among these are *The Blackwell Dictionary of Twentieth-Century Social Thought* (Blackwell, 1993); *The Social Science Encyclopedia* (2d ed., Routledge, 1996); and *The Dictionary of Critical Social Sciences* (Westview, 1999). This volume complements these titles and should be a useful addition to academic library collections, particularly those that support programs in the social sciences. Large public libraries will want to take a look to ascertain its potential usefulness in their settings.

Literacy in America: An Encyclopedia of History, Theory, and Practice. 2v. Ed. by Barbara J. Guzzetti. 2002. 779p. bibliogs. illus. index. ABC-CLIO, $185 (1-57607-358-0). 302.2.

Because without widespread, deep literacy there would be neither markets for nor creators of encyclopedias, it is surprising that a comprehensive encyclopedia on literacy and its many dimensions has not appeared earlier.

Written for an audience embracing both students being introduced to theories and terminology of literacy and specialists in the field, the A–Z entries fall into five categories. The first and most numerous covers "definitions, process, influences, issues, types, and theories." The others cover "literacy assessment, literacy instruction, literacy resources and organizations, and literacy professional publications and reports." Throughout, literacy is examined not just as the capability of an individual to read and write but also as a dynamic force in society. Entries such as *Gender and writing*, *Literacy and culture*, Social nature of literacy, and Television and reading demonstrate literacy's inseparability from the society in which it functions. So, too, do articles on forms of expression that express social trends; these include *Comics*, *Graffiti*, and *Instant messaging*. The great majority, however, treat concepts and terms related to the study, acquisition, and teaching of literacy. These include *Ebonics*, *Fluency*, *Reading clinics*, *Spelling*, and *Writing assessment*. Complementary articles treat both sides of controversial issues such as the phonics–whole language debate.

The encyclopedia's substantial articles, each signed by its author, typically run two to three double-columned pages. *See also* references to related topics and short unannotated bibliographies conclude the articles. The citations cumulate in an extensive bibliography at the end of volume two.

An article devoted to *The Literacy Dictionary: The Vocabulary of Reading and Writing* (International Reading Association, 1995) describes the narrower scope and purpose of that earlier work, whose brief definitional entries complement the encyclopedia's longer, more analytical articles.

Both have unquestionable value for library collections and curriculum centers serving teachers in training, practitioners in the field, and researchers.

American Social Leaders and Activists. By Neil A. Hamilton. 2002. 434p. bibliogs. illus. index. Facts On File, $65 (0-8160-4535-6). 303.48.

Written by a history professor at the University of Tennessee, *American Social Leaders and Activists* includes biographies of more than 285 people who have attempted to change the norms of their society. Most of the alphabetical entries are one or two pages in length, with those for well-known individuals ranging four to five pages in length. Fifty-five of the entries include a black-and-white picture, and each entry ends with a three-to five-title "Further Reading" section. In addition to a general index, entries are also indexed by activity and decade of birth.

Social reformers from colonial times to the present from a variety of fields are included. The author has selected well-known and lesser-known individuals from both ends of the spectrum (and places in between). Abbie Hoffman, Elizabeth Cady Stanton, and Gloria Steinem are here, as are Rush Limbaugh, Phyllis Schlafly, and Randall Terry (founder of Operation Rescue). Several Latino and Native American activists are included (two groups that are often overlooked). Individuals whose social reform activities are often overshadowed by other accomplishments are also covered (e.g., Dr. Spock and Joan Baez). Perhaps most interesting is the inclusion of David Duke, supporting the author's desire to include "those people I consider to be the most prominent, most controversial or interesting."

American Social Leaders and Activists is a fine book. When compared to similar sources—*American Social Leaders* (ABC-CLIO, 1993) and *American Reform and Reformers: A Biographical Dictionary* (Greenwood, 1996)—it is superior. *American Social Leaders* does have more entries, but it is nearly 10 years old and does not include as many biographies on those still living. *American Reform and Reformers* has longer entries but only covers about 50 individuals, all of whom are well known. The current title is a recommended purchase for high-school, public, and academic libraries.

East Asia and the United States: An Encyclopedia of Relations since 1784. 2v. Ed. by James I. Matray. 2002. 778p. bibliogs. indexes. maps. Greenwood, $175 (0-313-30557-9). 303.48.

Matray, professor of history at California State–Chico, has put together a list of experts from both sides of the Pacific to write this encyclopedia. China, Japan, Korea, and Vietnam are treated in various entries accessible through the index, rather than in concise overviews, but there are individual entries for almost every other nation in East Asia, including Burma, Cambodia, Indonesia, Laos, Malaysia, Micronesia, the Philippines, Thailand, and Taiwan. Other entries cover people (*Aquino, Corazon*; *MacArthur, Douglas*; *Pol Pot*); events (*Boxer uprising*, *Tokyo war crime trials*, *Pueblo incident*); and a variety of other topics germane to U.S. relations with East Asia (*Boat people*, *Exclusion acts*, *North Korean nuclear controversy*, *Ping-Pong diplomacy*, *Viet Cong*). The text focuses on diplomacy, economics, and politics, although there is also some coverage of military and cultural affairs.

Pinyin spelling of Chinese names and places is used, so familiar names to U.S. readers like Chiang Kai-shek and Sun Yat-sen are rendered in different spellings (Jiang Jieshi and Sun Zhongshan). Cross-references and a useful name index, along with a subject index, make it easy to locate the material that is needed. Both volumes contain several maps of the region as well as a chronology. The articles are brief (from around one-half to two pages) but thorough, giving the reader a quick look at the particular topic. The extensive set bibliography is divided into subject areas and includes numerous sources in languages other than English.

Better fact checking would have noted that Chinese general Sun Liren died in 1990 at the age of 91 and is not still living as indicated in his entry. On the whole, however, this is a set that students and interested patrons in most large public and academic libraries will find very helpful when researching the U.S. role and relations on the other side of the Pacific.

Encyclopedia of Terrorism. By Cindy C. Combs and Martin Slann. 2002. 339p. appendix. bibliogs. illus. index. Facts On File, $77 (0-8160-4455-4). 303.6.

Focused on a timely topic, this volume is a good companion to the news for the general reader. Recent enough to give coverage to the events surrounding the September 11, 2001, attacks on America, this encyclopedia also includes entries on the history of terrorism. The entries are arranged alphabetically. Most entries are short, but some cover several pages.

Included in this volume are an appendix with charts and graphs, a 33-page chronology called "Major Acts of Terrorism, 1946–2000," and a 27-page chronology called "U.S. and International Reaction to September 11, 2001." Entries include personalities, organizations, nations, techniques, weapons, and ideologies of terrorism. Examples of entries include *Anthrax, as a biological weapon*; *Begin, Menachem*; *bin Laden, Osama bin Mohammed*; *Black Hand*; *Christian patriotism*; *Federal Bureau of Investigation (FBI)*; *Iran*; *Ku Klux Klan*; *neo-Nazis*; *al-Qaeda*; *Rushdie, Salman*; *Stockholm syndrome*; and *Zionism*. Entries contain cross-references, and many have a short list of suggested readings. The illustrations are black-and-white photographs.

The great advantage that this encyclopedia has over similar works is currency. One excellent source, *Political Terrorism: A New Guide to Actors, Authors, Concepts, Databases, Theories, and Literature* (North-Holland; dist. by Transaction, 1988) is more comprehensive in scope but less up-to-date. A useful complement is Facts On File's *Terrorism* (2001), part of its Library in a Book series, which includes a bibliography better than those offered in *Encyclopedia of Terrorism* as well as information on how to research the topic. *Encyclopedia of Terrorism* will be a useful addition to most reference collections and is recommended for public, high-school, and academic libraries.

Encyclopedia of World Terrorism: 1996–2002. 2v. 2003. 1,028p. appendixes. bibliogs. glossary. illus. indexes. M. E. Sharpe, $249 (1-56324-807-7). 303.6.

This set continues the publisher's 1997 three-volume *Encyclopedia of World Terrorism*, which covered events through 1996. Its purpose is to reflect "the new global sweep of contemporary terrorism."

Volume 1 contains three sections. The first, "Twenty-first Century Terrorism," covers the 9/11 attacks, their impact, and America's response. It also offers A–Z entries on 27 key people and organizations, including Mohammed Atef, Rudolph Giuliani, and the Taliban. Section 2, "Global Terrorism, 1996–2002," lays out key issues and then surveys terrorism in different regions of the world. U.S. domestic terrorism is included. Section 3, "Future Trends in Terrorism and Counterterrorism," has entries for topics such as "Cyberterrorism and Information Warfare" and "Threats Involving Chemical and Biological Weapons." All entries include current bibliographies. Many also have a sidebar with key facts or dates. Appended are a chronology (from 1996 through August 2002), a directory of organizations, an extensive bibliography, and a volume index.

Volume 2 contains documents. Some of these are historical documents meant to show the development of world terrorism, such as an excerpt from the Assassins from The Book of Ser Marco Polo and "The Law of Suspects" from the French Revolution. The rest are UN conventions, legislation and enforcement policies related to the homeland defense of various nations, and declarations and manifestos from terrorist groups. In the appended matter are a chronology that begins in 1945 and an extensive glossary. The index includes the contents from the 1997 set, as well as volume 1 of the continuation set, but not the documents in volume 2.

Throughout the two volumes, readers are referred to the entries in the 1997 set for additional information, so it would be helpful to have the earlier set on hand. Even for libraries that don't own the earlier set, the new one would be an important addition. It is more comprehensive than Facts On File's *Encyclopedia of Terrorism* [RBB S 1 02], which is an accessible single-volume resource useful for secondary-school and public libraries.

Rebels and Renegades: A Chronology of Social and Political Dissent in the United States. By Neil A. Hamilton. 2002. 361p. appendix. bibliogs. illus. index. Routledge, $95 (0-415-93639-X). 303.48.

Hamilton, a professor of American history, examines significant people and incidents associated with radicalism and extremism in America. Hamilton's book is a new contribution to reference sources in this area, both because it is a chronology and because of its scope. For example, while the *Encyclopedia of Modern American Extremists and Extremist Groups* (Greenwood, 2002) investigates extremism since 1950, Hamilton's coverage is broader, beginning in 1620 and discussing moderate reformers as well as extremists.

The book is divided into nine historical periods based on the National

History Standards, beginning with "Colonization and Settlement" and ending with the "Contemporary United States." Essays on each era provide helpful historical background. Some 180 articles, arranged in chronological order, vary in length from 500 to 1,000 words and include recommendations for further reading. Use of cross-references is inconsistent, which could hinder readers' access to other relevant topics.

Topics span a wide array of social and political dissenters including civil rights campaigners, women's rights activists, abolitionists, white supremacists, anarchists, cults, and militia groups. Specific entries deal with the Pilgrims, the Boston Tea Party, the Montgomery bus boycott, the Ku Klux Klan, the destruction of the Murrah Federal Building in Oklahoma City, and the September 11 terrorist attacks. As the book is so broad in scope, it is useful for illustrating both historical and contemporary examples of extremism.

The main text is supplemented with numerous useful features. Sidebars present further details of events and people. An appendix of 18 primary documents, including excerpts from speeches and manifestos, is included. Illustrations, such as black-and-white photographs, cartoons, and art reproductions, further complement the text. The detailed index facilitates access to the main text and the appendix of primary documents.

Rebels and Renegades is well written and comprehensive and clearly illustrates how radicals and extremists have challenged and altered the status quo. This volume is appropriate for high-school, public, and academic libraries.

The Columbia Guide to American Environmental History. By Carolyn Merchant. 2002. 448p. bibliogs. index. Columbia, $50 (0-231-11232-7). 304.2.

This latest addition to the Columbia Guides to American History and Cultures series has 10 chapters on historical topics and themes; a 60-page dictionary of environmental agencies, concepts, laws, and people important in American environmental history; an environmental history time line; and a lengthy "Resource Guide." The 10 overview essays are good introductions to general topics. For example, chapter 7, "Conservation and Preservation, 1785–1950," discusses changing land policies and laws, social and scientific movements, and park creation—wide-ranging topics succinctly described and interrelated. "Urban Environments, 1850–1960" (chapter 6) is a reminder that the human environment is often far removed from the natural environment, though its impact is considerable. The chapters have bibliographies of the main sources consulted, useful to those whose interest has been piqued. The table of contents lists both chapter titles and the subheadings for the topics mentioned in each.

The "Resource Guide" offers lists of visual (films and videos) and electronic resources arranged by topic as well as a bibliographic essay and a bibliography of articles and books in 21 categories. The books in the bibliography could serve as a guide when developing a core collection on environmental history. This volume, like the others in the series, should prove to be a welcome addition to academic and large library collections.

How Geography Affects the United States. 5v. 2002. 720p. bibliogs. illus. indexes. maps. Greenwood, $199.95 (0-313-32250-3). 304.2.

This series is designed to explain to readers in grades six through eight the impact of geography in shaping the U.S. Arrangement is by region: the Northeast, the Southeast, the Midwest, the West, and the Southwest. Each volume begins with an introductory chapter that shows on a map the states that incorporate the region. The text discusses the characteristics of the region, including land formations, climate, and the people who settled on the land. Charts list the states and pertinent information such as capital, first permanent settlement, and date of statehood. Another chart lists each state's land mass, population, and ranking within region by size. Sidebars and maps provide supplemental information. Although the emphasis is on geography, the history of the development of the area and brief biographies of important individuals are included. Each volume concludes with a list of resources including books and Web sites pertaining to the region.

Although *How Geography Affects the United States* has been designed to meet curriculum needs and reflect the new direction of geography instruction, the fact that all of the many illustrations are in black and white lessens the appeal to the middle-grade reader. The maps would be more effective if color were used to highlight regions or locations. The magnificence of geographical formations is lost when they are only described and the accompanying photos are in black and white. Budget-conscious school librarians may feel that their money is better invested in one of the series that covers the individual states and employs many color photographs.

People around the World. By Anthony Mason. 2003. 256p. illus. index. maps. Kingfisher, $24.95 (0-7534-5497-1). 305.8.

This visually lavish, oversized volume is designed to give elementary- and middle-school students information about people on every continent. Large, colorful photographs, many featuring children, are to be found on almost every page. Although some of the concepts are quite sophisticated, such as globalization, Mason has managed to discuss them on the level of the intended audience. Unfamiliar terms are explained within the text; native words are italicized and explained.

The book is arranged by continent, with a color topographical map and several boxed facts at the beginning of each chapter. Each chapter is then divided into smaller geographical areas. This division is done by country for the larger nations or by region encompassing several smaller countries. Coverage in these sections includes history, geography, economics, cultural traditions, daily life, sports, and entertainment. Each chapter ends with a "Facts and Figures" section—quick reference information on every country including capital city, population and density, square mileage, life expectancy, religion and language, adult literacy rate, and currency.

The strength of this reference is its beautiful photography. All pictures are captioned, offering additional information to the reader. Unfortunately, some captions are so close to each other that younger readers may have trouble determining which picture they belong with, and one photograph showing a U.S. military amphibious landing seems incorrectly captioned with information about President Bush. Text is sometimes printed over a picture, making it difficult to read.

In trying to appeal to the younger reader, the author occasionally lapses into generalities and glosses over many of the world's problems. The volume is to be commended for its breadth of coverage, but 250 pages does not allow for much depth, making this more suitable for the browser than for the researcher.

Bowling, Beatniks, and Bell-Bottoms: Pop Culture of 20th-Century America. Ed. by Sara Pendergast and Tom Pendergast. 5v. bibliogs. illus. index. 2002. 1,329p. UXL, $225 (0-7876-5675-5). 306.

It is commonplace for students studying a pivotal historical issue—war, stock market crash, death of a president—to research its effect on American mores. A good place to begin is this ambitious set, a testimonial to "what a difference a century may make." From Betty Boop to anime; the cocktail hour to ecstasy; flappers to the Goth culture; Sears, Roebuck catalog to Home Shopping Network; and *The $64,000 Question* to *Who Wants to Be a Millionaire*? these volumes—packed with a myriad of provocative personalities, events, and underlying trends—make a fascinating read for the student researcher and the armchair historian alike.

The first level of arrangement is chronological, with each volume covering two decades. For each decade, A–Z entries are sorted into nine categories: "Commerce," "Fashion," "Film and Theater," "Food and Drink," "Music," "Print Culture," "Sports and Games," "TV and Radio," and "The Way We Lived." The foremost fads and styles emblematic of this century's culture are described and analyzed in more than 750 signed entries that vary in length from 150 to 1,000 words, with 500 words being the average. Special features make locating information almost effortless. Each volume, containing an index and a cumulative table of contents, has additional listings of all entries by alphabetical order and by the nine topical categories. A time line highlights key historic and cultural events. Introductory overviews of each decade and topical category provide more information. "At a Glance," a box offering examples of "What We Said," "What We Read," "What We Watched," "What We Listened To," and "Who We Knew," reveals how life was celebrated during that period. Cross-referencing, an awkward denoting of decade, topical category, *and* volume number (but not page number) that chops up the text, is used to redirect, but it is doubtful that a teen researcher would take the time to follow these leads. Sidebars might have been more helpful. Archival photographs, posters, and other black-and-white prints earn a mere glance. No color photographs are included. Bibliographies of additional sources—including Web sites—conclude all entries, offering an opportunity for more in-depth investigating in why historical events matter.

Sociology, Anthropology, Political Science

Any good school library media specialist can see the advantage of purchasing this clear, concise set because it has the potential for easy integration into curriculum planning with any school subject area. It is geared for middle-school and high-school users; public libraries with strong usage by teens should consider purchasing it as well.

Current Issues. 4v. 2003. bibliog. glossary. illus. index. Macmillan, $375 (0-02-865744-6). 306.

Here is a set that will be useful for student debates and research on controversial topics. Some 265 entries treat subjects ranging from *Abortion* and *Academic freedom* to *Women's rights* and *Work*. Entries are arranged alphabetically, with plenty of *see* and *see also* references.

Articles range from two pages (*Acid rain*, *Quality of life*) to seven or more (*AIDS*, *Mental health*), with most about three pages. Information is clearly presented, usually providing an overview, historical background, constitutional or legal principles, ethical or social aspects, and several different points of view. Often there are sidebars with vocabulary defined, quotes from the text, charts, and photos. Usually these add to the text, but the article on *Poverty* has a photo of a girl in Manila even though the article only discusses U.S. poverty.

Entries are unsigned but have been reviewed by the editorial board, which consists of university scholars. Many topics have been adapted from other Macmillan titles, such as *Encyclopedia of Bioethics* (rev. ed., 1995), *Civil Rights in the United States* (2000), *Encyclopedia of Sociology* (2d ed., 2000), and *Encyclopedia of the American Constitution* (2d ed., 2000). Additional articles created specifically for this set include *Taxation* and *War*. Information is current through 2001.

Each volume includes a cumulative table of contents, glossary, cumulative index, and a list of additional sources grouped by general topic ("Bioethics," "Civil Rights," etc.). There are a few minor problems with access. For example, *School choice* cannot be found in the index, even though several paragraphs are devoted to it in the article on *Public schools*. Students looking for information on chemical and biological warfare won't find it without turning to the index, because the entry that provides it has the odd and somewhat retro heading *Germ warfare*.

High-school, college, and public libraries that don't already own the other Macmillan titles or subscribe to CQ *Researcher* or SIRS may want to add this set for its concise introduction to many issues.

The Greenwood Guide to American Popular Culture. 4v. Ed. by M. Thomas Inge and Dennis Hall. 2002. 2,155p. bibliogs. illus. index. Greenwood, $399.95 (0-313-30878-0). 306.4.

Adopting Popular Culture Association founder Ray B. Browne's definition of popular culture as "all the experiences in life shared by people in common, generally though not necessarily disseminated by the mass media," the new version of this encyclopedia covers 58 topics in great detail. Combining the contents of the *Handbook of American Popular Literature* (Greenwood, 1988) and *The Handbook of American Popular Culture* (2d ed., Greenwood, 1989), the *Guide* has eliminated chapters on advertising, detective and mystery fiction, and gender studies as being exhaustively addressed in other works. Chapters have been added on amusement parks, do-it-yourself home improvement, housing, living history and reenactments, museums and collecting, and New Age movements. The introduction has been lifted intact from *The Handbook of American Popular Culture*, but the front matter includes a lengthy new essay on the study of popular culture by Michael Dunne.

Articles, written by subject experts in generally readable (if not scintillating) prose, run between 20 and 50 pages in length. Each chapter includes a brief chronological survey of the development of the subject under consideration; a critical guide in essay form to the standard or most useful reference works, bibliographies, histories, critical studies, and journals; a description of research centers or sources of primary and secondary sources; and a checklist of works cited in the text. Aimed at a wide cross section of users, from reference librarians to general readers, the *Guide* serves as a sound source for research purposes as well as for interest reading. Some chapters (e.g., "Fashion" and "Television") include a pictorial section following the text of the chapter. Aside from the chapter-end illustrations, the text is amply illustrated in black-and-white photos and reproductions. The very extensive index provides a sound navigational aid.

The lengthy topical essays of this resource make it a complement to the *St. James Encyclopedia of Popular Culture* (St. James, 2000), and it is recommended for large public and academic libraries.

International Encyclopedia of Marriage and Family. 4v. 2d ed. Ed. by James J. Ponzetti. 2002. 1,838p. bibliogs. illus. index. Macmillan, $495 (0-02-865672-5). 306.8.

High-school students, undergraduate and graduate students, and public library patrons will find this set provides a wealth of information on the dynamics of marriage and family life around the world. The set revises and significantly expands Macmillan's 1995 *Encyclopedia of Marriage and the Family*. The annotation "(1995)" after an entry title in the alphabetical list of entries at the beginning of the first volume indicates that the entry has been essentially reprinted from the first edition with an updated bibliography.

The work is particularly notable because of its broad scope. Marriage and family are interpreted in the broadest sense, and contemporary issues related to marriage and family are included. International and cultural coverage, absent from the earlier edition, offer added value. Fifty countries representing the regions of the world were selected for inclusion; coverage of family life in these countries was excellent. There are 12 entries on unique racial and ethnic groups, selected because they were either indigenous or prominent in heterogeneous nations and research was available about their distinct family patterns. In addition, 11 entries on specific religions or belief systems are included because of the impact these systems have in guiding and supporting lifestyle choices and patterns. *Adolescent parenthood*, *Commuter marriages*, *Dowry*, *Extended families*, *Hospice*, *In-law relationships*, *Jealousy*, *Menstrual taboo*, *Relationship metaphors*, *Sandwich generation*, *Wedding ring*, and *Work and family* are some of the other topics covered.

Signed alphabetically arranged entries are carefully documented and accompanied by bibliographies incorporating cited works and suggestions for further reading. Cross-references to related content facilitate use. A comprehensive and well-developed index of nearly 100 pages concludes the set. The encyclopedia would have been enhanced by the addition of two items to the end matter: a directory of key associations and a list of core Web sites for further information. Although the bibliographies do include Internet sites, they are few and far between—something to consider in future editions.

There have been only been a few reference works on family life published in the last decade. Oryx's *Statistical Handbook on the American Family* (2d ed., 1999) stands out. The five-volume *Encyclopedia of Family Life* (Salem, 1999) filled an important niche when it was published, because it was more comprehensive than the 1995 Macmillan set; that is no longer the case. The Salem set focuses on family issues that confront modern society in Canada and the U.S.; the new Macmillan set is broader in scope. In our rapidly changing multicultural world, purchase of this set is highly recommended for public, high-school and college libraries. There is no question that libraries owning the 1995 edition will serve their users well by investing in this update. Thumbs-up to Macmillan for both identifying a need in the reference literature in the social sciences and for significantly broadening the scope of their initial two-volume set.

Macmillan Encyclopedia of Death and Dying. Ed. by Robert Kastenbaum. 2v. 2002. 1,071p. appendix. bibliogs. illus. index. Macmillan, $240 (0-02-865689-X). 306.9.

This new encyclopedia from Macmilan offers another option in the popular field of death reference works. The 327 signed entries, written by scholars and expert care providers, range in length from a few paragraphs to several pages. The focus of the entries is on exploring "the place of death in contemporary life," although the encyclopedia also aims to provide a historical perspective of death and dying through the ages. Types of entries include causes of death (*Assassination*, *Cancer*, *Drowning*); practices surrounding death (*Cryonic suspension*, *Pyramids*, *Sympathy cards*); individuals and events that have influenced the way we think about death (*Sartre, Jean-Paul*; *Terrorist Attacks on America*); and entries on the nature or meaning of death from various multidisciplinary and multicultural perspectives (*Confucius*, *Ghost Dance*, *Maya religion*). *See also* references are included at the end of each entry along with a bibliography featuring monographic, periodical, and Internet resources. Many of the entries are accompanied by one of the 150 black-and-white photos scattered throughout the volumes. An appendix profiles and gives contact information for 75 organizations active in death-related education, research, advocacy, or other areas. This is followed by a comprehensive general index.

The release of this set unfortunately succeeds the very similar one-volume *Encyclopedia of Death and Dying* (Routledge, 2001), which offers more than 400 slightly more succinct entries and bibliographies as well as a separate name index. Both sets could serve as an update to the *Encyclopedia of Death* (Oryx, 1989), but libraries on tight budgets may not be able to afford both despite the fact that each has some unique content and perspective. Either title could be complemented by the more specialized *Death and the Afterlife: A Cultural Encyclopedia* (ABC-CLIO, 2000), which deals with the meaning of funeral and afterlife traditions in various cultures. The *Macmillan Encyclopedia of Death and Dying* is written in language suitable for the general reader and is recommended for academic and large public libraries.

Encyclopedia of Urban Cultures: Cities and Cultures around the World. 4v. Ed. by Melvin Ember and Carol R. Ember. appendixes. bibliogs. illus. index. maps. 2002. Grolier, $399 (0-7172-5698-7).

With global issues and internationalization becoming an integral part of everyday life, there is a definite need for information that helps people understand other cultures. *Encyclopedia of Urban Cultures* makes a contribution by describing and analyzing nearly 240 country capitals and urban areas with a population of at least 25,000. The editors are husband and wife and serve respectively as president and executive director of the Human Relations Area Files at Yale University, an international research organization in the field of cultural anthropology. As is the case with other Yale Human Relations Area Files products, there is a strong international flavor as many of the urban areas covered are from outside North American. This is one of the strong points of the encyclopedia. Places like Tallinn, Estonia, or Windhoek, Namibia, will not be discussed in most other urban-studies resources.

Following 16 overview essays on topics such as "Migration and Cities" and "Urbanization in Latin America," entries are arranged alphabetically by city name. The academic writing style reflects the scholarly training of the more than 300 contributors. The signed essays follow a uniform pattern, with sections on "Orientation" (i.e., location, population, distinctive features, and main attractions); "History"; "Infrastructure"; "Cultural and Social Life"; "Quality of Life"; and "Future of the City." Each entry includes a thumbnail map of the region with the location of the urban area highlighted, helping readers to get a sense of where the specified city is located. There is also a black-and-white photo as part of each essay. Each entry concludes with a short bibliography directing users to more in-depth work. Although some have greater narrative and analytical qualities, entries represent solid research, and there is a wealth of data that researchers will be glad is in one place. A strong reading of these entries will not only help readers understand a specific city but also underscore the forces at work in many urban environments. The 50-page index adds value by indexing categories like *class system* to help readers link to similar themes in different entries. There is also an appendix that provides finding aids to locate cities by country and region.

Although *Encyclopedia of Urban Cultures* is a place to get authoritative data on urban areas, a good general encyclopedia like the *Encyclopedia Britannica* also can do this job and often does it a bit better. For example, the *Vienna* entry in *Britannica* has a longer description of the cultural influences of Beethoven and Mozart and includes Viennese cultural and political figures, such as Freud, Herzl, and Hitler. On the other hand, a general encyclopedia will not provide nearly as much detail about a smaller city such as Asmara, Eritrea.

The editors have published other material in this field, including *Countries and Their Cultures* (Macmillan, 2001), which is valuable for students who are studying cultures by country, rather than by urban area. The other way that many people study different cultures is by the cultural group itself (Latinos, French Canadians, etc.). A strong resource for this type of approach is *Encyclopedia of World Cultures* (1991, G. K. Hall), which was also prepared under the auspices of the Yale Human Relations Area Files. For the range of international cities it covers and the convenience of having so much information about cities in a single reference tool, *Encyclopedia of Urban Cultures* is recommended for academic and public libraries.

American Political Scientists: A Dictionary. 2d ed. Ed. by Glenn H. Utter and Charles Lockhart. 2002. 516p. appendixes. bibliogs. index. Greenwood, $99.95 (0-313-31957-X). 320.

The first edition of this book, published in 1993, focused on political scientists who came into the profession prior to 1970. Most of the political scientists were white males because before 1970 few minorities or women were in the profession. In the second edition, political scientists who came into the profession after 1970 are included, and although those who were covered in the 1993 edition are still here, the selection shows greater diversity in terms of gender and ethnicity.

Of 193 entries, 22 are new and 110 have been revised. The preface explains the process by which the political scientists were chosen for the book: "Slightly over 80 percent of our new entries represent members of the 'consensus list'" that was compiled based upon various "reputational studies" and input from persons who had served as president of the American Political Science Association. The editors say they have "compiled *a*, not *the*, list of exceptionally valuable contributors to the profession."

The entries are arranged alphabetically by last name and contain birth and death information, educational background, and career summary as well as the major contribution each person made to the field. Each entry concludes with a chronologically arranged list of selected primary works chosen by other specialists in the field. Some entries also contain "works about," which are arranged alphabetically by the author's last name. Most of the entries are two pages, which is helpful for quick information. Appendixes list political scientists by degree-granting institution and also according to subfield.

As long as a researcher is aware that this is not a definitive work, it could be useful for beginning research or for finding quick answers. It is recommended for large public and academic libraries, especially where the first edition has been well used.

CQ Electronic Library. [Online database]. 2001. CQ, pricing from $500 for a single database. [http://library.cqpress.com/]. (Last accessed October 2, 2002).

CQ Electronic Library consists of six separate databases: *Supreme Court Collection, Public Affairs Collection, CQ Insider, CQ Researcher, Electronic Encyclopedia of American Government*, and *CQ Weekly*. Subscriptions are available for individual databases or bundled together to meet the needs of a particular institution. Because we have already reviewed *CQ Researcher* [RBB Ja 1 & 15 99] and *Electronic Encyclopedia of American Government* [RBB N 1 01], this review will focus on the other components.

The six databases are all informative and user-friendly. Of those covered here, *Supreme Court Collection* and *Public Affairs Collection* are the most similar. Both contain links to articles on a given topic from the many CQ publications. A particularly useful feature is the CiteNow! tab, which generates the correct citation of the article in APA, MLA, *Bluebook*, and *Chicago Manual of Style* format. Each database also contains a time line and an image library; however, these are quite limited and provide no additional substantive information.

Supreme Court Collection offers summaries for more than 4,000 cases from 1793 to the present, and more detailed coverage of analysis of 300 "key cases" such as *Brown v. Board of Education*. Content can be searched by case, justice, or subject in the basic search and by justice, date, term, area of the Constitution, and policy in the advanced search. Keyword searching, justices' biographies, and browsing by topic are also offered.

In *Public Affairs Collection*, content is derived from more than 15,000 documents and organized into 22 subject headings like Advocacy and Public Service, Education, and Transportation. A click on Health will bring several subheadings; a click on one of them (such as Hospitals) will reveal a results list with information from a variety of sources (encyclopedia entry, Web links, case summary, organization information, primary source, legislative information). This kind of general information will be the most use to high-school and public libraries.

The newest addition to the *CQ Electronic Library* is *CQ Insider*, which is mainly a directory of government offices, elected officials, organizations, and advocacy groups, arranged both alphabetically and by topic. One interesting feature of this section is the link to organizational charts for most of the federal agencies. Although much of the information included in this database is available for free and can be easily retrieved by a Google search, it is nice to have it available to the patrons in one place.

The well-known *CQ Weekly* is also included in the *CQ Electronic Library*. Articles and votes can either be searched by keyword or browsed by topic. Issues can be browsed by date, as can recent floor votes. The current issue is displayed upon log-in, but sections can only be viewed one at a time (in contrast to the print version). However, online issues are usually available about one week before their print counterparts.

Libraries with a significant collection of CQ's print resources will find

Sociology, Anthropology, Political Science

little that is new here. The user-friendly searches, online access, and integrated CQ publications do make the collection worthy of consideration as budgets allow.

Encyclopedia of Latin American Politics. Ed. by Diana Kapiszewski. 2002. 358p. appendixes. bibliogs. glossary. illus. index. maps. Oryx, $74.95 (1-57356-306-4). 320.98.

"Every Latin American country has its own rich and unique history," says Jeffrey Taggart, who wrote the introductory article for this book. This is certainly exemplified in this publication from the Center for Latin American Studies at Georgetown University. The title will dispel myths that all of the governments south of the U.S. border are the same. Latin America is defined as the "eighteen Spanish-speaking republics of the Western Hemisphere, together with Portuguese-speaking Brazil and French-speaking Haiti" and additionally Puerto Rico.

The book is broken into individual country chapters, each penned by a different author. Each chapter uses a standard format, which makes it easy to find comparative information. After a brief profile with demographic, business, and governmental structure information, there is an overview of the country's history, followed by between 20 and 40 A–Z entries on important people and political organizations, issues, and events. These entries are concise, well written, and well cross-referenced. A list of the heads of state, a bibliography, and a list of Web resources conclude each chapter. The appendixes contain brief articles on inter-American organizations and U.S. policies aimed toward Latin America. A glossary of terms used in many articles and a well-compiled index round out the text.

Information on these countries can be found in numerous other sources, among them *Encyclopedia of Latin American History and Culture* (Scribner, 1996), *Reference Guide to Latin American History* (Sharpe, 2000), and *Worldmark Encyclopedia of the Nations* (Gale, 10th ed, 2000), but this volume's country-by-country focus on twentieth-century politics makes it unique. Recommended for high-school, public, and academic libraries.

Encyclopedia of Modern American Extremists and Extremist Groups. By Stephen E. Atkins. 2002. 375p. bibliogs. illus. index. Greenwood, $74.95 (0-313-31502-7). 320.53.

An academic librarian has brought together information on a wide range of political, religious, economic, and social extremism in the U.S. over the past half century, with particular emphasis on the last two decades. According to the introduction, an extremist movement, group, or individual is one who pursues "policies or practices outside the societal norm," often through violence. The extremist agenda transcends personal gain and seeks to change the status quo. Although the focus of the book is on current American-developed extremism, links to Canadian and European movements are noted as well as roots earlier in the century. Foreign terrorists operating in the U.S. are excluded.

The 275 entries, varying from 200 to 1,500 words, cover leaders, ideas, organizations, and tactics. The largest category of groups and individuals advocates a transformation of the government. These include the Aryan Nations, Kathy Boudin, Ted Kaczynski, and the Michigan Militia. The second largest is religious extremism, followed by economic and social extremism practiced by Earth First! and People for the Ethical Treatment of Animals, among others. Reflecting the time period that is covered, most of the movements have a radical right orientation. The criminal and violent activities of the groups, the internal conflicts, and the shifting of allegiances between organizations and individuals are described. Birth and death dates, family background, motivation, education, and occupation of the individuals are provided when known. Several entries, such as *Animal rights movement* and *Anti-abortion movement*, provide a broad perspective. A list of suggested readings for each entry, current through 2001, directs the user to further information. Cross-references and black-and-white photos enhance the work, which concludes with a 13-page chronology of events and a selected bibliography (including some Internet sources).

While other books, such as *Encyclopedia of White Power* (AltaMira, 2000), cover specific aspects of extremism, this work offers a more comprehensive survey. It will be useful in high-school, public, and academic libraries.

The Malcolm X Encyclopedia. Ed. by Robert L. Jenkins and Mfanya Donald Tryman. 2002. 688p. bibliogs. illus. index. Greenwood, $74.95 (0-313-29264-7). 320.54.

Malcolm X has been dead for more than 37 years and is part of the pantheon of murdered American leaders, becoming one of the most controversial and heroic figures of the twentieth century.

The Malcolm X Encyclopedia is the most comprehensive resource on this historic figure. The major section of the volume consists of 500 essays that create a cross-disciplinary, textured description of the man, his life, his times, and events. The essays are written by 70 contributors representing a wide range of educators and scholars from all over the country but also including graduate students, middle-school administrators, high-school teachers, and even a baseball media consultant. Topics include *African nationalism*, *Civil rights movement*, *Police brutality*, *Socialism*, and *White liberals*, among others.

Also included are a detailed chronology as well as several thematic essays that provide a framework for the entries that follow. Among these introductory essays are "Elijah Muhammad Sr." and "Malcolm X and the Role of Women." All encyclopedia entries have a short bibliography, but there is an extensive bibliography of books, articles, newspapers, electronic resources, and oral interviews included as a separate section in the volume.

The editors state up front that with so many contributors on the subject of one man there is bound to be duplication among the entries. Where the duplication was redundant, they endeavored to eliminate it; where the duplication served to provide insight, substance, and greater understanding, the passages were left in place. For the public library reference collection, one must consider whether *The Malcolm X Encyclopedia* would not duplicate what might be found in other standard African American reference resources. But considering the stature of the subject and the ongoing interest on the part of the general public and students (as seen in more than 150 Web sites and several thousand Web pages devoted to him), the encyclopedia would add a first-stop resource for library users seeking information on this important figure of contemporary American history.

SYBWorld. Ed. by Barry Turner. 2002. [Internet database]. Palgrave, pricing from $450 [http://www.sybworld.com/]. (Last accessed December 9, 2002).

The Statesman's Yearbook is one of the reference librarian's standard resources for current political information. This electronic version, updated monthly, is very useful in a rapidly changing world. The home page has a world map and a column with search options on the left. Users may click on a region of the map, type terms in the search box, or use pull-down menus to browse by place, international organization, person, or abbreviation. Other features include an extensive directory of international organizations and a chronology of world events from 1999 to the present with a special link covering the war on terrorism. In the World Today offers analysis of current events, and Compare Statistics allows users to create a bar graph or table comparing population, per capita gross domestic product, or Human Development Index of two or more countries. The site also has an abbreviations list and a metric and Celsius converter.

The basic search is by keyword. The advanced mode allows three types of searches: Boolean, Concept, or Pattern. Concept means that using the term *naval* will also search *navy*, *maritime*, and *marine*. Pattern will include variant spellings, such as *defense* and *defence*. Searches can also be limited by one or more categories, such as "Culture" and "Natural Disasters."

The 192 country profiles contain basic maps and data such as capital and population as well as links to information on politics, the economy, international affairs, natural resources and environment, the military, and the legal, health-care, and educational systems, among other topics. Users will also find profiles of cities and biographies of key figures. All articles have lists of further reading and resources, and there are more than 3,000 links to relevant Web sites, including government departments, major companies, newspapers, and more. The In the World Today feature, which has sections on World News, Elections, Economy, and Political Conflict and Terrorism, is updated daily. Featured subjects on December 9, 2002, included President Bush's nomination of a new Secretary of the Treasury, the national strike in Venezuela, the state of the world economy in October and November 2002, and an agreement to end separatist violence in Indonesia. Links to information about the Bush administration, a biography of Hugo Chavez, and articles about the economic policies of Venezuela, the International Monetary Fund, and the territory and population of Indonesia helped to place these events in context. Nonsubscribers can access In the World Today, although they cannot use the links to other SYBWorld content.

SYBWorld describes itself as a "one-stop resource for students, teachers, scholars, journalists, policy makers, and government officials—indeed for everyone seeking to understand our times." Although it does not offer in-depth analysis, this site does an excellent job of providing detailed overviews of the world's countries and current events. It is easy to use, and it will be a welcome addition for academic, public, and high-school libraries.

The Citizen Action Encyclopedia: Groups and Movements That Have Changed America. By Richard S. Halsey. 2002. 385p. bibliogs. illus. index. Greenwood, $65 (1-57356-291-2). 322.4.

"Don't Agonize, Organize," is the slogan of OWL, the Older Women's League, and it is the animating force for this fine resource. Halsey, a library science educator and author, has brought together a wide-ranging yet carefully focused work on organizations, people, and events that created a more progressive nation in the twentieth century. In this alphabetically arranged work, the 160 national organizations described had a formalized identity and grassroots advocacy, were committed to making an impact on society, and achieved some success in their objectives.

The 88 citizen activists who have entries were prominent in dissent or activism; had sufficient reference value to be in biographical directories, books, or public media; and were given substantial coverage in major city newspapers. Examples are Dorothy Day, Abbie Hoffman, Jesse Jackson, Larry Kramer, Phyllis Schlafly, and Richard Viguerie. The work also includes 26 entries, such as *Activist think tanks* and *Senior movement*, that cover various aspects of activism. See also references and cross-references are included. Users are led to further information by the resource lists at the end of entries. Brief chronologies within some entries (*African American rights*, *Women's issues*) provide a helpful framework. Photos complement a number of articles. A "Directory of Organizations" with e-mail and URL addresses, an 11-page bibliography, and a detailed index complete the resource.

There is some overlap with other titles. *The Encyclopedia of American Activism: 1960 to the Present* (ABC-CLIO, 1998) has a more limited chronological scope. *Activists, Rebels, and Reformers* (UXL, 2001) is mainly biographical and intended for the middle-school audience. High-school, public, and academic libraries will find *The Citizen Action Encyclopedia* very helpful for a wide range of users.

Minority Rights in America. By Alan Axelrod. 2002. 411p. appendixes. bibliogs. index. CQ, $125 (1-56802-685-4). 323.1.

Written by a seasoned author of more than 30 reference books, this is a comprehensive source consisting of nearly 600 entries on various aspects of civil, social, and political rights in U.S. history. Entries are arranged alphabetically and focus on all aspects of minority rights, particularly those pertaining to African Americans, Asian Americans, and Hispanic Americans. Most entries describe seminal events, prominent individuals, or critical court cases and legislation. Broader subjects, such as H*ispanic civil rights movement*; *Islam*, N*ation of*; and W*omen's civil rights movement*, are covered as well. Entries contain cross-references and conclude with suggested reading.

Although the entries are brief, the scope is impressive, ranging chronologically from the colonial (William Penn), to the contemporary (Ruth Bader Ginsburg) and covering subjects like the *Amistad* mutiny, euthanasia, Jackie Robinson, Japanese internment, and voter registration drives. Three appendixes are included, the first of which lists historic documents, speeches, legislation, and Supreme Court decisions. The second appendix contains, in alphabetical order by name, all court cases mentioned within the volume along with their case numbers. This is a valuable tool for anyone wishing to pursue further research. The final appendix is a directory of current civil rights groups, with mailing addresses, phone numbers, and often an e-mail, Web site, and fax listing as well.

It is not entirely clear why some entries are included. For example, entries on Crispus Attucks, an African American killed in the Boston Massacre, and Joe Louis, the great boxer, are quite interesting, but no obvious relation to minority rights is indicated. Also, the "Suggested Reading" is usually only one resource, sometimes two, which seems paltry for complex issues such as affirmative action or slavery. Still, although not as exhaustive and scholarly as other similar reference sources, such as *Civil Rights in the United States* (Macmillan, 2000) and *The Encyclopedia of Civil Rights in America* (Sharpe, 1998), this volume is an excellent source for quick summaries and descriptions of crucial people, places, and events in the history of minority rights in the U.S. Recommended for public and academic libraries.

Chronological History of U.S. Foreign Relations. 3v. By Lester H. Brune. 2002. 1,549p. appendix. bibliog. illus. index. maps. Routledge, $350 (0-415-93914-3). 327.73.

The update of a title first published in 1985 "is designed as a reference for scholars, librarians, students, researchers, journalists, and citizens seeking a straightforward explanation of particular events regarding the United States' relations with other nations." When first looking at the three volumes of this book, one might be overwhelmed by the sheer quantity of information contained. However, upon closer examination the volumes are arranged in such a way as to be usable by a wide audience.

Each volume offers a table of contents and a list of maps. The material is arranged chronologically from the arrival of settlers at Jamestown, Virginia (May 24, 1607), to George W. Bush's inauguration as U.S. president (January 20, 2001). Each event is described in summaries ranging from a paragraph to two pages in length. More than 30 percent of the material is new. A select bibliography of reference guides and general titles is arranged in a way that mirrors the chronological organizations of the main text.

Maps and cross-references add value, as does the appendix, which contains brief biographies of U.S. Secretaries of State from 1781 to 2001. The extensive index cites only page numbers and provides a volume key at the bottom of each page; including the volume number with the citations would save researchers a step.

Though there are numerous chronologies available, this one is unique—and timely—in its focus on U.S. relations with the rest of the world. The update will be a welcome addition and valuable resource for almost any library, whether academic or public. It is a useful complement to titles such as Scribner's *Encyclopedia of American Foreign Policy* [RBB My 15 02] and the *Encyclopedia of U.S. Foreign Relations* (Oxford, 1997).

The Greenwood Encyclopedia of International Relations. 4v. By Cathal J. Nolan. 2002. 2,128p. bibliog. index. maps. Greenwood, $475 (0-313-30743-1). 327.

From the vast (*Anti-Semitism, Containment, Nationalism, World War I*) to the particular (*Cook, James; Depth charge; Petty officer; Vertical takeoff and landing*) and all along the intervening scale, this encyclopedia defines terms, explains the significance of events, identifies influential individuals, and analyzes important ideas in international relations throughout the world. Its temporal scope reaches very selectively to ancient times with entries on Alexander the Great and the Punic Wars; however, the emphasis falls on places, people, events, and ideologies of the past several centuries since the start of the European voyages of discovery.

In A–Z order, more than 6,000 straightforward and clearly written entries range in length from two or three lines to two or three pages. Even brief entries are punctuated by words in italics, the encyclopedia's convention for internal *see also* references. These cross-references provide historical, political, economic, or theoretical context for topics treated rather narrowly in their own entries. Users are well advised to follow these linkages even though doing so in a print source demands more than clicking a mouse on hyperlinked terms in an online document. The general index adds further depth through extensive subdivision of topics and by differentiating page references for main entries from those for secondary mention of a topic. Some of the longer entries conclude with one or more bibliographic citations to suggested readings. These are cumulated in a general bibliography in an appendix. A series of gray-scale historical maps depicts various regions of the world at key times in their histories.

The breadth of scope ensures this set's utility in finding an explanation for little-known facts such as the origins of the term *green line* as the geographic line separating would-be combatants (derived from the color of a crayon a British UN officer drew on a map in 1964 to separate Greeks and Turks on Cyprus) or an explanation of *Birobizhan*, a desolate area on the Chinese-Soviet border designated in the 1920s by Stalin to serve as a giant ghetto to which the Bolsheviks hoped Soviet Jews would migrate en masse. The set will also be useful to those who need an explanation of more garden-variety terminology, events, concepts, and persons significant to the field of international relations as they have unfolded in history. Its emphasis on the particular complements the lengthy analytical essays on topics and country-to-country relations in Scribner's *Encyclopedia of American Foreign Policy* [RBB My 15 02] and the *Encyclopedia of U.S. Foreign Relations* (Oxford, 1997).

Mexico and the United States. 3v. 2002. 960p. bibliogs. illus. indexes. maps. Marshall Cavendish, $279.95 (0-7614-7402-1). 327.73072.

Students have long needed an encyclopedia that investigates the close and complex ties between Mexico and the U.S. *Mexico and the United States* is a balanced and affordable work that will be welcome in most school collections.

The alphabetically arranged entries are signed and include *see also* references. Most articles are a page long; others cover two to five pages. Each entry has an introductory paragraph in bold type that summarizes the contents. Text is enhanced by photographs (many in color), sidebars, maps, and chronologies. Each volume has a short index and bibliography for the volume. The bibliographies include Internet sites, movies, and novels as well as informational books. Volume 3 provides a general bibliography, a time line, a general index, and several subject indexes: biographical, cultural, economics and environment, geographical, historical, political, population, and society and law.

Entries cover topics in history, biography, geography, culture, sociology, politics, and economics. Some focus more on Mexico, and some focus more on the U.S, but all have relevance, expressed or implied, for relations between the two nations. Examples include *Agriculture*, *Arizona*, *Bilingual education*, *Corridos*, *Elections in Mexico*, *Elections in the United States*, *Mexican Revolution*, *NAFTA*, *Oil*, *Sonoran Desert*, and *Zapata, Emiliano*. The color photographs evoke the richness of the Mexican culture: murals, celebrations, crafts, family life, and the historical sites from ancient times to present. There are no pronunciation guides for Mexican terms.

This set will be of use to most junior-high and high-school libraries, especially for the study of Spanish, world history, American history, multicultural topics, and social justice issues. The writing is clear and understandable by the target audience of eighth through twelfth grades. Marshall Cavendish has given schools another great resource.

Business, Economics, Resources

Worldmark Encyclopedia of National Economies. 4v. Ed. by Sara Pendergast and Tom Pendergast. 2002. bibliogs. glossary. illus. index. maps. Gale, $295 (0-7876-4955-4). 330.9003.

The ultimate aim of this resource is stated in an introductory essay written by contributor Gerald W. Fry: "It is our hope that this set will enhance both economic and geographic literacy critically needed in an increasingly interconnected world." The editors and contributors attempt to accomplish this by presenting a series of accessible articles that methodically analyze the economic structures and financial climates of 198 countries and territories.

Countries are arranged in alphabetical order within four regional volumes. The country entries have two goals: to present a clear picture of current economic conditions and to provide statistical data that will allow for comparative interpretations. Within entries, information is divided into 14 standardized subdivisions, among them a country overview; an overview of the economy; a section on politics, government, and taxation; and a section on infrastructure, power and communications. Subsequent sections treat economic sectors, agriculture, industry, services, international trade, money, poverty and wealth, working conditions, the country's history and economic development (in timeline format), and future trends. A fifteenth subdivision looks at the economies of any dependencies, colonies, or territories. A country-specific bibliography of print and electronic sources completes each entry.

Fact boxes, maps, charts, and tables, all rendered in crisp black-and-white, accompany the text. The statistical data comes from various sources, including the World Bank's *World Development Indicators*, the U.N.'s *Human Development Report*, and the *International Financial Statistics Yearbook*, published by the International Monetary Fund. There is some unevenness in the statistics due to reporting irregularities or idiosyncratic procedures of reporing agencies, but in many cases researchers will be able to make direct comparisons and contrasts. A 16-page insert repeated in each volume features small but detailed, full-color reproductions of paper currency. Each volume ends with a glossary a set index.

The appeal of this work is that a tremendous amount of often-elusive information has been neatly sorted into manageable units. There is an increased call for this sort of data as the social studies curriculum evolves to reflect a global perspective. Accessible to students in tenth grade and up, this set will be of primary interest to high-school and academic library collections. Public libraries will want to consider it as well.

Encyclopedia of Careers and Vocational Guidance. 4v. 12th ed. Ed. by Andrew Morkes. 2002. 3,216p. appendixes. bibliogs. glossaries. illus. indexes. Ferguson, $159.95 (0-89434-418-8). 331.7.

One need only consider recent swings in the airline and Internet industries, not to mention the stock market, to understand the need for libraries to have up-to-date career guides. Now in its twelfth edition, *Encyclopedia of Careers and Vocational Guidance* is, like that other standard of the career reference section, the *Occupational Outlook Handbook* (U.S. Bureau of Labor Statistics, annual), essential. Volume 1 devotes 71 pages to career guidance topics and more than 375 pages to overviews of 93 career fields (similar to the industry profiles of earlier editions), while volumes 2 through 4 cover the essentials of some 677 careers, alphabetically arranged. With some 3,200 pages of up-to-date information engagingly presented, this is truly a one-stop source.

The opening section on career guidance is organized into four areas: "Preparing for Your Career," "Finding a Job," "Applying for a Job," and "You're Hired!" Along the way is practical advice on choosing a career, networking, resumes and cover letters, interviewing, salaries and wages, and employment laws. Each of these and other topics are accompanied by a well-annotated list of Web sites to consult for further information. The next section profiles 449 career fields. Each profile looks at the background, structure, and employment outlook of the field and offers sources of further information (with address, phone number, and Web address); references to related articles; a glossary; one or more black-and-white photographs; and the occasional interesting sidebar. Volume 1 concludes with appendixes on career resources for those with disabilities and information on internships, apprenticeships, and training programs and indexes to various job classification systems (such as the Dictionary of Occupational Titles and the Guide for Occupational Exploration), organizations and Web sites, and job titles. Volumes 2 through 4 profile specific careers. For each, there is an overview followed by sections on history, description of the job, requirements, earnings, work environment, outlook, and more. Each profile also offers sources for further information, and, usually, a photograph. Often there is a bibliography or an interesting sidebar; the article on home health-care aides, for instance, provides an interview with a home health physical therapist. Volumes 2 through 4 contain an identical job title index.

This resource continues to be a key library resource, highly recommended for high-school, public, and academic libraries.

Business: The Ultimate Resource. 2002. 2,172p. glossary. illus. index. maps. tables. Perseus, $59.95 (0-7382-0242-8). 658.

Weighing in at seven pounds and running to more than 2,100 pages, this colossus (200 contributors, 2.5 million words, 700 illustrations, 150 maps) is most definitely not your father's reference book. Although it fits into the traditional category of specialized desktop encyclopedia, the editors have done a wonderfully innovative job of designing it for the time-pressured, eye-weary business executive. The liberal use of white space, graphics, sidebars, and boxed features, plus a concisely informative writing style, will remind business research veterans of the Hoover's Handbook titles that were launched by Reference Press a decade ago.

B*usiness* is arranged into stylishly presented sections. "Best Practice" provides dozens of two-page, signed essays covering topics such as "Strategic Agility," "Intellectual Capital," and "Mentoring." These essays are really executive summaries, and they include mini–case studies, tips, and suggestions for finding more information. The "Management Checklists" and "Actionlists" sections are organized into subsections on training, e-commerce, etc., and are intended to serve as a "comprehensive handbook of practical answers to everyday business challenges." "Management Library" summarizes highly influential business books.

The next sections, "Business Thinkers" and "Management Giants," profile individuals such as Peter F. Drucker, John Jacob Astor, and F. W. Woolworth. The "Dictionary" gives definitions of more than 5,000 international business terms, acronyms, and abbreviations, and the "World Business Almanac" contains statistics, facts, and figures, including profiles of more than 150 countries, 50 U.S. states, and 24 key industry sectors. The final section, "Business Information Sources," lists more than 3,000 Web sites, books, journals, magazines, and organizations. The volume closes with an exhaustive 32-page index.

A nice bonus for *Business* purchasers is that they may choose to register for monthly, PDF-format updates, and these will be archived on a Web site. Registration is via [http://www.ultimatebusinessresource.com/], with a subscriber password provided upon purchase of the print volume. A quick, online "walk-through" of this process proved it to be extremely simple and user-friendly. *Business* is highly recommended both for library and individual purchase.

Law, Public Administration, Social Problems and Services

World Atlas of Biodiversity: Earth's Living Resources in the 21st Century. By Brian Groombridge and Martin D. Jenkins. 2002. 340p. appendixes. bibliogs. illus. index. maps. Univ. of California, $54.95 (0-520-23668-8). 333.95.

A revision and updating of *Global Diversity: Earth's Living Resources in the 21st Century* (World Conservation Monitoring Centre, 2000), this atlas was published to coincide with the World Summit on Sustainable Development held in Johannesburg. It is meant to provide "a comprehensive and accessible view of key global issues in biodiversity." Filled with an amazing breadth of textual information, the volume is arranged into eight thematic chapters. The first four of these cover the biosphere, the phylogenetic tree, the changes in biodiversity on a geological timescale, and human needs and impacts. The next three chapters deal with issues in terrestrial, marine, and inland water biodiversity, and the final chapter addresses global management responses.

Information is delivered in the form of essays, tables, figures, color photographs, and elegant maps that require thoughtful study to feel the impact of what they contain. The two map pairs that contain some of the most important information in the book are those that show possible future scenarios of biodiversity change as identified by two different models. These maps are less than one-fourth the size of other maps, so lose some of their visual strength while containing powerful ideas.

The appendixes are an eclectic group. Appendix 1 lists the phyla of living organisms. Appendixes 2 and 3 contain descriptions of the origins and current statuses of plant and domestic livestock species important for human consumption. Appendix 4 is a 16-page listing of recent vertebrate extinctions. The index is detailed, and index headings include map pages in boldface type.

The preface states that this is "a resource pack and a survival kit for the future." It also could have said that the volume is probably one of the highest value-for-price books on the environment currently in print. Every academic and large public library should purchase it.

Legal Systems of the World: A Political, Social, and Cultural Encyclopedia. 4v. Ed. by Herbert M. Kritzer. 2002. 1,883p. bibliogs. charts. glossary. index. maps. ABC-CLIO, $385 (1-57607-231-2). 340.

This hefty set contains a wealth of information about legal concepts, procedures, and developments throughout the world. Although the emphasis is on current legal systems of political entities, some articles, such as *Napoleonic Code* and *Inquisitorial procedure*, address historic matters and others deal with broader concepts, such as *Indigenous and folk legal systems*, *Islamic law*, and *Natural law*. Of obvious value to anyone interested in comparative analyses of legal matters, the set will also be useful to persons contemplating business or legal activities around the world and anyone wanting to comprehend the social operations of another country.

More than 400 signed, alphabetically arranged entries provide historical background, describe the legal structures and the types of personnel required to maintain them, and explain key concepts. Additional information includes legal education requirements, specific oddities of particular systems, and the impact of political and legal developments on other systems. Most of the 350 contributors are identified with universities, law schools, law firms, and government agencies.

Simple maps accompany the country articles and include inset globes that help the reader locate the less-familiar places. Organizational charts included in the country and U.S. state and Canadian province entries show relationships among the various courts in each jurisdiction. The lists of references and further reading at the end of each entry direct the readers to additional sources.

A work of this magnitude is created over time, and some of the articles already need updating (such as the one that includes a chart of salaries of state court judges dated 1999 and, of course, the one on Afghanistan that was written before September 11, 2001). Nevertheless, this is a valuable compilation of information on a subject that affects us all. Recommended for legal, academic, and large public libraries.

Encyclopedia of the United Nations. By John Allphin Moore Jr. and Jerry Pubantz. 2002. 484p. appendixes. bibliogs. illus. index. Facts On File, $75 (0-8160-4417-1). 341.23.

The purpose of this encyclopedia is to provide a guide to the key activities, institutions, and personalities of the UN and to illustrate the role that this organization has played in world events. Written by two history professors with the help of 25 contributors, this excellent examination is very timely in light of current world events.

Locating information is straightforward. The more than 300 entries are arranged alphabetically and range from a single paragraph to several pages. Access is aided by easily identifiable cross-references directly in the text of the articles and *see also* references at the end of each article. Recommendations for additional readings are included at the end of most of the entries. Finally, a detailed index facilitates access to the main text.

The entries cover a wide range of issues pertinent to the UN, including peace and security (*Disarmament, Peacekeeping*); justice (*Human rights, International law*); humanitarian activities (*Office for the Coordination of Humanitarian Affairs, United Nations Children's Fund* [UNICEF]); and development (*Sustainable development, United Nations Development Programme*). The book also focuses on key individuals (*Annan, Kofi Atta; Roosevelt, Franklin D.*); historical origins (*Fourteen Points, League of Nations*); nations and events in which the UN has been involved (*Bosnia, Suez crisis*); and agencies (*World Bank, World Health Organization* [WHO]). The broad scope effectively illustrates the UN's range of activities and role in world events.

The main text of the book is complemented by excellent supplementary material. For example, the several appendixes include a listing of member states as of June 2002 and a chronology of key UN dates and events. There are also an extensive bibliography and a listing of UN Web sites.

Less comprehensive than Routledge's four-volume *Encyclopedia of the United Nations and International Agreements* (3d ed., 2003), this user-friendly and clearly written guide is suitable for public libraries and academic libraries.

Encyclopedia of the United Nations and International Agreements. 4v. 3d ed. By Edmund Jan Ozmanczyk. 2002. 2,941p. bibliogs. index. Routledge, $550 (0-415-93920-8). 341.23.

This reference was originally compiled in 1975 by Ozmanczyk, a Polish correspondent, author, and politician. English editions appeared in 1985 and 1990. This third English edition has undergone substantial revision, including changes in format. Many articles relating to the post–Second World War era have been dropped as not being as relevant today. The arrangement has been changed to letter-by-letter alphabetization, and there is now a single index at the end of volume 4.

The encyclopedia has approximately 6,000 entries ranging from one sentence to many pages in length. The editor states in the preface that the cutoff date for updating material was December 31, 2001, but we found many citations to information well into 2002 (e.g., *Timor, East* and *Trachoma*). Some discrepancies still show up in the text even after being criticized in previous editions (e.g., under the Ireland entry, *Gill History of Ireland* is cited wrongly). There are entries on individual countries, diseases, geographical locations, weapons, international terms, and excerpts and full text of important treaties and documents. For example, the full text of the 1968 Nonproliferation Treaty is given. There are no biographical entries in this work. Most entries include bibliographic citations to other sources, many of them foreign-language materials. Assisting users of this reference is a 51-page alphabetical list of entries at the front of volume 1 and a 144-page index at the end of volume 4.

Numerous references provide information on international organizations. Although there is some duplication among these works, a random sampling showed the *Encyclopedia of the United Nations and International Agreements* covers organizations not listed elsewhere. In addition it has terms and treaties that are not listed in other works. It is more scholarly and detailed than Facts On File's one-volume *Ency-*

clopedia of the United Nations (see above), and large academic and public libraries will want to seriously consider it.

The U.S. Constitution A to Z. By Robert L. Maddex. 2002. 646p. bibliogs. illus. index. CQ, $125 (1-56802-699-4). 342.73.

Librarians familiar with previous volumes of CQ's Ready Reference Encyclopedia of American Government series will welcome *The U.S. Constitution A to Z*. The 250 alphabetically arranged entries, running from *Abortion* to *Zoning*, clearly describe the concepts, issues, events, and persons that have kept the "world's oldest written national constitution still in force" a dynamic work in progress.

The author, an attorney who specializes in international law, presents this volume as a useful overview of our constitutional history rather than an exhaustive work. But the inclusion of primary source documents (such as the First Charter of Virginia and both Virginia's and New Jersey's plans for the U.S. Constitution), a table of relevant court cases, a selected bibliography, and a list of Internet resources make it more than a simple introduction. Each entry's additional readings and the black-and-white illustrations throughout the book enhance its value for students wanting to learn more.

Whether to purchase this volume, however, might depend on other similar holdings and space available. Many excellent reference sources on the U.S. Constitution have appeared in recent years, including *Encyclopedia of Constitutional Amendments, Proposed Amendments and Amending Issues, 1789–1995* (ABC-CLIO, 1996), and *Constitutional Amendments, 1789 to the Present* (Gale, 2000). In addition to these one-volume works, there are the four-volume *Constitution and Its Amendments* (Macmillan, 1999) and the six-volume *Encyclopedia of the American Constitution* (2d ed., Macmillan, 2000).

CQ's entry into the field is more current, including as it does coverage of the 2000 presidential election and alluding to some of the antiterrorism measures proposed after 9/11. It is recommended for academic, public, and high-school libraries that do not already own some of the above-mentioned works or could use an additional single-volume resource on the Constitution.

Landmark Decisions of the United States Supreme Court. By Paul Finkelman and Melvin I. Urofsky. 2002. 687p. appendixes. bibliogs. indexes. CQ, $225 (1-56802-720-6). 347.73.

More than 1,000 of the Court's most important decisions are discussed in this title. The cases selected for inclusion fall into three categories: decisions recognized as the most important (*Dred Scott* v. *Sandford*, *Roe* v. *Wade*); cases that are significant but of lesser impact; and those that were narrow in influence. Cases in the latter group include some of the first decisions made in the eighteenth century. The length and depth of the case explications reflect the importance of a decision in terms of its impact on American society.

Summaries are preceded by the type and date of the decision, the vote of each justice, and the authors of the majority and dissenting opinion. The summaries give the background, relevant legal points, and impact of each decision. Underlying principles are clearly explained. References to additional resources and related cases are also included. In addition to an alphabetical case index, there is a subject index that offers a useful way for a researcher to find a justice's voting patterns and positions on specific topics. Appendixes list Supreme Court nominations by president and Court members by chief justice. The seating chart of the court is also provided. A glossary would have been useful.

Although they will need to turn elsewhere for the actual text of a decision, students and researchers without a legal background who are seeking an overview of a Supreme Court decision can't go wrong with this resource. It covers considerably more cases than CQ's *Illustrated Great Decisions of the Supreme Court* (2000) or *The Oxford Guide to Supreme Court Decisions* (1999). Recommended for public and academic libraries.

The Oxford Companion to American Law. Ed. by Kermit L. Hall. 2002. 912p. bibliogs. indexes. Oxford, $65 (0-19-508878-6). 348.73.

This title bills itself as "a comprehensive guide to every aspect of law in America." Although that statement is hyperbole, this is perhaps the best one-volume encyclopedia of American law to be published in a long time. Editor Hall, president of Utah State University and a specialist in the history of law, has overseen another Oxford title—*Oxford Companion to the Supreme Court of the United States* (Oxford, 1992)—that will be a standard for many years. His group of contributors includes legal and historical scholars, faculty of law schools, judges, and legal writers.

The book contains nearly 500 articles arranged in an A–Z format. Numerous *see also* references direct readers to similar topics in the book. Cross-references are denoted within the text for easy travel between articles. Individual cases of American law have, for the most part, been left out of the list of entry headings. There is an index to cases though; that leads readers to the article(s) where the case is discussed. A few extremely important or popular cases are included as entries (*Brown* v. *Board of Education*; *Leopold and Loeb case*; *Simpson, O. J., trials of*). The same is true for people—only well-known or important historical figures are given individual articles.

Articles are generally several pages long and written at a level that is easily understood. Topics as arcane and confusing as intellectual property law and torts are explained with a minimum of legalese. With the ease of comprehension and the thorough main index, the volume is a good place for students to start school papers. College students will find the bibliography after each article useful in going further in their selected topics. Like law itself, the book is already out-of-date, as topics such as internment and privacy must be reconsidered after laws passed following the September 11, 2001, tragedy. However, this should not deter any library from purchasing this title. Readers will find a sometimes difficult topic covered in a simple, concise, and clear manner.

Gale Encyclopedia of Everyday Law. 2v. Ed. by Shirelle Phelps. 2002. 1,259p. bibliogs. glossary. index. Gale, $225 (0-7876-5759-X). 349.73.

This work is designed for the layperson who wants background information about legal issues and procedures that affect our everyday lives. It is not a dictionary, although it includes a glossary, and it is not a do-it-yourself legal guide. Approximately 200 articles provide historical information, brief descriptions of relevant federal laws and regulations, variations in state and some local laws, directions to print and electronic sources of additional information, and contact details for potentially useful national and state organizations and agencies.

The articles are arranged in alphabetical order within broad categories, such as "Attorneys," "Consumer Issues," "Education," "Immigration," "Real Estate," and "Taxes." Some sections are surprisingly brief, while others are rather comprehensive. *First Amendment Law* merits only 3 pages, while *Healthcare* gets 70 and *Internet* gets 60. There is some unevenness in writing and editing. The article on international travel, for example, has several grammatical errors and still shows $400 as the maximum value of foreign-acquired goods to bring back duty-free. Otherwise, most of the information provided seems to be useful, and the editor offers the caveat to verify current status of laws and regulations and Web addresses.

Under *Attorneys*, there are suggestions for finding a good lawyer—and guidance regarding malpractice! The *Automobiles* entries include the basics for buying and leasing a vehicle, recommendations regarding insurance, and information on safety requirements (including seatbelts and child restraints). *Immigration* offers background material on asylum, deportation, and dual citizenship. *Real estate* provides the expected information on buying and selling property but includes sections on renters' liability, time-shares, and zoning as well. The section on *Taxes* explains how corporate and personal income taxes are structured, spells out what might be involved in an IRS audit, and shows sales tax rates by state. The index points to specific pages, but most users will find the comprehensive table of contents and the general arrangement by broad topic the easier way to find what they need. Recommended for academic and public libraries.

Guide to the Presidency. 2v. 3d ed. Ed. by Michael Nelson. 2002. 1,760p. illus. index. CQ, $315 (1-56802-714-1). 352.23.

This third edition updates and revises the 1995 edition of a preeminent reference source on the U.S. presidency. Updating incorporates Bill Clinton's second term and many aspects of George W. Bush's first, generally ending with the 2002 State of the Union address. Revisions reflect new research published during the 1990s and early 2000s.

The two volumes provide a narrative and also almanac-type information. The history of the presidency; the powers of the office (for example, chief diplomat, commander-in-chief, chief executive); the president as a public figure; relations with other branches of government; the vice presidency; presidential succession; and many other topics are covered in 37 chapters authored by academic scholars. Of special note is a collection of charts scattered throughout the work, covering an eclectic range of facts: number of presidential press conferences, percentage of voting-age population casting votes in presidential elections, presidential campaign funding, press secretaries, and more. Many of these charts have been extracted from other CQ publications. In addition, the work contains the texts of notable speeches, pertinent Supreme Court decisions, inaugural addresses, and State of the Union messages, among many other primary source materials. Each volume contains a helpful keyword index to the contents of both volumes.

Guide to the Presidency is an essential purchase for public and academic libraries. In these tight economic times, however, small public and college libraries already owning the second edition may reluctantly resist purchasing this one, especially if they have other information on the presidency since 1995.

African American Recipients of the Medal of Honor: A Biographical Dictionary, Civil War through Vietnam War. By Charles W. Hanna. 2002. 189p. appendix. bibliog. illus. index. McFarland, $45 (0-7864-1355-7). 355.1.

Here are the stories of 88 African Americans who have been awarded the Medal of Honor. Among them are Clement Dees, a deserter whose medal was later revoked; several of the "buffalo soldiers" who fought in the Indian Wars; and Naval Landsman Aaron Anderson, a recipient during the Civil War whose medal was erroneously issued under the name Aaron Sanderson.

Within chapters that correspond to major conflicts, from the Civil War to the Vietnam War, summaries are arranged alphabetically by recipient's name and generally range from just under a page to three or four pages in length. Entries often include quotes from citations, and some are accompanied by black-and-white illustrations, mostly of grave sites. An appendix lists total numbers of medals awarded by wars and campaigns.

This is a useful text to better grasp the discrimination that has been inherent in the military for much of its existence. Discrimination is discussed particularly in relation to the First and Second World Wars, where just eight African American individuals have been awarded the Medal of Honor. One medal was awarded for service in World War I, out of the 370,000 African Americans who served, but President George H. W. Bush did not award it until 1991. Seven medals were awarded for actions in World War II, but President Clinton did not issue them until 1994. The seven medals for African Americans are out of a total of 439 awarded to WWII servicemen.

This book adds to the collection of materials available on the Medal of Honor. Previous books—*Medal of Honor Recipients, 1863–1994* (Facts On File, 1995); *The Congressional Medal of Honor: The Names, The Deeds* (Sharp and Dunigan, 1984)—look at the whole of the recipients and provide much less specific descriptions of the individuals and their actions. *African American Recipients of the Medal of Honor* is a valuable addition to collections on military history, government, and African American studies.

Air Warfare: An International Encyclopedia. 2v. Ed. by Walter J. Boyne. 2002. 771p. bibliogs. illus. index. maps. ABC-CLIO, $185 (1-57607-345-9). 358.4.

Ground Warfare: An International Encyclopedia. 3v. Ed. by Stanley Sandler. 2002. 1,065p. bibliogs. illus. index. maps. ABC-CLIO, $295 (1-57607-344-0). 355.

Boyne and Sandler are distinguished military history scholars. Boyne is the former director of the National Air and Space Museum, and Sandler is a retired historian for the U.S. Army. They have respectively authored *Air Warfare* and *Ground Warfare*, which complement the earlier *Naval Warfare* [RBB S 15 02], by Spencer Tucker. These references cover their subjects from the earliest times possible to the present, *Ground Warfare* reaching back to ancient times and *Air Warfare* beginning its coverage with World War I. They are international in scope and have international contributors. According to the introductions, the intended audiences are scholars and general readers.

With only a few differences, both sets are arranged in a similar manner. Each accompanies its A–Z entries with an introduction; an alphabetical list of entries; a list of contributors; a list of abbreviations, terms, and acronyms; a select bibliography; and an index. Each signed entry is one-quarter to several pages in length and concludes with a short bibliography and, in most cases, cross-references. Scope encompasses biographies, battles, wars, raids, and weapons. *Air Warfare*'s more than 900 entries are heavy on particular kinds of aircraft (*Bell AH-1 Cobra, Grumman F4F Wildcat*). Among its more than 1,200 entries, *Ground War-*

fare includes some unusual discussions like *Music, military; Religion and war;* and *Reporting, war*. Both sets have entries for treatment of their subjects in the arts and for the roles played by women.

Each set is enhanced by appropriately placed black-and-white maps, illustrations, and photographs. Information is fairly current. *Air Warfare* covers *Enduring Freedom*, the U.S.'s post-9/11 bombing campaign in Afghanistan, and *Ground Warfare* covers the troubles in Peru, Rwanda, Somalia, and Yugoslavia through 2000. Interestingly, *Air Warfare* has an entry for Scott O'Grady but none for the air war in the former Yugoslavia.

Other military reference tools, whether more general, such as *The Oxford Companion to Military History* [RBB Ja 1 & 15 02], or more specific, such as *Encyclopedia of the Korean War* [ABC-CLIO, 2000], may treat some of the same topics but do not offer the same perspective. These unique surveys of aerial and ground combat would be useful additions to reference collections in academic, public, and high-school libraries.

Directory of Military Aircraft of the World. By Peter R. March. 2001. 480p. glossary. illus. index. Sterling, $75 (1-85409-527-7). 358.4183.

March has authored *Military Aircraft Markings*, an annual reference book on aircraft recognition, for more than 20 years. His current project covers all known military aircraft flying through early 2001. Included are 412 aircraft of combat, combat support, training, and a miscellaneous category surveying communications, transport, VIP planes, and more. Each entry is illustrated with at least one color photograph and a second color photograph or computer illustration showing a side or angled view. A typical entry provides a history of the development of the aircraft, information on its current service, and special features of the plane. A sidebar presents standard technical data—range, endurance, crew, and so on. Coverage includes all branches of the military or the equivalent national services.

Information is arranged alphabetically by name of manufacturer and then name of aircraft. A page header quickly allows users to locate the desired plane and provides information on the manufacturer, aircraft name, type of aircraft, and national origin. This is followed with about half a page of text and technical data. At the top and bottom of each page are attractive photographs and digital artworks showing the plane.

Assisting users are several well-designed tools, including a 50-page "World Air Arms Inventory," which is arranged alphabetically by country, service organization, type of aircraft, and manufacturer. Near the back of the book is a two-page glossary of all abbreviations used in the text. This is followed by a subject index.

The only comparable resource is *Jane's All the World's Aircraft*, the massive annual that lists all known powered aircraft. *Jane's* is arranged by country and manufacturer, but users will not find listings there for countries that do not produce aircraft. A user seeking information on the air arms of countries such as Uruguay, Vietnam, and Zimbabwe would need to consult *Directory of Military Aircraft of the World* instead. This current, comprehensive, easy-to-use resource is an excellent complement to *Jane's*, and all libraries with an interest in military aviation should consider it for their collections.

Encyclopedia of American Submarines. By Wilbur Cross and George W. Feise Jr. 2002. 304p. appendixes. bibliog. glossary. illus. index. Facts On File, $65 (0-8160-4460-0). 359.9.

This A–Z work brings together the technical and human side of dangerous and sometimes deadly undersea missions and explorations. Most of the more than 300 entries provide information on individual submarines, such as the *H. L Hunley*, a Confederate submarine and the first to sink a ship in wartime in 1864, and the *Tang*, a World War II submarine that sank itself with its own torpedo, all the way up to the *Greeneville*, the submarine that collided with a Japanese vessel off the coast of Hawaii in 2001, killing several Japanese crew members. Biographical information about significant individuals ranges from David Bushnell, who in 1776 created the first operational submarine, to Hyman George Rickover, the "father" of the navy's nuclear program. Other entries cover submarine weaponry like Trident and Polaris missiles, terms such as *Subsafe* and *Wolf pack*, and general topics such as *Logistics, Lost boats*, and *World War I*.

The heart of the work is the attention paid to individual submarines and their missions, failures, and successes. For security reasons, less detail is provided regarding the missions of submarines currently in use. A selected bibliography has material published from the World War II era to the present, which is appropriate for the historical coverage

Law, Public Administration, Social Problems and Services

the authors strived to achieve. Other back matter includes a chronology of significant events, Navy submarines listed by commission date, a list of submarine museums in the U.S., a listing of related Web sites, definitions of acronyms, and a glossary.

This very accessible work provides an interesting and informative overview and is recommended for most libraries.

Encyclopedia of the Navy Seals. By Charles W. Sasser. 2002. 270p. bibliog. illus. index. Facts On File, $60 (0-8160-4569-0). 359.9.

This monograph from a prolific author who has been a police officer, teacher, U.S. Navy journalist, and U.S. Army Special Forces soldier covers the Navy Seals from their World War II predecessors (e.g., *Alamo Scouts*, *Underwater demolition teams*) to their present units and service in Vietnam, Grenada, Panama, the Persian Gulf War, and Bosnia. Coverage includes organization, personnel, equipment, weapons, terms, and training.

More than 300 alphabetical entries vary from a paragraph to several pages in length. There are numerous cross-references at the end of each entry. About 50 black-and-white photographs illustrate the volume and are appropriately placed throughout the text. Assisting readers is a select bibliography with approximately 100 citations to books, periodicals, and one Web site. An examination of the bibliography shows the citations to be current and representative of the substantial amount of literature available. Rounding out the reference is a detailed index. Within the index, boldface page numbers represent main entries, and italics denote illustrations.

This reference will be popular with military aficionados, scholars, and general readers. Although there are dozens of books regarding the Navy Seals, this is the only reference in an encyclopedia format. This volume should be considered for acquisition by high-school, public, and academic libraries.

Naval Warfare: An International Encyclopedia. 3v. Ed. by Spencer C. Tucker. 2002. 1,231p. bibliogs. glossary. illus. index. maps. ABC-CLIO, $295 (1-57607-219-3). 359.

Tucker is editor of some well-known military reference titles, including the *Encyclopedia of the Korean War: A Political, Social, and Military History* (ABC-CLIO, 2000) and the *Encyclopedia of the Vietnam War: A Political, Social, and Military History* (ABC-CLIO, 1998). This new resource is international in scope, covering the subject of naval warfare from ancient times to the present. Some 157 contributors are responsible for more than 1,500 signed entries. Most entries include *see also* references and a short bibliography with one to four citations.

According to the introduction this work covers the standard topics of battles, ships, and commanders but also goes further by covering subjects like equipment (*Boarding pike*, *Chronometer*), tactics and strategies (*Broadside*, *Coastal assault*), food and medicine (*Burgoo*, *Grog*, *Scurvy*), and more. Information is current up to July 2001, when operations to recover the Russian submarine *Kursk* began. Recent discoveries and scholarship on the battleships *Bismarck* and *Maine* and the spy ship *Liberty* are mentioned in the text. Appropriately placed throughout the text are about 209 illustrations and 11 area maps and 19 battle maps. There is also a glossary with approximately 390 terms. A select bibliography has about 350 citations. Assisting users is a contents list that provides a snapshot of entry headings as well as a lot of quick information (e.g., year built and type are noted next to names of ships; birth and death years are noted next to names of people). Also assisting users is a detailed index.

An excellent comparable work is the one-volume *An Encyclopedia of Naval History* (Facts On File, 1998) with approximately 1,000 entries covering a 500-year time period. The Tucker work is more current and has more entries and fuller bibliographic citations. Academic and public libraries with an interest in military history should consider this well-designed resource for their collections.

Opposing Viewpoints Resource Center. [Internet database]. 2002. Gale, pricing from $1,250 [http://www.gale.com/OpposingViewpoints/]. (Last accessed September 9, 2002).

Gale has lost little time between purchasing Greenhaven Press and producing this "resource center." For the uninitiated, the Opposing Viewpoints series provides pro and con arguments for various current-events-related topics. The print series has long been a staple in secondary school and young adult collections for research and debate preparation on hot topics in social studies and science. The *Opposing Viewpoints Resource Center* (OVRC) includes more than 2,000 articles from more than 170 titles in the Opposing Viewpoints, Current Controversies, and other Greenhaven series; 1,000 topic overviews from Gale and Macmillan reference books; more than 3,000 statistical tables, charts, and graphs; almost 800 images; 30 full-text periodicals and newspapers; links to more than 1,000 Web sites; and 24 titles from Gale's Information Plus series, which provides statistics, laws and legislation, and more.

OVRC may be searched several different ways. The Browse Issue Search allows the researcher to select from an alphabetical list of 68 topics that reflect the series' book titles, such as abortion, censorship, gangs, and terrorism. Or a patron may enter a term and, selecting from the pull-down menu, search by subject, keyword, or full text. The Advanced Search allows Boolean searching by Title/Headline, Source, Author, Subject, and Full-Text. Entering a date or range of dates limits the search to newspapers and periodicals. Another limit is by document type, such as court Case Overview, Image, Magazine, and Website Listing.

Results lists are tabbed to make it easy to select from among the various kinds of information. A search for *endangered species* yielded 27 essays from Greenhaven titles published from 1998 to 1999; 12 reference documents; 24 statistical tables from sources such as the U.S. Forest Service; 172 magazine and newspaper articles (several published in 2002); 17 images; 4 primary documents (for example, the Endangered Species Act of 1973); and 13 Web sites. If a library subscribes to *Student Resource Center*, OVRC will automatically perform a cross-search, which greatly expands the possibilities.

Icons at the top of the page offer Help, Search Tips, Dictionary, Research Guide, and Toolbox. Dictionary provides access to *Merriam-Webster's Biographical Dictionary*, *Merriam-Webster's Collegiate Dictionary*, and *Merriam-Webster's Geographical Dictionary*. The Research Guide links to a series of critical-thinking guidelines ("Review the author's credentials and affiliations," and so on) that should be applied to all research sources and are excellent for lesson plans. The Toolbox offers work sheets in PDF (portable document format) and examples to help teachers and students actually do something with the research. Other features include Spotlight On and This Week's Poll. On August 31, 2002, the Spotlight On assembled documents related to pollution laws. The poll asked, "Should oil exploration and drilling be permitted in the Arctic National Wildlife Refuge (ANWR) in Alaska?" However, there does not seem to be a way to view current or past poll results.

OVRC is an excellent addition to public and school libraries' digital offerings. Undergraduate institutions should also consider it. It will probably remain one publishing cycle behind the print version.

Notable American Philanthropists: Biographies of Giving and Volunteering. Ed. by Robert T. Grimm Jr. 2002. 388p. appendixes. bibliogs. illus. index. Oryx, $69.95 (1-57356-340-4). 361.7.

Many people believe philanthropy is a practice limited to the wealthy and powerful. But this collection of 78 profiles that describe 110 individuals and in some cases families reveals that some people of modest means have helped shape American life through voluntary service or charitable donations. Although most readers will have heard of the Rockefellers or the Guggenheims, or are aware of Jane Addams' work in the early 1900s at Hull House in Chicago, fewer might be familiar with Oseola McCarty, a laundress who gave $150,000 to the University of Southern Mississippi in 1995, or Rebecca Gratz, who established the first independent Jewish women's charitable association in 1819. Among other names that appear here are Clara Barton, Andrew Carnegie, Cesar Chavez, and Bill Gates. One entry describes the strong commitment of the Lakota nation to giving and sharing. There is little awareness of American Indian philanthropy, and yet it is one of America's oldest philanthropic traditions.

The entries, varying from 1,500 to 2,500 words in length for individuals and 2,500 to 9,000 for families, examine early life and education, career, philosophy, motivations, and actions. Some short examples of a person's writings may be included, and the contributions to society are evaluated. The entries conclude with compact bibliographies and are cross-referenced. The appendixes include "Timeline of American Philanthropy" (from the 1600s to 1999), a list of videos and a list of children's books about some of the people who are profiled, and an index that interfiles personal or family names, organizations, and subjects.

This volume complements other information on the more famous persons and also introduces readers to some forgotten or lesser-known persons. It is recommended for large public and academic libraries.

The Directory of Independent Ambulatory Care Centers. Ed. by Laura Mars-Proietti. 2002. 986p. indexes. Grey House, paper, $185 (1-930956-90-8). 362.1.

Medical professionals and patients will welcome Grey House's addition to its outstanding line of health-care directories. This volume bridges a gap in health-care directories by bringing together into one comprehensive listing those centers and clinics that focus on diagnostic imaging tests, outpatient surgical procedures, or specialities such as pain management and sleep disorders. It must be emphasized that the 7,000 or more facilities that are listed are not affiliated with hospitals or medical centers. The clinics associated with hospitals and medical centers have been omitted because they are located easily through their hospital ties.

The overall arrangement is by state and then by city. Within each state, facilities are grouped by their services: ambulatory clinics (for general care), ambulatory surgical centers, and diagnostic imaging centers. Profiles vary in length and detail. Most contain the basics: name, address, telephone and fax numbers, services offered, and key executives. The more extensive ones contain statistics on physicians, employees, and operating rooms; year founded; and Web site addresses. Some of the profiles need more clarity. For example, Borg Imaging Group in Rochester, New York, has several entries with no distinction between the central and branch locations, and two of the locations are listed twice for no apparent reason. However, that minor flaw in no way detracts from the overall quality or usefulness of the directory. The user's guide and user's key, located at the front of the text, are essential for accurate interpretation of the profiles. Content is indexed by facility name and by services and specialties.

The directory is available in both print and subscription-based electronic formats. Regardless of format, it should be widely used by health professionals, medical libraries, and public libraries with sizable health-care collections.

The Encyclopedia of Blindness and Vision Impairment. 2d ed. By Jill Sardegna and others. 2002. 333p. appendixes. bibliogs. index. Facts On File, $65 (0-8160-4280-2). 362.4.

Updating the 1991 edition, the more than 500 entries in this resource address a range of issues related to vision impairment and vision loss. Arranged alphabetically, topics include key people, aid devices, diseases, medical procedures, legislation, social issues, and companies and organizations. Although the book is intended for the general public, undergraduate and high-school students should find articles discussing issues such as *Employment disincentives* or *Myths* about blindness useful for research papers and speeches. Article length averages half a page.

The second edition contains several new topics, 100 updated entries, and 11 completely redone appendixes. For example, readers can now find information about guide horses, LASIK surgery, and the possible damaging effects of air bags. Selected articles include contact information or a short bibliography. Many bibliographies have been updated to include Web page addresses while retaining print resources dating from the 1980s. Appendixes provide contact information for dog-guide schools, national organizations, and other useful resources. Most entries listed in the appendixes include Web page addresses. However, none of the 36 federal agencies listed in appendix 4 contain a Web page address. In some cases, cross-referencing appears incomplete. Of four diseases mentioned in *Cataract*, only one is cross-referenced although all four have their own entries. Like the previous edition, this new publication contains one illustration, a labeled drawing of the eye. Although the authors explain topics using precise and easy-to-understand terminology, the lack of charts, drawings, and pictures, in some cases, slows comprehension.

Some of the information in this resource can be found in other sources. For example, readers can find a description of cataracts in the *Gale Encyclopedia of Medicine* (2d ed., Gale, 2002), or find periodical articles on eye damage caused by air bags. However, its coverage and convenience make *The Encyclopedia of Blindness and Vision Impairment* unique. Those with the older edition will want to update. Suitable for academic and public libraries.

Encyclopedia of Abortion in the United States. By Louis J. Palmer Jr. 2002. 420p. bibliog. graphs. index. McFarland, $75 (0-7864-1386-7). 363.46.

The history of abortion in the U.S. has been written in the courtroom, beginning with the landmark case of *Roe v. Wade* in 1973. This A–Z encyclopedia covers every Supreme Court opinion since that date. Legal coverage also includes the majority of abortion laws in each state.

Entries for the Supreme Court cases are meticulously thorough. Complete citations are given along with all the case specifics such as date argued, date decided, concurring and dissenting opinions, and names of counsels. The background of each case is provided, as is significant text of the majority opinion. Every Supreme Court justice who rendered an opinion in an abortion case also has an entry giving a brief biographical sketch of the justice and comments on the pertinent case(s). Voting records of the justices are included.

State law summaries begin with a brief overview of the state's legislative history regarding abortion, followed by text of the current state code. Additional coverage includes short paragraphs summarizing the philosophy and purpose of many pro-choice and pro-life organizations. The position of religious denominations appears in an entry entitled *Religion and abortion*. Abortion-related medical terms are covered, but details are brief. Examples of these terms are the various methods of abortion and contraception and genetic disorders.

Supplementary statistical information accompanies some entries, but there is no main entry for statistics such as appear in *Abortion: A Reference Handbook* (2d ed., ABC-CLIO, 1996). The alphabetical index of names and entry headings does not make information retrieval easy; a subject index would have been more useful. Despite these problems the strong legal focus and currency of information make the encyclopedia a useful resource for public and academic libraries. Because of the focus on the period since *Roe v. Wade*, researchers will need to turn to sources such as *Encyclopedia of Birth Control* (ABC-CLIO, 2001) for historical perspective.

Encyclopedia of Fire. By David E. Newton. 2001. 294p. bibliog. illus. index. Oryx, $69.95 (1-57356-302-1). 363.37.

As the author states, the subject of *Encyclopedia of Fire* is more than combustion. The book is also about the science of fire; the social and cultural explanations and uses of fire; the images of fire in philosophy, mythology, religion, music, and art; and the natural phenomena of fire at work in the world. From *Air pollution* to *Yule log*, the entries are serious, entertaining, whimsical, surprising, and sometimes gloomy.

It is impossible to describe the breadth of topics without listing them all. Some examples in adjacent entries as they appear in the encyclopedia are: *Bessemer, Sir Henry* and *Biblical allusions to fire*; *Heat and Hell*; *Lamps and lighting* and *Lavoisier, Antoine Laurent*; *New-fire* and *Nuclear winter*; *Smoking (tobacco)* and *Space exploration fires*. The entries vary in length, with many several pages long. The writing is clear, accessible, and graceful. Most entries are accompanied by references to books, journals, and Web sites. Some have contact address information. There is a six-page bibliography of books related to fire, covering topics as varied as pottery making, steam engines, and medical treatment. Pages have adequate white space, readable fonts, and good use of boldface and italics to assist the reader in locating information.

Most public and academic libraries will want to own this fine resource. When a reference book is not only a straightforward accumulation of information but also an appealing browsing book even with very few pictures, one knows it is a success.

Encyclopedia of Forensic Science: A Compendium of Detective Fact and Fiction. By Barbara Gardner Conklin and others. 2002. 329p. appendix. bibliogs. illus. index. Oryx, $64.95 (1-57356-170-3). 363.25.

The *Trace evidence* entry in the *Encyclopedia of Forensic Science* states a principle of forensic science. According to French criminologist Edmond Locard, "Every contact leaves a trace." This resource is a guide to those traces and their use in the courtroom. The editorial team has collaborated on other projects, including *From Talking Drums to the Internet: An Encyclopedia of Communications Technology* (ABC-CLIO, 1997).

The book has an alphabetical arrangement, with a subject index at the end. Entries cover forensic techniques; types of crimes; famous criminal cases (*Lindbergh kidnapping and trial*, *Oklahoma City bombing*); and infamous criminals (*Bundy, Theodore*; *Jack the Ripper*; *Unabomber*). Also included are fiction writers (for example, Patricia Cornwell) and fictional characters (for example, Sherlock Holmes). Many of the entries—for example *DNA evidence*, *Hair evidence*, and *Tool marks*—describe a notable case where the evidence was key to a conviction. Each entry has a recommended reading list, including Web sites. There are a bibliography and an appendix of useful Web sites at the end of the book. Cases are primarily American, though some are British and Australian.

The *Encyclopedia of Crime and Justice* [RBB Ap 15 02] presents a broader coverage of the justice process than *Encyclopedia of Forensic Science*. For example, the index of the former source includes references to *blood alcohol level, blood feuds,* and *blood money,* but there is no entry on the evidentiary use of blood. The *Encyclopedia of Forensic Sciences* (Academic, 2000) is highly scientific. Public and academic libraries will appreciate the less scholarly but informative *Encyclopedia of Forensic Science*.

Environmental Encyclopedia. 2v. 3d ed. Ed. by Marci Bortman and others. 2002. 1,641p. bibliogs. illus. index. Gale, $275 (0-7876-5486-8). 363.7.

There are a surprisingly small number of encyclopedias covering environmental science and environmental issues. The expanded and updated edition of Gale's *Environmental Encyclopedia* does little to improve on the quality of such offerings.

Entries range from 100 to more than 2,000 words. Some are complemented by black-and-white photographs and diagrams. Each entry is signed, and topical coverage includes a broad range of environmental perspectives, including scientific, political, and social issues. Most of the entries are followed by a brief bibliography. However, these bibliographies are inconsistent, some pointing to a large number of standard and useful sources, others leading the user to an odd selection of works that do not represent comprehensive or core treatments of the issue at hand.

Additional sections include a brief (five-page) "Historical Chronology" of environmental events, a five-page chronology of "Environmental Legislation in the United States," organizations mentioned within the bibliographies accompanying encyclopedia entries, and an index to entries and terms.

The factual information presented in the encyclopedia is generally accurate, although the entries are inconsistent in their tone. That is, although the entries on more scientific topics are quite good and objectively presented, the social issue and biographical entries have a less objective, more chatty tone. In large part, this stems from an editorial perspective that often takes sides with the environmentalists. The result is a work that is not appropriate as the only source for beginning students.

There are other choices for coverage of the human and social aspects of environmental issues. *Encyclopedia of Environmental Issues* (Salem, 2000) and *Encyclopedia of Global Change: Environmental Change and Human Society* (Oxford, 2002) are useful for the high-school level and up, while *The Encyclopedia of the Environment* (Grolier, 1999) and *The Environment Encyclopedia* (Marshall Cavendish, 2001) offer attractive presentations for school and public libraries. Issue-based treatments should be supplemented by more scientifically oriented works, such as *Encyclopedia of Environmental Science* (Oryx, 2000) or *The Environment A to Z* (CQ, 2000). The present work is appropriate only for comprehensive environmental collections.

Famous First Facts about the Environment. Edited by Ronald J. Formica. 2002. 573p. indexes. H. W. Wilson, $140 (0-8242-0974-5). 363.7.

This volume is the latest in the respected Wilson Facts Series and utilizes the same formula as *Famous First Facts: A Record of First Happenings, Discoveries, and Inventions in American History* (5th ed., H. W. Wilson, 1997). Editor Formica seeks to "expand the record of important and interesting" environmental firsts and presents them in this format from a global perspective. The nearly 4,000 facts are organized into alphabetically arranged subject categories from "Activist Movements" to "Zoos, Aquariums, and Museums." Many categories contain further subcategories. For example, the subject heading "Wildlife" is divided additionally into "Breeding," "Conservation," "Control," and "Preserves and Restoration." Entries range in length from one sentence to one paragraph and are arranged chronologically within each category or subcategory. Each entry is assigned a four-digit indexing number, beginning with 1001.

Nearly one-half of the volume contains the five indexes: a subject index of topics mentioned in the entries, an index by years (through 2002), an index by month and day, an index to persons referred to in the main entries, and a geographical index. A "How to Use This Book" page begins the work and is useful to readers unfamiliar with the arrangement of other Famous First Facts books.

Although much of the information contained in this work could be located in other reference tools, the variety of environmental issues covered and the chronological presentation complement other environmental resources. This comprehensive, detail-oriented, and accessible compilation is a timesaving and valuable reference tool for environmental researchers. Academic and public libraries alike will find this a worthwhile purchase for their science reference collections.

Guns in American Society: An Encyclopedia of History, Politics, Culture, and the Law. 2v. Ed. by Gregg Lee Carter. 2003. 756p. appendixes. bibliogs. illus. index. ABC-CLIO, $185 (1-57607-268-1). 363.3.

Carter, professor of sociology at Columbia University and author of several books, including *The Gun Control Movement* (Twayne, 1997), has pulled together a fine group of 82 contributors for this title on the legal and social aspects of guns in America. The set represents an attempt to bring together research on all sides of an often murky and divisive issue. Designed for "researchers, teachers, students, public officials, law-enforcement personnel, journalists, and members of the general public," its purpose is to help the reader "become educated enough on any particular aspect of the gun issue to make an informed decision."

Entries cover a variety of information and present a wide spectrum of opinions. Biographical entries treat legal scholars on the Second Amendment, political leaders, and prominent social activists from all sides. Court cases that featured Second Amendment interpretations are described and feature summations of the pertinent issues. Historical articles, such as *Boomtowns, cowtowns, and gun violence* and *Vigilantism*, give a social context to the interaction between American culture and guns. Other articles focus on various gun makes, bullet types, and recent events, such as the Waco, Texas, raid and Columbine High School tragedy, that have driven discussion of gun policy.

Appendixes cover federal laws that have had an impact on the Second Amendment, state gun law, and organizations participating in pro-gun-control and pro-gun-rights activities. Brief entry-specific bibliographies and an extensive selected bibliography will facilitate further research for advanced students or interested citizens. A welcome resource on a topic that will continue to be debated for many years to come, this set is recommended for academic and public libraries.

Encyclopedia of Juvenile Justice. Ed. by Marilyn D. McShane and Frank P. Williams III. 2002. 416p. appendixes. bibliogs. index. Sage, $125 (0-7619-2358-6). 364.36.

This volume, edited by two criminal justice scholars, provides a comprehensive overview of juvenile justice in the U.S. Readers will find information on the history of the juvenile justice system as well as material on theories of delinquency, treatment and punishment of juvenile offenders, and the institutions and legal framework of the system.

The encyclopedia includes more than 100 alphabetically arranged entries written by more than 120 scholars and practitioners and ranging from a few paragraphs in length to several pages. Examples of specific entries include *Alcohol abuse; Gangs; Boot camps; Cambridge-Somerville Youth Study; Death penalty; Law, juvenile; Public opinion on juvenile justice issues;* and *Truancy.* Approximately 20 of the entries are biographical. In addition, the book contains articles on issues that have recently been sensationalized in the media, such as *Missing children* and *School violence.* The entries are clearly written, and many include useful historical background. Each article is signed and includes a bibliography and cross-references.

Some of the additional features detract from the overall quality of the main text. The index is too broad and has several inaccuracies. In addition, the appendix of print and online resources provides a general description and examples of juvenile justice resources such as reference books, journals, standards, and statistics instead of a more comprehensive bibliography of books and journal articles.

Despite some weaknesses, the *Encyclopedia of Juvenile Justice* is generally thorough and informative. It is particularly helpful for placing juvenile justice issues that have received a great deal of media attention into perspective and dispelling some of the myths surrounding juvenile crime. This reference work is suitable for public, academic, and law libraries.

Education, Commerce, Custom

Encyclopedia of Education. 8v. 2d ed. Ed. by James W. Guthrie. 2002. 3,357p. appendixes. bibliogs. index. Macmillan, $850 (0-02-865594-X). 370.

Though this is called the second edition of the 1971 Macmillan set, all of the articles are new. They cover policy and curriculum issues

(*Accreditation in the United States, Class size and student learning, Scheduling, Single-sex institutions*); learning (*Categorization and concept learning, Learning theory*); assessment (*General educational development test, Statewide testing*); standards (*School reform, Standards movement in American education*); history and culture (*G.I. Bill of Rights; Islam; Special education: History of*); legislation (*No Child Left Behind Act of* 2001); and profiles of organizations, schools, and people (*Gary schools; Harvard University; Military academies; Montessori, Maria*). The writing is well edited and accessible, with more than 850 signed articles from nearly the same number of experts.

Articles range from 1 to 20 pages or more. Topics that are quite broad (e.g., *Risk behaviors*) are divided into multiple sections (e.g., *Drug use among teens, Suicide, Teen pregnancy*, etc.). Such sections contain individual bibliographies. Bibliographies cite both primary and secondary literature as well as Internet resources, such as government or association sites, when appropriate.

The primary focus appears to be on U.S. practices and institutions, from preschool to higher education. However, international coverage can be found throughout the set in articles on countries or regions (Canada, South Asia), as well as within topics (e.g., "Comparing Science Education Requirements around the World" in the essay on Science Education, or Rural Education: International Context). Readers will have to look elsewhere for an overview of some subjects, such as adult education and academic libraries, for which there are no entries.

Volume 8 contains some useful appendixes as well as a detailed subject index. Appendix 1 lists assessment and achievement tests, with a summary of audience and purpose, and contact information. Next is a listing of state departments of education, followed by the large appendix 3, titled "Court Cases, Legislation, and International Agreements." These original source documents—46 in all—were deemed "essential." They include *Wisconsin v. Yoder* (1972), Morrill Land-Grant Act of 1862, and Convention on the Rights of the Child (1989). Appendixes 4, 5, and 6 list Internet resources (international and domestic), a very brief general bibliography, and an outline of contents in conceptual format, respectively.

With its wider range and in-depth treatment of topics, this new edition of the *Encyclopedia of Education* will complement more specialized education references and those with shorter entries, such as *Encyclopedia of American Education* (2d ed., Facts On File, 2001). It will be a standard in academic libraries supporting education programs.

The Encyclopedia of Learning Disabilities. By Carol Turkington and Joseph R. Harris. 2002. 304p. appendixes. bibliog. glossary. index. Facts On File, $65 (0-8160-4075-3). 371.9.

Dr. Sam Kirk coined the term *learning disabilities* in 1963. One in five children in the U.S. struggles with a learning disability, defined by law as "a severe discrepancy between potential and achievement." This book does a nice job of pulling together the terms and concepts related to a growing area of concern for parents and educators—what is a learning disability and what is not?

More than 600 alphabetically arranged entries cover conditions, means of identification, treatments, legal issues, and individuals who have made a contribution to research in the field. Examples include *Acalculia* (also known as anarithmia), the inability to do simple mathematics; *Angelman syndrome*, a childhood disorder characterized by hyperactivity; *Cylert (pemoline)*, a drug sometimes used to treat ADHD (attention deficit/hyperactivity disorder); and *Zone of proximal development* (ZPD), the gap between the level of a student's independent function and how he or she may perform learning tasks with help. Entries are complete and informative, and the language is easy to understand. Appendixes include a list of national organizations that deal with various learning disorders along with descriptions, contact information, and Web sites; sources of government information and assistance; assistive technology resources; hot lines; commercial technology resources; bulletin boards and discussion groups; and books of interest to people with learning disabilities. There are also a short glossary of terms and an up-to-date bibliography.

Overall, coverage is excellent, and there seems to be little else available that is as current, complete, and easy to use. Recommended for public and academic libraries.

Higher Education in the United States: An Encyclopedia. 2v. Ed. by James J. F. Forest and Kevin Kinser. 2002. 831p. appendixes. bibliogs. illus. index. ABC-CLIO, $185 (1-57607-248-7). 378.73.

With the recent changes in U.S. higher education, a new encyclopedia is welcome. These volumes provide articles on higher-education history (particularly since 1945) and trends, contributed by almost 200 university scholars and other experts in the field. Authors were suggested by the editors' advisory board and by colleagues in the Association for the Study of Higher Education and the American Educational Research Association.

Alphabetically arranged, the articles range in length from a page to more than a dozen pages (e.g., *History of higher education in the United States*). Most entries are several pages long; a few black-and-white photographs provide visual relief from the text. In general, articles include an overview of the topic, historical or social context, and current issues. The historical perspective usually extends back at least to the beginning of the twentieth century, and in most cases treatment of current issues is very up-to-date. However, the article on academic freedom shies from some current concerns, such as intellectual property. The number of contributors results in some unevenness, as in the articles that address topics such as *Affirmative action, Asian Americans in higher education, Multiculturalism*, and *Native American studies*, some of which tend to advocate for a particular view rather than present a balanced picture. In some cases, large overlaps occur.

Writing is usually straightforward; happily, "educationese" seems to have been avoided. Cross-references help the reader find more information on related topics. This feature is particularly useful because some article headings, such as *Theories of research in higher education*, are not obvious choices. Appendixes provide a survey of "Important Books about Higher Education" and a chronology of important events. These are followed by an extensive bibliography and a detailed index.

Generally, this set provides a useful introduction to the world of higher education. Indeed, beginning faculty would do well to delve into this reference book to help them navigate higher-education waters. College students will also derive a clearer picture of the "underbelly" of institutions of higher education and their driving forces. Recommended for public and academic libraries.

Women in Higher Education: An Encyclopedia. Ed. by Ana M. Martinez Aleman and Kristen A. Renn. 2002. 637p. appendixes. bibliogs. illus. index. ABC-CLIO, $85 (1-57607-614-8). 378.1.

Researchers looking for a feminist slant in the reference literature on education will find it here. Designed for scholars, students, and "first-time inquirers," this volume aims to record "the knowledge gained from a half-century of intensive research relating to women in higher education." Instead of the strictly A–Z arrangement found in most resources described as encyclopedias, a "selective compilation" of entries is arranged under nine broad categories, including "Historical and Cultural Contexts," "Feminism in the Academy," and "Women Administrators." Within these categories, individual entries address topics such as *Military colleges, Sexual harassment, Medical education, Title IX, Black sororities, Lesbian faculty*, and *Leadership in Catholic institutions*.

Each section begins with an overview, followed by from 2 to more than 30 entries that are the work of more than 120 academic contributors. Length varies from two pages for *Black women's colleges* and *Sexual assault*, among others, to nine pages for *Psychology of sex differences*, with three or four pages being the norm. Each entry includes a list of references, some of them quite extensive. In some cases there are *see also* references to entries that are related. Following the encyclopedia portion of the book are an essay on women's studies resources and a list of institutions that identify themselves as women's colleges. A 38-page bibliography and a detailed index complete the book.

The "explicitly feminist approach" sets this volume apart from works such as *Encyclopedia of Education* (2d ed., Macmillan, 2003) and makes it worth considering for education and women's studies collections in academic libraries.

World Consumer Lifestyles Databook: Key Trends. 2002. 470p. bibliog. maps. tables. Euromonitor, 122 S. Michigan Ave., Ste. 1200, Chicago, IL 60603, paper, $1,090 (1-84264-140-9). 380.1.

Founded in 1972, Euromonitor is a leading international publisher of marketing information. This new collection of statistical data, presented in tables, features detailed statistics on the lifestyles of consumers in 71 countries. Consumers are grouped by their income; household profiles; eating, drinking, and smoking habits; home ownership; and education. The three main sections are "Rankings," "Cross-Country Comparisons," and "Country Data." The comparative world rankings and cross-country sections present standardized data for all 71 countries, and the country-specific section covers the data in greater detail. Coverage is generally for 1990 to 2000, and tables often display the full 11-year time-series to enable the monitoring of trends.

Section 1 contains maps of the countries arranged by region: Europe, Americas, Asia and Australasia, and the Middle East and Africa. Section 2 is a series of unique rankings showing the position of each country as measured by a variety of criteria. The cross-country data in the third section provide a standardized, comparable overview of lifestyle data for all countries. Units are in terms of percentages, U.S. dollars, and per capita figures for easy comparisons. Section 4, the country-specific data, is a detailed analysis of consumer lifestyles for each country. The last section is a list of sources for the marketing information with current contact details and a brief description of data available from these organizations. Examples of the sectors covered in both the cross-country and country-specific sections include home ownership, savings and investment, eating habits, leisure habits, personal care and clothing, transport, tourism, and crime.

Focusing on people rather than products, this reliable, quick reference is updated by a team of researchers with extensive country-specific knowledge. Business collections serving students, corporations, researchers, and small to medium-sized businesses will see this data book used frequently.

Gale E-Commerce Sourcebook. Ed. by Deborah J. Baker. 2002. 970p. index. Gale, $195 (0-7876-5750-6). 384.4.

The *Gale E-Commerce Sourcebook* strives to fill a need for a comprehensive reference providing detailed directory information, resource contact data, practical knowledge, and "how to" topics for students, entrepreneurs, researchers, and faculty as well as interested laypersons and consumers. An introductory essay presents a brief history of the Internet and e-commerce. Following the essay, the alphabetically arranged section "'How To' Topics in E-Commerce" discusses 100 topics like authoring software, business-to-government (B2G) e-commerce, data integrity, digital authentication, network topologies, performance metrics, and voice commerce. Each article is generally one to four pages long, includes trends or outlooks where appropriate, and always concludes with a short further reading list of print and electronic references. The articles are reprinted from journals, Web sites, and other sources.

The directory section, also arranged alphabetically, covers more than 4,700 associations, consultants, educational programs, publications, trade shows, and Web site designers and hosting companies. Entries include name, contact name, address, phone, toll-free and fax numbers, e-mail and URL addresses, and brief descriptions of purpose and services as well as descriptive information such as number of employees, date founded, publications, and awards. Leading e-commerce companies are also profiled with ranking by revenue and number of employees. An index at the end of volume 2 provides more access points to users. The index is explained in the "Preface and User's Guide" in volume 1; it would be helpful to have the explanation repeated at the start of the index in volume 2.

Readers will better understand the e-commerce big picture after consulting this valuable tool. Public, academic, and special libraries will want to add this unique resource to their business reference collections.

★**South Asian Folklore:** An Encyclopedia. Ed. by Margaret A. Mills and others. 2002. 710p. bibliogs. illus. index. Routledge, $175 (0-415-93919-4). 398.

Edited by three well-known folklore scholars, *South Asian Folklore* contains about 500 entries on the local traditions of Afghanistan, Bangladesh, India, Nepal, Pakistan, and Sri Lanka. The editors point out that cultural production is not bound by modern political boundaries and acknowledge that, because of the size of the region and the uneven nature of prior research, the work presents only a "suggestive sample of the huge range of South Asian cultural practices and production." These limitations notwithstanding, there is an impressive wealth of information here, the work of more than 250 contributors. Entries on the architecture of Afghanistan, bangles as symbols of status and ethnic identity, traditional carpet weaving, the caste system in India and Nepal, the ritual practice of firewalking in Sri Lanka, Hindu goddesses, the Indian classical dance called Kathakali, the Tibetan hero Kesar, and the uses of turmeric as a sacred plant are just a few examples. Although there are some entries related to music, such as *Film music* and *Women's songs*, detailed articles on folk music were omitted because *The Garland Encyclopedia of World Music* devotes one volume to South Asia.

Most of the alphabetically arranged articles are divided into two categories: general concept articles and case study articles. The former recognizes topics that are applicable to the entire region and provides an overview of a topic (e.g., *Folk art*, *Pilgrimage*, *Pottery*, *Puberty rituals*). Generally two or three pages long, these articles are intended to pique the reader's interest and provide *see also* references to the more detailed case study articles. Usually shorter, the case study articles focus on one specific topic (e.g., *Bhakti saints*, *Jain folklore*, *Jihad poetry*). Geographic (*Bangladesh*, *Gujarat*); definitional (*Bhand pathar*, a form of Kashmiri theater; *Panch Pir*, five Sufi saints venerated by South Asian Muslims); and biographical (*Tagore*, *Rabindranath*) entries are also included. Each article concludes with bibliographic references. Though there is no classified contents list, the index helps the reader pull together all the information related to a specific place or activity. Index entries that are also main entry headings are indicated in bold type. Black-and-white illustrations, though few in number, are well chosen.

This fine book provides a readable introduction to topics that are often neglected by Western study. In recent years there has been an increase in scholarship on the folklore of the region, but until now there have been no encyclopedic overviews. Although this area of the world receives some coverage in publications with an international focus, such as *Folklore: An Encyclopedia of Beliefs, Customs, Tales, Music and Art* (ABC-CLIO, 1997), more general works cannot, obviously, give the same depth of study as this single volume. With its thorough scholarship and unique coverage, *South Asian Folklore* is recommended for large public and academic libraries.

Language

The American Heritage Dictionary for Learners of English. 2002. 999p. Houghton, $24 (0-618-24951-6). 423.

The American Heritage Thesaurus for Learners of English. 2002. 326p. Houghton, $18 (0-618-12990-1). 428.1.

Together, these two volumes provide an excellent language resource for the intended audience of learners of English as a second language.

The dictionary, a revised edition of *The American Heritage English as a Secondary Language Dictionary* (1998), is adapted from the *American Heritage Dictionary of the English Language* (4th ed., 2000) and defines more than 40,000 words, among them newer terms such as ATM, Internet, and on-line. Reasonably portable, it includes homonyms such as *rote* and *wrote*, which often confuse ESL speakers. Synonyms are also provided, with degrees of emphasis added. For example, synonyms for *anger* include *rage* and *fury*, with explanations as to their usage. Definitions for common idiomatic phrases such as *here you go* and *look alive* provide additional value, as do word-building lessons such as the ones on *neo-* and *–oid*, explaining how word parts are attached to existing words (e.g., *neoclassicism*, *humanoid*). *Somebody* and *something* are strangely abbreviated as *sbdy* and *sthg*, a space-saving measure that will only serve to further confuse ESL learners, who are already confused enough. New to the revised edition is a reference section containing basic grammar, forms of address, U.S. states and capitals, and a few other items.

The thesaurus provides more than 6,000 synonyms. The list of synonyms for any given word lacks the depth and breadth of word choice provided by a standard thesaurus such as *The Oxford American Thesaurus of Current English* (1999), with 350,000 synonyms. However, unlike a standard thesaurus, the synonyms are not just listed but defined and also used in sample sentences. Two bonus features are a section on irregular English verbs and a section on idiomatic use of prepositions such as *attest to*, *estranged from*, and *proficient at*. Both works are done in an extremely readable larger font with plenty of white space. They are recommended for libraries serving ESL communities.

The Firefly Visual Dictionary. By Jean-Claude Corbeil and Ariane Archambault. 2002. 952p. illus. index. Firefly, $49.95 (1-55297-585-1). 423.

A picture is sometimes worth a thousand words, and this bulky visual dictionary is definitely designed with that premise firmly in mind. Approximately 6,000 entries, containing a total of 35,000 terms, cover everything from cheetahs to heat pumps. Seventeen broad subject classifications from "Astronomy" to "Sports and Games" aid users in finding the illustrations they are seeking. The sections are color coded and can be easily located by looking at the side of the volume, though a detailed table of contents gives equally good access. The full-color computer-generated illustrations, though they have a bit of a homogenized look, are admirably clear and vary in size from a full page to two square inches. The small type used for labeling may pose problems for some readers, but upper-elementary, middle-, and high-school students should find reading the terms unproblematic, and the arrows pointing to the items labeled are clearly and unequivocally placed.

An excellent teaching or browsing book, this is a fine extension of the authors' earlier *The Facts On File Junior Visual Dictionary* (Facts On File, 1989), including many items not in the previous, smaller work as well as updating and extending pictures related to technology. A caveat may be in order: upper-elementary students could find pictures of women's undergarments and the cross sections of the human reproductive system unduly engrossing. Regardless, this thoroughly indexed, attractive volume is certainly a good addition to public and school library collections.

The McGraw-Hill Children's Dictionary. By the Wordsmyth Collaboratory. 2003. 830p. illus. index. maps. McGraw-Hill Children's, $24.95 (1-57768-298-X). 423.

This hefty dictionary is targeted at the students in elementary through middle school. The more than 30,000 entries are easy to read, with definitions arranged in three columns. "Word History," "Homophone Note," and "Synonyms" boxes give extra information about some words. Frequent small photographs and drawings (one to two per page on average) illustrate some definitions and add to the appealing look. An alphabet strip runs down the outer edge of each page, allowing for easy location of each section. Large, easy-to-read guide words are placed in a blue strip at the top of each page, while entry words, broken into syllables, are clearly denoted in bold, with the definitions slightly indented. Part of speech, in red italics, follows the word directly, and the pronunciation is situated at the end of the entry. There are no usage labels, but British and Canadian spellings are included. Each alphabetic section begins with a colored box that gives pronunciation information and a list of hard-to-spell words.

A series of icons is located at the bottom of each page. These stand for broad topics such as "Human Body" and "Natural Environment." When one of these icons is located in a definition, it refers the student to the "Lexipedia Word Explorer" at the back of the dictionary. Here all words pertaining to a given topic area are grouped together, providing cross-referencing to related terms. Full-page and double-page colored sections address a plethora of popular topics, such as dinosaurs, stars, and money. A "How to Use" section at the front of the dictionary, which lays out in detail all the features mentioned above, is followed by a brief history of the English language, a pronunciation key, and a sound and spelling guide. The reference section that concludes the volume contains a world history time line; a section on "Symbolic Communication" (road signs, Braille, etc.); a mini world atlas; pictures of flags of the world; lists of U.S. presidents and Canadian prime ministers; facts about U.S states and Canadian provinces; and weights and measures.

Picture placement is sometimes problematic. For example, a photo of a tree placed between *lofty* and *log* could refer to either one and does a good job of illustrating neither. While the cartoons used to illustrate words with several distinct meanings are helpful in some instances, a few of the more tortured sentences (for example: "At the Silly Things Bowl, Martin bowls a strike with a ceramic bowl") may be more confusing than not.

With the exception of these caveats, this attractive dictionary is a fine work, suitable for use in school and public libraries.

Microsoft Encarta College Thesaurus. Ed. by Susan Jellis. 2001. 1,166p. St. Martin's, $21.95 (0-312-28906-5). 423.

This companion to the *Microsoft Encarta College Dictionary* [RBB N 15 01] has 40,000 alphabetically arranged entries with 350,000 synonyms and antonyms. *Microsoft Encarta* combines both an A–Z and a thematic approach; most other thesauruses use one or the other.

In addition to single words the alphabetic section contains phrases like *full of beans* and *walk a tightrope*. Interspersed between the entries are "Compare and Contrast" boxes that explain nuances in meaning. There are also boxes for lists of types or parts—types of sports, parts of an engine. Advertised as up-to-date with terms for technology, science, and business, the thesaurus even includes words that are not in the *College Dictionary*, such as *cybermarketing*. Other current words with synonyms are *extreme sport*, MBO (*management buyout*), and *superstore*.

The alphabetic section serves as an index to the thematic section, and the editor has done a good job of linking the two. The thematic section groups more than 50,000 related words under 1,279 topics. Many of the numbered entries begin with a quotation. (Garry Trudeau on lifestyle: "I'sve been trying for some time now to develop a lifestyle that doesn't require my presence.") The lack of a guide to the abbreviations (for example: n, adj. v., UK) that are used throughout the volume is a slight drawback. Another is that since the vocabulary is derived from the British Bloomsbury Database of World English, some British words and meanings like *signboard* (billboard) and *tailback* (traffic jam) are included.

Since the *Microsoft College Encarta Thesaurus* is based on the Synonym Finder in Microsoft Office 2000 and has the familiar ("well-known, recognizable, common") words *Microsoft* and *Encarta* in the title, it will be a popular resource for high-school and college students. It is an excellent choice for libraries or individuals that need a current thesaurus that reflects today's culture.

Shorter Oxford English Dictionary. 2v. 5th ed. 2002. 3,750p. index. Oxford, $150 (0-19-860575-7). 423.

Considering it was 20 years between the third and fourth editions of this work, this "abridgement" of Oxford's flagship OED after fewer than 10 years is most welcome. Given some of the advance publicity and advertisements, Oxford is clearly aware that to win in the dictionary wars (at least in the eyes of the general public), it is necessary to emphasize newer words added to the dictionary. The general coverage of the volumes remains largely unchanged from the fourth edition, however, even retaining the previous edition's preface and adding a briefer preface for the current edition. Still, some welcome changes have been made.

Like the previous edition, this work "sets out the main meanings and semantic developments of words current at any time between 1700 and the present day." Words such as *achtande*, *knottle*, or *pompal* (all present in OED *Online*) that are obsolete, obsolete variations, or rare are therefore not included. Words obsolete by 1700 are still included, however, if used by authors such as Shakespeare or other "influential literary sources." Headwords are traced back to their earliest usage. The dust jacket from the work claims it has "more than one third of the coverage of the OED" and more than half a million definitions, with 83,500 illustrative quotations from 7,000 authors. Although the preface does not cite the number of new entries, publicity from Oxford states that 3,500 new words have been added to this edition. An actual headword count is not given, though the publisher's Web site puts the number at 97,600.

The most welcome change to this edition is that the text is much easier on the eyes than in the fourth edition. Most notably, the illustrative quotations are placed within a tinted text box, making them very easy to spot. In the main entries, each definition sense is now started on a new line in clear, bold numbers (the older edition had all the senses grouped together in one paragraph), and etymologies are spelled out, with *Old English* or *Middle Low German* replacing the fourth edition's OE or MLG, respectively. Addressing a criticism RBB had of the fourth edition, abbreviations are now within regular alphabetical order rather than placed at the beginning of the alphabet.

Unfortunately, one thing the *Shorter* OED has not changed is its tradition of abbreviating dates of first use—and, when needed, of last use—for a headword (L19 for late-nineteenth century, M20 for mid–twentieth century). Because even collegiate dictionaries now routinely spell out a date range for first use, it is time Oxford adopted a similar approach. It would also be useful to attach a date to the illustrative quotations used rather than just citing the author.

With both OED *Online* and the print *Oxford English Dictionary* too expensive for many libraries, this is a reasonably priced work that includes the requisite neologisms (*Bollywood*, *full monty*, and *phat*, among others) to make it a *goof-proof* purchase for all libraries, even those owning the parent work. The *Shorter* OED has some entries (*Jedi*, *Klingon*, and *warp drive*) that are not even included in OED *Online*. In short, this is one *badass* dictionary deserving a place in almost every library.

The Oxford Dictionary of Word Histories: The Life Stories of over 12,000 Words. Ed. by Glynnis Chantrell. 2002. 560p. Oxford, $35 (0-19-863121-9). 422.

Dictionaries of etymology and word histories differ greatly in what is increasingly being called "accessibility" or "user-friendliness." This new work from Oxford, which provides the histories of more than 12,000 words, is definitely on the accessible side. Virtually all of the words are common, "everyday" words—core words—with only a handful of the exotics to which editors of other collections of word histories are drawn. Chantrell discusses the words straightforwardly and with a bit more vivacity than might be expected. In addition, her information is undoubtedly fresher than anyone else's, drawn as it is from the database of ongoing research for the Oxford English Dictionary.

Each entry includes the date of first recorded use and a brief discussion of the term's origin and evolution. Prefixes are treated in boxed "Wordbuilding" features. A distinct gesture of friendliness on Chantrell's part is her decision to spell out words that would ordinarily be abbreviated in scholarly works and even in some nonscholarly dictionaries. T. F. Hoad's Concise Oxford Dictionary of English Etymology (Oxford, 1993), perhaps the most accessible of the scholarly choices, is prefaced by a list of almost 400 abbreviations, the use of which no doubt contributed substantially to its conciseness. In another nod to user-friendliness, many of the words abbreviated in Hoad—*ablative, substantival, indeclinable, frequentative,* and so on—are not to be found in Chantrell's word histories.

Still, within the zone of popular word histories, Chantrell sets herself against several formidable and well-established competitors, among them John Ciardi's *Good Words to You: An All-New Dictionary and Native's Guide to the Unknown American Language* (Harper, 1987), John Ayto's *Dictionary of Word Origins* (Arcade, 1993), and Adrian Room's *A Dictionary of True Etymologies* (Routledge, 1986). The *Oxford Dictionary of Word Histories* is recommended for libraries that need to freshen or expand their collection of word history resources.

Science

Life on Earth: An Encyclopedia of Biodiversity, Ecology, and Evolution. 2v. Ed. by Niles Eldredge. 2002. 793p. bibliogs. illus. index. ABC-CLIO, $185 (1-57607-286-X). 333.95.

Life on Earth is intended to introduce "younger generations" to biological diversity, "the variety of life on Earth at all its levels, from genes to biogeographic regions, and the ecological and evolutionary processes that sustain it." The encyclopedia's activist perspective and conversational style will appeal to high-school and beginning college students, especially those writing position papers. Eldredge is curator of paleontology at the American Museum of Natural History (AMNH), and a number of the 60 contributors are AMNH scientists. Most other contributors are associated with major universities and research institutions in the U.S.

Four introductory essays outline the definition, importance, and preservation of biodiversity. Many of the 194 articles are about specific phyla or species (*Annelida—the segmented worm, Giant ground sloth, Lagomorpha*) or important concepts (*Botany, Human evolution, Meteorology, Soil*). Others address issues that will appeal to students and general readers (*Ethics of conservation; Medicine, the benefits of biodiversity to; Tourism, ecotourism, and biodiversity*). Essays and articles incorporate many tables with sources cited, line drawings, and unremarkable black-and-white photographs. Articles are clearly written, usually define specialized terms, and include bibliographies of books and popular and scholarly periodical articles. An index leads readers to topics mentioned within articles (e.g., *deep ecology, ecofeminism, urban sprawl*). Rachel Carson is listed in the index as *Louise Carson*.

The five-volume *Encyclopedia of Biodiversity* (Academic Press, 2001) set the standard for academic reference works on biodiversity. *Life on Earth* is an alternate choice for high-school or smaller college and public libraries that cannot afford *Encyclopedia of Biodiversity* or need a more accessible source.

Science of Everyday Things: Volume 3: Real-Life Biology. Ed. by Neil Schlager. bibliogs. glossaries. illus. index. 2002. 430p. Gale, $85 (0-7876-5634-8). 500.

Science of Everyday Things: Volume 4: Real-Life Earth Science. Ed. by Neil Schlager. bibliogs. glossaries. illus. indexes. 2002. 507p. Gale, $85 (0-7876-5635-6). 500.

The first two volumes of this series are *Real-Life Chemistry* and *Real-Life Physics*, released in 2001. The purpose of the series is to explain scientific phenomena using common real-world examples. *Real-Life Biology* and *Real-Life Earth Science* each have about 40 entries covering various scientific phenomena and principles. Information in each entry includes "Concept" (defines the scientific principle or theory), "How It Works," "Real-Life Applications," and "Where to Learn More." A "Key Terms" section defines terms from the text. Examples of topics covered in *Real-Life Biology* include biochemistry, nutrition, reproduction and birth, immunity, infection, and the biosphere and ecosystems; topics from *Real-Life Earth Science* include study of the earth, geology, geomorphology, soil science, geochemistry, and meteorology. Under "Real-Life Applications" we can learn about the fate of the dodo bird (under *Species*); working the night shift (under *Biological rhythms*); the greenhouse effect (under *Ecosystems and ecology*); mass extinction (under *Paleontology*); and the 1812 New Madrid, Missouri, earthquake (under *Seismology*).

Entries, written at a level accessible to high-school students and the general reader, average about 10 pages in length. The "Where to Learn More" section provides about 10 books and Web sites for further information. Black-and-white line drawings and photographs supplement the text. There are no color illustrations. An index offers subject access to the contents of each volume; in addition, there is a cumulative subject index of all 4 volumes. The basic facts provided in these books are available elsewhere, but the "Real-Life Applications" may be interesting to some. Recommended for high-school and public libraries.

Space Sciences. 4v. Ed. by Pat Dasch. 2002. 1,057p. bibliogs. glossary. illus. indexes. Macmillan, $395 (0-02-865546-X). 500.5.

In this wonderful encyclopedia designed for middle-and high-school students, 341 entries explore the wonders of space. Each volume has a theme. *Space Business* (volume 1) covers topics such as *Communications satellite industry, Law of space,* and *Space tourism. Planetary Science and Astronomy* (volume 2) covers the more scientific aspects, including planetary explorations. *Humans in Space* (volume 3) treats manned missions and various astronauts, and *Our Future in Space* has entries for topics such as *Asteroid mining, Mars bases,* and *Military uses of space*. The entries in each volume are in alphabetical order and range from a single paragraph to several pages in length, with most being one or two pages long.

The front and back matter are the same in each volume and include a few pages of reference tables such as conversion charts, time lines of milestones in space history and human achievements in space, a list of contributors, a table of contents for the set, and a glossary. Volume 1 has a unique time line of "Major Business Milestones in U.S. History." The index in the first three volumes is specific to the volume only, and there is a cumulative index in volume 4.

Numerous sidebars provide additional information throughout the set. Words that appear in bold type in the entry are defined in the page margins and also in the glossary. The color illustrations and photographs are beautifully reproduced and appear on almost every two-page spread. Additionally, there are smaller portraits and black-and-white illustrations. Almost every person mentioned has a portrait somewhere in the set.

The entries are well written and should be easily understood by the target audience of YA students. The breadth and depth of information will fascinate students and be very helpful in preparing reports and projects on a wide variety of space-related topics. School and public libraries should eagerly add this set to their collections.

Chronology of Science. Ed. by Lisa Rosner. 2002. 566p. appendixes. bibliog. glossary. illus. index. ABC-CLIO, $85(1-57607-954-6). 502.

The material in this chronology is arranged by five time periods: "Earliest Discoveries," "The Medieval World," "The Scientific Revolution," "The Industrializing World," and "The Twentieth Century." These chapters are also divided into shorter time periods, then by scientific disciplines in alphabetical order, from astronomy to physics. (Some users may have preferred having the book arranged first by scientific disciplines, with a separate time line for each discipline.). There are 16 feature essays placed throughout the text in appropriate time periods. Some examples are "The Origins of Mathematics," "Pioneering Experiments on the Digestive System," and "The History of Plastics."

Each section has an introduction that summarizes the important discoveries and concepts of each discipline by era. Entries are usually two to three sentences long, and many have longer explanations of the concept. The diagrams and illustrations are abundant and very helpful. The longer essays give interesting histories of concepts and discoveries. Every page has a guide tab at the top that lists the discipline and the time period on that page.

Following the chronological portion are brief biographies. Not every scientist mentioned in the text is included in the biography section. The bibliography, which is divided by discipline and annotated, lists many Web sites. The glossary is quite extensive and has some detailed entries (*atom, cell*). Of special interest to many high-school chemistry programs is the list of elements with their discovery dates, names of scientists who discovered them, and uses.

The text is well written and enjoyable to read, especially the longer essays. The 20 contributors succeed in making some of the most difficult concepts understandable to the layperson. This is originally a British publication, and though it retains British spelling, coverage is more universal than American publications tend to be. More up-to-date than *Asimov's Chronology of Science and Technology* (HarperCollins, 1994), this volume is a wonderful chronology to add to most high-school, academic, and public libraries.

The American Heritage Student Science Dictionary. 2002. 376p. illus. Houghton, $18 (0-618-18919-X). 503.

This attractive volume was designed to help users in grades seven and up understand the important concepts of science. In an accessible manner that does not talk down to users, the 4,500 entries provide pronunciation, part of speech, and definition, with enough detail to explain the scientific meaning and relevance of each term. Entries may also include irregular plurals, run-ons, and other forms, and cross-references that direct the user to other entries for more information or for purposes of comparison.

Although easy enough for a fifth-grader to use, the work provides more than just a simple definition of an elusive term. It also offers sidebars entitled "Did You Know?" which clarify 100 important terms, such as *plate tectonics*. In a conversational tone, these "Did You Know?" features challenge readers to use their observation skills or own experiences to understand the scientific concepts. "A Closer Look" examines a dozen topics in even more detail. For example, *Leaf* has a useful illustration that helps users understand (and see) the difference between monocotyledon and dicotyledon leaves. Additional boxed features called "Usage " and "Word History" also add to the user's understanding. (For example, the "Usage" box on *infectious/communicable/contagious* helps to clarify what the three terms mean in relation to each other.)

Another welcome feature are the 300 biographical entries, which identify men and women from around the world who have made a contribution to science. These short entries include birth and death dates, nationality, and importance and often have a photograph or illustration. Some 20 individuals are treated in longer biography sidebars. The biographies would be especially helpful for small libraries that have a limited range of reference materials for children in science.

More than 400 full-color illustrations and photographs as well as graphics, charts, and tables enhance the text. The typeface, the amount of white space, and the overall design of this work will appeal to students who might be intimidated by larger scientific dictionaries. Overall, this is an excellent addition to school and public libraries.

McGraw-Hill Dictionary of Scientific and Technical Terms. 6th ed. 2002. 2,380p. appendix. illus. McGraw-Hill, $150 (0-07-042313-X). 503.

It has been 30 years since the first edition of this encyclopedia was published. Over this span of time, the terminology in science and technology has expanded at a rapid rate, resulting in the addition of some 5,000 new terms in each edition. The sixth edition continues that expansion and now has some 110,000 terms and 125,000 definitions, accompanied by 3,000 black-and-white illustrations. The format continues as in the past, with letter-by-letter alphabetization. Synonyms, acronyms, and abbreviations are given within the definition. Pronunciation of each and every term continues to set this dictionary apart from other science and technology dictionaries. It is a large, heavy volume that lies flat when open. It may be time for the publisher to consider a two-volume work for ease of handling by the patron.

Each entry is classed into one or more of 104 fields, from "Acoustics" to "Zoology," for which abbreviations are inserted in the definitions. These fields have been revised to reflect modern usage with some new ones added, including "Forensic Science" and "Neuroscience." A detailed scope note for each field is included near the front of the dictionary. The 3,000 illustrations are in the outside margin of each page near the appropriate term and are crisp and clear. One change that would be useful in future editions is referring the reader to the appendix when appropriate. *Periodic table* is defined in the main part of the dictionary but there is no reference to the periodic table in the appendix, which would be missed if one did not browse through the back matter. Among other items in the appendix are information on measurements systems, mathematical signs and symbols, and very brief biographies of Nobel laureates and individuals after whom scientific terms are named.

This continues to be the most comprehensive science and technology dictionary for the student, researcher, and layperson. It is recommended for most libraries.

Van Nostrand's Concise Encyclopedia of Science. Ed. by Christopher G. DePree and Alan Axelrod. 2003. 821p. illus. Wiley, $40 (0-471-36331-6). 503.

This desk reference is based on the new two-volume, ninth edition of *Van Nostrand's Scientific Encyclopedia* (Wiley, 2002). Written at a level accessible to the general reader, the alphabetically arranged entries range in length from about a sentence to a page. The 5,000 entries cover physics, chemistry, earth sciences, space sciences, life sciences, energy, environmental sciences, materials sciences, and information sciences. Sample entries include *Arachnida, Bubonic plague, Celery, Constellations, Direct-current circuits, Gravitation, Green flash, Kohoutek (comet), Laser, Phenol, Sidereal day, Silurian period, Television* (TV), and *Units and standards*.

For the abbreviated encyclopedia, some entries were reduced in length and others were omitted. There is an entry for *Mercury (planet)* but none for mercury, the chemical element; unless they have "significant biological or industrial importance," the elements are covered in the entry *Chemical elements* instead of having entries of their own. There are no entries for popular topics such as human cloning, red tide, and the Internet. There are a few cross-references, but more would be useful. For example, there is no *see also* reference from *Periodic table of the elements* to *Chemical elements*. Scattered black-and-white line drawings and photographs supplement the text.

This desk encyclopedia is recommended for high-school and public libraries in need of a compact, up-to-date, relatively inexpensive science reference source.

A to Z of STS Scientists. Elizabeth H. Oakes. 2002. 372p. bibliog. illus. index. Facts On File, $45 (0-8160-4606-9). 509.2.

This source's title shares a difficulty with some other Facts On File books. Online catalogs use A as a stop word, so the book will not show up on a title search in an online catalog even if a library owns it. The second problem with the title is the use of STS, which stands for the interdisciplinary field of Science, Technology, and Society (covered in the *Facts On File Encyclopedia of Science, Technology, and Society* [1999]) but is not an acronym that will be familiar to all readers.

Those difficulties aside, this is a useful reference source. In text written at a level appropriate for high-school students or undergraduates, it chronicles 208 men and women scientists and inventors, both recent and historical, whose scientific or technological achievements have had a major impact on society. Entries are about 1,000 words each and list nationalities, dates, and discipline and describe the experiences and contribution of the featured scientists and inventors. Some, but not all, entries contain photographs or portraits of the notable person. Cross-references are indicated in small capitals. Entries do not have bibliographies for further reading.

Some of the biographies are for well-known people (Rachel Carson, Charles Darwin, Joseph Lister, J. Robert Oppenheimer); others are for less-well-known individuals. Reflecting the multidisciplinary nature of the STS field, coverage is diverse, extending to explorers Ferdinand Magellan and Marco Polo and pottery manufacturer Josiah Spode. Controversies, such as that between Steven Jobs and John Sculley at Apple Computer, or Rosalind Franklin and the discovery of DNA, are presented with balance. Some of the choices seem unusual. For instance, Paul Allen, cofounder of Microsoft, is covered, but Bill Gates, the other cofounder, is not. The writing is clear and nontechnical and includes personal experiences. Appendixes include a chronology and lists of entries by year of birth, country of birth, country of major scientific activity, and field of study. This title will be a useful addition to science biographical collections of both smaller and larger high-school, academic, and public libraries.

★**History of Modern Science and Mathematics.** 4v. Ed. by Brian S. Baigrie. 2002. 1,040p. bibliogs. illus. indexes. Scribner, $350 (0-684-80636-3). 509.

Baigrie, associate professor at the Institute for History and Philosophy of Science and Technology at the University of Toronto, has created a very useful reference source. *Modern science* is defined as post-Copernican, but the thematic coverage of 23 scientific disciplines includes their global historical origins. For example, the history of algebra encompasses Babylonian, Chinese, and Islamic along with the familiar Greek mathematics. Emphasis is on the natural rather than the applied sciences.

This attractive set first presents topical essays, such as "The Relationship Between History of Science and Science" and "What Is a Proof?" followed by overview essays on biology, mathematics, and physics. Histories of the specific disciplines, from "Algebra" to "Systematics," average about 35 pages in length. The longest is "Chemistry," at 95 pages, and the shortest is "Algebra," with 19 pages. Volume 4 concludes with an "Interdisciplinary Timeline" and a name and subject index. The name and subject indexing is very solid. The bibliographies at the end of each essay contain mostly books, but Web sites are also mentioned. The coverage in the bibliographies is impressive. For example, the bibliography after the overview essay on physics includes works by Albert Einstein and J. Robert Oppenheimer.

The audience for this resource includes advanced high-school students, undergraduates, and general readers. Although some articles, such as "Atomic and Nuclear Physics" and "Calculus," assume prior knowledge, the essays are carefully written to present technical subjects in jargon-free terms. The text is broken up with sidebars, illustrations, graphs, and charts. The use of bold type refers readers to definitions or cross-references in the margins. Sidebars add biographies or information related to scientific instruments, practices, or methods; institutions; connections between science and society; and other topics. Examples include "Scientific Institutions: The Smithsonian and the Practice of Anthropology," in "Anthropology," and "Science and Society: Endangered Species Act, 1973," in "Ecology."

The *History of Modern Science and Mathematics* will find a home in the reference collection on the history of science. Its topical essays nicely complement the dictionary format of the *A Dictionary of the History of Science* (Parthenon, 2001), and it has broader coverage in both time and place than recent one-volume history of science encyclopedias, such as *Encyclopedia of the Scientific Revolution* (Garland, 2000), *The History of Science in the United States: An Encyclopedia* (Garland, 2001), or *The Scientific Revolution: An Encyclopedia* [RBB Mr 1 02]. Highly recommended for high-school, public, and university libraries.

History of Science. 10v. 2003. 800p. bibliogs. glossaries. illus. index. Grolier, $279 (0-7172-5729-0). 509.

This set presents readers in grades six and up with information surveying the study of science through the ages. Each volume discusses a specific time period, region, or area of science. Arrangement is, for the most part, chronological. Volumes 1 through 6 cover science history beginning with the ancient Egyptians and ending with the eighteenth century. There is good coverage of the science of Islam, and volume 3 is devoted to science in China, India, Mesoamerica, and other regions. The nineteenth and twentieth centuries are treated in two volumes each, one covering physical sciences and the other covering life sciences.

Each volume contains 20 well-written topic entries, each covering a region, a branch of science, or a significant concept, discovery, or development. These entries range in length from two to five pages and contain numerous charts, graphs, and illustrations in an appealing layout. Brief biographical outlines for various scientific figures are included where appropriate. Words underlined in the text are defined in the volume-specific glossary. Each volume also contains a table of contents, a time line for the period being covered, resources for further study, and a set index.

A comprehensive glossary, pronunciation guides, cross-references, and volume-specific indexes would have made the set more accessible. Still, these volumes provide a general introduction to many topics in a single source and would appeal to students and browsers alike. Public and school libraries needing science history reference materials for the middle-school level and up will find this purchase suitable.

The Nobel Scientists: A Biographical Encyclopedia. By George Thomas Kurian. 2002. 420p. bibliogs. indexes. Prometheus, $75 (1-57392-927-1). 509.2.

The Nobel Prize was established by Alfred Nobel for discoveries that "confer the greatest benefit on mankind." This source covers the award from its beginning in 1901 to 2000. Entries are arranged by award categories of chemistry, physics, and physiology or medicine, and then by year of award. If an award went to more than one individual, each recipient has an entry. There are indexes by name, nation, and scientific work. Each entry includes the recipient's name, prize, brief biographical information, a citation of the award, a summary of his or her life's work, selected publications, and a bibliography. Also included in each entry are a bibliography of selected publications of the award winner and a bibliography of works about the award winner.

There are several other reference works devoted to biographies of Nobel Prize winners. Specifically, the fourth edition of Louise Sherby's *The Who's Who of Nobel Prize Winners*, 1901–2000 (Oryx, 2002) and *Nobel Prize Winners: An H. W. Wilson Biographical Dictionary, 1997–2001 Supplement* (H. W. Wilson, 2002) have recently been published. The Kurian and Sherby books are similar. Both include educational achievements, a summary, recipient publications, and a bibliography. Kurian doesn't list award recipient's parents; Sherby does. The Wilson title has longer biographical entries, similar to those in its *Current Biography*.

The Nobel Scientists: A Biographical Encyclopedia is informative, well written, and nicely laid out, and libraries can select it with confidence. But if a library has to pick only one Nobel Prize biographical source, the choice would be the Wilson volume because of its longer entries.

Science in Everyday Life in America. 5v. 2002. bibliogs. illus. indexes. Greenwood, $160 (0-313-32235-X). 509.73.

Written for the upper-elementary through middle-school environment, *Science in Everyday Life in America* is a chronological approach to science and history in America from precontact to the present time. Each volume includes an introduction, a short bibliography with Web sites, and a volume index. There is no table of contents to guide the reader. Inventions and technologies, an average of 24 in each volume, are alphabetically arranged. Entries are between three and seven pages long and include background, related inventions and technologies of the period covered, and further refinements that have occurred after the indicated period. The information is well written for the intended audience. The lightning rod, refrigeration, the bicycle, mass production, and the personal computer are some of the topics covered. Captioned black-and-white photographs enhance the text.

In an attempt to make the reading accessible for the younger reader, phonetic spelling follows many terms. This may be useful for scientific, technical, and geographic terms like *tectonics* (tek-TAHN-iks), *genome* (JEEN-ohm), and *Massachusetts* (mass-uh-CHOO-setz), but it is distracting for words like *especially* (es-PESH-ul-ee) and *experience* (ex-PEER-ee-ense). Each mention of *scientist* (SYE-en-tist) in every volume is handled in the same manner.

Because of the lack of a comprehensive index or a table of contents for the individual volumes, the use of the set is limited unless one knows when something was invented or locates the information in another source first. For those with an interest in science or history, this set would be interesting general reading. For research, it is recommended with reservations for school and public libraries.

Science, Technology, and Society: The Impact of Science in the 20th Century. 3v. Ed. by Phillis Engelbert. 2002. 476p. bibliogs. glossary. illus. index. UXL, $139 (0-7876-5649-6). 509.04.

Before there were six degrees of separation from Kevin Bacon, there was the Erdos number—1 for someone who cowrote a paper with popular mathematician Paul Erdos, 2 for someone who cowrote a paper with a mathematician who cowrote with Erdos. This is one fascinating fact students will learn when they use this encyclopedia. The set's purpose is to help students understand the impact that twentieth-century discoveries and inventions had on the course of human history.

Each volume begins with the same table of contents, chronology, and list of words to know. Volumes cover specific fields of science: volume 1, *Life Science*; volume 2, *Mathematics and Medicine*; volume 3, *Physical Science and Technology*. The format for each of the five topics is the same: "Chronology," "Overview," "Essays" on specific discoveries and inventions, "Biographies" (nine or ten two-page profiles), "Brief Biographies" (additional paragraph-length treatments), "Research and Activity Ideas," and a bibliography for more information. Sidebars are placed liberally throughout the volumes. They may be biographical sketches, glossaries for the topic, or further explanations of ideas mentioned in the essay. Most of the black-and-white illustrations are photographs of scientists.

Some of the topics covered in the essays are "Evolution and Creationism in the Public Schools"; "The Emergence of Women in Mathematics";

"The Development of Public Health Services"; "The Discovery, Importance, and Limitations of Antibiotics"; and "America Becomes the Automobile Nation." Some of the longer biographies cover Niels Bohr, Rachel Carson, Srinivasa Ramanujan, Florence Sabin, Carl Sagan, and Orville and Wilbur Wright.

Although there are many science resources for students at the middle-school level and up, this one offers a refreshing perspective. The Facts On File Encyclopedia of Science, Technology, and Society (1999) covers some similar ground but is designed for an older audience. The UXL set fits in perfectly with the curricula and should be on the A list for purchase by most school and public libraries.

World Book Biographical Encyclopedia of Scientists. 8v. 2002. 1,536p. bibliog. glossary. illus. indexes. World Book, $289 (0-7166-7600-1). 509.2.

Intended for students in grades six and up, World Book's new biography set on scientists covers more than 1,300 individuals from ancient times to the present. The alphabetically arranged entries vary in length from around one-half to two double-columned pages. Each begins with a brief summary of basic facts: date and place of birth and, where relevant, death; nationality; and occupation. The readable essays clearly state the scientist's importance in the first sentence or two and provide personal as well as professional information. Many entries include portraits, and longer entries, such as those for Elizabeth Blackwell, Albert Einstein, and Antoine Laurent Lavoisier, have a short chronology. Cross-references link entries for scientists whose work is related. There are no entry-specific lists of further reading. Pronunciation guides for some of the scientists' names are a helpful feature.

Interspersed among the biographies are a number of two-page "Special Reports" that provide a more thematic approach. For example, following the entry for Otis Barton, who designed the bathysphere for undersea exploration, there is a report on "Exploring the Ocean Floor." A detailed cumulative index is repeated in each volume, and indexes by occupation, nationality and ethnicity, and century appear in volume 8. Volume 8 also has a glossary, a "List of Other Reference Sources," and list of Nobel Prize winners.

There are several other science biography reference sources for a similar age group. The World Book set has some advantage in currency over The Grolier Library of Science Biographies (1996), which gives brief summaries of 2,000 professional careers. Marshall Cavendish's Biographical Encyclopedia of Scientists (1998) covers just 500 people but generally provides more information, including bibliographies that list major works by as well as about each scientist. UXL's Scientists: Their Lives and Work (1997–2002) is now up to seven volumes treating around 280 scientists in profiles of three to seven pages. Despite the fact that it deals with so many scientists, World Book's coverage in some areas, such as African American scientists, seems skimpy—there are just 14. School and public libraries could purchase this set to provide breadth, knowing they may need to supplement it with other resources.

A Dictionary of Quotations in Mathematics. Ed. by Robert A. Nowlan. 2002. 314p. bibliog. indexes. McFarland, paper, $45 (0-7864-1284-4). 510.

Quotients rather than *quotations* may come to mind when thinking of mathematics, but that certainly isn't the case here. Nearly 3,000 quotations are carefully divided into 38 chapters subdivided into hundreds of smaller sections offering a wide array of mathematical topics. Like an intriguing puzzle or elaborate maze, there is always something to discover in this densely packed compendium of arithmetic erudition. Quotations are presented under carefully designated subject headings. For example, the chapter "The Theory of Probability" is divided into eight smaller sections: "Calculating Probabilities"; "Probability, Ignorance and Certainty"; "Miscellaneous Views of Probability"; "Chance"; "Gambling"; "Permutations and Combinations"; "Discrete Mathematics"; and "Making Predictions." Many other subjects are similarly subdivided, and three chapters are devoted to the words of some 92 "mathematical people," from Niels Abel to Zeno of Elea.

Quotations are fully credited, with the speaker and title of the source duly noted. Author and keyword indexes are provided, as is an extensive bibliography composed of the sources quoted. The range of topics covered surpasses mere figures and number crunching: the nature of mathematics and its relationship to language, philosophy, religion, and the arts are among the subjects addressed. In short, you can count on this book to supply appropriate mathematical bits of wisdom for any occasion.

Real-Life Math: Everyday Use of Mathematical Concepts. By Evan M. Glazer and John W. McConnell. 2002. 165p. bibliogs. illus. Greenwood, $49.95 (0-313-31998-7). 510.

"Why do we have to learn this?" is a common question relative to mathematics study. This reference book intends to answer that query by providing examples of real-life applications related to high-school mathematical concepts.

The authors, both with academic mathematical backgrounds, posit more than 40 concepts that appear in the U.S. mathematics education standards, among them *Matrices*, *Plane*, *Pythagorean theorem*, *Rotations*, and *Series*. The intended audience includes high-school students, teachers, and librarians, although mathematics teachers are the ones most likely to understand all the concepts and formulas.

The entries, arranged alphabetically, range from two to six pages. After an opening paragraph definition, various applications in science, sports, business, architecture, and other topics are explained. The term *everyday* usually refers to public activity rather than school or home life. A few diagrams and graphs accompany the text. Related URLs complete the entry. Some cross-references exist, but they are not consistently used. A bibliography of sources concludes the volume; an index is sorely needed.

Entries on *Probability*, *Perimeter*, and *Quadrilaterals* are very thorough and almost too elementary at points, although those same entries also describe related advanced math concepts. On the other hand, entries such as *Tangent* and *Polynomial functions* are at once too brief and complex. Although natural logarithms are briefly mentioned, no accompanying application is clearly noted. Nearly a page is devoted to symmetry, but Markov chains and fuzzy logic are vaguely explained in a sentence or two. The absence of entries on algorithms, measurement, modeling, set theory, transformations, and limits is puzzling.

The book's approach makes it more useful as a reference tool than a math enrichment volume. It does provide some useful application ideas across the math curriculum, more for the adult educator than the teenager, and might be useful in high-school libraries.

Astronomy Encyclopedia: An A–Z Guide to the Universe. Ed. by Patrick Moore. 2002. 456p. illus. maps. Oxford, $50 (0-19-521833-7). 520.3.

This encyclopedia is actually a revised and expanded edition of *The Astronomy Encyclopedia* (Orion, 1987), edited by Moore. The field of astronomy has expanded, new discoveries have been made, new theories developed, and new interpretations voiced. The general public has always been fascinated with the mysteries of the heavens, which makes the revised work a must-have for most libraries.

Moore's numerous publications are the "granddaddies" of books for the general reader that explain all that one needs to know about stars, planets, moons, and other heavenly bodies. Here, some 3,000 alphabetically arranged topics and definitions have been brought together with beautiful photographs (most in color), star maps, and explanatory diagrams. With the capability of sending more space probes into outer space, we have seen more photographs of far-off planets and their moons. Many of these photographs are in this encyclopedia, for example, Proteus, the largest of the inner satellites of Neptune discovered by *Voyager* 2 during its 1989 flyby. Most of the articles are brief but informative and understandable by any educated layperson. Definitions are concise, and there is a generous use of *see* references. Brief biographical information is given on individuals who have been associated with astronomy and related fields.

The two-column text makes good use of white space and boldface headings. There is at least one photograph, diagram, or chart on every page. All photographs are fully described. Throughout the book are highlighted boxes of information or articles that focus on objects in the sky, from planets to stars to asteroids. Eight star maps at the end of the book cover northern, equatorial, and southern stars. There is no index, but words and terms encountered in an article that have their own entries are printed in full capitals. This is a beautiful book, replacing many older encyclopedias that may be on the reference shelves. If a library has funds to purchase only one encyclopedia covering astronomy, this is the one to select.

The Facts On File Space and Astronomy Handbook. By Joseph A. Angelo Jr. 2002. 278p. appendixes. glossary. illus. index. Facts On File, $35 (0-8160-4542-9). 520.

Written by the author of several other books on space, this handbook is designed for a general audience. It is organized into four sections: a

1,200-entry glossary, 400 short (one sentence to one paragraph in length) biographies, a 45-page chronology of 8,000 years of discoveries in astronomy and space science, and 17 pages of charts and tables.

The glossary provides brief descriptions or definitions for terms such as *Blastoff*, *Extraterrestrial catastrophe theory*, *Gemini Project*, *Galactic cannibalism*, *Habitable payload*, *Orion Nebula*, *Planck's radiation law*, and *Zenith*. Biographies include well-known people such as Galileo Galilei, John Glenn, and Sally Ride as well as some that one would not expect to find in an astronomy resource, for example, Italian artist Giotto, who witnessed the 1301 passage of Halley's comet and depicted it in a fresco. Charts and tables cover topics such as stellar spectral classes, an Apollo Project summary, and physical and dynamic properties of the planets. Appendixes provide a short bibliography and Web sites.

The index to this handbook could use some improvement. Some index entries—for example, *astronauts* and *stars*—have very long lists of page references. Many users would not have the time or patience to go through this number of undifferentiated references. Topics covered by the charts and tables are not uniformly included in the index. A few black-and-white line drawings and photographs supplement the text. Cross-references link entries to related entries.

The *Space and Astronomy Handbook* is recommended for libraries in need of a concise, up-to-date reference in this area.

The Facts On File Dictionary of Atomic and Nuclear Physics. Ed. by Richard Rennie. 2002. 250p. appendixes. bibliog. illus. Facts On File, $49.50 (0-8160-4916-5). 539.7.

The Facts On File Dictionary of Biochemistry. Ed. by John Daintith. 2002. 247p. appendixes. bibliog. illus. Facts On File, $49.50 (0-8160-4914-9). 572.

The Facts On File Dictionary of Cell and Molecular Biology. Ed. by Robert Hine. 2002. 248p. appendixes. bibliog. illus. Facts On File, $49.50 (0-8160-4912-2). 571.6.

The Facts On File dictionaries of *Atomic and Nuclear Physics*, *Biochemistry*, and *Cell and Molecular Biology* are part of the 15-volume Facts On File Science Dictionaries set. Written in clear, easy-to-understand language, basic terminology and concepts are covered in entries that range in length from one sentence to several paragraphs.

The *Dictionary of Atomic and Nuclear Physics* covers areas such as atomic theory, the structure of matter, spectroscopy, quantum theory, nuclear physics, particle physics, and cosmology. Examples of specific entries are *Bohr model*; *Carbon dating*; *Grand unified theories* (GUTs); *Hadron*; *Hawking, Stephen William*; *Rydberg constant*; and *Self-organization*. Appendixes provide tables of fundamental constants, elementary particles, chemical elements, and a selected list of organizational Web pages.

General areas included in the *Dictionary of Biochemistry* are basic organic and physical chemistry, classes of compounds, cytology and histology, nutrition and metabolism, and natural-product chemistry. Examples of specific entries are *Beta-pleated sheet*; *Cyanobacteria*; *Enzyme*; *G protein*; *Guanine*; *Isomerase*; *McClintock, Barbara*; *Pollution*; *Sex determination*; *Sugar*; *Vector*; and *Zeolite*. Appendixes provide a chronology of major events in the development of biochemistry and molecular biology, a table of the genetic code, amino acid structures, the periodic table, chemical elements, the Greek alphabet, and suggested Web pages.

Cell structure, basic molecular biology and biochemistry, molecular genetics, cell metabolism, and laboratory techniques are among the general topics covered by the *Dictionary of Cell and Molecular Biology*. Examples of specific entries are ATP (*adenosine triphosphate*); *Chloroplast*; *Desmosomes*; *Krebs cycle*; *Micromanipulation*; *Osmosis*; *Pauling, Carl Linus*; *Senescence*; *Shine-Dalgarno sequence*; and *Zygotene*. Appendixes provide a chronology of major events in the development of biochemistry and molecular biology, amino acid structures, the genetic code, and Web sites.

Black-and-white line drawings supplement the texts. All volumes conclude with short bibliographies. Aimed at high-school students taking advanced placement science courses, these dictionaries could also be useful to students enrolled in introductory college courses. High-school, public, and academic libraries might consider their purchase.

A to Z of Chemists. By Elizabeth H. Oakes. 2002. 276p. bibliog. illus. index. Facts On File, $45 (0-8160-4579-8). 540.

A to Z of Chemists is the first volume of a series from Facts On File called Notable Scientists. The author, Oakes, has also written the *Encyclopedia of World Scientists* (Facts On File, 2001) and the *International Encyclopedia of Women Scientists* (Facts On File, 2002). This volume was designed for high-school through early college students and is also a good resource for general readers who are interested in chemistry. It covers more than 150 chemists from the first century A.D. through the present who have made significant contributions to their field, as determined by consulting established reference works such as the *Dictionary of Scientific Biography* (Scribner, 1970–1980). Among the chemists who are covered are St. Elmo Brady, Alfred Nobel, Linus Pauling, and Maxine Singer.

The volume is arranged by surname, with cross-references to other scientists included in the book. Entries range in length from 750 to 1,200 words and focus on the scientists' work and the scientific achievements that place them as leaders in the field. Some black-and-white photos are scattered throughout the text. Appended matter includes listings of the entries by country of birth, country of major scientific activity, and year of birth; and a chronological chart by year of birth. The volume is completed by a bibliography and an excellent index.

Although there are numerous reference sources that supply biographies of scientists, there are few that cover this particular area. The older, four-volume *A History of Chemistry* (St. Martin's, 1961) and *The Biographical Dictionary of Scientists: Chemists* (P. Bedrick, 1984) are ones to mention, but this new volume is more current as well as being both easy to read and fairly comprehensive. It is recommended particularly for high schools and undergraduate collections as well as public library reference collections.

World of Earth Science. 2v. Ed. by K. Lee Lerner and Brenda Wilmoth Lerner. 2003. 736p. bibliog. illus. index. Gale, $150 (0-7876-7739-6). 550.

Intended to challenge new students and provide a solid foundation for more advanced students, this set offers information in an encyclopedic format on the concepts, theories, discoveries, pioneers, and issues relating to topics in the earth sciences. It is the latest in a series that includes *World of Genetics* [RBB Je 1 & 15 03] and *World of Chemistry* (Gale, 2000). Contributors and their affiliations are listed at the beginning of volume 1. The set includes approximately 650 entries, from *Abyssal plains* to *Zeolite*. Students will appreciate the clearly written articles as well as the fact that special attention is placed on current ethical, legal, and social issues pertaining to the earth sciences, such as pollution, global warming, and ozone depletion.

Each of the entries ranges in length from a few paragraphs to a few pages. The table of contents provides an alphabetical listing for all of the entries but does not indicate on which page they are found nor in which volume. Within each entry, boldface terms direct readers to related entries, and each entry concludes with a list of *see also* references. Approximately 150 to 200 black-and-white photographs and illustrations are included throughout the text. In addition, at the center of each volume are eight pages of color plates that are referenced throughout the text. Volume 2 concludes with a list of sources consulted that includes books, periodicals, and Internet sites. Volume 2 also contains a chronology that lists milestones in human scientific achievement or observation from prehistory to 2002 as well as a general index.

Although students and the general public will appreciate having all of this accessible, easy-to read information on both concepts and individuals in one collection, some of the information is available in other Gale resources, such as *Notable Scientists from 1900 to the Present* (2001), that many libraries may already own. Recommended for college and high-school libraries or any public library that has a large science collection.

A to Z of Earth Scientists. By Alexander E. Gates. 2002. 336p. bibliog. illus. index. Facts On File, $45 (0-8160-4580-1). 551.

Intended for high-school and early college students and general readers, this volume in the Notable Scientists series contains entries on approximately 200 earth scientists. Most are currently or recently active, but some significant older scientists have also been included. Among the subdisciplines covered in the text are geochemistry, geophysics, mineralogy, paleontology, petrology, sedimentology, structural geology, and tectonics. Although the coverage spans the globe, there is an emphasis on Americans. In the preface, Gates explains that the book is shorter than planned mainly because of the difficulty of obtaining information on currently active scientists.

Each entry consists of an entry head with the subject's name, dates, nationality, and field(s) of specialization. This is followed by an essay ranging in length from 750 to 1,500 words, with most averaging about 1,000 words. The essays generally cover basic biographical information such as educational background, positions held, prizes awarded, etc. The rest of the essay is devoted to the scientist's work. Though very readable, the text includes many technical terms that not always explained. In the preface readers are encouraged to keep an earth science dictionary handy, especially if they have no course background in the subject.

The book concludes with lists of entries based on country of birth, country of major scientific activity, year of birth, and field of study for each scientist. The book also includes a chronology, which would be of use to students looking for a scientist from a particular time period, as well as an extensive bibliography.

The list of biographical dictionaries of earth scientists is short, if not nonexistent. Generally, current reference information for students on earth scientists is limited to that which may be found in single-and multivolume sets on scientists in general. This would be a useful resource for high-school, college, and public libraries requiring reference material devoted solely to earth scientists.

The Oryx Resource Guide to El Nino and La Nina. By Joseph S. D'Aleo with Pamela G. Grube. 2002. 230p. bibliog. glossary. illus. index. Greenwood, $49.95 (1-57356-378-1). 551.6.

In this volume two meteorologists seek to explain the basic causes and effects of El Nino and La Nina, also known as the El Nino and Southern Oscillation, or ENSO. Once thought to be a weather phenomenon that affected only the tropical Pacific, nowadays El Nino and its climatological opposite, La Nina, receive widespread media interest and attention. This work chronicles what is known about ENSO in 12 short chapters. Topics covered include a history of ENSO and its causes, the effects of ENSO on weather in the U.S., global weather, and world ecosystems. The authors discuss how scientists study and track the ENSO phenomenon, and the advances made in prediction, as well as how governments around the world are using this information. One chapter is devoted to two past super El Nino events (1982–83 and 1997–98). Brief biographies of nine "key people" in ENSO research are provided as well as a directory and description of organizations involved with ENSO, with relevant Web sites. A chronology of milestones in the study of ENSO, from the fifteenth century to the present, concludes the work. A detailed glossary and an extensive bibliography are provided. Numerous charts, maps, and diagrams are included as well as color plates comparing strong and weak El Ninos and La Ninas.

Well written and easily accessible, this work will appeal to anyone interested in learning more about the ENSO phenomena. A solid choice for public and academic libraries looking for materials on this topic.

Mapping the World. 8v. 2002. bibliog. glossary. illus. index. maps. Grolier, $239 (0-7172-5619-7). 562.

This set of brief volumes is intended to describe the history of cartography, discuss its importance in the development of various cultures, and explain how it is done. Each of the individual volumes examines a particular aspect of mapping: "Ways of Mapping the World," "Observation and Measurement," "Maps for Travelers," "Navigation," "Mapping New Lands," "Mapping for Governments," "City Maps," and "Mapping for Today and Tomorrow." Within each volume, around 12 or 13 separate topics are presented in sections of two to six pages. In addition to the numerous maps that appear throughout the set, every page is enhanced with nicely captioned illustrations, most in color. At the bottom of each left-hand page there are cross-references to other sections in the set that expand on some aspect of the subject under discussion. Many of the topics are classroom oriented and encourage students to carry out activities for further study. Words appearing in a volume's glossary are indicated in italics. Each volume concludes with further reading and Web sites as well as a comprehensive index.

Although this set fills a need, is nicely arranged, and has an appealing layout, it is somewhat weak on content. This would be an additional purchase for upper-elementary and middle-school libraries wanting to supplement their map curriculum.

★Encyclopedia of Evolution. Ed. by Mark Pagel. 2002. 1,205p. bibliogs. illus. index. Oxford, $325 (0-19-512200-3). 576.8.

The study of evolutionary biology has become increasingly important as scientists try to better understand the natural world. Research in areas such as hominid evolution and hereditary disease frequently makes the headlines. This outstanding encyclopedia brings together 365 well-written, alphabetically arranged articles covering all aspects of evolution, from fundamental theory to popular topics such as cloning. Editor-in-chief Pagel is professor of evolutionary biology, University of Reading, U.K. The 330 contributors include anthropologists, biochemists, biologists, ecologists, geneticists, paleontologists, and zoologists, primarily from academic institutions in the U.S. and the U.K.

A topical outline in the first volume organizes the articles into general categories such as concepts and definitions, molecular evolution, population genetics, developmental biology, biodiversity, social behavior, evolution of disease, human evolution, mathematical models, and history. Entries range from a half page to more than 15 pages in length. Examples of specific article titles include *Antibiotic resistance*; *Cnidarians*; *Creationism*; *Franklin, Rosalind*; *Genetically modified organisms*; *Mutation*; *Natural selection*; *Phylogenetic inference*; *Plagues and epidemics*; *Plants*; and *Red queen hypothesis*. Although many of the articles are on subjects that would be of interest mostly to specialists or students, some, such as *Mate choice*, would have broader appeal.

A unique feature is the inclusion of an extraordinary collection of essays by nine eminent scientists and philosophers including Stephen Jay Gould, Jane Goodall, David L. Hull, and John Maynard Smith. These articles, totaling about 90 pages, provide an excellent overview of topics such as culture of chimpanzees, human genetic and linguistic diversity, motherhood, and Darwinian medicine. Written at a level accessible to the general reader, these thought-provoking essays demonstrate what insights are possible when a subject is approached from an evolutionary perspective.

Entries are written for users with varying backgrounds. For example, overview articles and biographies would be useful to advanced high-school and general undergraduate students. More technical and specialized entries are directed at readers with further training. Bibliographies are included at the end of most articles. Black-and-white line drawings and photographs supplement the text, and a 35-page index facilitates access.

No other recent encyclopedias provide comparable authoritative in-depth coverage of biological evolution. The *Encyclopedia of Evolution* is highly recommended for large public and academic libraries.

Genetics. 4v. Ed. by Richard Robinson. 2002. 1,144p. bibliogs. glossary. illus. index. Macmillan, $395 (0-02-865606-7). 576.

This encyclopedia set, part of the Macmillan Science Library series, is intended for use by middle-and high-school students, college nonspecialists, and beginning researchers. More than 100 contributors are responsible for approximately 250 signed entries from *Accelerated aging: Progeria* to *Zebrafish*. Articles range from a few paragraphs to a few pages in length and focus on a variety of topics, including inheritance, genes and chromosomes, genetic diseases, biotechnology, history, careers, and the ethical, legal, and social issues associated with genetically modified foods and cloning. The entries appear in alphabetical order and include cross-references to related entries. Most have a list of suggested readings and Internet resources to examine for further information.

Each volume begins with a complete table of contents as well as a "For Your Reference" section that includes a group of diagrams and illustrations to help students visualize the various structures related to DNA and RNA. Words that appear in bold in the text are defined in the page margins and collected in a glossary at the conclusion of each volume. Each volume also includes a topical outline and an index, and volume 4 includes a cumulate index as well.

The attractive layout features a wealth of colorful diagrams and photographs that will appeal to students as well as the casual browser. The clear and well-written articles are informative and should meet the needs of most students. In addition, users will appreciate the thorough indexing and cross-referencing, which make navigation straightforward. Though it has more extensive coverage, *World of Genetics* [RBB Je 1 & 15 02] lacks suggested readings at the end of each entry and is not as attractively designed. It is aimed at the high-school level and up, while *Encyclopedia of Genetics* (Salem, 1999) is designed for use by undergraduates and others with a general understanding of science. *Genetics* would be a useful resource for middle-and high-school libraries as well as undergraduate and public libraries.

World of Microbiology and Immunology. 2v. Ed. by K. Lee Lerner and Brenda Wilmoth Lerner. 2002. 699p. bibliog. illus. index. Gale, $150 (0-7876-6540-1). 579.

Microbiology and immunology are sometimes seen as esoteric and highly specialized sciences with few interpreters to students and the lay public. The authors have selected 600 entries that highlight selected important persons, research facilities, terms, and concepts of both these fields. There are brief biographies of the well known (*Salk, Jonas*) and the lesser known but important (*Milstein, Cesar*); and explanations of common terms (*Epidemics and pandemics*), uncommon terms (*Retroposons and transposable elements*), and acronyms like AIDS and SCID (*Severe combined immunodeficiency*).

The entries are in alphabetical order with many cross references. Though there are no bibliographies with the entries, there are 13 pages of book and journal-article citations and 10 pages of Web addresses in the "Sources Consulted" section. This is followed by an 18-page "Historical Chronology" of milestones in human scientific achievement, showing how ancient (circa 10,000 B.C.E.) ideas eventually led to germ theory and the burgeoning of microbiology and immunology through 2002. The extensive, detailed general index indicates the main entries' volume and page numbers in boldface type. Sometimes the same page information is repeated in regular type, an unnecessary redundancy. Using the index one can find that the Irish potato famine is mentioned in the entry on F*ungal genetics* along with other similarly embedded bits of information. One important, but missing, finding aid is an index to the biographies, as browsing biographies is often a way to interest students in a discipline.

The language is straightforward and only as technical as required. The aim is to increase curiosity and interest in these diverse and important disciplines, and to show the development and growing importance of both fields to human health. Though the editors emphasize student use, the major users will probably be persons wanting to learn a bit about terms they hear or read in scientific and medical news. In no way does this publication compete with professional encyclopedias designed for researchers and medical practitioners such as E*ncyclopedia of Microbiology* (Academic, 2000) or E*ncyclopedia of* Immunology (Academic, 1998). Recommended for public libraries and general interest in academic libraries.

Magill's Encyclopedia of Science: Plant Life. 4v. Ed. by Bryan D. Ness. 2003. 1,263p. bibliogs. glossary. illus. indexes. maps. Salem, $435 (1-58765-084-3). 580.

Written by subject authorities, this encyclopedia provides approximately 380 articles on botany and related sciences. About half of the articles were updated and revised from other Salem publications, among them M*agill's Survey of Science: Life Science* (1991), M*agill's Survey of Science: Life Science, Supplement* (1998), E*ncyclopedia of Environmental Issues* (2000), and E*arth Science* (2001). The rest were written specifically for this encyclopedia. The easy-to-understand, alphabetically arranged, signed entries are written at a level appropriate for high-school and undergraduate students as well as the general reader. Averaging several pages in length, discussions begin with an overview of the topic and end with an annotated bibliography of books and articles. All bibliographies, even those attached to articles taken from previous sets, are new. Examples of topics covered include A*cid precipitation, Carbon cycle, Deforestation, Estrogens from plants, Fruit crops, Ginkgos, Medicinal plants, Rubber, Soil, Stems, Taiga,* and Z*ygomycetes.*

Black-and-white line drawings, photographs, charts, tables, sidebars, and maps augment the text. About 200 pages of useful supplemental materials are provided, including one-paragraph biographies of important botanists, a plant classification overview, a 35-page glossary, a time line of important advances in plant science, common-to-scientific plant names, scientific-to-common plant names, Web sites, and an annotated bibliography. A well-constructed 50-page index provides subject access to the set.

Two other recent encyclopedias on the topic, Macmillan's P*lant Sciences* (2001) and Grolier's P*lants and Plant Life* (2001), are designed to meet the needs of middle-school students and up. Salem's entry on the plant science shelves is recommended for high-school, public, and undergraduate libraries in need of a general encyclopedia of plant science.

The Illustrated Encyclopedia of Trees. By David More and John White. 2002. 800p. glossary. illus. index. Timber, $79.95 (0-88192-520-9). 582.16.

First published in England, this volume could be described as a labor of love. More worked for many years painting the more than 2,000 illustrations of trees, bark, flowers, leaves, cones, and fruits. White is a retired dendrologist who wrote the accompanying text. The trees are varieties that grow in Britain, France, Germany, Belgium, and Holland, but the introduction notes that most are found in the U.S. and many are native to North America.

The volume is arranged by scientific order beginning with the ginkgo family and ending with palms. Each two-page spread has an average of a quarter page of text with the rest devoted to illustrations of the trees and detailed pictures of the cones, leaves, etc. In addition to the descriptions of more than 1,000 species and varieties of trees, there are notes indicating height, hardiness, choice, and wood. The hardiness table is calculated by a percentage based on the minimum temperature. C*hoice* refers to a tree's garden value as expressed by a rating of from one (excellent for ornamental and practical value) to four (not recommended because of susceptibility to disease or other reasons). The illustrations of mature trees (often in two or three seasons) sometimes have an animal or person under the tree to indicate scale. There are some omissions of common trees in the U.S., such as the mountain laurel and shadbush. Other oddities include the use of the term *lime* instead of *linden*.

In the last four years there have been a number of books published on trees. For the U.S. gardener D*irr's* H*ardy Trees and Shrubs* (Timber, 1998) is recommended. However, T*he Illustrated Encyclopedia of Trees* is more than a reference book and will be read for pleasure. The beautiful illustrations and informative text make it a perfect source for anyone interested in this important part of our environment. An appropriate purchase for academic and public libraries.

Firefly Encyclopedia of Insects and Spiders. Ed. by Christopher O'sToole. 2002. 240p. bibliog. glossary. illus. index. Firefly, $40 (1-55297-612-2). 595.7.

Firefly Encyclopedia of Reptiles and Amphibians. Ed. by Tim Halliday and Kraig Adler. 2002. 240p. bibliog. glossary. illus. index. Firefly, $40 (1-55297-613-0). 597.9.

With lush color photographs and lavishly detailed illustrations, these encyclopedias present a striking abundance of information at a glance. Also noteworthy is the scholarly text, a comprehensive overview of these frequently studied—and uniquely different—phyla.

The format of both volumes is similar. A major article introduces the main classes: amphibians, reptiles, and arthropods (insects and arachnids). Articles pertaining to specific species follow. For example, 23 species of the class I*nsecta*—with a separate article for millipedes and centipedes, members of the superclass M*yriapoda*—are featured. Entries vary in length, depending upon the complexity of the species. Information on S*toneflies* is covered in two pages, while C*rickets and grasshoppers* requires twelve pages of text. All articles—penned by authorities in the field of biological study—provide current scientific information and research findings relating to physiology and to behavior.

Several valuable features are standard in each article. Most significant are the "Factfiles," which provide a quick summary of valuable statistics, including the order, class, physical features, life cycles, population, habitat, color, reproduction habits, and longevity of the species. Conservation status, a key consideration for many researchers, is also noted, using IUCN (World Conservation Union) categories as a descriptor. Boxed "Special Feature" (for example, "Fly-Borne Diseases" and "Decoding the Frog Chorus") and "Photo Story" (such as "Building Nests of Mud and Paper" and "Harvesting Snake Venom") articles supplement the erudite text with fascinating sidelights concerning behavior, morphology, and economic and medical importance, among other topics.

Although glossaries of biological terms are included, sidebars defining these terms on the pages on which they appear might have been a better placement because most students will not turn to the ends of the volumes. A bibliography of sources and an index complete each book.

One thinks short and concise when perusing an encyclopedia. Such is not the case with these resources, which are strongly recommended for high-school, public, and academic libraries. For students in grades four through eight, Marshall Cavendish's multivolume I*nsects and Spiders* [RBB F 1 03] and R*eptiles and Amphibians* [RBB F 15 03] offer less scholarly but equally attractive coverage.

Insects and Spiders of the World. 11v. 2002. 704p. bibliog. glossary. illus. indexes. maps. Marshall Cavendish, $329.95 (0-7614-7334-3). 595.7.

Insects, spiders, and other related arthropods account for almost 75 percent of all species. This set presents readers in grades four through eight with information about these creatures as well as general topics such as insect evolution, migration, and insecticide.

Nearly 200 entries are arranged alphabetically and range in length from one to six pages. Each entry is color coded into one of four categories: insects (*Ant*, *Bedbug*, *Termite*); spiders (*Black widow*, *House spider*, *Tarantula*); other arthropods (*Centipede*, *Millipede*, *Scorpion*); and overview (*Arachnology*, *Communication*, *Metamorphosis*). Many articles include a "Key Facts" box with basic details concerning habitat, breeding, and so on as well as a distribution map that indicates where the insect or spider lives in the world. Many longer articles also have sidebars that provide more detailed information about one particular aspect of the topic. Entries are further enhanced by diagrams, illustrations, and vivid color photographs. All entries include a *see also* box of headings to refer to within the set for more information.

Volume 1 contains a reader's guide and table of contents to the entire set. Each volume has its own table of contents as well as a glossary of terms mentioned in the text and an index. The final volume offers a comprehensive glossary and index for the set as well as several subject indexes, including "Insects," "Spiders," "Behavior," and "Habitat." Also included in the final volume are an arthropod tree, a key to arthropod identification, and facts about arthropod diversity. In addition, listings of Internet sites, books, organizations, and museums to contact for further research are provided.

This comprehensive encyclopedia is easily accessible and provides a nice introduction to insects and spiders. An excellent purchase for school and public libraries.

Reptiles and Amphibians. 11v. 2002. 1,568p. bibliog. glossary. illus. indexes. maps. Marshall Cavendish, $459.95 (0-7614-7390-4). 597.9.

This appealing set provides thorough coverage of the field of herpetology for students in grades eight and up. The first 10 volumes contain 70 alphabetically arranged entries on topics ranging from *African reed frogs* to *Worm lizards*. Each of these volumes is 144 pages in length and includes a three-page index to the species, places, and behaviors presented in that volume. The articles range in length from 18 to 20 pages and begin with a boxed summary of key facts and information on classification. The first part, "Profile," gives an overview of the family of reptiles or amphibians under discussion and also touches on interesting idiosyncrasies and environmental challenges. This section is followed by heavily illustrated two-page spreads covering "Family Tree," "Anatomy," "Habitats," "Food and Feeding," "Survival," and other topics.

Volume 11 includes a comprehensive index and glossary as well as indexes of scientific names, biological classification, habitats, geographical distribution, and behaviors. In addition, listings of Internet sites, books, organizations, and museums to contact for further research are provided. The final volume also includes two articles explaining the shared features of reptiles and amphibians as well as the meaning and use of taxonomic terms. The complete set includes more than 1,500 colorful and attractive photographs, drawings, diagrams, distribution maps, and anatomical charts. Students will appreciate the appealing layout and the simple accessibility of information.

Current reference information for students on herpetology is generally limited to field guides or a single volume of a multivolume set on animals. This set would be an outstanding addition for school and public libraries, as it provides an abundance of in-depth information devoted solely to reptiles and amphibians.

World of Animals: Mammals. 10v. Ed. by Pat Morris and Amy-Jane Beer. 2003. bibliogs. glossaries. illus. index. maps. Grolier, $419 (0-7172-5742-8). 599.

Grolier has released *Mammals*, the first cluster of a five-set *World of Animals* collection intended for the middle-school level and up.

Closely related mammals with similar lifestyles are grouped in 10 volumes. For example, volume 6 covers ruminant herbivores, and volume 10 covers marsupials. Each 128-page volume follows a well-organized format. In clear, concise text intermingled with many color photographs and illustrations, information is presented in three types of articles. The first, introducing major animal groups such as ruminants and marsupials, emphasizes similarities. The second provides overviews of families or closely related groups like deer and their relatives and American opossums. A third type, which constitutes the bulk of the text, with articles ranging from two to six pages, describes individual species such as the Muntjac and the Virginia opossum. More than 250 animals are covered. The vivid, detailed photographs and illustrations alone provide great pictorial data that would satisfy the investigation of a younger learner. Cross-referencing—located in the bottom margin—denotes animal, volume, and page number, making additional searching easier. Each volume concludes with a volume-specific species list and glossary, lists of further reading and Web sites, and a full set index.

Especially noteworthy is the feature called a "data panel." Placed on the introductory page for each individual animal, the panel includes the common and scientific names, family, order, size (in imperial units and metric equivalent), a visual comparison of an adult mammal and a six-foot tall human being, key features (habits, breeding, voice, diet, habitat, distribution, and International Union for the Conservation of Nature status), and a locator map showing the normal range. Solid information is presented for the most minimal inquiry. Volumes have reinforced bindings, a critical feature because it is predictable that this set will be used frequently based on traditional grades 6–12 curricula.

Public schools and libraries should plan to include this and future *World of Animals* publications in their yearly budgets. Subsequent sets—each also consisting of 10 volumes—will cover birds, insects and other invertebrates, fish, and amphibians and reptiles.

Medicine, Health, Technology, Management

The American Heritage Stedman's Medical Dictionary. 2d ed. 2002. 923p. appendix. illus. index. Houghton, $27 (0-618-25415-3). 610.

First published in 1995, *The American Heritage Stedman's Medical Dictionary* "is designed for general readers and professionals in the allied medical fields, law, and the insurance industry." Words have brief definitions that are meant to provide "an appropriate level of technical language without including excessive detail."

The entries are alphabetical, letter by letter, with cross-references for variants, symbols, and synonyms. Some entries have black-and-white line drawings. To enhance accessibility, the editors have avoided the traditional subentry format in most medical dictionaries, which puts a long list of terms under a main entry. For example, Tourette's syndrome is found under *Tourette's* rather than under *syndrome*. A "Subentry Index" serves to group terms under the more general headings. In addition, nonspecialist terms are preferred; a user looking up the word *leukocyte* will find a *see* reference to *white blood cell*. However, those unfamiliar with medical terminology will need further clarification after reading the definition: "Any of the colorless or white cells in the blood that have a nucleus and cytoplasm and help protect the body from infection through specialized neutrophils, lymphocytes, and monocytes." Individual entries for each of these cells do not offer much assistance.

The dictionary also has more than 300 very short biographical entries for those who have contributed to medical science, such as Marie Curie, Rene Laennec, and Ivan Pavlov. There are anatomical charts, a periodic table, measurement and metric conversion tables, a chart of first aid for burns, and dietary guidelines and Recommended Daily Allowances (RDAs) at the end of the book. The RDA information is from 1989, rather than the revised 2001 allowances.

Although this dictionary would be sufficient for a small office or home collection, libraries serving students and the public will find the sixth edition of *Mosby's Medical, Nursing, & Allied Health Dictionary* (6th ed., 2002) more useful. It has more entries; clearer, more detailed definitions; and 2,200 color illustrations.

A Biographical Dictionary of Women Healers: Midwives, Nurses, and Physicians. By Laurie Scrivener and J. Suzanne Barnes. 2002. 340p. appendixes. bibliogs. index. Greenwood, $74.95 (1-57356-219-X). 610.

Scrivener and Barnes have posted a long-delayed valentine to female health professionals.

Among the more honored female health workers—Clara Barton, Margaret Sanger, Faye Wattleton—the book elevates the undervalued, for example, colonial midwife-herbalist Ann Hutchinson and Marie-Henriette LeJeune Ross, an Acadian healer who applied Turkish-style inoculations to Nova Scotians of Cape Breton to ward off smallpox. Emphasis is on women from the U.S. and Canada. Missing from the lineup is commentary on the Hispanic *curandera*, a folk healer and adviser vital to Latinos into the twenty-first century.

Assisting the researcher, student, teacher, librarian, and health professional are excellent reference aids. Alphabetically arranged entries cover one or two pages and contain names, dates, education, professional organizations, photos, and innovations. References to books, journals, newspapers, and a sprinkling of Web sites point the user to other sources of information. Some entries include a portrait. Appendix 1 lists entrants by occupation (midwives, nurses, and physicians). A second appendix provides a five-page time line of events forming the milieu in which women established practices in communities where gender restrictions limited the medical profession to men only.

These women can be found in other resources; more than 70, primarily physicians, have entries in The Biographical Dictionary of Women in Science (Routledge, 2000). But A Biographical Dictionary of Women Healers offers a distinct context and is recommended for high-school, public, and academic libraries.

Women in Medicine: An Encyclopedia. By Laura Lynn Windsor. 2002. 259p. bibliogs. illus. index. ABC-CLIO, $85 (1-57607-392-0). 610.

Following on the heels of a similar publication, A Biographical Dictionary of Women Healers [RBB O 1 02], comes another encyclopedia documenting the contributions of women in medicine. Biographies of more than 250 women from a broad range of medical areas give evidence of the many contributions women have made in the field. The entries span the centuries in recording the growth and impact of women's accomplishments in this traditionally male-dominated discipline.

There are biographies of St. Fabiola, who lived in the fourth century, as well as contemporary women who made their mark in the past decade. Not all are physicians. Researchers, nurses, midwives, and women active in medically related social issues are also covered. The biographical sketches run from three sentences to three pages. Most include information about the subject's early life followed by a discussion of her contribution to the field of medicine. Most of the subjects are from North America and Western Europe. Four Asian women, many African American women, and a good representation of Native American women are included. In addition to the biographies there are more than 20 entries on related topics, such as Female genital mutilation and Footbinding, as well as for organizations, institutions, and medical terms. References to source material follow each entry, as do cross-references. An extensive bibliography is included.

Most of the women can be found in other sources such as American Women in Science, 1950 to the Present: A Biographical Dictionary (ABC-CLIO, 1998) and the aforementioned A Biographical Dictionary of Women Healers. The latter title contains as many women and also includes useful appendixes that list entrants by occupation (midwives, nurses, etc.) and a time line, but it has no topical entries. Women in Medicine is recommended for public, secondary-school, and college collections that need more coverage in this area.

The Encyclopedia of the Brain and Brain Disorders. 2d ed. By Carol Turkington. 2002. 369p. appendixes. bibliog. glossary. index. Facts On File, $65 (0-8160-4774-X). 612.8.

Hardly a week goes by without a news story about brain disorders such as Alzheimer's disease, autism, multiple sclerosis, Parkinson's disease, and stroke. General readers who are regularly exposed to information about the brain and brain disorders will appreciate this accessible reference from a medical writer. Containing more than 800 clear, concise entries, the volume also includes three directories (of self-help, professional and governmental organizations), a glossary, and an extensive list of references. An index facilitates access to the wide range of terms that are covered. The first edition, called The Brain Encyclopedia, was published in 1996.

Entries treat Aging and the brain, Brain scans, Circadian rhythm, Down syndrome, Friedreich's ataxia, Mapping the brain, Narcolepsy, Postconcussion syndrome, and Slow viruses of the brain, to name just a few topics. The introduction notes that almost every entry has been revised, many with extensive updates. Among the new entries are Ecstasy (MDMA), Mad cow disease, Multiple intelligences, Neurological manifestation of AIDS, Shaken baby syndrome, and entries for each of the four drugs approved to treat Alzheimer's disease. Students interested in the brain and brain disorders will find much of interest here—information on the causes, cures, key research, symptoms, treatments, and trends of each field of study. The Encyclopedia of the Brain and Brain Disorders is useful for brief definitions of terms and ready-reference questions. Lay readers and students will undoubtedly appreciate the jargon-free language.

Encyclopedia of the Human Body. By Richard Walker. 2002. 304p. glossary. illus. index. DK, $29.99 (0-7894-8672-5). 612.

If you have ever wanted to know why your blood is red, how fast your hair grows, or the role of different types of vitamins and minerals in the body, this is the tool for you. This encyclopedia provides a wealth of information associated with the human body in an eye-catching format. Nearly 900 full-color photographs, illustrations, electron micrographs, models, and diagrams accompany the text and are clearly labeled.

Content is organized in seven sections. "Working Parts" includes information on topics such as cells, DNA, and tissues. "Moving Framework" discusses skin, hair, skeletal system, and muscles. "Control and Sensation" includes the nervous system, the five senses, and the brain. "Supply and Maintenance" provides information about blood, the heart, the respiratory system, and digestion. "New Generations" discusses reproduction, birth, aging, and inheritance. The "Body through Time" section at the end of the book contains information about how humans have studied the body throughout the millennia. Double-page spreads provide information on each topic and are succinctly written with numerous illustrative materials. A final reference section provides a time line of significant health-related events from 100,000 B.C.E. to the present and a glossary of simple definitions of almost 300 scientific terms. The comprehensive index is necessary for navigation as topics are not presented alphabetically.

A characteristic DK publication, this encyclopedia is attractive and a good beginning reference source for basic information or quick answers. Browsers will appreciate the appealing layout, especially the close-up images of various body structures. Public and school libraries will be well served by this title.

World of Anatomy and Physiology. 2v. Ed. by K. Lee Lerner and Brenda Wilmoth Lerner. 2002. 734p. bibliog. illus. index. Gale, $150 (0-7876-5684-4). 612.

This reference provides basic information on human anatomy and physiology. The 650 alphabetically arranged entries, ranging in length from several paragraphs to several pages, are written at a level accessible to high-school students and the general reader. Topics covered range from classical human anatomy and physiology to developmental and reproductive biology. Examples include Amino acids, Blushing, Breathing, Endocrine system and glands, Gene therapy, Sexual reproduction, Sleep, Space physiology, and Veins. Lengthy biographies of about 200 famous as well as lesser-known scientists, among them Francis Crick, Herophilus, Rita Levi-Montalcini, Susumu Tonegawa, and Otto Heinrich Warburg, are also included.

Black-and-white line drawings and photographs supplement the text. Sixteen color plates illustrating topics such as basic anatomical nomenclature, the circulatory system, and the endocrine system are inserted in the center of both volumes. (Excellent detailed anatomical illustrations are available from MEDLINEplus: Anatomy [http://www.nlm.nih.gov/medlineplus/anatomy.html].) Cross-references to related articles, definitions, and biographies are provided. Other features are a 15-page bibliography that lists worthwhile books, articles, and Web sites and a historical chronology of significant events in the advancement of anatomy and physiology. A comprehensive 91-page index provides subject access to the contents.

Although primarily aimed at high-school students and general readers, this reference source could also be of use to undergraduate students in introductory courses. It is recommended for high-school, public, and academic libraries.

Drugs and Controlled Substances: Information for Students. Ed. by Stacey L. Blachford and Kristine Krapp. 2002. 495p. appendix. bibliogs. glossary. illus. indexes. Gale, $115 (0-7876-6264-X). 613.8.

Written for the teen reader, with many references to teen usage, Drugs and Controlled Substances is a comprehensive reference work for students and would be useful for adult readers as well. It "covers illegal drugs, legal addictive drugs and other substances, and commonly abused classes of prescription and over-the-counter drugs."

The volume encompasses a wide range including Caffeine, Designer drugs, Herbal drugs, and Rohypnol plus the standard Alcohol, Heroin, and Steroids. Each of the 50 main topical essays includes the names of the substance—brand names, generic names, and chemical names as well as street names. Overviews, chemical composition, usage reason and method, the effects of usage as well as reaction with other substances, consequences (personal, social, and legal), and treatment and rehabilitation are some of the subtopics addressed within each essay. In addition to the well-written essays, sidebars discussing legal issues, misconceptions, history, and news stories add depth to each topic.

Additional features are many, including a general index, a variant name index, and a chronology of key events from 5,000 B.C.E. to 2002. Photos, illustrations, and charts to assist in identifying particular drugs give added information. The additional resources that are listed—books, periodicals, and Web sites by known authorities—match the high standards of the rest of the content.

Currency, scope, and authority are the hallmarks of this highly recommended reference work that should be found in most school and public libraries. For the high-school level, it offers much more depth than *The Encyclopedia of Drugs and Alcohol* (Watts, 2002), which has been a standard resource in middle and high schools.

Drugs, Alcohol, and Tobacco: Learning about Addictive Behavior. 3v. Ed. by Rosalyn Carson-DeWitt. 2002. 839p. bibliog. glossary. illus. indexes. Macmillan, $275 (0-02-865756-X). 613.8.

Alcohol, drugs, and tobacco cause a multitude of effects in the lives of children and teenagers. Drawing on the previously published *Encyclopedia of Drugs, Alcohol, and Addictive Behavior* (Macmillan, 2d ed., 2001), this set is designed to interest and educate students in middle school and older as well as general browsers. This work contains more than 200 alphabetically arranged articles addressing the nature of, treatments for, and social issues surrounding addictive substances and behaviors. Articles from the previously published set have been revised to suit the needs of younger readers, their teachers and parents, and nonspecialists.

Articles range in length from several paragraphs to several pages and introduce such topics as *Anabolic steroids*, *Binge drinking*, *Creativity and drugs*, *Ecstasy*, *Gambling*, *Gangs and drugs*, *Treatment types*, and *Risk factors for substance abuse*. Articles are clear and well written, and the appealing layout includes photographs, diagrams, and sidebars that mention interesting facts or suggest fiction titles that deal with similar issues. For example, *Cut*, by Patricia McCormick (Scholastic, 2002), is suggested for the article *Cutting and self-harm*. Words highlighted in the text are defined in page margins (in addition to the glossary). *See also* references conclude each article.

Each volume begins with a complete table of contents and concludes with a comprehensive glossary, annotated bibliography (including Web sites), and index (volume 3 contains a cumulative index). A listing of organizations (including addresses, phone numbers, and Web sites) to contact for further information or assistance is also provided. We came across one error: the article *Alcohol: Withdrawal* states that the process of detoxification "usually takes fifteen to twenty years."

Containing sufficient information to serve the needs of a variety of student users, this set will appeal to the casual browser as well. It is recommended for junior-and senior-high-school and public libraries. It is broader in scope than Gale's *Drugs and Controlled Substances: Information for Students* (2002) [RBB Mr 15 03], which has entries for 50 drugs but not for other, related topics.

Health Matters! 8v. Ed. by William M. Kane. 2002. bibliog. glossary. illus. index. Grolier, $409 (0-7172-5575-1). 613.

This set serves two purposes: it is a means of answering young adults' questions about their health and empowering them to make sound decisions and also a reference source for school reports pertaining to health topics.

Each of the eight volumes focuses on a different health-related topic, such as addiction, mental health, sexuality and pregnancy, weight and eating disorders, and sexually transmitted diseases. Within each volume the topics are organized into six different sections.

In the first section, "Healthy Living: Teen Choices and Actions," readers are encouraged to contemplate the consequences of their choices. In "Who Me? Check It Out!" users can take quizzes to assess how their current behavior may affect their health. By far the largest section of each volume is "Just the Facts," which is an alphabetical listing of entries. "Concerns and Fears" examines various topics that are of particular concern to young adults; and in "It Can't Happen to Me," teens will read about others who have faced health problems and overcome them. Finally, "Straight Talk" provides answers to some of the difficult health questions facing teens today. The writing is straightforward and concise and should be accessible to young adult readers, although the intended audience may be put off by the at-times condescending tone.

Color photographs are included on almost every page as well as plenty of charts and graphs. There is cross-referencing within and among the volumes. In addition, sidebars are used to highlight keywords and to debunk common myths pertaining to health matters. Each volume concludes with a directory of services, organizations, help sites, and hot lines; a glossary; and lists of further reading and Internet sites. There is also a comprehensive index at the conclusion of each volume.

This set is more thorough than *Healthy Living* (UXL, 2000) and would be a useful addition to high-school or public libraries.

Biological Hazards: An Oryx Sourcebook. By Joan R. Callahan. 2002. 385p. bibliogs. glossary. illus. index. Greenwood, $64.95 (1-57356-385-4). 615.9.

The theme of this book seems to be adapted from a sign at one time used in military and industrial settings: "Everything is dangerous if you're stupid" but not so if citizens are well informed, keep risks in perspective, and take sensible precautions. Starting with an overview of the nature of hazards and continuing through the glossary and index, Callahan has produced a very readable book of introductory information on a wide range of biological hazards, ever present somewhere in the environment. Chapters divide hazards into categories: human pathogens in water, food, and air; those transmitted by contact; plant and animal pathogens and pests; venoms, toxins, and allergens; and animals that are a threat for predatory or other behavior. Another chapter provides information on controversial topics such as immunization and biological warfare. These chapters generally conclude with "Outlook for the Twenty-first Century"; "The Good Old Days," which lends historical perspective; and "From the Author's File Cabinet," which offers anecdotes that help illustrate various points.

The chapters that deal with different kinds of hazards offer extensive references and recommended readings. Lists of additional resources, including statistics and documents, print resources, nonprint resources, and organizations, comprise the final chapters. The volume's topical arrangement makes a good index imperative, and the index here is accurate and thorough. All types of libraries should consider this addition to their collections because of the accessible writing and the lists of both technical and popular resources for further information.

The Encyclopedia of Addictive Drugs. Richard Lawrence Miller. 2003. 491p. bibliogs. indexes. Greenwood, $75 (0-313-31807-7). 615.

Miller, who has authored other books on drug-related topics, has produced a remarkably clear and informative work intended for a wide audience, "from a student doing a term paper to reporters preparing a story, from parents reading that story to a narcotics law enforcement officer needing extra information."

Preceding the A–Z entries is a section on drug types that defines five major categories of drugs (e.g., stimulants, steroids), with subclasses where necessary. General information for each type of drug is given in detail, and all the alphabetical entries refer back to this section for descriptions of broad characteristics. The alphabetical listing of drugs that follows lists only substances "which have been declared a public concern by government officials, medical caregivers, or news media." Each entry includes the pronunciation of the substance, the Chemical Abstracts Service Registry Number (a unique identifier for every chemical), formal name or names, informal ("street") names, the drug type, Federal Schedule Listing (which ranks drugs according to their potential for abuse), U.S. availability (e.g., prescription or illegal), and pregnancy category (based on the risk a drug poses to the fetus). Following this information, highly readable discussions cover uses, drawbacks, abuse factors, some drug interactions, cancer risk, pregnancy effects, and any additional information that seems pertinent. Both notes and reliable sources of additional scientific information are listed at the end of each of the entries.

Entries are appropriately weighted. *Nutmeg*, for example, is a bit over two pages, while *Marijuana* runs to a little over eight (including two pages of informal names). A comprehensive list of print and Internet sources is included at the end of the volume, as are an exhaustive and accurate drug name index and a subject index.

More general and accessible than the *Drug Abuse Handbook* (CRC, 1998), *The Encyclopedia of Addictive Drugs* is recommended for high-school, academic, and large public libraries. It covers more addictive drugs than Gale's *Drugs and Controlled Substances: Information for Students* [RBB Mr 15 03], which is intended primarily for the high-school level.

Diseases. 8v. 2d ed. Ed. by Bryan Bunch. 2002. bibliogs. illus. index. Grolier, $299 (0-7172-5688-X). 616.003.

Written for middle-and high-school students, these volumes are a revised edition of a set originally published by Grolier in 1997 (and well reviewed in RBB). More than 500 diseases or conditions are arranged in alphabetical order, each identified as a disease (viral, mechanical, genetic, etc.), symptom (*Hives*), body system (*Thymus*), disorder (*Albinism*), injury (*Whiplash*), or reference (*Tropical diseases*). More than 40 entries are new or have been heavily revised. Most entries are at least a page or two, describing cause, incidence, symptoms, diagnosis, treatment, and prevention of disease and disorders. Often included are *see also* references, such as those to *Abscess*, *Digestive system*, *Inflammation*, *Large intestine*, and *Peritonitis* from the entry *Appendicitis*. *See* references are also found throughout the text (e.g., "*Babesiosis* see *Parasites and disease*").

Writing is understandable without being oversimplified, and many entries include pronunciations. The introductory pages claim "special attention has been paid to diseases and disorders that affect young people (ranging from *Acne* to *Warts*)," but many others are also included (*Finger and toenail fungus*, *Mastitis*, *Tourette's syndrome*). Often the text changes from narrative to give direct advice, such as "Tips to allergy-proof your home," "You can drain a painful blister," or "Call a physician immediately."

Illustrations are occasionally helpful (*Aneurysm* clearly shown, Heimlich maneuver demonstrated in a photo on *Asphyxia*), but many drawings are just cartoonish. A few first-aid books and newsletters plus health Web sites are listed in volume 1, but listing Web sites at the end of some articles would have been even more useful. Certainly this browsable set is appropriate for students or where an overview is adequate, and libraries where the first edition has been popular will want to update their collections.

The Encyclopedia of Asthma and Respiratory Disorders. By Tova Navarra. 2002. 410p. appendixes. bibliog. graphs. index. Facts On File, $71.50 (0-8160-4467-8). 616.2.

More than 1,000 entries define and explain causes of asthma and other respiratory diseases and disorders. Information on treatment protocols, medications, research, and prevention is given, as are definitions of key related health terms. Entries for professional and nonprofit organizations are also included.

Most definitions are very short, often just a phrase or a sentence. In one exception, the *Asthma* entry runs several pages and is nicely organized by subtopics such as "Symptoms and Signs of an Asthma Attack" and "Medications for Asthma." Entries for other respiratory diseases are several paragraphs long and, although the basics are covered, are not nearly as comprehensive as the asthma article. Some articles are accompanied by statistical charts and graphs. There are also tables listing things such as the weeds and trees that cause hay fever. The A–Z definitions and articles make up just over one-half of the book. The remainder is composed of extensive appendixes, most of which give statistical details about asthma.

The introduction states that the encyclopedia is a resource for patients and their families, but the vocabulary is geared to a professional reader and those familiar with medical terminology specific to respiratory disease. Health information consumers will find more accessible information in the *Lung Disorders Sourcebook* (Omnigraphics, 2002) and *Respiratory Diseases and Disorders Sourcebook* (Omnigraphics, 1995). Both of these titles are part of the consumer-friendly Health Reference Series. Other useful titles are *The 2002 Official Patient's Sourcebook on Asthma* (ICON, 2002) and the AMA's *Essential Guide to Asthma* (Pocket Books, 1998). *The Encyclopedia of Asthma and Respiratory Disorders* would be useful in libraries serving health-care professionals and students involved in a health curriculum.

The Encyclopedia of Diabetes. By William A. Petit Jr. and Christine Adamec. 2002. 374p. appendixes. bibliog. index. Facts On File, $71.50 (0-8160-4498-8). 616.4.

This work is a comprehensive reference source on diabetes, the complex metabolic disorder that afflicts nearly 20 million Americans. Beginning with a helpful 20-page historical overview, the book continues in an A–Z format and examines key aspects of the disease, including medical and physiological terms, treatment and self-care, related social issues, personal adjustment to having the disease, up-to-date research and statistics, and so on. All forms of diabetes are included: Type 1 (juvenile onset) and Type 2 (formerly "non-insulin dependent") as well as forms of the disease resulting from surgery, medication, malnutrition, pregnancy, and other causes.

The more than 300 entries cover such diabetes-related topics as diet, smoking, foot care, amputation, blood glucose monitoring, insulin use, legal issues, men's and women's issues, diabetes in various ethnic groups and nationalities, and more. Many helpful charts and sources of information are included in entries. Eleven appendixes cover organizations, periodicals, research centers, Web sites, medications, and so on. The bibliography is extensive.

The book strikes a good balance between the audiences of healthcare professionals working with this population and patients themselves. Because diabetes is a growing problem, with more than 800,000 new cases diagnosed annually, this promises to be a valuable source for academic, professional, and public libraries.

The Encyclopedia of Skin and Skin Disorders. 2d ed. By Carol Turkington and Jeffrey S. Dover. 2002. 436p. appendixes. bibliog. glossary. index. Facts On File, $71.50 (0-8160-4776-6). 616.5.

This is the book to turn to to find out why one shouldn't wear makeup during air travel until a few minutes before landing; why a southwestern critter with a name as innocuous as the Kissing Bug should be avoided if at all possible; whether you really do want to wash your face, and if so, how; or which slug's shells are crushed and used to provide the reddish pigment in many cosmetics. Readers will use this work as an initial source for information regarding such topics as the possible risks of suicide associated with the use of certain acne medication or the treatment of varicose veins with endovascular lasers.

More than 1,100 cross-referenced entries range in length from the single line devoted to *Tumbu fly bites* to multiple pages, such as the entry for *Burns*. Most seem to be in the two-to five-paragraph range. New to this second edition are entries on news makers like Botox and information on the possible link between the foaming agent diethanolamine and cancer. There certainly is enough updated information to warrant libraries replacing the first edition (called *Skin Deep: An A–Z Encyclopedia of Skin Disorders*, 1996).

The few images are clear black-and-white drawings. A nice example is the cross-section of a fingertip that accompanies the entry *Nails*. Several appendixes provide readers with helpful lists such as "Cosmetic Ingredients to Avoid," "Types of Lesions," and contact information for skin-related organizations as well as a glossary, a bibliography, and a well-developed index.

The volume will surely be welcome in high-school and college libraries, public libraries of all sizes, and consumer-health collections.

The Gale Encyclopedia of Mental Disorders. 2v. Ed. by Ellen Thackery and Madeline Harris. 2002. 1,173p. bibliogs. glossary. illus. index. Gale, $275 (0-7876-5768-9). 616.89.

Mental illness is a major cause of disability in the U.S. Thirty million people visit physicians and two million spend time in hospitals every year because of mental disorders. *The Gale Encyclopedia of Mental Disorders* provides a good overview of mental illness, psychotherapy, and other treatments. It includes both traditional and alternative therapies. Medical writers, pharmacists, and mental health professionals wrote and edited the 400 signed, alphabetical entries in the set.

The entries cover disorders (*Anorexia nervosa*, *Schizophrenia*); diagnostic procedures and techniques (*Kaufman Short Neurological Assessment Procedure*, *Magnetic resonance imaging*); therapies (*Behavior modification*, *Electroconvulsive therapy*); medicines and herbs (*Paroxetine*, *St. John's Wort*); and related topics (*Advance directives*, *Neurotransmitters*). Entries for disorders include a definition, description, causes and symptoms, demographics, diagnosis, treatments, prognosis, and prevention. Those for medications contain the definition, purpose, description, recommended dosage, precautions, side effects, and interactions. Entries for herbs and supplements have a leaf icon next to the heading. All entries have a resource list of print and electronic sources and organizations to contact. One hundred black-and-white photographs and charts illustrate the text. A color photo gallery repeated in both volumes has enhanced versions of some of the photographs. There are ample cross-references, making it easy to locate drugs, which are entered by generic name. Boxes with definitions of key terms help readers understand the material. A full glossary is at the end of volume 2. Users will find a symptom list here also. This list demonstrates patterns that are linked to various disorders.

Although there is some overlap with *The Gale Encyclopedia of Medicine* (2d ed., 2002), The Gale Encyclopedia of Mental Disorders offers more detailed coverage of psychiatric disorders and their treatments. The articles are more accessible than those in a medical textbook or the DSM (Diagnostic and Statistical Manual of Mental Disorders, published by the American Psychiatric Association), but they still require a fairly high level of literacy. This is an excellent resource for public, academic, and consumer-health libraries.

The Patient's Guide to Medical Tests: Everything You Need to Know about the Tests Your Doctor Orders. 2d ed. By Joseph C. Segen and Josie Wade. 2002. 418p. glossary. index. Facts On File, $44 (0-8160-4651-4). 616.07.

Medical tests can be intimidating, particularly if the patient is uninformed about the procedure. Written by a physician and a registered nurse, this updated guide provides basic facts on about 1,000 medical tests and terms. The alphabetically arranged entries are about a paragraph in length and usually include a description of the test, patient preparation, the procedure, the reference range of values for persons free of disease, abnormal values, cost, and special instructions or precautions. There are no illustrations, and the book does not provide much information on pain and other possible side effects. A 54-page glossary, a subject index, and a brief list of medical abbreviations and symbols are included.

Because rapidly evolving technology results in continual advances in the field of diagnostic medicine, recent knowledge must be made available. A good supplement to print sources is the MEDLINEplus Medical Encyclopedia Web site [http://www.nlm.nih.gov/medlineplus/encyclopedia.html], from the National Library of Medicine/National Institutes of Health, which offers authoritative updated facts on many common medical tests as well as a wealth of other health information.

The strength of this revised edition is its currency and the number of tests included. The book is recommended for public, special, and academic libraries in need of a recent concise guide to medical tests. However, because the information is very succinct, users may want to consult other sources, such as The Yale University School of Medicine Patient's Guide to Medical Tests (2d ed., Houghton, 2002), as well.

Encyclopedia of Bridges and Tunnels. By Stephen Johnson and Roberto T. Leon. 2002. 381p. appendixes. bibliog. illus. Facts On File, $75 (0-8160-4482-1); Checkmark, paper, $21.95 (0-8160-4483-X). 624.

A selective guide to bridges and tunnels worldwide, this volume presents information about circumstances, technologies, and people involved in these landmark projects. Entries for particular structures include name, dates of construction, and a short descriptive phrase (for example, London's Millennium Bridge is described as "Britain's wobbly symbol"), followed by a description of building materials and techniques and circumstances surrounding construction. Others among the more than 300 entries cover types of bridges and tunnels (Beam bridge, Cantilever bridge); principles, materials, and techniques of design and construction (Bridge aerodynamics, Concrete, Wetdrilling); events (Channel Tunnel fire, Lowe's Motor Speedway walkway collapse); personalities (reinforced concrete inventor Joseph Menier, Brooklyn Bridge designer John Augustus Roebling); and more. Length of entries ranges from three or four paragraphs to almost 10 pages for Golden Gate Bridge. Although there are no lists of further readings, there are an appendix for bridge and tunnel Web sites and a bibliography. An additional appendix lists longest bridges and tunnels by type.

The reading level is not too technical and is appropriate for general readers, although it may not be detailed enough for a practicing engineer. The writing style tends to veer away from reportorial objectivity (for example, the entry for the Mostar Bridge in Bosnia notes that it was "vindictively blasted into rubble by Croat troops"), which some readers might find distracting.

The Encyclopedia of Bridges and Tunnels nicely complements Encyclopedia of Architectural and Engineering Feats [RBB My 15 02]. Recommended for the technology reference collections of public and academic libraries.

The American Horticultural Society Encyclopedia of Plants and Flowers. Rev. ed. Ed. by Christopher Brickell and Trevor Cole. 2002. 720p. glossary. illus. index. DK, $60 (0-7894-8993-7). 635.9.

If only one gardening resource is purchased this year, let it be this book, a revision of The American Horticultural Society Encyclopedia of Garden Plants (1989). Tightly packed into a single volume is nearly everything that amateur landscapers and gardeners need to consider for outlining, designing, and planting their outdoor growing areas.

Two indispensable tools, the 2002 USDA plant hardiness zone map, upgraded to 15 zones, and the 1997 American Horticultural Society plant heat zone map, appear on the front and back endpapers. Of utmost importance is the "How to Use This Book" section, which explains how best to navigate through the charts, symbols, color codes, abbreviations, and special features of the text. Following this, the arrangement of information resembles the organized subconscious thought process associated with the planning and preplanting seasons. "Creating a Garden" takes the reader step-by-step through the entire process of creating an appropriate landscape and garden design. Everything is to be considered—plot size, style, structure, proportion, texture, colors, plant selection, and the year-round maintenance, appearance, and growth factor. Basically, this is how the professionals do it. "The Plant Selector" offers advice and recommendations for particular sites or uses. The main portion of the encyclopedia, "The Plant Catalog," is divided into 10 sections (for trees, shrubs, roses, perennials, rock plants, cacti, and more). Within each section, plants are arranged by size, season of interest, and color. Each description includes botanical and common names, portrait, plant size (height and spread), shape, cultivation and hardiness zones, color range, and toxicity.

Whether one is planning a full-scale garden, a postage-stamp garden, or simply a container garden, the plant catalog has the appropriate selection. The book's final section, "The Plant Dictionary," compiles more than 8,000 readily obtainable plants for temperate zones, with full descriptions for 4,000 of these not already covered in the catalog. A glossary completes the text. Authoritative, beautifully designed, and lavishly illustrated (but not to the point of overshadowing the text), this hefty practical gardening encyclopedia deserves far more than a mere glance.

The Botanical Garden: Volume 1: Trees and Shrubs. By Roger Phillips and Martyn Rix. 2002. 491p. bibliog. glossary. illus. index. Firefly, $75 (1-55297-591-6). 635.976.

The Botanical Garden: Volume 2: Perennials and Annuals. By Roger Phillips and Martyn Rix. 2002. 539p. bibliog.. glossary. illus. index. Firefly, $75 (1-55297-592-4). 635.9.

The strict botanical viewpoint of Phillips and Rix offers scholarly gardeners an alternative to popular horticulture guides. In two classy volumes illustrated with detailed photos of leaves and bracts, blossoms, rhizomes, and root structures, the text expresses the value of plants to ecology, farming, and the individual orchard, landscape, flower bed, and window box. Arranged into groups in evolutionary order, the plants appear on individual pages or multipage spreads alongside scientific name, concise description, locale, and designation of hybrids and cultivation methods. The commentary is reduced to the blunt shorthand of the scientist, but the 4,000 pictures are pure art. Rounding out each volume are a succinct two-page glossary of such terms as loess, raceme, and umbel and a brief bibliography organized by continent.

Examples of elegantly arranged illustrations are found under Albizia, Mahonia, and Yucca in volume 1 and under Acanthus, Dryopteris, and Molucella in volume 2. The accompanying plant data are, as the authors state, definitive and full of exacting details (e.g., the names and dates of botanists who located and classified individual flowers, ferns, herbs, bamboos, and evergreens). What is lacking in each entry and particularly in the index is the human touch. The authors ignore common names for many plants (the only way to find lilac is to know that its scientific name is Syringa) and avoid reference to plant uses in cooking, aromatherapy, and healing, thus confining the value of the set to college and university libraries. Whereas the botanist and grower will be overjoyed to find so brilliant a display of entries and plant photos, the high-school student, librarian, greenhouse manager, and ordinary gardener is more likely to experience frustration. Recommended for large botany collections.

Caring for Your Dog: The Complete Canine Home Reference. By Bruce Fogle. 2003. 448p. glossary. illus. index. DK, $35 (0-7894-8929-5). 636.7089.

Fogle, a Canadian with an extensive veterinary practice in the U.K., has produced a useful and comprehensive reference for both the public library and the pet-owner's library. Chapters are arranged into three sections: "Your Family Dog," "Diseases and Disorders," and "First Aid and Emergencies." The section on diseases is the most extensive, with chapters covering topics such as nutrition, the immune system, the various body systems, and geriatric health. Within these chapters are entries on specific conditions, terms, treatments, and so on. The text is clear and nontechnical, with a good glossary at the end. There are many sidebars, including weight charts, lists of breeds at risk for particular ailments, and questions and answers. Flow charts for specific processes such as whelping can tell a pet owner when something is normal and when the vet needs to be called.

A good introductory section covers selecting, living with, and training a dog. A thoughtful consideration of euthanasia comes essentially from the Western tradition but acknowledges that for other traditions the decision may be fraught with conflict. The "First Aid and Emergencies" section has a flow-charted "emergency action plan," a suggested first-aid kit, and recommended first-aid actions until one can get the animal to the vet. The section on poisoning covers dangerous household items, plants, and animals. A "Clinical Signs Rapid Reference" can be found at the beginning of the volume and a good general index at the end.

As with all DK titles, the text is liberally illustrated with high-quality diagrams and photographs. Illustrations of diseases or injuries are presented clearly. Recommended for public libraries for both the reference and circulating collections.

Dogs: The Ultimate Dictionary of Over 1,000 Dog Breeds. By Desmond Morris. 2002. 752p. bibliog. illus. index. Trafalgar Square, $24.95 (1-57076-219-8). 636.71.

Animal lovers have long been captivated by Morris' fascinating work in the field of animal behavior. This addition to his oeuvre will not disappoint. Morris says this is the reference book he always wanted. It didn'st exist so he wrote it! While most standard guides focus on a breed's physical standards for the show ring, this guide downplays that aspect and instead gives a historical perspective.

More than 1,000 dog breeds are covered. Breeds that are officially recognized and registered by major kennel clubs are included, but this dictionary also encompasses unrecognized breeds that have played a part in the history of domestic dogs. New breeds such as the Schnoodle, service dogs for the disabled, and even dogs once bred for human consumption are discussed, as are wild dogs, wolf-dog hybrids, and obscure and extinct breeds.

Presentation and organization of breed information is unique. Dogs are arranged first according to their original function—"Sporting Dogs," "Livestock Dogs," and "Service Dogs." Within these broad categories the animals are separated by functional specialty, such as "Sighthounds," "Sheep-herders," and "Rescue Dogs." For each group, a short overview essay is followed by entries for specific breeds, arranged by country of origin. The physical appearance and disposition of the dog are described, along with the breed's history and development over time, as well as the background of the breed name. (There was at one time a breed called a Turnspit whose name precisely described its function—running in a wheel that turned meat being roasted before a fire.) Information about relationships among breeds and controversies among canine experts adds an interesting dimension. Some breeds are represented in small black-and-white drawings. In addition to an extensive annotated bibliography, a list of references appears after many entries. There is an alphabetical index of 3,000 breed names, with those appearing in the dictionary in capital letters.

Although not replacing official kennel club guides, this title will be a valuable supplementary source of information for dog lovers. It offers hours of delightful browsing through the history of man's best friend.

★**The Advertising Age Encyclopedia of Advertising.** 3v. Ed. by John McDonough and Karen Egolf. 2002. 1,873p. appendixes. bibliogs. illus. index. Fitzroy Dearborn, $385 (1-57958-172-2). 659.103.

This comprehensive reference source takes a broad look at the advertising industry. Its focus is primarily historical because, as the editors point out, "much of advertising's past remains buried, reported only in rare press accounts and other primary sources." Included are profiles of 120 ad agencies from around the world, 80 of them contemporary. Also covered are 40 U.S. agencies of historic interest that have either merged with other entities or gone out of business. In many cases, the encyclopedia provides an agency's first formal written history.

In addition to the agency histories, one finds entries for advertisers, brands, and campaigns (*Airlines*; *Geritol*; *Kraft Foods, Inc.*; *Yahoo!*); individuals (*Burnett, Leo*; *Hearst, William Randolph*; *Packard, Vance*); practical and theoretical aspects of advertising (*Infomercial*, *Music and jingles*, *Package design*, *Psychographics*, *Targeting*); and social, cultural, and historical issues (*Consumer movement*; *Cultural symbols*; *Minorities: Representations in advertising*). There are also 52 entries dealing with the history of advertising in specific countries or regions (*Canada*, *Middle East*). Ad agency profiles start with brief chronologies of key dates and alphabetical lists of major clients. Advertiser profiles include lists of principal agencies. Most entries conclude with a list of further reading. Entry length generally ranges from one to six or seven pages. The set is richly illustrated, and each volume includes a 24-page section of color plates that are cross-referenced from related entries. The hundreds of illustrations, most of which came from the Hartman Center for Sales, Advertising, and Marketing History in Duke University's Rare Book, Manuscript, and Special Collections Library, enhance the usefulness of the volumes and bring the words to life.

The third volume ends with appendixes: "Advertising Hall of Fame," "Notable U.S. Advertising Degree Programs," "Top U.S. Advertising Agencies," "Top U.S. Advertisers," "Top Worldwide Advertising Agencies," and "Top Worldwide Advertisers." A lengthy, detailed index identifies acronyms and provides access by keywords, authors/titles, institutes, companies, individuals, associations, quotes/jingles from commercials, products, and more. The level of detail in the index helps compensate for the lack of *see also* references.

This encyclopedia complements Gale's *Encyclopedia of Major Marketing Campaigns* (2000), which profiles 500 specific advertising efforts (for example, Timex Corporation's "It Takes a Lickin' and Keeps on Tickin'"; Wendy International's "Where's the Beef?"). Well-researched, thorough, and fascinating, it belongs in all business collections and most academic and large public libraries.

A Student's Guide to Biotechnology. 4v. 2002. bibliogs. glossaries. illus. indexes. Greenwood, $160 (0-313-32256-2). 660.6.

This attractive series is designed to help students in grades 6 through 12 understand the issues that make up the biotechnology debate. It defines terms, profiles people who have made significant contributions to the field, provides a historical overview, and investigates the controversies associated with biotech research.

Each volume includes an identical time line as well as a volume-specific bibliography and index. Volumes 2 to 4 also have glossaries. The volume *Words and Terms* defines terms, gives examples of their use, and adds historical and technical information that shows how the term fits into the scheme of biotechnology. Some entries also include information on scientists or interesting facts associated with the term. Entries are heavily cross-referenced through the use of bold type. This is an excellent resource to help students understand complex issues or see connections. The volume *Important People in Biotechnology* profiles almost 40 individuals, from Anton van Leeuwenhoek (1632–1723) to Genentech founder Robert Swanson (1947–99). Entries are between two and four pages long, and each is accompanied by a picture of the individual. "The History of Biotechnology" begins its coverage with the processes of fermentation and composting in the ancient world and ends with speculation about the future. "Debatable Issues" presents a balanced look at some of the most controversial issues facing scientists today: DNA testing, genetic modification, stem cell research, cloning, and holding patents on the human genome. Each chapter begins with an overview, followed by fictitious speakers presenting a pro and con opinion on the topic. Although the individuals are not real, the ideas represent held opinions.

These volumes are sure to be useful for teachers or librarians who want to introduce research skills to middle-schoolers. Students will appreciate finding so much current information about topics that are hotly debated in the news. *A Student's Guide to Biotechnology* is recommended for school and public libraries.

Fine Arts, Decorative Arts, Music

Artists from Latin American Cultures: A Biographical Dictionary. By Kristin G. Congdon and Kara Kelley Hallmark. 2002. 314p. bibliogs. glossary. illus. index. Greenwood, $59.95 (0-313-31544-2). 709.

Profiling twentieth-century artists in a variety of genres, this biographical dictionary contains 75 alphabetical entries with two or three pages of basic information (date and place of birth and death), genre, places to view artist's works, and a bibliography for further reading. The clear, well-written essays discuss societal influences such as culture, politics, language, and economics. When available, quotations from the artist have been provided. Artists from the U.S. and 13 nations of Central and South American and the Caribbean and working in a variety of genres are included. Although many, such as Frida Kahlo, Wifredo Lam, and Diego Rivera, are well known, others are not as visible to the general public. Important works of each artist are described to help readers visualize them. Illustrations include black-and-white photographs in some of the entries and 13 color plates in the middle section of the book. Although many art terms are defined within the text, the glossary defines artistic styles and religious and political movements.

Artists from Latin American Cultures would be a useful tool in high-school, public, and undergraduate libraries seeking an introduction to Latin American art. It supplements related works such as the *Encyclopedia of Latin American & Caribbean Art* (2000), the second publication in the Grove Library of World Art series, which not only includes artist biographies and influential art movements but also provides almost 500 illustrations and nearly 100 color plates.

Contemporary Fashion. 2d ed. Ed. by Taryn Benbow-Pfalzgraf. 2002. 743p. bibliogs. illus. index. St. James, $170 (1-55862-348-5). 746.9.

The second edition of *Contemporary Fashion*, a revision of the late Richard Martin's 1995 edition, provides students and scholars with useful information on more than 400 fashion leaders from the 1940s to today. New entries include Stella McCartney, Vera Wang, and companies such as Abercrombie & Fitch and Victoria's Secret. Each alphabetically arranged entry contains a capsule biography or company history, a list of books and articles by or about the designer, an essay, and in some of the entries a brief quote from the subject on design philosophy or his or her work. Unique to this edition is an advisory board of industry professionals who helped choose approximately 50 new designers and companies. The number of photographs has doubled from the previous edition. A "Nationality Index" provides the only indexing.

A similar publication is Anne Stegemeyer's *Who's Who in Fashion* (Fairchild, 1996). Although it includes color photos, unlike *Contemporary Fashion*'s black-and-white photos, only 250 fashion designers are represented, with very brief entries and no individual designer bibliographies. Another recent title, *In an Influential Fashion: An Encyclopedia of Nineteenth-and Twentieth-Century Fashion Designers and Retailers Who Transformed Dress* [RBB Ag 02], focuses primarily on the U.S. and serves as a good general introduction for high-school and public libraries. Large public libraries and academic libraries serving fashion and design programs will find the more comprehensive *Contemporary Fashion* useful.

The Oxford Companion to Music. Ed. by Alison Latham. 2002. 1,434p. bibliogs. index. Oxford, $60 (0-19-866212-2). 780.3.

The new *Oxford Companion to Music* updates two earlier works: the original 1938 *Companion*, last published in 1970, and *The New Oxford Companion to Music*, a two-volume set published in 1983. Its focus is classical music from the Middle Ages to the present. In the preface, editor Latham notes that "non-Western and popular musics are included, but mostly in so far as they have had an impact on the Western classical tradition." According to the jacket blurb, there are more than 1,000 (out of more than 8,000 total) new entries, and more than 70 percent of the content has been revised or rewritten. Well over 100 scholars and writers contributed to this edition.

Entries, arranged alphabetically, vary in length from one or two lines (*Orchestral score*; *Rite of Spring, The*) to several pages (*Copyright*; *Form*; *Handel, George Frideric*; *Pianoforte*). Biographies (of composers, artists, etc.), instruments, well-known works, countries, societies, musical terms and types, and sociocultural aspects (*Music on the Internet*, *Politics and music*) are all covered. Nine major multipage essays on topics such as "The Baroque Era" and "Opera" are printed on a light gray background and arranged in sections. Some are new; some are repeats from the *New Oxford* with necessary revisions. Some entries show the British origin of the work, such as *Eighth-note*, defined as the American term for *quaver*. Tables and examples of notation are added where needed, but the photographs, portraits, and reproductions of paintings and scores found in the *New Oxford* have been omitted. The writing is accessible to a wide range of users, from students and professional musicians to the general reader and listener.

Libraries that own *Baker's Dictionary of Music* (Schirmer, 1997), which is somewhat similar in scope and size, will want to purchase this as well, because each title has many unique entries. In general, although *Baker's* has more references to popular music, *Oxford* includes more scholarly and technical detail as well as bibliographic references that have been expanded from other editions. This will be a standard purchase for smaller libraries that want to update the classical music section with a reasonably priced, one-volume work.

Women and Music in America since 1900: An Encyclopedia. 2v. Ed. by Kristine H. Burns. 2002. 747p. bibliogs. illus. index. Greenwood, $150 (1-57356-267-X). 780.

As the editor points out, "The major role that women have played and continue to play in the musical culture of the United States is indisputable." This encyclopedia is "the first major attempt" to document that role.

Approximately 300 of the A–Z entries are for women in a broad range of musical forms—Anonymous 4, Joan Baez, Cher, Judy Garland, Bernadette Peters, Leontyne Price, LeAnn Rimes, Barbra Streisand, and the Supremes, to give just a few examples. A number of educators, patrons, and researchers are also included. All of the women were born in or made most of their contribution in the U.S., were born in or lived chiefly during the twentieth century, and "advanced the role of women in music." The intent is not to be exhaustive but to identify major contributions, focusing on those who have won awards or been the first or most successful. In addition, there are entries for topics in education (*Children's choirs*, *Piano pedagogy*); gender issues (*Feminist music history*, *Male gaze*); genres (*Asian American music*, *Church music*, *Motown*); honors and awards (*Country Music Hall of Fame*, *Fulbright Fellowship Program*); organizations (*Grand Ole Opry*; *Performance ensembles, classical*); and professions (*Audio production*, *Music librarian*). Signed entries range in length from half of a page to just over four pages for *Garage rock and heavy metal bands*, *Rock and popular music genres*, and a few others, and each includes a list of further readings. A chronology and a topical list of entries appear at the front of each volume. Volume 2 concludes with a bibliography and an index in which entry headings are denoted with bold type.

Information on many of these women is readily available in other sources. However, combining selective biographical coverage with entries for topics that address a variety of related issues provides useful context and a unique perspective. This set would be a valuable addition to academic and larger public libraries as well as any library that specializes in music or in women's studies.

Encyclopedia of Contemporary Christian Music. By Mark Allan Powell. 2002. 1,088p. glossary. index. Hendrickson, paper, $29.95 (1-56563-679-1). 782.25.

Powell, a professor at Trinity Lutheran Seminary and former pastor, has created a work for a genre that, though popular and widespread, has received little reference coverage. Even in other music reference works, such as Salem Press' *Popular Musicians* (1999), this form of music is pushed into the categories of pop, rock, or gospel. Powell defines contemporary Christian as a musical style that was developed in the late 1960s and early 1970s and known then as "Jesus music." Since that time, it has evolved and borrowed from other popular musical styles such as metal, rap, rock, and ska. Gospel of any variety and other types of Christian music (hymns, sacred music, instrumentals) are excluded.

The alphabetically arranged entries cover individuals and groups. Each entry lists all albums produced, with date and record company. An essay provides biography and evaluation as well as partial lyrics for significant songs and notes on performance style. Group entries name all members (including dates for when various members came and went), the instruments they played, and who sang the vocals. Entries conclude with lists of chart hits and awards.

Powell drew upon every available issue of prominent and lesser-known Christian music periodicals, newspapers, and Web sites, then created a database of each artist and group discussed, interviewed, or reviewed in these sources. Some of the groups he includes are primarily known as rock or pop bands that occasionally have songs or albums with a spiritual nature, such as Moby and U2. Powell states that in these cases, he erred on the side of inclusion. More well known singers and groups have longer entries (for example, Amy Grant, the Winans, Jennifer Knapp), but even the less well known (for example, Phat Chance, Project 86, Jan Krist) have at least a long paragraph.

Given the sheer volume of material, the relatively modest price of this work is a wonderful bargain. Add to that the unique coverage, and this volume is highly recommended for music collections and Christian schools.

Haydn. Ed. by David Wyn Jones. 2002. 515p. appendixes. bibliogs. map. Oxford, $70 (0-19-866216-5). 780.

Similar in format to the Oxford Composer Companions book on J. S. Bach (1999), this well-planned, scholarly encyclopedia is a comprehensive and informative reference source on the life, music, and times of the prolific and influential eighteenth-century composer of classical music.

A "Thematic Overview" listing the book's entries under broad topics and then subdivided by specific subjects related to Haydn helps readers focus on the areas of knowledge they are researching (e.g., biography; composers; family, friends, and acquaintances; cities, towns, and villages; individual musical works). This is followed by a Haydn family genealogical chart and a sketchy map of Europe and England. The main body of the encyclopedia consists of almost 1,000 alphabetically arranged entries related to Haydn's life, music, and historical era. Each entry is followed by the initials of the author, whose full name can be determined by referring to a list of contributors located at the beginning of the book. Many entries also cite one or two sources used in the preparation of the entry. In addition, there are several megaentries that give in-depth treatment to subjects like Haydn's life, his compositional method, the keyboard sonata, and the symphony.

Appendixes include a list of Haydn's works in chart format, noting details like instruments scored for, musical key, date, and Hoboken number as well as a chart of "text incipits" noting movements in Haydn's vocal music cross-referenced to the Hoboken catalogue. There is unfortunately no index, which would help readers identify specific subjects within the text of entries.

This reference source provides comprehensive and accurate information similar to that found in the 100-page article on Haydn in *The New Grove Dictionary of Music and Musicians* (2d ed, Groves, 2001). It is most useful as a complement to *The New Grove Dictionary* in academic libraries supporting graduate-level programs in music and in large public libraries.

Chronology of Western Classical Music. 2v. By Charles J. Hall. 2002. 1,340p. indexes. Routledge, $225 (0-415-93878-3). 781.6.

This new chronology covers events in "cultivated/art music" from around the world for the years 1751 through 1900 and 1901 through 1999. Author Hall's previous chronologies, A *Chronicle of American Music, 1700–1995* (Schirmer, 1996), An *Eighteenth-Century Musical Chronicle: Events, 1750–1799* (Greenwood, 1990), A *Nineteenth-Century Musical Chronicle: Events, 1800–1899* (Greenwood, 1989), and A *Twentieth-Century Musical Chronicle: Events, 1900–1988* (Greenwood, 1989), have essentially been rolled into one, with some additions, corrections, and formatting changes.

Each year's entry begins with a couple of paragraphs outlining historical and arts and literature highlights. Nine categories of musical events follow, among them "Births" and "Deaths" (both further subdivided into composers, conductors, singers, performers, and others); "Debuts"; "Prizes/Honors"; and "Biographical Highlights." The last category in each year, "Musical Compositions," is the largest, encompassing chamber music, choral and vocal music, orchestral and band music, ballets, symphonies, and more. A "Composition Index" and a "Historical Index" (which indexes names of people, orchestras, places, and so on) complete the set. There is no source bibliography, which would undoubtedly fill an entire volume, but the author cites the *New Grove Dictionary of Music and Musicians* (Grove, 2001) and *Baker's Biographical Dictionary of Musicians* (Schirmer, 2001) as "the final word" when he found conflicting data.

Hall's earlier works have a cleaner layout, but there is better organization of compositions in the new set, with narrower subdivisions in each broad category. A comparison of entries in the latest chronology with those in the author's earlier works shows that several new names have been added in the various categories for each year, and many old names have been corrected or include additional data, such as what instrument a person played. Libraries that have the other works may not be able to justify purchase of the new set, but those with comprehensive music collections or high demand for chronologies will welcome it. Another music chronology, *Music since 1900* (Schirmer, 6th ed., 2001), takes a day-by-day rather than a subject approach and covers only the twentieth century.

Country Music: A Biographical Dictionary. By Richard Carlin. 2002. 497p. appendixes. bibliog. illus. index. Routledge, $125 (0-415-93802-3). 781.642.

Country music speaks to the downtrodden, the lonely, the rebellious, and the bruised. Where else can you find this type of lyric: "I've got tears in my ears from lyin' on my back in my bed while I cry over you" by Harold Barlow?

That type of song is described as a "Weeper—a song dripping with heavy sentiment, often dealing with romantic loss, death or betrayal" in a revised and expanded version of *The Big Book of Country Music* (Penguin, 1995). There is factual information here but also Carlin's personal opinion on the historic and current musicians of American country music. Following a short history of the genre, each entry includes birth and death dates, followed by biographical information that covers lives before, during, and after any commercial or critical success. The entry closes with a discography of selected currently available recordings on CD. Photographs occasionally accompany the entries, which range in length from a quarter page in one column to a whole two-column page.

A few entries on musical styles are included, for example, bluegrass, gospel, honky-tonk, and rockabilly. In addition, other significant aspects of country music have entries, among them such instruments as the banjo and the guitar and such places as the Grand Ole Opry. The majority of the entries are about the performers, both individuals and groups. Carlin includes current favorites such as Billy Ray Cyrus and Faith Hill (who sings "as if she were trying to launch her tonsils into the upper tier of seats at Yankee Stadium") along with historic names such as the Carolina Tar Heels, who were best known during the 1920s.

Following the more than 900 biographical and subject entries are a select bibliography, appendixes on selected entries by musical genre and selected entries by musical instrument, and finally a comprehensive name index, which also includes song titles and album titles. This spirited look at country music is recommended for large music collections as well as for any library serving fans of the genre.

A Chronology of American Musical Theater. 3v. By Richard C. Norton. 2002. illus. indexes. Oxford, $395 (0-19-508888-3). 782.1.

Designed as a companion to Gerald Bordman's *American Musical Theatre: A Chronicle* (3d ed., Oxford, 2000), this hefty set reproduces the program information for every musical, operetta, or other musical play that opened in a major New York City theater from January 1850 through May 2001. In addition, it includes selective coverage of productions from the previous 100 years, thus providing an impressive chronological record of 4,978 musicals (including revivals) produced on Broadway from 1750 to the end of the 2000–2001 season.

Norton devoted seven years to researching and preparing this compilation, relying on actual theater programs from opening nights or opening weeks, supplemented with information gleaned from *Variety*, *Billboard*, the *New York Times*, and other publications. Arranged by the date each musical opened, the entries provide extensive credits and cast lists, act and scene settings, the beginning and ending dates of the production's run, the total number of performances, and any changes of venue or return engagements. Most entries also include an act-by-act list of songs and other musical numbers and the performers for each. Meticulous footnotes give sources of information for material not found in the programs and additional details, such as revisions or added songs. Preceding the section for each theater season is a black-and-white photograph of a scene from one of the featured musicals. Volume 3 includes indexes to show titles, songs, and selected individuals.

In his lengthy preface, Norton provides useful historical background and detailed explanations regarding his criteria for inclusion. His interpretation of "musical theater" is quite broad, encompassing almost any entertainment with musical components, such as revues, burlesques, comic operas, and dance dramas. However, his geographical range is more confined, limited to those New York City venues generally considered to be within the Broadway theater district. As he himself regretfully notes, his exclusion of off-Broadway productions means that *The Fantasticks* does not appear in this set.

Although there is considerable overlap between this work and Ken Bloom's two-volume *American Song: The Complete Musical Theatre Companion, 1877–1995* (2d ed., Schirmer, 1996), each compilation includes productions that are not in the other. While Bloom's work covers slightly fewer shows (4,863), it encompasses not just Broadway but off-Broadway and off-off-Broadway musicals as well as regional theater and original television productions. On the other hand, Norton's chronology covers many Broadway shows not in Bloom's work, and it also provides more extensive information for each musical. By far the most comprehensive and scholarly chronology of Broadway musicals available, A *Chronology of American Musical Theater* makes a substantial contribution to the history of musical theater in the U.S., and it is highly recommended for larger public, academic, and research libraries.

Performing Arts, Recreation

Sports and Games of Medieval Cultures. By Sally Wilkins. 2002. 325p. appendix. bibliog. illus. indexes. Greenwood, $49.95 (0-313-31711-9). 790.

The Middle Ages are defined as spanning from 466 to 1476 for the purposes of this text. It is part of the Sports and Games Through History series, which for now also includes *Sports and Games of the Ancients* (2002) and *Sports and Games of the 18th and 19th Centuries* (2002).

Each chapter of the book covers a separate geographical area: Africa, Asia, Europe, Latin America, Middle East, North America, and Oceania. Within each chapter, there is an opening summary of sport in that part of the world, followed by sections on games ("sedentary pastimes with recognized rules of play"), play ("active games and outdoor play"), and sports ("organized, competitive physical activity"). Within each section, entries for individual activities are alphabetically arranged. Discussions generally range from a paragraph to a page and a half and cover development, equipment, and rules. Familiar sports, many of which appear in more than one chapter because they occurred in different parts of the world, include swimming, tennis, lacrosse, chess, and dice. Lesser-known examples include the Xhosa stone game (a version of jackstones, or jacks); *tsoro yematatu* (a version of ticktacktoe), from Zimbabwe; and *tako-no kiri-ai* (or kite fighting), from Japan and Korea. Many entries include suggestions for adapting games for modern use, and the appendix includes how-to instructions for making some of the sporting or gaming equipment using available materials. Black-and-white photos and some explanatory diagrams enhance understanding of the activity being described.

The bibliography lists a variety of sports history texts, articles, and Web sites. There are a geographical index listing countries within the larger regions and a subject index listing specific games or sports. Though its topic is specialized, this readable volume could be useful in several kinds of collections: sports, the Middles Ages, and multicultural studies.

African Americans in the Performing Arts. By Steven Otfinoski. 2003. 276p. bibliogs. illus. index. Facts On File, $44 (0-8160-4807-X). 791.
African-American Athletes. By Nathan Aaseng. 2003. 262p. bibliogs. illus. index. Facts On File, $44 (0-8160-4805-3). 796.

Here are two strong additions to the A–Z of African Americans series for students and general readers. Other titles in the series have included volumes on African American business leaders, religious leaders, and mathematicians and scientists.

The volume focusing on professional and amateur athletes is written by the veteran children's biography author Aaseng. Profiles cover more than 155 athletes, with information on their lives and their athletic accomplishments. Individuals were selected for inclusion based on a variety of factors—statistics, championships, recognition by peers, or pioneering efforts. Among them are Hank Aaron (baseball's career home-run leader), John Davis (two-time Olympic weightlifter), Emmitt Smith (professional football player), and Debi Thomas (Olympic figure skater). All but a handful are from the twentieth century. Failures and missteps of the athletes are not ignored, nor are they sensationalized.

African Americans in the Performing Arts features actors, dancers, singers, musicians, composers, and choreographers. Composers and choreographers such as Quincy Jones and Katherine Dunham are included when they are performers as well as creators.

The biographies mainly encompass performers from the early twentieth century through the 2002 Academy Awards. Selections were based on "personal preference, historical importance, variety, and level of achievement." Some 190 biographies treat notables such as Harry Belafonte, Duke Ellington, W. C. Handy, Roland Hayes, Ice-T, Frankie Lymon, and Bessie Smith. Entries describe each subject's life and how personal experience affected his or her art and, in many cases, his or her social activism. The unique individuality of the person is stressed in all cases.

The reader will be aided by the list of entries at the front of each book as well as the index, bibliography, and lists of entries by activity and year of birth at the back. Further reading is included at the end of each one-to two-page entry, and there are cross-references within each entry to the other entries. Some entries are accompanied by photographs.

Writing is clear and well suited for the audience. Both volumes will be useful sources for information and are recommended for school and public libraries.

The American Film Institute Desk Reference. Ed. by Melinda Corey and George Ochoa. 2002. 608p. bibliog. illus. index. DK, $40 (0-7894-8934-1). 791.43.

The American Film Institute (AFI) has created a unique reference source that captures the magic and excitement of the movies. Containing a wide range of information about cinema and the film industry, this volume is a feast for the eyes. Its striking and colorful page layouts feature more than 500 photographs and other illustrations and creatively integrate narrative text with sidebars and boxes highlighting miscellaneous facts, quotes, and trivia.

Relying on a small team of contributors (among them several Hollywood celebrities), the editors have produced a six-part compendium beginning with "Movie History," a chronology of motion pictures from 1830 through mid-2002. "Movie Basics" covers the fundamental components of the film industry, while "Movie Crafts" focuses on the skills and terminology involved in moviemaking, ranging from writing and directing to designing costumes and editing. Featuring brief biographies of principal figures, "People in Film" is subdivided by professions, such as actors, directors, and special-effects artists. "Films" includes lists of winners of major film awards, annotated versions of several of the AFI's lists of best movies, movie quotations, and brief overviews of cinema in other countries. The final section, "Sources," provides directories of studios, organizations, film schools, and other institutions associated with the film industry as well as lists of recommended publications and online resources.

Although the index is useful, it is not comprehensive, failing, for example, to provide access to such features as a sidebar about DivX and tips for finding an agent. In addition, because the numerous glossaries of film terms are not indexed, finding a specific term can be frustrating. More troubling is the apparent lack of rigorous fact checking. The biography of composer John Williams indicates that he is still conductor of the Boston Pops Orchestra, a position he hasn't held since 1993, and the membership of the American Society of Composers, Authors and Publishers is given as 39,000 although ASCAP's Web site indicates it currently has more than 140,000 members.

In spite of these problems, this attractive and fact-filled compilation is a bargain. Particularly suited for home libraries, it will also be a useful addition to high-school, public, and academic libraries.

The Baseball Filmography: 1915 through 2001. 2d ed. By Hal Erickson. 2002. 552p. bibliog. illus. index. McFarland, $45 (0-7864-1272-0). 791.43.

An interesting mesh of America's pastime with "America's second pastime" (the movies), this update to *Baseball in the Movies* (McFarland, 1992) covers 29 feature films produced in the U.S. between 1991 and 2001, plus the 81 theatrical and television releases included in the first edition. Also added are several silent films, such as *The Battling Orioles* and *They Learned about Women*.

Entries are alphabetically arranged by name of film and are between 2 and almost 20 pages in length (for *A League of Their Own*). The work details films exhaustively, with complete cast lists, production credits, release dates, and thorough plot summaries. Where applicable, the plot summaries compare the films to the books on which they were based. The author comments on production issues, actors, shooting problems, and studio-versus-producer conflicts. Interesting facts are obviously derived from extensive research, such as Jackie Robinson being "compelled to alter his familiar batting stance in order to accommodate the camera's limited field of vision" in *The Jackie Robinson Story*. Black-and-white photos appearing every few pages are a mix of actual film clips, ads, posters, and backstage moments. Sections following the main entries discuss "Baseball Short Subjects" and "Baseball in Non-Baseball Films." An excellent bibliography and index add value

The writing style makes this a very readable book suitable for secondary, public, and academic libraries. The author deserves a big "Atta boy!"

A Biographical Dictionary of Silent Film Western Actors and Actresses. By George A. Katchmer. 2002. 478p. appendix. illus. McFarland, $95 (0-7864-0763-8). 791.43.

People may not be aware that actors often began their careers in the Western genre only to gain their greatest successes in other forms of film. In this volume more than 1,000 entries represent a wide range of performers, including such well-known names as Wallace Beery, Walter Brennan, Boris Karloff, Mary Pickford, and Sally Rand as well as cowboy stars Hoot Gibson and Tom Mix. Each appeared in at least three silent western features "or was often seen in . . . one-and two-reel short subjects."

Arrangement is alphabetical, with each entry containing a biographical summary (sometimes very sketchy, depending on available information) and a list of film highlights. For each film the author provides the type of film ("Western," "one-reel," "farce"), release date, and names of the other stars. For supporting and bit players he also supplies the name of the character ("Slim," "a deputy sheriff," "the young Indian mother"). Films that are available on tape are identified by an asterisk and bold type. Most of the film highlights end in 1930, although some extend well into the sound era. Wherever possible a photograph of the person (and at times a scene from one of the films) accompanies the entry. There are cross-references to the predominant form of name. An appendix provides access by film title.

With the success of such cable stations as Turner Classic Movies (TCM) and American Movie Classics (AMC) and the continued development of such sites as the Internet Movie Database, early film, especially silent, is more accessible than ever. This book offers an opportunity for silent film fans and researchers to find some information, even if slight, about performers who exist today only as a name in film cast lists. Public libraries and academic institutions that support film studies, especially the history of early film and its performers, will welcome this volume.

British Film Institute Film Classics. 2v. Ed. by Edward Buscombe and Rob White. 2002. 1,248p. bibliogs. illus. Fitzroy Dearborn, $250 (1-57958-328-8). 791.4375.

In 1982 the British Film Institute (BFI) compiled a list of 360 classic films produced throughout the world from 1914 to 1981. After initiating a project to build an archive of perfect prints of these films, in 1992 the BFI began to publish a series of monographs providing an introduction to each film. Now, the first 50 titles issued in the BFI Film Classics series have been brought together in this compilation. Arranged chronologically by the year of each film's release, the volumes contain 25 essays apiece, beginning with *Das Cabinet des Dr. Caligari* (1920) in volume 1, and ending with *Annie Hall* (1977) in volume 2. Authored by a variety of well-known writers, including Richard Schickel, Camille Paglia, and Salman Rushdie, the commentaries are individualistic rather than following any set criteria concerning format or content. Some focus on the film's production history; others provide criticism, analysis, and interpretation; and others contain lengthy synopses of the story. Each is fascinating in its own way, providing insights and observations that illuminate the film anew for both cinema scholars and movie buffs. All of the essays include a selection of stills from the film, extensive film credits, and bibliographic references. Not all of the photographs and illustrations that appeared in the original series are reproduced here. In addition, all photographs are in black-and-white, although a number of the original monographs include color photographs.

The lack of an index greatly limits this set's usefulness as a reference source. Although each volume includes a chronological list of the films covered in that volume, access is hindered by the absence of an overall table of contents for the set. Also missing are an alphabetical list of the films and a breakdown of films by country of origin. Without these enhancements, there is no reason for libraries that already have the individual volumes in the BFI Film Classics series to add this compilation. However, academic and research libraries that are not purchasing the series may want to consider this set for their circulating collections.

The Edward G. Robinson Encyclopedia. By Robert Beck. 2002. 416p. bibliog. index. McFarland, $55 (0-7864-1230-5). 791.43.

Although he has been dead for 30 years, character actor Robinson's popularity continues. This compendium consists of alphabetically arranged entries detailing his life and career. Entries run from one sentence to a couple of pages and offer facts and commentary about all of the actor's known appearances and performances, ranging from starring roles in theater and feature films to commercials for Maxwell House coffee and a cameo on the *Batman* television series. Also covered are individuals, including wives and coworkers, and various aspects of Robinson's professional and personal life. The entry *Art*, for example, discusses his private collection of French impressionist paintings as well as the ways in which fine art figured in some of his films. A bibliography consisting of more than 230 print sources attests to the author's extensive research, and the exhaustive index should ensure that no particulars get overlooked.

The August 8, 2002, "Dear Abby" syndicated advice column devoted to a series of personal affidavits from readers attesting to Robinson's graciousness and generosity is proof of his enduring appeal. This volume is the only source entirely devoted to Robinson currently available (two books about his work, *The Cinema of Edward G. Robinson* [A. S. Barnes, 1972], by James Parish, and *The Complete Films of Edward G. Robinson* [Carol, 1990], by Alvin H. Marill, are out of print, as is the biography *Edward G. Robinson*, by Foster Hirsch [Pyramid, 1975], and Robinson's autobiography, *All My Yesterdays* [Hawthorn, 1973]). Of obvious interest to film and performing arts collections, this offering should also be considered by public libraries.

The Encyclopedia of American Television: Broadcast Programming Post–World War II to 2000. By Ron Lackmann. 2002. 528p. appendixes. bibliog. illus. index. Facts On File, $75 (0-8160-4554-2); Checkmark, paper, $21.95 (0-8160-4555-0). 791.45.

Lackmann previously authored *The Encyclopedia of American Radio: An A–Z Guide to Radio from Jack Benny to Howard Stern* (Facts On File, 2000). His latest work covers his other love, television, to which he was introduced at the 1939 New York World's Fair.

Alphabetically arranged entries cover many nationally televised programs, with information about the premise and actors or personalities, dates and time shown, and network affiliation. With the exception of some important specials and miniseries, programs must have aired for at least a season. Cable productions are excluded. Other entries offer biographies of popular, important, or award-winning personalities, among them Ed Asner, Milton Berle, Julia Child, Garry Marshall, Rosie O'Donnell, and Dan Rather. Pictures of cast members of various shows are interspersed. One appendix contains the top-rated shows for each season since 1952. Another appendix contains Emmy Awards, 1948 to 1999.

The Complete Directory to Prime Time Network and Cable TV Shows, 1946–Present (7th ed., Ballantine, 1999) and *Total Television: The Comprehensive Guide to Programming from 1948 to the Present* (4th ed., Penguin, 1996) have similar entries and descriptions but do not include biographies. The four-volume *Museum of Broadcast Communications Encyclopedia of Television* (Fitzroy Dearborn, 1997) is more selective in its coverage of programs and performers but has a broad range of topical entries. Lackmann's volume is a worthwhile addition for libraries needing a readable, popular guide.

The Encyclopedia of Ethnic Groups in Hollywood. By James Robert Parish. 2002. 722p. bibliog. illus. index. Facts On File, $75 (0-8160-4604-2). 791.43.

What do the movies *Hondo*, *I Passed for White*, and *The Mark of Zorro* have in common? All feature white actors portraying ethnic characters. This was a common practice in Hollywood in the past, as was the use of ethnic actors portraying characters of another ethnicity (for example, Hispanic American actors passing as Native Americans). It continues to this day, although to a lesser degree.

Arranged in five sections corresponding to major ethnic groups ("African Americans," "Asian Americans," "Hispanic Americans," "Jewish Americans," and "Native Americans"), this encyclopedia examines the stereotypes and treatment of such groups in movies and television. More than 1,200 entries cover movies and television programs, actors, themes, and specific genres. Each movie or television listing begins with the name, year, director, screenplay, and cast list. This is followed by a plot summary and some discussion of major themes and significance. The entries for actors give birth and death dates, followed by biographical material, including a list of roles. Information is generally current and in some cases mentions 2003 films that have not yet been released, although the entry for Salma Hayek does not include her role in *Frida* in 2002.

Thematic entries in each section discuss genres, such as combat films, situation comedies, and science fiction series; directors; impersonations; and pressure groups. Each of the sections also has entries related to specific themes or character types, such as Anti-Semitism, Blackface, Geishas, and Half-breed. The encyclopedia concludes with a bibliography and an extensive index.

The topic of this encyclopedia has been mined before in such titles as Blacks in American Films and Television: An Encyclopedia (Garland, 1988) and Hispanics in Hollywood: An Encyclopedia of Film and Television (Garland, 1994). But this work brings the topic to bear on five ethnic groups in an accessible, clearly written manner that will be helpful for anyone interested in learning more about the subject. It will be a useful overview for both academic and public libraries, particularly those with ethnic or film collections.

Horror Films of the 1970s. By John Kenneth Muir. 2002. 662p. appendixes. bibliog. illus. index. McFarland, $59.95 (0-7864-1249-6). 791.43.

The 1970s is one of the great decades for horror films. Classics such as Carrie, The Exorcist, Jaws, Halloween, and Texas Chainsaw Massacre all debuted during this time. Works by directors Stephen Spielberg, John Carpenter, Brian de Palma, Wes Craven, and others helped shape horror cinema. Focusing mostly on American films, this resource examines 200 movies released from 1970 to 1979.

The book is organized into 10 year-by-year sections, with the films arranged alphabetically by title and given ratings of between one and four stars. Most of the entries begin with excerpts from reviews, information on cast and crew, a synopsis, commentary by the author, and in some cases comments about the film's legacy. The cast and crew information and plot summaries are important reference resources. The commentary, which can go on for several pages, puts each film in context and discusses style and filmmaking techniques. It also explores how topics such as racism, religion, and women's rights are represented in films like Blacula, The Exorcist, and The Stepford Wives, respectively.

Perhaps the best part of the work is the beginning essay, "The History of the Decade (in Brief . . .)," which explains why horror films were so unique during the 1970s and explores some of the common themes, such as post-Vietnam distrust of government, nature run amuck, and the failure of science. The work ends with five appendixes: "Horror Film Conventions of the 1970s," "The 1970s Horror Hall of Fame," "Memorable Movie Ad Lines," "Then and Now—Recommended Viewing," and "The Best Horror Movies of the 1970s."

Horror Films of the 1970s is an important reference tool for film collections in academic and public libraries and a must for fans.

Sitcom Factfinder, 1948–1984: Over 9,700 Details from 168 Television Shows. By Vincent Terrace. 2002. 226p. index. McFarland, paper, $25 (0-7864-1243-7). 791.45.

Almost 170 sitcoms—from The Abbott and Costello Show to WKRP in Cincinnati—are listed in alphabetical order. For each show, details such as character names (and variations), addresses, cars and license plate numbers, pets, favorite foods, and important episode plots appear in narrative form, which makes for good reading but also makes it difficult to find answers to reference questions. The shows were broadcast between January 1, 1948, and December 31, 1984. Related information includes reunion shows, radio origins, syndication, and spin-offs.

Entries range in size from one paragraph for shows that were not on very long or for which there are only a few existing episodes (The Hathaways, Karen, My Little Margie), to several pages for those that were long-running and popular (Andy Griffith, Cheers, Leave it to Beaver). Defining a sitcom would have been helpful and might have explained the omission of shows such as F-Troop and Julia.

What could have been an excellent manual for TV trivia buffs has several errors. For example, in the entry for The Addams Family, one of Gomez's nicknames for Morticia is given as "Caita," not "Querida." In the entry for M*A*S*H, Major Winchester's sister is mistakenly called "Hanoria" rather than "Honoria." Cheers' Cliff Claven belongs to the Knights of the Scimitar, not, as it is spelled here, "Semitar." These are small details, but in a resource like this, details count.

The book is fun, nicely written, and filled with facts, much of them just what people want to know. It is clear that the homework has been exhaustively done for the shows that are included and that the author has a love for the subject. A little more research, editing, or clarification would have made this an even better book.

The Continuum Companion to Twentieth Century Theatre. Ed. by Colin Chambers. 2002. 866p. bibliogs. Continuum, $150 (0-8264-4959-X). 792.

This theater companion features more than 2,500 alphabetically arranged entries on a broad array of stage-related topics. Although the emphasis is on English-speaking theater in the twentieth century, the scope is surprisingly comprehensive. Entry types include people, companies, countries, branches of theater making, trends, genres, definitions, and historical surveys. The objective is to "define theater broadly and as a live and continuing activity." The geographical scope spans five continents, and the 280 contributors hail from 20 different countries.

Entries vary in length from a few sentences to several pages, with the majority accompanied by a brief list of monographs to open the door to further research. A "Selective Reference Bibliography" also appears at the beginning of the book. There is no index, though there are cross-references. The lack of an index and of entries for individual plays means that in order to read about Who's Afraid of Virginia Woolf? for example, one would have to recall that the playwright is Edward Albee and go to his entry.

This work differs from other single-volume theater reference works because of the diversity of its contributors. Whereas coverage is similar in scope to The Cambridge Guide to Theatre (Cambridge, 1995), the latter features only entries written by scholars. Continuum offers not only entries by scholars but additional boxed entries written by active professional theater insiders, including voice teacher Cicely Berry, lighting designer Jennifer Tipton, and actress Billie Whitelaw. The result is a less academic, more interesting style than the typical reference work. Although there is overlap, Continuum covers a wider geographic terrain than the Concise Oxford Companion to the Theatre (Oxford, 1992) and is more contemporary. Only in the Continuum volume, for example, are there entries on digital performance and the Internet.

Libraries with active theater collections will want this lively addition, but the price may be a bit steep for those already owning the Cambridge or Oxford volumes. Recommended for academic and public libraries with strong theater collections.

A to Z of American Women in Sports. By Paula Edelson. 2002. 278p. bibliogs. illus. index. Facts On File, $44 (0-8160-4565-8). 796.

Edelson provides a biographical look at more than 150 women who have had a significant impact in sports. Although the title would lead the reader to assume these are all women from the U.S., they are not. For example, Sonja Henie, Martina Navratilova, and Monica Seles are imported athletes, and Henie and Navratilova achieved citizenship long after their professional careers were set. Other women included are not athletes in the traditional sense, but their contributions include coaching, refereeing, and being the "first" in their fields. Examples are rock climber Lynn Hill, markswoman Annie Oakley, baseball umpire Pam Postema, commentator Robin Roberts, and coach Pat Head Summitt. Women in organized sports include basketball player Teresa Edwards, soccer player Mia Hamm, golfer Nancy Lopez, gymnast Mary Lou Retton, and skier Picabo Street.

Each entry is one to two pages long, with biographical information, further reading, and sometimes an accompanying photograph. In addition to the general index, entries are indexed by sport and by year of birth, from 1850 to 1989.

Other recent titles on this subject are The Women's Sports Encyclopedia (Holt, 1997) and Nike Is a Goddess: The History of Women in Sports (Atlantic Monthly, 1998). A to Z of American Women in Sports provides an update to this area of the reference collection at a moderate cost and is a good selection for junior-high, high-school, public, and community college libraries.

The Encyclopedia of North American Sports History. 2d ed. By Ralph Hickok. 2002. 594p. bibliog. illus. index. Facts On File, $75 (0-8160-4660-3). 796.

First published in 1992, The Encyclopedia of North American Sports History is now in its second edition. Entries fall into eight categories: sports; general history; biography; sporting events; major awards; cities; stadiums, fields, and arenas; and sports organizations, such as leagues, college conferences, and halls of fame. Among the more than 150 new entries are Ford Field; Snowboarding; Williams, Venus E. S. (but no entry for Serena); and XFL. Content is arranged alphabetically; each entry is from 250 words to several pages in length, with the longer entries reserved for histories of the major American sports, such as baseball and football. Some of the entries include illustrations, and Web site addresses are given for associations, teams, and stadiums.

Besides the obvious biographical entries and sports entries, there are topical essays that provide good overviews, among them *Arenas, Blacks in sports,* and *Women in sports*. Results of various sports events, such as the Super Bowl, the U.S. Open, and the World Series, have been updated through 2001, as have entries for golf, the Goodwill Games, Seattle's Kingdome, Michael Jordan, and many others.

The importance of this volume is in its coverage of a variety of minor sports, such as women's synchronized swimming, steamboat racing, skin diving, and sled dog racing, for which finding information may be difficult. This is a recommended purchase especially for those who do not have the first edition. Those who have the first edition would have to weigh what other resources the library has at hand—including Web site access—to justify the purchase of the volume.

The Olympic Century: The Official History of the Modern Olympic Movement. 24v. 2002. bibliogs. illus. indexes. maps. World Sport Research & Publications, $599 (1-888383-00-3). 796.48.

This joint project with the International Olympic Committee (IOC) and the U.S. Olympic Committee (USOC) covers the Olympic movement from its beginnings in Greece through modern times. Following volume 1, which surveys the ancient Olympiads and efforts to reestablish the Olympic Games in the nineteenth century, the set progresses from 1896 to 1998. A twenty-fifth volume, scheduled for publication in 2004, will deal with Sydney 2000 and Salt Lake City 2002.

Each volume contains between 176 and 180 pages and is lavishly illustrated. Lively narrative is accompanied by photographs of athletes, events, posters, medals, and more. Maps show various venues. Sidebars highlight particular sports or personalities or offer interesting sidelights. For example, a sidebar in the volume that covers 1936 to 1948 tells about the fate of several Jewish medal winners and a version of the games held in German prisoner-of-war camps in 1944. An appendix in each volume offers programs of events, selected statistics, and medal counts, along with lists of IOC members. Because this is a history of the Olympic movement rather than just the games, a considerable amount of page space is devoted to behind-the-scenes IOC and USOC activities. The writers do not avoid controversial topics such as drug use and bribery scandals.

There is a great deal of useful information here, both visual and textual, but there are also several impediments to the work's value as a reference tool. Each volume has its own index, but there is as yet no comprehensive index to the set. A reader who consults a volume's table of contents to locate coverage of specific Olympiads will not find chapter titles such as "A Soaring Spirit" and "Shades and Shadows" helpful. Finally, in several volumes, the table of contents gives incorrect page numbers.

For a more accessible A–Z arrangement or more exhaustive statistics readers will need to turn to other reference sources, such as *Historical Dictionary of the Olympic Movement* (Scarecrow, 1995), *Historical Dictionary of the Modern Olympic Movement* (Greenwood, 1996), and volumes in McFarland's Results of the Early Modern Olympics series. Public libraries where there is a strong interest in the Olympics might consider *The Olympic Century* for its scope and visual appeal. Plans for an online component with curriculum guides and other material should make it attractive to high-school libraries as well.

The Scribner Encyclopedia of American Lives: Sports Figures. 2v. Ed. by Arnold Markoe. 2002. 1,097p. illus. index. Scribner, $250 (0-684-80665-7). 796.

The Scribner Encyclopedia of American Lives (or SEAL, as it is known to reference librarians) is the continuation of the now-defunct retrospective standard, *Dictionary of American Biography* (DAB). SEAL: *Sports Figures* is the first of a planned multivolume series based on thematic special areas of interest. According to the publisher a projected set on personalities of the 1960s will be made available in November 2002.

The sports volumes consist of 614 new biographies of athletes, coaches, team owners, sportscasters, and writers—in short, anybody famous connected with American sports. Each entry includes family background, the influences that formed the character of the athletes, and the achievements both in and outside of the context of sports. Consistent with the parent SEAL set, each entry includes a photograph. However, unlike the parent set, SEAL: *Sports Figures* includes living sports personalities. Amateur athletes are covered, but the weight of the entries is tilted to the professional. Some 205 contributors went about collecting the biographical information by selecting and reviewing the source material and interviewing the biographee and his or her family.

Selection of only 614 subjects in the history of American sport must have been a daunting task. Statistical rankings and memberships in the respective sports halls of fame were significant indicators for inclusion. But other elements were also considered. For instance, biographies that tell a story or illuminate some less-known aspect of sports history are included. That being said, there is room for some vociferous debates among sports fans over the selection of some current sports personalities. For instance, Nomar Garciaparra, a fantastic shortstop who has played for the Boston Red Sox since 1996, was picked over Wade Boggs, a former Red Sox–Yankee–Tampa Bay shortstop who is now retired and is a sure bet to be elected to the Baseball Hall of Fame. While Garciaparra has done great things and is expected to be one of the top shortstops to have ever played the game, Boggs has already made his mark. Garciaparra's future may be cut short because of injuries.

For libraries continuing DAB with SEAL, the thematic series will add value to the entire set, making DAB and SEAL a one-stop biography reference center.

Sports and Games of the Ancients. By Steve Craig. 2002. 271p. bibliogs. illus. index. Greenwood, $49.95 (0-313-31600-7). 796.

Sportswriter Steve Craig has assembled a good introductory reference source on major games and sports played all over the world during ancient times, from the first Olympiad (776 B.C.E.) to the fall of Rome (C.E. 476). This is a volume in Greenwood's Sports and Games through History series. Selective rather than comprehensive, it is an excellent resource for teachers who want to liven up their history lesson plans.

The main body of the work is organized geographically, with sections on Africa, Asia, Europe, Latin America, the Middle East, North America, and Oceania. Each section begins with a brief introduction to the sport and game culture of the region, followed by individual entries of 300 to 1,500 words on each sport or game. Games that persist, such as lacrosse and boxing, are at home here alongside a wide variety of more obscure activities. The author has downplayed Greek and Roman games with the intent of offering some balance to an area that has been dominated at times by discussion of those cultures.

For each sport or game, we learn the culture of its play, the basic rules, and the importance of it within its culture, as well as the influence of the game or sport on or from other societies. Every entry also includes "Suggestions for Modern Play" and a short list of sources. A good 10-page bibliography and brief index complete the work. More diagrams of game play and sports fields would have been useful. It also would have been helpful if the author had included a table of contents showing the activities covered for each region.

The writing style is straightforward and easy to follow, and there is much of interest here for general readers. Comprehensive research on sports and games would require supplementation with other more scholarly works, such as *Encyclopedia of World Sport* (Oxford, 1999). The bibliography of Craig's work is a good starting place for such research. Recommended especially for school and public libraries, as well as college or curriculum collections needing a concise introduction to sports and games.

Sports Nicknames: 20,000 Professionals Worldwide. By Terry W. Pruyne. 2002. 423p. bibliog. index. McFarland, $55 (0-7864-1064-7). 796.

Professional sports are, at their core, kid's games played by the best for others to watch and enjoy. Nicknames add color and flare for the fans and the players. This title is a unique resource for those who want to know the "why" behind nicknames that have stuck or failed to stick to individual and groups of professional athletes. Examples include "Air Jordan" (Michael Jordan, basketball), the "Steel Curtain" (the Pittsburgh Steelers defense, football), and "Tiger" Woods (real name Eldrick Woods, golf), along with 19,000-plus more athletes.

This work is divided into six sections. The first five cover athletes or teams in baseball, football, basketball, hockey, and "Other Sports," listed alphabetically within each section by last name. Most entries are one or two sentences long, and all cite sources for the nicknames. The last section is an alphabetical index by nickname. Coverage includes historic and modern players, but as indicated in the title, no collegiate and only a few Olympic athletes are included.

Although the coverage is stated to be worldwide, football is defined as American-style football and soccer is included in the "Other Sports" section. Also included in "Other Sports" are tennis players, skateboarders, bullfighters, and jockeys. Most of the nicknames are ones given by fellow players or managers, but those given by Chris Berman, an ESPN sports commentator, come only from his fertile imagination and are designed to make his reporting humorous. These nicknames include "You De Manning" (Peyton Manning), "Bert Be Home Blyleven," and "Three Blind Weiss" (Walt Weiss).

So just who was "The Round Mound of Rebound" ? Charles Barkley, the professional basketball player, of course, who was also known as "Sir Charles." This is a specialized but comprehensive reference source for all libraries that can afford it.

World Soccer Yearbook, 2002–3: The Complete Guide to the Game. By David Goldblatt. 2002. 496p. illus. index. maps. DK, paper, $30 (0-7894-8943-0). 796.334.

Authored by a writer for a major British newspaper, this sports yearbook aims to examine the game of soccer at a global level. Whereas works such as *The World Encyclopedia of Soccer*: *A Complete Guide to the Beautiful Game* (Lorenz, 2001) profile select international teams and championships, *World Soccer Yearbook*, 2002–3 examines "the beautiful game" from a truly worldwide perspective.

The major focus of *World Soccer Yearbook* is on the 204 soccer nations affiliated with Federation Internationale de Football Association (FIFA), the governing body of world soccer. Dominant soccer nations, such as England, Argentina, and Italy, are given in-depth coverage ranging from 20 to 30 pages. Brief overviews and tabular data of approximately one to two pages are dedicated to less prominent soccer nations, such as those in the Caribbean. The main section of the yearbook is arranged by major soccer federation and then by country in what appears to be an arbitrary order. Fortunately, the book's detailed table of contents and accurate index overcomes any difficulties that the work's arrangement may present.

In addition to country data, the yearbook addresses global soccer themes in the opening and closing chapters of the book, entitled "The World Game" and "World Issues," respectively. Topics such as the global origins of the game and the migration of South American and African players to Europe are considered in these sections. This coverage is innovative and further demonstrates the international scope of this reference book.

One of the most outstanding features of the yearbook is its variety of illustrations. Full-page color maps of major soccer cities identify the location of important soccer landmarks such as team offices and stadiums. The work also contains an inclusive selection of color and black-and-white photographs of teams, individual players, championships, and the game in action. In addition, detailed diagrams supplement the sections on the rules of the game and playing styles, which helps the reader grasp these concepts.

World Soccer Yearbook, 2002–3 is a comprehensive and engrossing resource that is essential reading for any fan or player of the game of soccer. This work is suitable for public libraries and college libraries supporting physical education programs and sports history programs. High-school libraries might also consider it.

Literature

Lit Finder. [Online database]. 2002. Roth, pricing from $600 [http://www.litfinder.com/]. (Last accessed September 4, 2002).

Lit Finder consists of three modules—*Essay Finder*, *Poem Finder*, and *Story Finder*. Of the three modules, *Poem Finder* is king, providing full text to 100,000 poems (including copyrighted poems) and indexing to 800,000 poems by more than 80,000 authors. *Story Finder* contains 2,500 full-text stories by 500 authors; *Essay Finder*, the smallest module, includes 1,310 full-text essays by 400 authors. K–12 schools can substitute *Poem Finder* with the smaller *The World's Greatest Poetry*.

Moving from one module to the next, screen layout appears consistent. A row of seven selectable tabs lines the top, and a short column of selections borders the left side of almost every Web page. Tabs provide easy access to each of the three modules. Some tabs seem unnecessary (e.g., "Register for a FREE Trial!").

Choices on the left include help options and a useful browse feature titled Table of Contents where users can peruse areas such as Authors or Subjects. *Lit Finder* appears to place a strong emphasis on browsing. Other browse options include the Year's Best Poetry, Kids' Korner [sic], and a hierarchical Subject Navigator in *Poem Finder*. In Subject Navigator, one can browse Poetic Forms and Genres (for example, Young Adult Poetry, Zambian Poetry) as well as subjects. One category in Kids' Korner, God, strongly favors Christianity while ignoring other faiths. Users can browse Just Published Stories (published 1999–2001) in *Story Finder* and also scan Genre Navigator in both *Essay Finder* and *Story Finder*.

Basic Search consists of a single text-entry box. Results present title and author ranked by relevancy. A search in *Poem Finder* for *frost* and *apple* retrieved 172 poem titles. Selecting the second title, "After Apple Picking," by Robert Frost, displayed a picture of Frost, text of the poem, a list of references, and links to Biography, Poem Explanation, and Other Poems by Author. *Lit Finder* includes biographical information on selected writers and explanatory information on selected works.

Advanced Search offers three text-entry boxes linked by choice of Boolean operator (AND, OR, and BUT NOT). A pop-down menu accompanies each text-entry box within Advanced Search. For example, in *Essay Finder* users can choose from 27 fields (e.g., Author Name, Author Nationality, Essay Title, Essay Subject) arranged under three general categories: Author, Essay, and Reference. Users must limit searches to one category.

Story Finder and *Essay Finder* contain obvious gaps. We could not find stories by William Faulkner, Ernest Hemingway, Franz Kafka, or Flannery O'Connor or locate essays by James Baldwin, Ralph Waldo Emerson, Michel de Montaigne, or George Orwell. However, Roth plans to add 2,000 new entries annually for both *Essay Finder* and *Story Finder*.

Compared to *Poem Finder*, *The Columbia Granger's World of Poetry Online* (Columbia Univ., 1999) is smaller and more selective. Wilson's online *Essay and General Literature Index*, covering 62,000 essays, is much larger than *Essay Finder* but contains no full text. *Short Story Index* via WilsonWeb covers 76,000 stories (1,300 full text).

No doubt, *Lit Finder*'s triple pack of essays, stories, and poems will be a time-saver for students and the general public. It is a good choice for academic, public, and school libraries.

Christian Fiction: A Guide to the Genre. By John Mort. bibliogs. index. 2002. 339p. Libraries Unlimited, $55 (1-56308-871-1). 809.3.

Christian fiction has crossed over into the mainstream, and the latest installments of Tim LaHaye and Jerry Jenkins' Left Behind series and Jan Karon's Mitford series regularly find places on the *New York Times* bestseller lists. But despite increased demand, Christian fiction is still new territory for many librarians. This new title in the Genreflecting Advisory Series tackles the growing popularity and complexity of fiction that "has something to do with Christian principles."

Mort, who writes the Christian Fiction column for *Booklist* (on which much of the book is based), discusses almost 2,000 classic and contemporary titles, from *Pilgrim's Progress* to *The Red Tent*, with emphasis on fiction of the past 10 or so years. In an introductory chapter he explains that even though evangelical fiction dominates the genre (and the book), Christian fiction is in fact quite diverse. Along with works by Janette Oke ("the gold standard") and other evangelical writers, Mort includes works by Madeleine L'Engle, Andrew Greeley, John Updike, and many more not necessarily thought of first as "Christian." And even within the evangelical mode, there are books to serve almost every reading taste.

Following a chapter on readers' advisory sources, books are grouped into various types, such as "Biblical Fiction," "Mysteries and Thrillers," "Catholic Fiction," and "Young Adults." Within these categories there are more refined subcategories—"Problem Romance," "African Americans," "Nuns and Priests as Sleuths." Each title entry provides full bibliographic information and an annotation. As in other books in the Genreflecting series, icons are used to help librarians identify award winners and adult titles suitable for young adults. Unique to *Christian Fiction* is an icon designating works that adhere to the publishing code of the Evangelical Christian Publishers Association and the Christian Booksellers Association—no profanity, no explicit sex. Mort also identifies works that are good book club and discussion group choices. The index references authors and titles.

The lists of titles are useful, but novices to the genre will find the thoughtful explanations and annotations just as valuable, and few librarians will come away from this volume without learning something new. *Christian Fiction* covers the genre much more extensively than *What*

Inspirational Literature Do I Read Next? (Gale, 2000) and is recommended as a readers' advisory and collection development tool.

Critical Companions to Popular Contemporary Writers. [Online database]. Greenwood, pricing from $79 [http://www.gem.greenwood.com]. (Last accessed February 27, 2003).

Greenwood's new database consists of all 46 titles from the Greenwood Critical Companions print series. Each title is devoted to a single author who is a popular best-seller but in most cases has not yet received a book-length academic literary analysis. Among the included authors are V. C. Andrews, Maya Angelou, Mary Higgins Clark, and John Grisham. A 1999 CD-ROM version featured 25 titles, but this updated networked database will lend itself to increased access.

Actual content of the database is identical to the print version and includes a biographical chapter drawing on published information; a section on genres and how the author fits into the larger literary context; and an analysis of the author's most important, popular, and recent novels featuring sections on plot and character development, themes, and an alternative reading of the novel (such as Marxist or archetypal). Sometimes, sections on generic conventions, narrative, point of view, symbols, language, and historical or social contexts are included. Each title concludes with a generous list of primary and secondary sources, both biographical and critical.

Once a user selects an author, a screen with the full text of the book appears, accompanied by the table of contents on the left (each chapter is a hypertext link). Clicking on a chapter heading will break down the chapter further into sections, also hot-linked. In addition to the table of contents, navigational aid is offered via a Search button at the top of the screen; clicking on this allows users to search across the full text of the entire title they are in or within individual chapter headings. Boolean searching is available, but searches are only possible across the entire full text. There is no subject index for the database, unlike in the back of the print titles; trying to search for themes like *good versus evil* does not work as well across full text. Results will show in bold where the search terms appear in the text. The advanced search mode offers the option to search in all, or a selection of, the 46 titles.

A citation is present at the bottom of every page, which students will love. However, printing is only available one page at a time rather than for the entire chapter or book, which is cumbersome. An e-mail option is coming soon but will have the same limitations.

Running from $79 to $164 per title, the online version is more expensive than the print version of the series, which on average costs $49.95 up to $70 per title. But the online version is more up-to-date; each title receives regular annual updates. Print titles seem to eventually get updated and rereleased, costing the library more money each time with the potential for endless revisions because of the prolific nature of many of the authors covered.

The content in this series is unique in that it attempts to treat best-selling authors from a serious literary standpoint. Although most of the authors get some light coverage in Gale's Literature Resource Center database, users will not find discussion of individual titles in great detail like they do here. Public, academic, and high-school libraries will want to consider purchasing this database, especially if they do not already own the print series. Including a subject index would be a major improvement.

Critical Survey of Poetry. 8v. 2d rev. ed. Ed. by Philip K. Jason. 2002. 5,029p. bibliogs. illus. indexes. Salem, $475 (1-58765-071-1). 809.1.

A new edition of a familiar reference work is usually a cause for celebration, and there is much to cheer about here. This work incorporates all the material from the 1984 *Critical Survey of Poetry: Foreign Language Series* and its 1987 *Supplement* as well as that of the 1992 *Critical Survey of Poetry: English Language Series Revised Edition* in addition to entries for well over 100 additional poets. The result is a wealth of background material on nearly 700 poets from ancient times to the present from many nations around the world.

The first seven volumes contain signed, alphabetically arranged articles on individual poets from Dannie Abse to Stefan Zweig, ranging in length from a half-dozen to a dozen pages. Each entry includes a listing of the subject's major collections of poetry, a description of work done in other literary genres, a list of awards and honors, a biographical sketch, an analytic essay, a list of other literary works, and a bibliography of secondary print sources. More than half of the entries include something not always found in works like these: a picture of the writer. Volume 8 is a virtual mini–reference library on poetry consisting of 7 essays on various types of theory and criticism, 45 essays surveying poetry around the world, a selection of "research tools" including a list of poetry awards and award winners, explanatory essays on language and linguistics and poetical terms, and a chronological list of poets. A 20-page bibliography completes the volume, while a trio of indexes (geographical, categorical, and subject) provides easy access to individual entries and essays throughout the set.

Intended for students in high school and college, the *Critical Survey of Poetry* provides a solid foundation for any student of poetry. The selection of poets is wide and varied, with contemporary poets like Rita Dove, Martin Espada, Robert Pinsky, Mark Strand, and Wislawa Szymborska represented along with such predecessors as Catullus, Sappho, Cynewulf, and Homer and just about every other major poet in between. This will be a valuable addition to reference collections in public, high-school, and college libraries.

Cyclopedia of Literary Places. 3v. Ed. by R. Baird Shuman and R. Kent Rasmussen. 2003. 1,320p. indexes. Salem, $290 (1-58765-094-0). 809.

In this set focusing on the "use of place in individual literary works," *place* is defined as any physical location appearing in a work of literature, either real or imaginary. Types of places range from the broad to the particular: examples include countries (Spain), cities and towns (Grover's Corners), neighborhoods (Upper East Side), buildings (Wicker Bar), or individual rooms (Chairman's bedroom). The aim of the encyclopedia is to show "how place matters within the literary work and then how it functions as a literary device." The set is intended to complement two others from the same publisher: *Masterplots* (2d ed., Salem, 1996), which offers plot analysis of popular literary works, and *Cyclopedia of Literary Characters* (rev. ed., Salem, 1998), which offers character analyses. All of the 1,304 literary works (novels, plays, and a small selection of poetry) covered were selected from *Masterplots* because they lend themselves to place analysis.

The entries, written by scholars, are arranged alphabetically by title of work and are typically between 300 and 1,000 words, 700 words on average. Each entry contains brief standard information about the work such as title, author, dates, type, and a short paragraph discussing the setting within the context of broader themes. This is followed by a discussion of the major places; 6,000 places get their own paragraphs as subentries within title entries. In addition, other places appear in bold type within paragraphs, despite not having their own entries. Asterisks are used to identify places that are real rather than imaginary. The place index lists all real and many fictional places and groups together locations that are subsets of larger places, such as *American West* or *Japan*. Also included are a title index (including title variants) and an author index.

Cyclopedia of Literary Places differs from the few other similar-minded reference works because of its title-driven focus and its inclusion of both real and imaginary places. The *Dictionary of Imaginary Places* (Harcourt, 2000) is arranged by place and only includes fictional locations. The *Dictionary of Real People and Places in Fiction* (Routledge, 1993) is the opposite, as it includes only real places upon which fictional entities are based in English-language novels and short stories. None of these works get past the "where" of a place to explore how it establishes mood, how it reflects the action or characters, or how it contributes to symbolism in a particular work. Therefore, *Cyclopedia* is a welcome work on a subject not fully exploited. It may not have sufficient background information about each literary work to stand on its own, but libraries already owning the *Masterplots* and *Cyclopedia of Literary Characters* sets will want to add it to the collection. Recommended for high-school, public, or academic libraries.

Encyclopedia of African Literature. Ed. by Simon Gikandi. 2002. 629p. bibliogs. index. Routledge, $150 (0-415-23019-5). 809.

Edited by an author of many books on African writers and literature, this encyclopedia covers all aspects of African literature produced in all of the major languages. Both sub-Saharan and North African literatures are represented, although for works in Arabic the focus is on the modern period.

More than 600 signed articles by academic specialists treat mostly individual authors, both well known and less established. Longer essays deal with historical and cultural issues concerning the study of

African literature, including criticism and theory and its development as a field of scholarship. Essays on *Autobiography*, *Feminist criticism*, and *Islam in African literature*, as well as regional overviews such as *Gikuyu literature* and *West African literature in English*, make this a useful starting point for exploration of African literature. Because these more general articles are one of the strengths of the work, it would have been helpful to list them in the fore matter, as it is a guessing game to find them. Most articles, including the biographical entries, have a very small list of references for further reading. Although reasonably up-to-date, these lists are often a mixture of a few primary and secondary works, not the most impressive feature of the volume.

African Writers (Scribner, 1997) treats only 65 authors but in considerably more detail, with more critical commentary and with extensive bibliographical references to books by and about the authors. The Dictionary of Literary Biography series from Gale has several volumes devoted to African writers, once again with lengthy articles on major writers and good bibliographies. It is the breadth of coverage that makes *Encyclopedia of African Literature* stand out, especially with the inclusion of lesser-known and newer writers as well as those writing in African languages. It would be helpful to have lists of authors by country and by category or genre and, as mentioned earlier, a list of the longer overview essays. Although the inclusion of a map of the continent is useful, it is almost 10 years out of date. On the whole, however, the volume is a worthwhile addition to academic and larger public libraries, especially as there is an increased interest in creative expression from the continent.

★**Encyclopedia of Holocaust Literature.** Ed. by David Patterson and Alan L. Berger. 2002. 263p. appendixes. bibliogs. index. Oryx, $54.95 (1-57356-257-2). 809.

This important and sensitive work presents a detailed look at the writings and lives of authors who survived, perished in, or were closely connected to the Holocaust (1933–1945). It gives fresh voice to the Holocaust Studies subject area, which has seen many new publications in the last few years and thus needs a strong survey text that helps put these writings into historical and literary context.

About 130 authors are covered in this work. All are first generation and wrote personal testimonies in the form of novels, memoirs, diaries, or plays in response to the Holocaust. Most, but not all, of the writers are Jewish. The writers did not all live in Europe during the Holocaust, but all were deeply influenced by its legacy.

Readers familiar with this genre will recognize important names that have subject entries: Aharon Appelfeld, Anne Frank, Viktor Frankl, Primo Levi, Elie Wiesel. Many others are given prominent treatment, including Adam Czerniakow, Anatoli Kuznetsov, and Isaiah Spiegel. People from all the European countries are included, although there is an understandable emphasis on those who wrote in English. Each entry answers several basic questions: the writer's literary response to the Holocaust, how that response is unique or distinctive, and how the author's work contributes to an overall understanding of the Holocaust. Each entry also contains detailed biographical data that helps put the writings into context, such as when and where the writer was in a death camp or at what age he or she became a refugee. The contributors provide powerful documentation and original research in presenting their subjects' literary messages and biographies. In addition to the bibliographies of primary and secondary works attached to the entries, the volume's "Bibliography of Primary Works of Holocaust Literature" is very comprehensive and will be a great aid to those doing primary research. Helpful appendixes include authors by date of birth, authors by country of birth, and birth names for authors writing under pen names.

The volume's arrangement and detailed, analytic treatment make it unique. *Holocaust Literature: A Handbook of Critical, Historical, and Literary Writings*, edited by Saul Friedman (Greenwood, 1993), has a subject approach, and some may want to consult that volume for a different access point to the topic. The authoritative *Bibliography of Holocaust Literature* (Westview, 1986) and its supplement classify more than 10,000 works of all types. The Oryx volume will be a strong addition to public and academic libraries, especially the many with Holocaust classes at the graduate or undergraduate level. Many librarians will be able to use the extensive bibliography as a collection development tool. *Bearing Witness: A Resource Guide to Literature, Poetry, Art, Music, and Videos by Holocaust Victims and Survivors* [RBB Ap 15 02] covers some of the same writers and is a good choice for public and school libraries.

Encyclopedia of Literature and Science. 2002. 575p. Ed. by Pamela Gossin. bibliogs. index. Greenwood, $94.95 (0-313-30538-2). 809.

As stated in the preface, the purpose of this book "is to introduce the emergent field of interdisciplinary literature and science (LS) studies to those just discovering it and provide a ready reference tool for those already working in a specific area." There are more than 650 alphabetically arranged entries, varying in length from 50 to 3,500 words and covering a wide range of topics: themes (*Astronomy*, *Dystopias*, *Environment*); writers (*Asimov, Isaac*; *Milton, John*); scientists (*Feynman, Richard Philips*; *Kepler, Johannes*); theories (*Darwinism*, *Poststructuralism*); and more. Among the longer entries (two to three pages) are *Anthropology/psychology/sociology*; *Culture*; *History of science*; and *Literary representations of the scientist*. Literary topics are discussed in terms of their relationship to science, and scientific topics in terms of their relationship to literature. Cross-references abound. Each entry is signed, and most have a brief bibliography. An extensive general bibliography includes works used to compose the entries and titles for further reading.

The intended audience is "undergraduate college and university students and their instructors," so although the volume is meant as an introduction, the language can be quite technical. Young adult authors such as Madeleine L'sEngle and William Sleator have been excluded—perhaps they have not yet been absorbed into the LS field.

Literature and science traditionally come together in the science fiction genre, but this volume shows that the two disciplines merge in other, diverse ways. Most academic libraries will need a copy of this encyclopedia, and large public libraries should consider adding it to their collections.

Favorite Children's Authors and Illustrators. 6v. Ed. by E. Russell Primm III. 2002. bibliogs. illus. index. Tradition; dist. by Child's World, $357 (1-59187-026-7). 809.

Kids love to find out about their favorite authors and illustrators. In addition, most students have to write a biography report of an author or illustrator at some point during their school career. If all those volumes of *Something about the Author* intimidate the kids wanting or needing to research an author in your library, this is the reference tool for you. In it, 222 biographical essays on "young readers' favorite authors and illustrators" are arranged alphabetically by last name. A cross-section of authors and illustrators is represented, primarily from the twentieth century. Some popular authors, such as Patricia Wrede and Caroline Cooney, are omitted, while new authors with few works to their credit, like Kate DiCamillo and Ian Falconer, are included.

Each essay is a brief but informative four pages in length and contains a wealth of information useful to student researchers. All entries include a photograph of the author or illustrator, dates of birth and death (if applicable), quotes from and about the subject, reproductions of book covers, and footnotes of interesting facts. For example, after World War II, author Joan Aiken lived for a time in a bus with her husband and children. A selected bibliography of each person's work through 2002 is included as well as a listing of major literary awards won (if any). A list of suggested print and Internet resources is provided for those interested in further study.

The first volume in the set begins with an introduction to the set and includes information about where students can send their picks for authors and illustrators to be included in future editions. Each volume begins with a volume-specific table of contents and a list of major children's author and illustrator literary awards, along with a brief description of each, and concludes with a comprehensive index. Designed to satisfy the browsing and research needs of middle-grade readers, this set is well designed and easily accessible. An excellent purchase for school and public library reference collections.

The Gay and Lesbian Literary Heritage: A Reader's Companion to the Writers and Their Works, from Antiquity to the Present. Rev. ed. Ed. by Claude J. Summers. 2002. 718p. bibliogs. index. Routledge, $55 (0-415-92926-1). 809.

The original edition, also edited by Summers, came out in 1995 to generally good reviews. It was published by Henry Holt, and it won a Lambda Literary Award. The book has changed little in the intervening years and still has all of the redeeming qualities discussed in the RBB review of the first edition. Articles are thorough and predominately brief. Longer articles cover topical themes and national or ethnic literatures. Each article is followed by a bibliography. Cross-references are good.

There are 32 new entries for this edition, including *Comedy of manners*; *Kushner, Tony*; *Norwegian literature*; and *Sand, George*. Few of the entries or the attached bibliographies from the previous edition have been updated. The articles on African American literature stop in the early 1990s. Missing are such well-known names as Donna Allegra, Marci Blackman, Thomas Glave, James Earl Hardy, and April Sinclair, all of them prime examples of writers who would be discussed if these articles were current. An article on author Elana Dykewomon seems to stop late 1980s, as her most recent work (*Beyond the Pale* and *Nothing Will Be as Sweet as the Taste: Selected Poems 1974–1994*) is not discussed.

Those libraries that already own the 1995 Holt edition should keep it. Those that don't own it might consider this edition for articles that orient readers into gay and lesbian literature and to authors of historical note. However, don't expect the revised edition to be up-to-date. There is room on the shelf for a current reader's companion to gay and lesbian literature, but this isn't it.

★**Holocaust Literature:** An Encyclopedia of Writers and Their Work. 2v. Ed. by S. Lillian Kremer. 2002. 1,499p. appendixes. bibliogs. glossary. index. Routledge, $250 (0-415-92985-7). 809.

A major addition to Holocaust Studies, this encyclopedia synthesizes a wide range of literary voices and provides a compelling look at more than 300 novelists, poets, memoirists, dramatists, and others writers who experienced the Holocaust (1933–45) or otherwise integrated the subject into their works. Some experienced the Holocaust firsthand in places like Auschwitz, the Warsaw Ghetto, or Babi Yar, while others lived through it in the U.S., Europe, or elsewhere. Still others were influenced as second-and third-generation writers, as children of survivors, or via other routes. The editor is a professor of English at Kansas State University, where she teaches courses in Holocaust literature and film. The wide range of contributors (from Europe, the U.S., Israel, and elsewhere) greatly enhances the relevance of this work, as scholars from around the world interpret the Holocaust from a variety of perspectives.

The encyclopedia provides comprehensive coverage of authors who made the Holocaust the primary focus of their writings (Aharon Appelfeld, Elie Weisel, Viktor Frankl, Nava Semel, and Primo Levi, among others). It also has a significant number of Jewish and some non-Jewish authors who may not be viewed as "Holocaust writers," such as Yehudah Amichai, Cynthia Ozick, Jean-Paul Sartre, and William Styron. The authors have written in Hebrew, English, Yiddish, Polish, German, French, and other languages, but most if not all have had their works translated into English.

The detailed entries (between 2,000 and 8,000 words long) treat how each author used her or his literary talents to respond to the Holocaust. Each entry follows a similar pattern of describing the author's work and then placing that work within the framework of Holocaust literature and other forms of literary expression. Generous quotes from the writers' works enhance the analysis and give the entries a powerful journalistic feel without detracting from the academic integrity. Each entry ends with an exhaustive bibliography of primary and secondary sources related to the author's work.

The appendixes bring together key events, historical figures, Holocaust literary themes and genres, authors' birthplaces and language composition, and other topics. These appendixes will greatly enhance research by tying together different subcategories of Holocaust studies. For example, researchers will be able to identify which writers experienced specific events, such as *Kristallnacht* or the *Kindertransport*, and which wrote on specific themes, such as postwar Jewish identity and resistance to Nazi persecution.

This work has a number of similarities with the recently published one-volume *Encyclopedia of Holocaust Literature* [RBB S 1 02]. The alphabetically arranged entries in both are well written, and some of the same scholars contributed to both titles (including the editor of this encyclopedia). Both are strong survey texts that help put Holocaust writing into a historical and literary context. But the current work is much more comprehensive and includes both first-and second-generation Holocaust writers (and some third-generation). *Encyclopedia of Holocaust Literature* has about 130 entries and includes only first-generation writers.

Libraries with Holocaust studies courses and others with an interest in this topic should purchase this title, as the number of authors covered and the strong bibliographic component make it an impressive resource for researchers and other serious students. This would also be an excellent purchase for large public libraries.

Literary Movements for Students: Presenting Analysis, Context, and Criticism on Literary Movements. 2v. Ed. by David Galens. 2002. bibliogs. glossary. illus. indexes. Gale, $125 (0-7876-6517-7). 809.

Another valuable title in the Gale For Students line, this set is meant to "provide readers with a guide to understanding, enjoying, and studying literary movements." Twenty-eight literary movements are described in their historical and cultural contexts. Volume 1 includes literature before the twentieth century (alphabetical chapters from "Bildungsroman" to "Transcendentalism"), and volume 2 covers the twentieth century ("Absurdism" to "Symbolism").

Each chapter consists of an introduction, brief entries for representative authors and works, and discussion of themes, styles, variations, and historical context. An original signed critical essay is included in each chapter along with, in most cases, lengthy excerpts from one or more previously published critical works. Black-and-white photos, sidebars listing such items as media adaptations and suggested topics and resources for further study, bibliographies of source material, and annotated further reading lists complete most chapters. A particularly useful feature is "Compare and Contrast," in which the cultural and historical background of each movement is compared to conditions in the late twentieth and early twenty-first centuries.

Front matter for each volume includes a volume-specific table of contents, a literary chronology, and a list of contributors (mostly freelance writers). Three indexes are found at the end: a "Cumulative Author/Title Index," a "Nationality/Ethnicity Index," and a "Subject/Theme Index." Also at the end of each volume is a useful glossary defining and cross-referencing terms from *abstract* to *zeitgeist*.

There are a few problems with the indexing. Chinua Achebe isn't in the "Author/Title Index" although his novel *Things Fall Apart* is. The "Subject/Theme Index" is not detailed enough—under *Fate and chance*, for example, are 47 undifferentiated page number citations. Edward Said is pictured and mentioned briefly in the chapter "Postcolonialism" but does not appear in any index; a general index would capture items that do not fit within the indexing system. Despite these minor flaws, high-school English and social studies teacher will snap this work up, and it will be well used in school, college, and public library collections.

Literature and Its Times: Supplement 1: Profiles of Notable Literary Works and the Historical Events That Influenced Them. 2v. By Joyce Moss. 2002. 590p. bibliogs. illus. index. Gale, $190 (0-7876-6550-9). 809.

The five-volume set *Literature and Its Times* was designed to help high-school and undergraduate students make connections between literature and history or society. Works are selected for inclusion by scholars based upon frequency of study, ties to significant events, or enduring appeal to readers either in or outside the culture that produced it. Classic as well as contemporary writings are included and are limited to works written in or translated into English. All works span a variety of genres and countries as well as historical periods. *Supplement 1* discusses works not included in the first five volumes.

The first volume of the supplement treats the period from ancient times to the 1920s and contains 49 signed entries for works that deal with, though they may not necessarily have been written during, those times, among them *Crime and Punishment*, *The Importance of Being Earnest*, *On the Origin of Species*, Plato's *Apology*, and *The Sound and the Fury*. The second volume, covering the 1930s and forward, has entries for 50 works, among them *Dinner at the Homesick Restaurant*, *The Glass Menagerie*, *Lolita*, *On the Road*, and *Song of Solomon*. Arrangement is alphabetical by title. Each entry has the same elements as entries in the five initial volumes: an introduction to the work, including a synopsis and its relation to the author's life; a discussion of events in history at the time the work is set; a detailed discussion of the work itself that includes plot, sources used by the author, and its relation to other writings; a description of history at the time the work was written; and, finally, a list of sources cited in the entry and a list of further readings. Many entries also include time lines, anecdotes, and illustrations.

Time lines preceding the text list only those events related to the works in each supplement. Each volume of the supplement has tables of contents by title and author. The index that closes each volume is cumulative for the entire *Literature and Its Times* set. Recommended for libraries that have found the foundation volumes useful.

Major Authors and Illustrators for Children and Young Adults: A Selection of Sketches from Something about the Author. 8v. 2d ed. 2002. 5,132p. bibliogs. illus. index. Gale, $495 (0-7876-1234-0). 809.

This compilation of biographical, bibliographic, and critical information is a subset of Gale's long-running series, Something about the Author (or SATA; 142 volumes covering more than 10,000 authors, 1971–present). The current work includes almost 1,100 articles, representing an international array of poets, novelists, biographers, storytellers, and playwrights from antiquity (Aesop) to modern day (Francesca Lia Block). Each multipage entry provides name and pseudonyms, personal data, contact information, professional memberships, awards and honors, a complete list of writings including interpretive pieces, a list of adaptations, works in progress, "Sidelights," and print biographical and critical sources. The "Sidelights," the only narrative portions of the entries, offer readable and engaging essays on each artist's development, motivation, critical reception, and personal thoughts and revelations. As with SATA, the information on living individuals was compiled through personal surveys and telephone interviews. When individuals were not available for direct consultations, numerous resources were consulted.

This second edition includes 950 completely revised and updated entries plus 150 new articles. The editors indicate that other enhancements include a nationality and a genre index. Though well intentioned, these guides are not that helpful. For example, almost 750 individuals (out of 1,100) are identified as "American," including those whose works reflect other cultures, such as Naomi Shihab Nye and Jamake Highwater. Conversely, Eve Bunting is identified as "Irish," and Isaac Asimov as "Russian," despite little apparent cultural emphasis in their works. One suggestion would be to designate "Heritage" or "Cultural Background" as alternate identifiers. Some of the genre designations are too broad to be of much use; more than 500 names are listed under "Novels" and about 350 under "Illustrations." Other more limited categories ("Animal Tales," "Horror Fiction," "Music," etc.) better lend themselves to practical applications for teachers and researchers. Another consideration for future editions would be the inclusion of a time line.

However, these are minor concerns, as are a few discrepancies in coverage (Robert Louis Stevenson is included, but curriculum staple Edgar Allen Poe is not; Ben Bova and Robert Heinlein are profiled but not Ray Bradbury, another standard presence in most American literature textbooks). Overall, this resource provides a tremendous amount of reliable and accessible information. Recommended for all public and secondary school collections that do not subscribe to SATA.

Make Mine a Mystery: A Reader's Guide to Mystery and Detective Fiction. By Gary Warren Niebuhr. 2003. 548p. appendix. indexes. Libraries Unlimited, $65 (1-56308-784-7). 809.

This addition to the Genreflecting Advisory Series is "intended to help readers' advisors, librarians, and others develop a greater understanding of the mystery genre so they can make reading recommendations and successfully answer questions raised by readers who enjoy reading mysteries." The book is divided into two parts. In part 1, "Introduction to Mystery Fiction," Niebuhr devotes considerable space to background material: discussion of readers'-advisory service in general and the appeal of mystery fiction in particular, and how to build and manage a mystery collection, followed by a history of the genre beginning in 1845. Part 2, "The Literature," annotates more than 2,500 titles by more than 200 authors.

Niebuhr take a fairly purist view of mystery, omitting crime, intrigue, thrillers, suspense, adventure novels, and true crime. This leaves "mystery detective novels where a fictional character tries to solve a puzzle concerning a crime to the administration of justice." Chapters correspond to three types of detectives—amateur, public, and private—with several variations, such as lawyer detectives and ex-cop detectives. For each different type, as appropriate, Niebuhr identifies those writers who are "historical founding members," "golden agers," and "modern practitioners." Under each writer, titles are grouped by detective and arranged in chronological order by publication date. This grouping by detective is useful because it corresponds to the way mysteries tend to be chosen and read. Each title entry includes publisher, date, and a brief annotation. An appendix lists print and electronic resources, organizations, and publishers. The volume concludes with author, title, character, subject, and location indexes. Niebuhr's type-of-detective approach is a useful way of classifying the factors that appeal to mystery readers, and the indexes offer alternative pointers to titles that readers might like.

Among guides to mystery fiction, this one stands out as being thorough and current. Essential for public libraries.

Reference Guide to World Literature. 2v. 3d ed. Ed. by Sara Pendergast and Tom Pendergast. 2002. 1,730p. bibliogs. indexes. St. James, $320 (1-55862-490-2). 809.

Featuring entries on nearly 500 writers and approximately 550 works, this new edition "represents a comprehensive and authoritative survey of literatures written in languages other than English." The chronological range is vast, beginning with the Vedas and the *Epic of Gilgamesh* and ending with contemporary works such as Isabel Allende's *The House of the Spirits* and Gabriel Garcia Marquez's *Love in the Time of Cholera*.

Volume 1 provides two-to three-page profiles of authors from *Abe Kobo* (Japanese) to *Carl Zuckmayer* (German); in between are authors from France, Haiti, Egypt, Spain, Lithuania, Ukraine, Iceland, and Tunisia, to name but a few. The editors state that this edition "provides expanded coverage of literatures in less represented languages, the primary focus being Arabic, Chinese, and Japanese, as well as previously unrepresented languages including Albanian, Estonian, Indonesian, Kurdish, and Thai." In addition, more contemporary women writers are profiled than in earlier editions.

In the author entries, brief biographical data are given when known: birth date and place, education, family, career summary, awards given, and death date. This is followed by a selected list of publications, references to bibliographies on the author, and references to full-length critical studies for further research. Finally, signed essays provide a critical evaluation of the author and his or her work. A list of contributors is available, as are a chronological list of writers and an alphabetical list of writers and works.

Author articles are cross-referenced to volume 2, which contains detailed entries on individual literary works presented in alphabetical order by title. Here, again, coverage is expansive—one finds essays on, among others, *Around the World in Eighty Days*, *Hansel and Gretel*, *Kiss of the Spider Woman*, *Les Liaisons Dangereuses*, *Madame Bovary*, and *The Rubaiyat*. This volume also provides a section of notes on advisors and contributors from universities worldwide, an index of authors and titles by language, and an alphabetical title index.

Reference Guide to World Literature is indeed a useful tool for researchers and aficionados of international literature. It is a worthy companion to works such as *Contemporary World Writers* (St. James, 1993), *Cyclopedia of World Authors* (Salem, 1997), *Encyclopedia of World Literature in the 20th Century* (St. James, 1998), and Gale's World Literature and Its Times series. Although not inexpensive, it is especially recommended for academic and large public libraries lacking coverage in the area.

The Social Impact of the Novel: A Reference Guide. By Claudia Durst Johnson and Vernon Johnson. 2002. 393p. appendix. bibliogs. indexes. Greenwood, $74.95 (0-313-31818-2). 809.3.

This new reference guide surveys 200 landmark novels that have made a notable impact on society or, more specifically, "the way individuals think and society acts." The novels are examined from a social and historical perspective, rather than a literary one, to show how they transformed society or changed readers' minds on important social issues. Entries are organized geographically by continent, and within the continent, alphabetically by country. Thirty different countries are represented, but the concentration is on novels that had an impact on Western thought. Novels had to be written in or translated into English for inclusion, but they do not have to be critically acclaimed (in fact, many were popular with the masses only). For each individual country, there is a time line of important social events to help place the literature that follows into perspective. Within specific countries, entries are arranged chronologically by date of publication.

Entries are typically between one and one-and-a-half pages. Most list the title, author, and date of publication; describe the historical context in which the work was written; and give an assessment of the public's reaction to the novel and its ultimate influence on society. Each entry concludes with a short "Additional Readings" list of monographs. Four reader aids are in the back of the book—author, title, geographical, and issues indexes. There is also an appendix of additional protest novels to facilitate further investigation.

Reference books examining literature from multidisciplinary perspectives seem to be on the rise. *Social Protest Literature: An Encyclopedia of Works, Characters, Authors, and Themes* (ABC-CLIO, 1999) is the closest parallel to The Social Impact of the Novel in scope, but it has a broader definition of literature and includes poetry and plays (about 130 of its 450 entries deal with individual literature works) rather than just novels. Entries in Social Protest Literature appear to have more detailed plot summary than in The Social Impact of the Novel but to the exclusion of more in-depth analysis on a novel's effect. Pricewise, the two volumes are comparable, and libraries may want to invest only in one.

This is a useful new reference tool for researching the development of social concerns in specific areas via literature or for comparing the treatment of specific issues in the literature of different cultures. Recommended for public, high-school, and academic libraries.

Supernatural Fiction Writers: Contemporary Fantasy and Horror. 2v. 2d ed. Ed. by Richard Bleiler. 2002. 1,048p. bibliogs. index. Scribner, $240 (0-684-31250-6). 809.3.

These volumes update the two-volume work first published in 1985 as a companion to the first edition of Scribner's Science Fiction Writers. The editor, Richard Bleiler, is the son of the first edition's editor, Everett F. Bleiler, and the author or editor of other works on genre fiction, including Science Fiction Writers (2d ed., Scribner, 1999) and Reference Guide to Mystery and Detective Fiction (Libraries Unlimited, 1999). Everett F. Bleiler makes an appearance here as a contributor.

The 1985 edition profiled supernatural writers who were primarily "of historical interest." For the new edition, it was decided to "largely eschew historical coverage and profile instead the most significant contemporary British and American writers of fantasy and horror." According to the introduction, contemporary is defined as someone who has been active since 1985. Some of the 116 writers, such as Ray Bradbury, Stephen King, and Joyce Carol Oates, appeared in the first edition, but many, including Paul Auster, Clive Barker, Ian McEwan, Philip Pullman, and J. K. Rowling, are new. Although they died before 1985, Robert Aickman and Shirley Jackson have entries in the new edition because their reputations continue to grow.

Whereas arrangement in the first edition was broadly chronological, the second is organized alphabetically by writer. Articles range in length from 5 to 12 pages. There is some biographical information but emphasis is on the works, with analysis of important themes, types of work, and, in many cases, individual series and titles. Each article concludes with a selected bibliography of works by the author under discussion, critical and biographical studies, and Web sites if they are available. The index in volume 2 lists authors and titles.

Librarians turn to the Scribner Writers Series for more in-depth treatment than can be found in most other literary reference sources, and Supernatural Fiction Writers does not disappoint. It is recommended for high-school, public, and academic libraries. Because the second edition extends rather than supersedes the first, the first edition should be retained.

Whodunit? A Who's Who in Crime & Mystery Writing. By Rosemary Herbert. 2003. 215p. Oxford, $35 (0-19-515763-X). 809.3.

The Oxford Companion to Crime and Mystery Writing, edited by Rosemary Herbert, appeared in 1999. Now Herbert has drawn on that earlier volume and also updated it by adding 101 new entries.

Whereas The Oxford Companion to Crime and Mystery Writing had 666 entries covering not only writers and characters but also settings, themes, subgenres, and terminology, this whittled-down version has 380 entries for writers, characters, and character types, such as Coroner, Genteel woman sleuth, and Gentleman thief. It reprints most of the entries from the parent volume that can be considered even remotely to answer the question "who"—even Animals and Corpse. Many of the new entries are for American writers, among them Nevada Barr, Edna Buchanan, James Lee Burke, Patricia Cornwell, Loren Estleman, Elizabeth George, and Scott Turow. There is also a new entry for Culinary sleuths. Among the "who" entries that have not been carried over are several related to adventure and espionage (for example, Bond, James; Fleming, Ian; Gentleman adventurer). Also gone are the references attached to some of the entries in the older volume. With a few exceptions, such as a slight shortening of Dalgiesh, Adam and expansion of Morse, Chief Inspector Endeavor, existing entries have not been revised.

Perhaps a second edition of The Oxford Companion to Crime and Mystery Writing will incorporate both volumes. In the meantime, libraries that already own the more comprehensive work will question whether this is a necessary purchase. Although numerous authors have been added, information on most of them is not hard to find in other reference sources. For other libraries, Whodunit? is worth considering as a way to update and refresh the mystery reference shelves.

Who's Who in Lesbian and Gay Writing. By Gabriele Griffin. 2002. 226p. bibliog. Routledge, $29.95 (0-415-15984-9). 809.8920664.

The title of this work conjures up the image of a compendium of authors, subjects, and publishers who happen to be gay or lesbian. It may also bring to mind people who are predominantly English speaking. Griffin realized that the contemporary development of lesbian and gay culture has been uneven, at best, across countries and continents, and with this work, she has attempted to level that ground.

More than 400 alphabetical entries range in length from several sentences to an entire page. Although the majority of the writers are from the U.K. and the U.S., many countries are represented, including Canada, Cuba, Finland, France, Ireland, Italy, Japan, and Portugal. The majority of the individuals lived and wrote during the past 150 years, with a smattering of biographies before the late 1800s, such as British poet Richard Barnfield (1574–1627) and Sappho, from the sixth century B.C.E.

Griffin uses the phrase "lesbian and gay writing" to refer to "texts with a lesbian and/or gay content" and "texts written by writers who identify publicly as lesbian and gay, or who are known to be lesbian or gay." That stated, it may be noted that not all individuals seem to fit these criteria. Eleanor Roosevelt is one example.

This volume may be of value in undergraduate libraries and in medium-sized to large public libraries with a significant lesbian and gay collection. Some of the same writers are covered in The Gay and Lesbian Literary Heritage [RBB S 15 02], which has thematic as well as biographical entries.

Encyclopedia of American Literature. 3v. By Carol Berkin and others. 2002. bibliogs. index. Facts On File, $225 (0-8160-4121-0). 810.

American literature is probably one of the most heavily represented subjects in U.S. libraries. One would think that this topic has been wrung out and hung out to dry. But despite standard works such as The Oxford Companion to American Literature (1995), despite all the varieties of coverage in more specialized reference tools, there is still room for this set on your reference shelves.

The three volumes are divided into chronological order: The Colonial and Revolutionary Era, 1607–1814; The Age of Romanticism and Realism, 1815–1914; and The Modern and Postmodern Period from 1915. Alphabetical entries encompass all forms of writers—novelists, diarists, essayists, historians, pamphleteers, poets, and editors. Some literary characters, such as Blanche DuBois, are included, as are historical figures, like Daniel Boone, about whom books were written. Other entries cover significant publications, such as the Federalist and the New Yorker, and documents, such as the Gettysburg Address. Genres, movements, and styles are covered in Drama, African-American literature, Minimalism, and other entries. In addition, significant organizations, social movements, and historic events are treated with regard to their relevance to literature.

Each of the approximately 1,900 entries is at least a paragraph long, with some entries (for example, the one on Norman Mailer) covering more than a page. In addition to the lists of primary and secondary source material attached to the entries, each volume has a more general bibliography. Each volume also includes a specific chronology and index; unfortunately, there is no index to the complete set.

This is an excellent source for students who need more than the Oxford Companion but less than Scribner's American Writers series, and its chronological arrangement offers a different slant. Recommended for high-school, public, and academic libraries.

★**Great American Writers:** Twentieth Century. 13v. Ed. by R. Baird Shuman. 2002. 1,887p. bibliogs. glossary. illus. indexes. Marshall Cavendish, $459.95 (0-7614-7240-1). 810.9.

This is an amazing encyclopedia that most high-school libraries should include in their collections. The 90 American and Canadian authors who are profiled are those who "most frequently appear in high-school and college anthologies or have had a profound influence upon some of the most notable authors of the twentieth century"—a balanced collection of classic (Theodore Dreiser, William Faulkner) and modern (Maya Angelou, Amy Tan), popular (Judy Blume) and literary (Saul Bellow), fiction (Carson McCullers, John Irving) and nonfiction (James Agee), poetry (E. E. Cummings), drama (Lorraine Hansberry), and song (Bob Dylan).

Each volume profiles seven or eight writers in chapters that are up to

25 pages long. Arrangement is alphabetical. The first page of a chapter has a picture of the author and lists birth and death dates and locations. Also found on this page are an "Identification" that defines the author's genres and what he or she is most noted for and a paragraph that summarizes the details of the longer profile that follows. A biographical essay, "The Writer's Life," chronicles upbringing, education, adult family life, work history, and writing history and is accompanied by a chronology. The discussions include details about hardships and mistakes as well as successes. For instance, the biography about Truman Capote tells about his wild partying and alcoholism. "The Writer's Work" summarizes the literary career and includes a table listing works by genre and date.

The next section, "Reader's Guide to Major Works," analyzes two or three of the most important writings in terms of plot, character, themes, and impact. A bibliography of secondary sources is attached to each title entry. "Other Works" briefly discusses some additional writings. Each chapter concludes with a list of resources, including archival collections, videos, and Web sites. The illustrations that enhance most pages are a blend of photographs and well-chosen examples of American artwork. The artwork is beautifully reproduced in full color and is large enough for students to see important details. In addition to artist's name and title of the work, each caption relates the artwork to some aspect of the author's life and writing. It is rare to see the fine arts so well represented in a resource about literature. Other illustrations show book covers, movie posters, or album covers.

The final, index volume has a glossary, lists of award winners, and a list of writers by genre. Multiple indexes provide access by writers, literary works, visual artworks, visual artists, films, literary characters, and geographic location.

The contributors are experts in their fields and have a good sense of how to present the material in a manner that is informative without being boring or verbose. *Great American Writers* is a work that a reviewer is happy to read cover to cover, and, more importantly, that makes a librarian excited to (finally!) have something to give a student who is trying to write that literary criticism research paper for a hard-driving English teacher.

Harlem Renaissance: A Gale Critical Companion. 3v. Ed. by Janet Witalec. 2002. bibliogs. illus. index. Gale, $325 (0-7876-6618-1). 810.9.

Intended for upper-high-school and undergraduate students, *Harlem Renaissance* spans three volumes. Volume 1 focuses on five topic areas, starting with an overview and background information, then moving on to chapters on social, economic, and political factors; publishing and periodicals; performing arts; and the visual arts. Each chapter averages about 100 pages and follows a standard pattern of organization. For example, the chapter discussing the performing arts begins with a two-page introduction followed by a list of representative works and a collection of primary materials. Essays reprinted from other sources provide overviews of performing arts during the Harlem Renaissance and discussions of drama, film, and music. Each chapter ends with a list of further readings. Reading lists are excellently annotated and current but neglect Internet sites.

Volumes 2 and 3 are devoted to writers. Eleven female and twenty-two male authors are discussed, among them Arna Bontemps, Marcus Garvey, Angelina Weld Grimke, James Weldon Johnson, and Dorothy West. Entries average 30 to 50 pages, the shortest being 7 pages. Most author entries include biographical profiles, lists of principal works, some primary source material, critical essays, and further reading lists. For example, the entry on Zora Neale Hurston includes, among other items, the short story "Spunk," nine complete critical essays reprinted from other sources, and a one-and-one-half page listing of further readings, including cross-references to other Gale titles. Two illustrations are included within the section on Hurston, a photo of the author and a playbill cover. Illustrations are in black and white and of good quality but used sparingly throughout the set. Each volume contains a cumulative author index, title index, and subject index plus a chronology outlining key events between 1890 and 1937.

Although much of the content is available elsewhere, including other publications from Gale (according to the preface there is 15 percent or less overlap with Gale's Literary Criticism series), it is useful to have so much material brought together and presented in this particular context. The breadth and depth of *Harlem Renaissance* make it a valuable and unique reference source for academic, public, and high-school libraries. A resource with a similar title, *Harlem Renaissance* (UXL, 2000), is better suited for younger audiences.

The HarperCollins Reader's Encyclopedia of American Literature. 2d ed. Ed. by George Perkins and others. 2002. 1,126p. HarperCollins, $49.95 (0-06-019815-X). 810.9.

Last published in 1991 as *Benet's Reader's Encyclopedia of American Literature*, this compendium focuses primarily on the U.S., although it also encompasses the literatures of Canada and Latin America. Its more than 6,000 entries include authors, filmmakers, songwriters, titles of literary works, characters, historical events, periodicals, groups and movements, and a variety of other topics. In addition, a number of lengthy articles provide broad overviews of the literary history of particular geographical areas, ethnic groups, and genres.

The most significant feature of this edition is the inclusion of 300 new entries for writers who have risen to fame in the last two decades. Among those added are Madison Smartt Bell, Charles Frazier, John Grisham, Tony Kushner, Frank McCourt, Jane Smiley, and Amy Tan. Editors George and Barbara Perkins have also authored several new general articles (*Globalization of American literature* and *Hispanic-American literature*), and they have updated more than 1,300 entries from the previous edition, primarily those on writers who remain active (e.g., Gayl Jones, Larry McMurtry, Bobbie Ann Mason) and overview articles, such as *Afro-American literature* and *Drama in the United States: since 1960*. An extensive search yielded only one new title entry—*All the Pretty Horses*—and no new entries for other categories of topics. Moreover, many lesser-known writers who appeared in the previous edition have been dropped, as have almost half of the entries for U.S. presidents and numerous titles (including Willa Cather's *O Pioneers!*).

Broader in geographic scope than *The Oxford Companion to American Literature* (6th ed., Oxford, 1995), the HarperCollins title also includes approximately 1,000 more entries, and its coverage of contemporary writers is more extensive. However, the paucity of new entries in categories other than biographical and survey articles creates an imbalance in the work as a whole because the last three decades are underrepresented by such types of entries as titles, characters, and events. Although its unevenness detracts somewhat from its usefulness, this encyclopedia continues to be a valuable source for high-school, public, and academic libraries.

Twayne Companion to Contemporary Literature in English: From the Editors of the Hollins Critic. Ed. by R. H. W. Dillard and Amanda Cockrell. 2002. 1,195p. bibliogs. illus. index. Twayne, $175 (0-8057-1703-X). 810.9.

Part of the new Twayne Companion to Literature series, this set features 101 select essays reprinted from *The Hollins Critic* (produced by Hollins University in Roanoke, Virginia) during the period between 1975 and 2002. A chronology of that period's important literary publications, awards, and events sets the context for the essays at the beginning of volume 1. Each essay, usually between 5,000 and 6,000 words, surveys a contemporary author's entire body of work and is intended to "do something more than merely offer a review of his (or her) books and something less than deliver a verdict on his (or her) 'place' in literary history." Essays also feature a brief biography accompanied by a line-art portrait of the writer, a bibliography of the author's works, and, where applicable, a career update. The essays, written by literary scholars, were chosen because of the excellence of the writing and a perceived lack of subject coverage elsewhere.

Included authors are mostly novelists or poets, primarily American but also Canadian, English, or Irish. Coeditor Dillard takes pains to discuss the collapse of the traditional literary canon in his introduction, thus banishing all expectation of national figures and trying to exonerate himself from a canon debate. Instead, he offers examples of the current "openness and . . . genuine diversity of style and content far more complex, varied, and interesting than one shaped merely by the demands of political correctness." Indeed, the authors covered have an impressive range of styles: among the included are postmodernists Thomas Pynchon and Paul Auster, science fiction writer Octavia Butler, historical fiction writer Thomas Flanagan, popular novelist Anne Tyler, cutting-edge novelist Richard Powers, and poets Mary Jo Salter and John Ashbery. An index at the back of volume 2 facilitates locating people and titles.

Because the original *Hollins Critic* essays are indexed only in MLA *Bibliography*, ABELL, and *American Humanities Index*, these volumes provide a welcome additional point of access. The authors covered are a nice representation of the "postmodernist chaos" arguably present in contemporary fiction. Recommended for academic libraries.

African American Poets: Lives, Works, and Sources. By Joyce Pettis. 2002. 357p. bibliogs. illus. index. Greenwood, $59.95 (0-313-31117-X). 811.009.

Audre Lorde, in an essay entitled "Poetry Is Not a Luxury," stated, "Poetry is not only dream and vision; it is the skeleton architecture of our lives. It lays the foundations for a future of change, a bridge across our fears of what has never been before." This is especially true for African American poets, who have the added weight of a history of bondage and inequality to inform their art.

The 46 poets examined here range from Jupiter Hammon and Phillis Wheatley in the eighteenth century to contemporary poets such as Maya Angelou, Rita Dove, and Quincy Troupe. Each entry begins with birth and death dates and a photograph of the poet, when available. After a brief overview, there is a discussion of the poet's work, including the main themes, and an analysis of selected major works. Each entry ends with a list of book-length works, where applicable; anthologies that include the poet's works; and references for further reading. The entries range from very short (2 pages) to lengthy (11 pages), averaging 8 pages. The book concludes with a list of 37 anthologies for further research and a complete index.

This book is a clear and understandable resource for students in high school and college to use to begin a research project on any of the poets. Unfortunately, samples of the poetry discussed are not included, which can be a drawback for students. Many of the same poets are covered in other works, such as *African American Writers: A Dictionary* (ABC-CLIO, 2000) and volumes in Gale's Contemporary Authors series. This work will be most useful for school and public libraries that do not have other resources for biographical and critical information on African American poets.

Asian American Playwrights: A Bio-Bibliographical Critical Sourcebook. Ed. by Miles Xian Liu. 2002. 407p. bibliogs. index. Greenwood, $94.95 (0-313-31455-1). 812.
Asian American Poets: A Bio-Bibliographical Critical Sourcebook. Ed. by Guiyou Huang. 2002. 376p. bibliogs. index. Greenwood, $99.95 (0-313-31809-3). 811.

The growing popularity of ethnic studies and the study of literature not included in the traditional canon can lead to difficult reference questions, and sources that cover these topics are always welcome. These two books from Greenwood offer substantial entries on prominent Asian American poets and playwrights. The information in the entries is useful, but the basis for inclusion is muddled. Both sources include twentieth-century authors from the U.S. and Canada. For *Asian American Poets*, a list of a hundred names was compiled. Those not represented from this original list were excluded because no contributor chose to write about them or because the promised contributions were not provided. The definition of Asian American is also confusingly broad. In *Asian American Playwrights*, the biography provided for Shih-I Hsiung gives no indication that he ever even visited North America. Other authors seem to have been included on the basis of rather short stays.

Asian American Playwrights contains 52 entries, among them performance artist Genny Lim; Santha Rama Rau, acclaimed for her dramatization of E. M. Forster's novel *A Passage to India*; and Laurence Yep, better known as a writer of children's books. *Asian American Poets* contains 48 entries for writers such as Meena Alexander, Virginia R. Cerenio, and Cathy Song. All entries were written by scholars in the field. The entries range from 2 to more than 20 pages and consist of four sections: biography, major works and themes, critical reception, and bibliography. The bibliographies include works by the entry subject as well as critical works. Both volumes end with a selected general bibliography and an index.

Though these books are not exhaustive sources on their subjects, they cover more poets and playwrights than Gale's *Asian American Literature* (1999). They are recommended as good introductions for academic and large public libraries, which can round out their collections with Greenwood's *Asian American Novelists: A Bio-Bibliographical Critical Sourcebook* (2000).

Black Drama: 1850 to Present. [Internet database]. Alexander Street, subscriptions from $1,000 [http://www.alexanderstreet2.com/bldrlive]. (Last accessed December 19, 2002). 822.

Framers of electronic databases can take lessons from Alexander Street Press, which has mounted 502 full-text plays on its new online source, *Black Drama*. With the aid of drama expert James V. Hatch, the company projects the list will grow to 1,200 entries, 25 percent of them previously unpublished. Playwrights from North America, English-speaking Africa, and the Caribbean are represented, among them Ossie Davis, Angelina Grimke, Langston Hughes, Zora Neale Hurston, Sonia Sanchez, Jean Toomer, Melvin Van Peebles, and Derek Walcott.

The beauty of this database is its anticipation of the user's needs. Enhancing the site are clear fonts and hypertexts, uncluttered page layouts, and speedy resolution from PhiloLogic software, which the University of Chicago developed. The table of contents lists Authors (125 of these on the day we looked), Years (from 1846 to 2001), Characters, Plays, Productions, Theaters, Companies, Subjects, and Related Resources, such as playbills, posters, and production stills. If one selects Authors, a neat, organized author list pops up with life data and number of plays, divided into published and unpublished. Under biographical details are a wealth of possibilities, including sexual orientation, education, and differentiation of nationality, ethnicity, and race plus instant links to titles and character lists. Selecting one of the plays leads to a record that has links to the electronic text as well as to author information, bibliographic details, related resources, and character information. Under Theaters, a list of 120 theaters that produced black drama provides information about productions, theater style, seating capacity, and theatrical companies, including players and their birth dates. A Find tool allows searching by Authors, Plays, Characters, Scenes, Production, Theater, and Resources. Very specific criteria such as the school the author attended or the seating capacity of the theater can be used to narrow these searches. Keyword full-text searching is also available, and here the researcher can again combine multiple fields.

Flaws are few. Biographies lack the depth one might find in other resources, such as various volumes of Gale's Dictionary of Literary Biography series. The focus of this sophisticated research tool is on the plays themselves rather than on background or context. Another 350 plays will be added this spring, and the update that follows will bring the number up to the projected 1,200. *Black Drama* is an indispensable tool for research collections in African American and world literature.

Contemporary American Women Fiction Writers: An A-to-Z Guide. Ed. by Laurie Champion and Rhonda Austin. 2002. 407p. bibliogs. index. Greenwood, $94.95 (0-313-31627-9). 813.
Contemporary American Women Poets: An A-to-Z Guide. Ed. by Catherine Cucinella. 2002. 402p. bibliogs. index. Greenwood, $94.95 (0-313-31783-6). 811.

Into the crowded field of biographical reference sources come two new works from Greenwood. Each covers 60 to 70 women writers who have written the majority of their works since 1945. Some authors, such as Toni Morrison, are established authors, while others, such as Sandra Cisneros, are still building their reputations. The writers are racially and ethnically diverse. However, in neither volume have the editors clearly explained the criteria they used in choosing authors. In *Contemporary American Women Fiction Writers*, the editors state the women selected have all been writing since 1945 and have made "significant contributions to the contemporary literary scene." Except for a few, such as Judy Blume and Sara Paretksy, all are literary authors, but why Amy Hempel and Linda Hogan were chosen over Susan Isaacs, Sue Miller, or Rosellen Brown is never made clear. Genre authors are generally excluded except for Paretsky. The editors of *Contemporary American Women Poets* say that the selected poets have written since 1945, represent a wide variety of ethnic and racial backgrounds, and come from all parts of the U.S. but offer no further explanation that justifies why some poets were chosen over others.

Each book is set up in an A–Z format with each author having a five- to six-page essay. Each essay includes a biography, an analysis of the writer's major works, and a bibliography of works by and about the author. The essays themselves are very readable and would be appropriate for high-school students and general readers who need a good overview of the writer's life and works. Because the essays are relatively short, college students would not have enough information for research papers but would find the articles helpful introductions.

Reference works on literary biography abound. The writers in both of these volumes are all included in Gale's Contemporary Authors series. Many are also included in Gale's Dictionary of Literary Biography series and Contemporary Literary Criticism series, which give more extensive biographical and analytical information. At least 20 of the fiction writers are also included in the H. W. Wilson Authors series. Approximately

Encyclopedia of Pulp Fiction Writers. By Lee Server. 2002. 304p. bibliogs. illus. index. Facts On File, $60 (0-8160-4577-1); Checkmark, paper, $19.95 (0-8160-4578-X). 813.

Written by established pulp fiction and popular culture author Server, *Encyclopedia of Pulp Fiction Writers* includes information on more than 200 nineteenth-and twentieth-century writers. Arranged in alphabetical order, each entry includes a biographical sketch and list of the author's works (arranged by pseudonym). Also included is an introduction that serves as a concise overview and traces the start of the industry of pulp serials to the genre that it is today.

Rather than being comprehensive, the encyclopedia aims to provide "a representative sampling," and in some cases leaves out better-known and widely covered writers in favor of others who are more obscure. Among the names one will find here are James M. Cain, Zane Grey, Mary Roberts Rinehart, Mickey Spillane, and Jacqueline Susann. Approximately 30 percent of the writers do not appear in other author sources like *Contemporary Popular Writers* (St. James, 1997), and for those who do, the emphasis is often not on any contributions to pulp fiction. Many authors who have become mainstream, such as Edgar Rice Burroughs and Ian Fleming, are included, and their humble beginnings are the focus of these articles. Some readers may be miffed to discover that their favorite (and often best-selling) authors—such as Tom Clancy and Mario Puzo—are identified with the pulp genre, but Server makes a good argument for inclusion. *Encyclopedia of Pulp Fiction Writers* fills a niche in sourcebooks on authors and is recommended for libraries with large literature criticism collections.

Mammoth Encyclopedia of Modern Crime Fiction. By Mike Ashley. 2002. 780p. appendixes. bibliog. index. Carroll & Graf, paper, $12.95 (0-7867-1006-3). 813.0872.

When faced with the challenge of producing a new encyclopedia on the topic of crime fiction, Ashley chose to include only those authors whose stories contain actual crimes, thereby eliminating related genres such as suspense or horror fiction. He focuses primarily on material written since the 1960s by writers from the U.S., the UK, and several other countries.

Written in an entertaining style, more than 500 author entries contain a discussion of writings; biographical details; information concerning Web sites, awards, and pseudonyms; a pointer to authors writing in a similar style; and a recommendation as to which title to read first. Each entry ends with a personal item of interest, such as the fact that James Patterson's first book was rejected 31 times before it was published.

Adding depth and interest is the section "Television Series and Major Films," which describes more than 400 major productions. Two appendixes follow: "Award Winners" and "Current Magazines and Websites." There is also an index to important characters and series.

Other more comprehensive reference works exist, including *The Encyclopedia of Murder and Mystery* (St. Martin's, 1999) and *The Oxford Companion to Crime and Mystery Writing* (1999). *Mammoth Encyclopedia of Modern Crime* provides a great deal of information that will appeal to aficionados of the crime-fiction genre and is recommended for libraries needing an economical guide.

A Zora Neale Hurston Companion. By Robert W. Croft. 2002. 256p. appendix. bibliog. index. Greenwood, $74.95 (0-313-30707-5). 813.

One of the best known figures of the Harlem Renaissance get volume-length reference treatment in this guide. A chronology and a brief overview of Hurston's life are followed by A–Z entries covering Hurston's works, characters, themes and motifs, family members, and acquaintances.

The entries for important works are generally the longest—two pages each for *Dust Tracks on the Road* and *Their Eyes Were Watching God*, for example—and include discussion of the work's genesis, plot, and critical reception. These entries also provide lists of materials for further reading. Entries for themes and motifs such as *death*, *love*, and *trains* offer brief explanations of the theme's overall meaning in Hurston's work as well as the use of the theme in individual works. Remaining entries treat individuals both real (such as anthropologist Franz Boas, who encouraged her folklore research, and convicted murderer Ruby McCollum, about whom she wrote several articles) and fictional. Because some characters, such as Jim Weston, the protagonist of the play *Mule Bone*, show up in several different works, this book is especially helpful for sorting through what the author calls "the intertextuality of Hurston's writing."

An appendix lists the contents of collections of Hurston manuscripts, correspondence, and other materials. An extensive bibliography lists primary materials by Hurston (including book reviews and newspaper articles as well as books, plays, short stories, and essays) and selected secondary materials.

Researchers will need to turn to other sources for more biographical and critical information, but this volume should be valuable to have on hand to support the study of Hurston's writings and life. It is recommended for public and academic libraries; high-school libraries might also consider it.

African American Autobiographers: A Sourcebook. Ed. by Emmanuel S. Nelson. 2002. 416p. bibliogs. index. Greenwood, $94.95 (0-313-31409-8). 818.

When African Americans began to write in the late eighteenth century, they often produced slave narratives and other autobiographical prose. They were encouraged in this by abolitionists who used these writings to support their cause. Additionally, for a people who had been denied recognition, autobiography allowed African Americans to define themselves and assert their selfhood as people rather than as property. The work of "claiming and defining the self" continues today in the writings of Maya Angelou, Henry Louis Gates Jr., and others.

This book spans the historical range of African American autobiographies. Most entries are between 5 and 10 pages long, and each entry begins with birth and death dates, when known. These are followed by a succinct biography, then an analytical discussion of the works and themes and their critical reception. Each entry ends with a list of autobiographical works by the author and a bibliography of studies of those works. Because the entries are arranged alphabetically, it would have been useful to include a chronological listing of the authors.

Other reference sources, such as Gale's Contemporary Authors and Nineteenth-Century Literature Criticism series, *African-American Writers: A Dictionary* (ABC-CLIO, 2000), and *Bearing Witness: Selections from African-American Autobiography in the Twentieth Century* (Pantheon, 1991), cover some of the same writers, but none of them have all of the authors included here. This book provides readers and researchers with the ability to examine African American autobiography as a genre and can also be used by students interested in delving into the autobiographical aspects of the work of those who are better known for their novels, poems, and other writings. It will be useful for libraries with African American collections as well as public and academic libraries that wish to have comprehensive coverage of African American autobiographical writings.

All Things Shakespeare: An Encyclopedia of Shakespeare's World. 2v. By Kirstin Olsen. 2002. 804p. appendix. bibliog. illus. index. maps. Greenwood, $150 (0-313-31503-5). 822.3.

Olsen has done the reference world a service by compiling a crackerjack guide to the Elizabethan milieu. In 207 entries she covers topics such as astrology, courtship and marriage, clothing, music, medical treatment, household objects, occupations, and coins of the era, with references to their representation in the plays. Entries vary in length from a few sentences for *Pomander* and *Windmill* to 16 pages for *Food*. Employing an abbreviation system (H8 V.v.l 31–32 for *Henry the Eighth*, Act V, Scene 5, lines 31–2), Olsen compresses into small space a wealth of data.

Especially useful to students are lists such as 77 insults and their sources and meanings and a similar survey of 50 birds, 34 units of measure, and 18 types of coins. A generous assortment of line drawings and woodcuts illustrating, for example, a crossbow and arrows, bloodhound, sea monster, and coins, particularize references. A 12-page entry on place-names points out 200 European settings for Shakespeare's plays. Back matter provides a trove of information for the teacher, historian, or dramaturge, beginning with a chronology of historical events referred to in the plays. Following a bibliography separated by topic, the work concludes with a 47-page index covering such minutia as *garters*, *harquebusier*, *marzipan*, and *typeface*.

The handbook has a few weaknesses. For example, there is no commentary related to the setting of *The Tempest* in Bermuda. Some illustrations lack detailed captioning and dates of sources, and too many name no source. Despite these omissions, students, teachers, librarians, actors, and readers will have little difficulty navigating the text to explain tidbits from Shakespeare's writings. Recommended for highschool, public, and undergraduate libraries.

Shakespeare's Words: A Glossary and Language Companion. By David Crystal and Ben Crystal. appendixes. 2002. 650p. Penguin, paper, $18 (0-140-29117-2). 822.33.

The main lexical references for Shakespeare scholars in the twentieth century were first Alexander Schmidt's two-volume *Shakespeare Lexicon* (1874) and later C. T. Onions' *Shakespeare Glossary*, which appeared in 1911 and was revised by Onions in 1919. A further revision in 1986, by Robert D. Eagleson, kept Onions in print but failed, to some extent, to satisfy scholars. The new *Shakespeare's Words* seems likely to fill the void created by the superannuated Onions.

Using the *New Penguin Shakespeare* as their text, the editors, linguist David Crystal and his actor son Ben Crystal, first collected all of the "problem" words flagged by the Penguin editors and then scoured the plays and sonnets for additional "difficult" words—especially words that are no longer current or that have developed a different sense since Shakespeare's time. After a few further additions, their entries totaled 21,263 under 13,626 headwords.

Rather than defining a word by listing a single near synonym, the Crystals decided that a system called lexical triangulation would better reflect the complexity of Shakespeare's language. Most entries have three glosses, each providing a slightly different slant. For example, *englut* is glossed as "swallow up, gulp down, devour." Each entry includes part of speech, an illustrative quotation (with text and context identified), and selected references to other occurrences. Sidebars contain brief tutorials on address forms, money, weapons, and more.

Readers newly acquainted with Shakespeare will benefit greatly by browsing through the Crystals' list of 100 frequently encountered words, which are accompanied by more illustrative quotations than are provided elsewhere. Other useful features are a chronology, plot synopses, diagrams illustrating interactions of characters, and 16 appendixes providing brief definitions for historical people, places, foreign terms, and other vocabulary not found in the A–Z section.

This is a most ambitious work that will be of immense value to student and scholar alike, a worthy successor to the landmark volumes that preceded it. Recommended for large public and academic libraries.

Thomas Hardy A to Z: The Essential Reference to His Life and Work. By Sarah Bird Wright. 2002. 430p. appendixes. bibliog. glossary. illus. index. Facts On File, $65 (0-8160-4289-6). 823.

Hardy's place in the curriculum as well as the "Hardy industry," which extends even to films (one as recent as 2001) and musical adaptations, help keep interest in the great, prolific English novelist and poet alive. Here is almost all that a general reader of Hardy might want to know about Hardy or that a reference librarian might need to find out, including the name of his beloved terrier (Wessex). The more than 700 alphabetically arranged entries treat family and friends; provide chapter-by-chapter summaries and critiques of the novels (eight and one-half pages on *Tess of the d'Urbervilles*); and discuss other creative writings, principal characters in the novels, interests and concerns reflected in miscellaneous writings, writers and poets whom Hardy knew or whose works had significance for him, aspects of the fine arts and the publishing field related to his writings and life, institutions and organizations, places and events, and honors and prizes. The appendixes include a topical list of entries, lists of media adaptations, a chronology of Hardy's writings, family trees, a glossary of place-names, a list of translations, and a comprehensive bibliography.

Other recent reference sources on Hardy include *The Cambridge Companion to Thomas Hardy* (1999), which contains 12 scholarly essays; and the *Oxford Reader's Companion to Hardy* (2000), which lacks separate entries for characters. *Thomas Hardy A to Z* is highly recommended for academic and large public libraries.

The Feminist Encyclopedia of Spanish Literature. 2v. Ed. by Janet Perez and Maureen Ihrie. 2002. 736p. appendix. bibliogs. index. Greenwood, $175 (0-313-29346-5). 860.9.

The fourth volume in a series that also looks at German, French, and Italian literature from a women's studies perspective covers literature from Spain written in Castilian Spanish. The publisher plans a separate volume on Latin American feminist writers.

Arranged from A to Z, articles range in length from one page to five or six pages. All are signed and include a bibliography of works by the author and periodical articles and books about the author. Many of the works cited in the bibliographies are in Spanish, although some English-language books and articles are included. The vast majority of entries cover Spanish women writers from the Middle Ages to the present and male writers who have important female protagonists in their works. Thus, there is no entry for Cervantes himself, but his work *Don Quijote de la Mancha* is discussed in light of Cervantes' portrayal of women. There are also articles on Spanish women who have been important in history; significant themes, characters, and character types; specific literary works; and philosophical works on feminism.

Other articles, such as *Cosmetics in Medieval and Renaissance Spain*, *Courtly love*, and *Feminism in Spain: 1900–2000*, offer cultural and historical background. Surveys of writing in certain genres, such as the series of entries on drama by Spanish women writers, provide good overviews, but the reader does need some background in Spanish literature because there are references to many authors and books that may not be well known. An appendix lists all entries arranged by time period.

For academic libraries and public libraries with large literature collections, this will be an invaluable reference source on a topic where there is very little information in English.

American Writers Classics: Volume 1. Ed. by Jay Parini. 2002. 388p. bibliogs. index. Scribner, $130 (0-684-31248-4). 913.009.
British Writers Classics: Volume 1. Ed. by Jay Parini. 2002. 393p. bibliogs. index. Scribner, $130 (0-684-31253-0). 823.009.

Scribner launches a new literature reference source with these volumes, accompaniments to its well-established American Writers and British Writers series. While those series focus on writers, the new ones concentrate on works. Each volume contains extensive essays on 20 literary classics in various genres, selected after researching the curriculum and consulting with professors. Although many of the choices, such as *The Adventures of Huckleberry Finn*, *Great Expectations*, and *The Red Badge of Courage*, are unsurprising, others, such as *Middlemarch*, *Tristram Shandy*, and *The Waste Land*, are not typically given to beginning students of literature, reflecting the fact that the new series are intended for a somewhat advanced audience.

An essay of around 20 pages in length is devoted to each classic and enhanced by a chronology of events in the author's life and a select bibliography of primary and secondary materials. Although most of the essays include background and a discussion of importance and influence as well as analysis, they do not adhere to a uniform structure. Some, like the essay on *The Scarlet Letter*, address biographical, literary, or cultural context in considerable detail, while others, such as that for *The Portrait of a Lady*, focus mainly on the text. Each volume concludes with an index (presumably this will be cumulative as the series grow) and a helpful listing of all authors covered in the American Writers or British Writers series.

In contrast to other reference sources that take a title approach to literature, such as volumes in Gale's For Students line (*Drama for Students* [1997], *Poetry for Students* [1997], etc.) and Salem's Masterplots series, the essays in American Writers Classics and British Writers Classics use fairly academic language and generally assume familiarity with literary concepts and terms. These new series should prove to be very useful complements to the American and British Writers families of literary reference tools.

Geography, Biography

Timelines of World History. By John B. Teeple. 2002. 666p. illus. maps. DK, $40 (0-7894-8926-0). 902.

Intended for quick reference or for trivia buffs rather than for any kind of genuine historical research, this volume uses time lines to provide "a visual chronicle of human history and development" from 10,000 B.C.E. to the present. Time lines appear in four columns—one each for Asia, Africa, Europe, and the Americas and Australasia—and are accompanied by gorgeous illustrations and maps. The outer column of each page has sidebars containing summaries of key events, condensed biographies, or descriptions of places. There is no index but rather a concordance, which occupies more than 200 pages at the back of the book, containing its own individual country chronologies, more brief biographies, and cross-references.

As might be expected from a work of this nature, its breadth is so wide that it renders the depth of coverage extremely shallow. In terms of volume of information, there is not much more conveyed here per subject than there would be in a good dictionary. For example, there are a total of about five brief paragraphs on World War I and about seven on World War II. Because world events are segregated by continent and presented in parallel fashion on the page, *Timelines* seems most valuable for comparing contemporaneous significant events at a glance. This also means that numerous pages contain blank columns for Africa and the Americas because of the relative lack of historical information about those parts of the world. The book's greatest strength is its graphics—13 full-color, foldout maps; more than a dozen smaller color maps; and more than 500 attractive illustrations and trenchant photographs.

This is a kind of deluxe version of the popular *The Timetables of History: A Horizontal Linkage of People and Events* (3d ed., Simon & Schuster, 1991), though that work is subdivided by subject (history, literature, religion, science, etc.) rather than by continent. This new title can only be the starting point of any meaningful inquiry, but the colorful graphics may grab the attention of younger readers and casual browsers. Recommended for public libraries.

Encyclopedia of the World's Nations. 3v. By George Thomas Kurian. 2002. 2,508p. bibliogs. index. maps. tables. Facts On File, $330 (0-8160-4139-3). 903.

Planned as a triennial, *Encyclopedia of the World's Nations* replaces three Facts On File publications: *Encyclopedia of the First World* (1990), *Encyclopedia of the Second World* (1991), and *Encyclopedia of the Third World* (1992). Its volumes contain entries for 190 independent countries. Each entry includes a map and a basic fact summary and covers major aspects of national life such as geography, climate, environment, economy, politics, legal system, ethnicity, and languages. The amount of statistical information for each country naturally varies, and some of the categories are simply left blank when the information is unavailable. Each entry also includes a bibliography, chronology, list of official publications, contact information, and a list of Internet resources. The bibliographies and lists of Internet resources are welcome inclusions. The third volume provides a useful index. The set contains some errors. For example, the title of the hereditary ruler of Liechtenstein is given as *prince con und zu Liechtenstein* rather than *prince von und zu Liechtenstein*, and the entry for Qatar gives the date for independence as 1981, although the correct date, 1971, is found in the chronology.

Encyclopedia of the World's Nations is one of many in a competitive field of reference sources. Similar information is available free online from the Library of Congress Country Studies [http://lcweb2.loc.gov/frd/cs/] and the CIA World Factbook [http://www.odci.gov/cia/publications/factbook/index.html]. Among print sources, *The Europa World Year Book* offers more comprehensive coverage that includes territories and dependencies, not just independent countries. Other print sources include the standard *Worldmark Encyclopedia of the Nations* (Gale, 10th ed., 2000) and *Statesman's Year Book* (Palgrave), which is also available as an online subscription database called SYBWorld [RBB Ja 1 & 15 03]. *Encyclopedia of the World's Nations* is a good effort, but it doesn't supersede or replace other print tools and reliable resources available online.

Man-Made Catastrophes. Rev. ed. By Lee Davis. 2002. 402p. bibliog. illus. index. Facts On File, $60 (0-8160-4418-X). 904.

The first edition of this work covered events from the burning of Rome in 64 C.E. to the explosion of Pan Am Flight 103 over Lockerbie, Scotland, in 1988. This version adds more than 70 incidents and 22 new photographs, including many of the terrorist events of recent years. It is a companion volume to *Natural Disasters* [RBB Je 1 & 15 02].

The author attributes most man-made disasters to some combination of stupidity, neglect, and avariciousness. Most war-related events are not included here; the author deems them "useless" in that, unlike tragic events—which provide opportunities for bravery and knowledge and growth—there is no "surviving dignity" attached to war.

Within each category of disaster ("Air Crashes," "Civil Unrest and Terrorism," "Explosions," and more), entries are listed geographically and then chronologically. Accounts are factual and include quotes from observers and participants. All chapters include contents lists and chronologies. "Civil Unrest and Terrorism" features a key to major terrorist organizations. The two-page list of electronic sources also appears to cite specific stories and articles instead of suggesting places students would go to learn more about a type of activity. There is an extensive index.

Although there are several sources that address natural disasters and some that combine natural and man-made disasters into a listing of the worst, this seems to be the only one that focuses on catastrophes caused by human error or malevolence. Depressing though it may be, its compilation of facts and opinions about those events might prove educational. It is recommended for high-school, public, and academic libraries, especially where the previous edition has been well used.

Assassinations and Executions: An Encyclopedia of Political Violence, 1900 through 2000. By Harris M. Lentz III. 2002. 291p. bibliog. index. McFarland, $55 (0-7864-1388-3). 909.81.

RBB praised the 1986 edition for its completeness. The author, an independent scholar, has compiled a number of other subject encyclopedias. The preface notes the work provides a concise look at "major world figures" who met their end through political assassination or execution. The entries cover (when known) the basic facts of the act, the motive, the assassin, and the subsequent effect. Earlier assassinations in history, from Julius Caesar through 1899, are briefly described in the prologue.

The approximately 1,200 entries are arranged chronologically by year and then date of the event. The length of each entry varies from one sentence to two columns, depending on the importance. In some instances, several persons executed by a tyrant are grouped together. Attempts that failed are also noted. The bibliography of secondary sources includes the works used in the first edition. The index lists people, nations, and topics such as *drug traffic*.

The work is accurate although minor English errors were noted. Some might question the author's choice of individuals to be included; a Kentucky political party head and a New York City crime boss are here though they are hardly "major world figures," while the execution of labor organizer Joe Hill by the state of Utah in 1915 and the first killing of a prominent civil rights leader, Harry T. Moore, in Florida in 1951, are not covered. Nevertheless, the work is recommended for public and academic libraries. *Encyclopedia of Assassinations* (rev. ed., Facts On File, 2001) covers 300 such acts throughout history.

Black Firsts: 4,000 Ground-Breaking and Pioneering Historical Events. 2d ed. By Jessie Carney Smith. 2003. 787p. bibliog. illus. index. Visible Ink, $58 (1-57859-142-2). 909.

This update to the first, 1994 edition has been expanded by more than 1,000 firsts, arranged in 16 chapters. The chapters survey broad fields such as "Arts and Entertainment," "Government: Local," and "Science and Medicine" and are broken down into more specific subject headings. "Arts and Entertainment," for example, encompasses "Architecture," "Dance," "Music," and "Television," among others. Under each of these headings, firsts are arranged chronologically. Each is described in an entry ranging from a line or two to half a page, and sources are always cited.

New entries extend coverage into 2002 but also add pre-1992 firsts that did not appear in the previous edition. Although a new chapter documents accomplishments in international government, emphasis is on African Americans. Frequent sidebars add information ("Blacks Commemorated on Postage Stamps") as well as drawing attention to particular firsts ("The First Black Car Dealership"). Many of the sidebars highlight achievements by women, and the author notes in her introduction that she made a deliberate effort to seek our firsts by women for the revision. Missing from this edition is the useful index of major black achievements by year.

Black Firsts remains an important part of the reference collection, and school, public, and academic libraries will welcome this updated version.

Dictionary of World Politics. By George Kurian. 2003. 391p. bibliog. maps. CQ, $75 (1-56802-561-0). 909.8.

More than 200 alphabetically arranged entries are included in this "world map of the global political landscape at the beginning of the twenty-first century." The entries cover a broad range of topics about modern politics of the world: political institutions; concepts and ideologies; governmental institutions; political events; parliamentary procedure terminology; elections and electoral politics; political parties (mostly related to the U.S.); diplomacy; territorial divisions, countries, and places; and notable political scholars.

The entries are clear, concise, and brief (one to four sentences long), except for those of countries and political concepts and movements, which are two to three paragraphs long. However, there are some glaring omissions and inconsistencies: there are no entries for Stalinism (though there are short entries on Trotskyism and Leninism); the Fair Deal (though there are entries for the New Deal, the Square Deal, the Great Society, and the New Frontier); the Tutsi tribe in Rwanda (though there is an entry for the Hutu tribe); and neoliberalism (though there is an entry on neoconservatism). The entries on the countries accurately describe their political structure and systems, but because of the brevity of each entry, they sometimes neglect to mention important historical facts. Also, some definitions of political terms lack information on the origin of the term—e.g., *pork barrel* and *straw poll*. An appendix includes 16 unclear and small maps, some with and some without capital cities. There is also a three-page bibliography.

Other established reference works such as almanacs and yearbooks (*The World Almanac*, *Statesman's Yearbook*), general dictionaries, multivolume encyclopedias, and one-volume political reference works cover the same territory as this dictionary. The revised edition of *Oxford Companion to Politics of the World* (2d ed., Oxford, 2001) is more thorough and equivalent in price. Because of the brevity of information and the duplication of its coverage, *Dictionary of World Politics* is a supplemental purchase.

Encyclopedia of the Stateless Nations: Ethnic and National Groups around the World. 4v. By James Minahan. 2002. 2,241p. appendixes. bibliogs. index. maps. Greenwood, $475 (0-313-31617-1). 909.82.

This set is an expansion of the author's earlier work *Nations without States: A Historical Dictionary of Contemporary National Movements* (Greenwood, 1996). It provides an up-to-date guide to more than 300 national groups, meaning groups that identify themselves as separate nations. Among the factors that were used to determine inclusion are "display of the outward trappings of national consciousness," particularly a flag, and "formation of a specifically nationalistic organization or political grouping" tied to a claim to self-determination. Basques, Chechens, Cherokee, Kurds, Palestinians, and Sikhs are some of the groups that are covered.

Each entry in the A–Z survey begins with the name and alternative names of the group. This is followed by information on population (with the author's estimate of population statistics for 2002), homeland, flag, culture (including ethnic makeup), language and religion, and history. Text is accompanied by black-and-white illustrations of the group's flag or flags and small maps that place the homeland in a specific geographical setting. Entries average five to ten pages in length and conclude with short selected bibliographies. Volume 4 includes two appendixes: one listing dates of independence declarations; the other, a continent-by-continent listing of stateless nations and their organizations. These appendixes are followed by an extensive index.

Some of the same groups have entries in *Worldmark Encyclopedia of Cultures and Daily Life* (Gale, 1998). As its name implies, *Worldmark*'s emphasis is more cultural, and among its 500 or so entries are many groups that do not necessarily have a national identity. *Encyclopedia of the Stateless Nations* is an excellent introduction to the resurgence of nationalism since the end of the cold war and is recommended for all academic libraries and those public and school libraries whose budgets will absorb the cost.

Great Events: 1900–2001. 8v. Rev. ed. Ed. by the Editors of Salem Press. 2002. 3,318p. illus. indexes. Salem, $475 (1-58765-053-3). 909.82.

This set revises the publisher's *The Twentieth Century: Great Events* (1992) and supplement (1996) and *The Twentieth Century: Great Scientific Achievements* (1994) and its supplement (1997). About 25 percent of the 1,000-plus articles are updated, and more than 200 articles have been added, offering a wide-ranging overview of events from 1900 until the 2001 terrorist attacks on the U.S. Arrangement is chronological. Each volume has a complete list of contents as well as a "Category Index" that lists entry headings alphabetically under more than 60 topics, such as *agriculture* or *weapons technology*.

Each one-thousand-word article begins with a headline-style title that announces the event (e.g., "Allies Fight Turkey at Gallipoli," "Nepal's Crown Prince Murders His Royal Family"), followed by a sentence or two summarizing the event and its significance. A shaded box pinpointing the "What," "When," "Where," and "Who" of the event is followed by a more detailed description and a discussion of the immediate impact of the event as well as its impact over time. Black-and-white maps and photographs add value.

The last volume of the set offers a time line of each event, noting the category and the country or region involved. The "Geographical Index" lists selected articles under the names of more than 225 localities. The "Personages Index" is an alphabetical list of the more than 3,000 individual names that appear under the "Who" category in the shaded box of each entry. Finally, the "General Subject Index" includes all names in the "Who" boxes as well as anyone found in the article text.

It is debatable whether some events, such as "Pets.com Announces Withdrawal from the Internet," truly qualify as "great." Nevertheless, this well-organized set provides useful summaries for middle-school students and up and should be considered by every library that serves them.

Medieval Jewish Civilization: An Encyclopedia. Ed. by Norman Roth. 2002. 701p. bibliogs. glossary. illus. index. Routledge, $150 (0-415-93712-4). 909.

The Diaspora, or Exile, refers to Jewish communities living outside the land of Israel. Although there is a temptation to think only of the religious aspects of these exiled communities, the editor of this new reference work points out that what survived the Diaspora was "a civilization, embracing a common history, language, literature, laws and communal structure." This encyclopedia, the latest volume in the Routledge (formerly Garland) Encyclopedias of the Middle Ages series, addresses the interaction of Jewish civilization in the medieval period with the Christian and Muslim worlds.

More than 150 entries are alphabetically arranged and written by a scholarly team of international contributors. Coverage includes important Jews from the period, such as the philosopher Maimonides and the Talmudic commentator Rashi. Non-Jews include political figures whose policies toward Jews were favorable (e.g., Frederick II) or unfavorable (e.g., Philip IV), along with Christian thinkers such as Thomas Aquinas and Bernard of Clairvaux, the entries for which detail their views on Jewry. Spain's importance for medieval Jewry is well known, but entries from *E*ngland to *E*gypt and for cities such as *F*rankfurt and *F*ustat provide a more complete geographic picture. The discussion of the Hebrew language shows how medieval Jews saved it from oblivion. Other entries describe Jewish poetry and literature in Hebrew and other languages as well as the importance of medieval Jews as translators of biblical, literary, and scientific texts. Contributions to *M*edicine and *Sci*ence and *mathematics* are chronicled, as are Jewish art and music. Also here are treatments of Jewish philosophy and the branch of mysticism called *Q*abbalah. That daily life of Jews is described in entries such as *C*lothing, *M*arriage, and *W*omen.

Medieval Jewish Civilization is a unique addition to reference shelves, providing a focus on the medieval period and contemporary scholarly positions not found in a standard reference work such as *Encyclopedia Judaica* (Macmillan, 1972). Its coverage of the many aspects of Jewish civilization, from art to science, will make it useful to a diverse audience. Recommended for academic libraries.

Terrorism, 1996–2001: A Chronology. 2v. By Edward F. Mickolus and Susan L. Simmons. 2002. 559p. bibliog. indexes. Greenwood, $175 (0-313-31785-2). 909.82.

Mickolus, a well-recognized authority and lecturer on terrorism, continues a series begun in 1980. The previous sources include *Transnational Terrorism: A Chronology of Events, 1968–1979* (Greenwood, 1980); *International Terrorism in the 1980s: A Chronology of Events* (Iowa State Univ., 1989); *Terrorism, 1992–1995: A Chronology of Events and a Selectively Annotated Bibliography* (Greenwood, 1993); and *Terrorism, 1988–1991: A Chronology of Events and a Selectively Annotated Bibliography* (Greenwood, 1993). The new volumes bring the series up-to-date through December 2001.

Like the previous volumes, the current work attempts to be comprehensive and not analytical, listing in chronological order every act of terrorism committed in the world since 1996. The book's working definition of *terrorism* is "the use or threat of use of violence by any individual or group for political purposes." Material is organized into three main sections: "1996–2001 Incidents," "Updates of 1969–1995 Incidents," and a bibliography. Entries provide the date (some are listed with just the year or month and year), the countries involved, and a short description of the event, groups, or individuals involved. The "Updates" section provides follow-ups to incidents that were first reported in earlier volumes,

Geography, Biography

from 1969 to 1996, such as the outcomes of trials or later information on terrorists or their victims. The 500-entry selected bibliography is topically arranged under headings such as "General Topics," "Regional Approaches," and "Internet Sites." The list of Internet sites is new and includes the Web site addresses of various terrorist groups. A country and date index, a name index, and a subject index enhance usability.

For many smaller public libraries the steep price may make this purchase hard to swallow, especially where other sources could provide a worthwhile, if less extensive, chronology. For those libraries needing a comprehensive source dedicated to the topic, and especially if the earlier chronologies are available in the collection, *Terrorism, 1996–2001* is certainly a worthy purchase.

Financial Times World Desk Reference. 5th ed. 2003. 736p. glossary. illus. index. maps. DK, paper, $30 (0-7894-8356-4). 910.3.

This desk reference contains three sections: "World Factfile," "The Nations of the World," and an index and gazetteer. Serving as part almanac, part statistical abstract, part atlas, and part encyclopedia, it provides thousands of facts, statistics, maps, charts, photographs, and illustrations in a colorful and user-friendly format. *Financial Times* became part of the title in 2002; previously editions were called the *Dorling Kindersley World Reference Atlas*. According to the publisher, it will be updated every one to two years.

"World Factfile" is a 60-page overview of the physical, political, historical, and economic characteristics of the modern world. It provides topographic maps with brief descriptive paragraphs for each continent or geographic region as well as thematic maps depicting major historical "ages" ("The Age of Discovery," "The Age of Revolution"), the global climate, the world economy, time zones, and more. There is also a chronology of world history with major events highlighted as far back as 400,000 B.C.

"The Nations of the World" profiles 193 nations, from Afghanistan to Zimbabwe, and briefly describes 33 territories and dependencies. Each country profile is two to eight pages long and includes the nation's official name, capital, flag, population, currency, and a map. Summaries accompanied by charts and relying heavily on symbols and icons address climate, transportation, tourism, people, politics, defense, environment, crime, education, and more. A twentieth-century chronology of events related to the nation is added as a sidebar. Statistics come from authoritative sources such as the World Bank and the World Health Organization. The final section of the guide, the "Index-Gazetteer," provides the reader with a glossary of geographical terms and a detailed alphabetic index (including alternative spellings and recent place-name changes).

In contrast to resources such as *The Statesman's Yearbook* (Palgrave Macmillan, annual), this volume relies less on text and more on graphics to convey information. Compact and cleanly designed, it would make an excellent addition to any library collection in need of another ready-reference tool on countries.

Geo-Data: The World Geographical Encyclopedia. 3d ed. Ed. by John F. McCoy. 2002. 704p. appendix. bibliogs. glossary. index. maps. Gale, $195 (0-7876-5581-3). 910.

The first new edition since 1989 of *Geo-Data*, formerly edited by George Kurian, is a splendid example of what a reference book can be. Its purpose is to provide the reader with the most detailed and comprehensive description available of the physical geography of the countries of the world. It achieves this purpose in an easy-to-use alphabetical arrangement for all of the world's 207 countries and dependencies. Each entry begins with the key facts about that country including longest rivers and highest mountains and other key statistics. All place-names and geographical features such as mountains and lakes have been listed in the most easily recognized versions of their names.

Entries adhere to the same basic structure with key facts followed by overall geography and geology; then mountains and hills; inland waterways, coasts and oceans; climate and vegetation; human population; natural resources; and finally further readings. This information is enhanced by a relief map of the country that is both clear and easy to read. Additional features of the volume include an extensive index plus 19 tables of world rankings and a glossary. The glossary is perhaps the weakest feature, as it could have been more extensive.

Other geographical dictionaries such as *The Columbia Gazetteer of the World* (Columbia Univ., 1998) and *Merriam Webster's Geographical Dictionary* (1997) define place-names in one A–Z listing. *Geo-Data's* arrangement lends itself to readers who want to take a country-by-country approach. This is an excellent reference book that will be valuable for high schools and public libraries as well as academic reference collections. Highly recommended.

Worldmark Encyclopedia of the Nations: World Leaders, 2002. Ed. by Susan Bevan Gall. 2002. 657p. bibliogs. illus. index. maps. Gale, $85 (0-7876-6610-6). 910.

World Leaders was first published as volume 6 of the tenth edition (2001) of *Worldmark Encyclopedia of the Nations*. In an earlier life, it was a loose-leaf volume entitled *Current Leaders of Nations* (Gale, 1997). To add more confusion, the 1997 information is now part of Gale's online *Biography Resource Center*. So here is a case of a print volume being more up-to-date than an online version.

The 2002 edition has the same format as volume 6 of the *Worldmark Encyclopedia of the Nations*. Entries for all 193 countries of the world were updated, with more than 50 having a change of leadership. The entries are arranged alphabetically by country, with the country as the header on the left page and the leader's name as the header on the right page. In most cases the profiles are accompanied by a photograph of the leader (the prime minister of Vanuatu has no photograph), a location map of the country, and a quotation from the leader. There is also a pronunciation guide to the leader's name ("JORGE BUHSH"). Entries follow a relatively standard form, with an introductory paragraph on the country, political and personal background of the leader, his or her rise to power, leadership, domestic and foreign policy, and business address. Length is generally around three pages, with the entry for Jorge Ibanez (Uruguay) and George Bush (U.S.) almost identical in length. Five to 10 relatively current references (including articles and Web sites) complete each discussion. The author or authors of each profile are listed, with both the date of the original writing and the update.

Gale has not announced the publication of the eleventh edition of the *Worldmark Encyclopedia of the Nations*, so it is unclear whether *World Leaders* will continue to be part of that set or only sold separately. With no comparable title, this is a current, readable resource for public, high-school, and academic libraries.

Historical Atlas of the United States. By Mark C. Carnes. 2002. 304p. charts. index. maps. Routledge, $125 (0-415-94111-3). 911.

More than 300 maps divided into 21 chronologically arranged parts cover the history of the U.S. from the formation of the North American continent to the September 11, 2001, attacks. There are special sections for presidential elections and territorial growth. The maps are in color and are generally easy to read. They include the expected maps of territorial changes and military campaigns but also include some more unusual additions, such as Harlem during the period of the Harlem Renaissance, Hollywood movie studios in 1919, and Lower Manhattan on September 11, 2001.

Overall, this atlas is a useful companion to the study of American history. Unfortunately, it is marred by mistakes that could have been avoided with more careful editing. For example, on the map "The Fate of Empire Loyalists, 1776–92," the king of England is identified as James III rather than George III. On "Civil Aviation, 1918–30," the beginning date for air service to Havana, Haiti, and Venezuela is given as 1839. On "New European States Emerge, 1991–93," the Estonian islands of Hiiumaa and Saaremaa are given a different color from the rest of the country. The Eastern Shore of Virginia is often not delineated or is given the wrong color. The Canadian Manitoulin Island is sometimes mistakenly shown as U.S. territory. These mistakes and others detract from an otherwise useful source.

There is no shortage of good, if older, atlases of American history. The excellent *Atlas of the Historical Geography of the United States* (Greenwood, 1975) is a reliable source. Newer sources, such as *Atlas of American History* (Facts On File, 1993), also give good service. If the many errors are corrected, *Historical Atlas of the United States* will be an extremely valued addition to reference collections. Even with the errors, most of the information is accurate. The currency and unique content make it worth considering, and it is recommended with reservations for public and academic libraries.

Historic Hiking Trails: A Directory of over 900 Routes with Awards Available to Hikers. By Steve Rajtar. 2002. 163p. index. McFarland, paper, $45 (0-7864-1196-1). 917.304.

There are guides to national parks, guides to state parks, campground directories, and guides to hiking trails in specific geographical areas. This little book is unique in that its focus is on historic trails for which hikers receive awards such as patches or medals upon completion of the trail. H*istoric* means that the trails are historically significant (for example, the Trail of Tears National Historic Trail) or take the hiker into or past buildings or sites that have some relationship to an event or person. Some trails are primarily recreational or scenic but provide access or proximity to historic sites.

Nine hundred routes in the U.S. (including Alaska and Hawaii) are listed. The trails range in length from two miles to more than a thousand. They vary in terrain; some are wilderness trails, while others run through cities. All are maintained and sponsored by youth groups (such as the Boy Scouts), historical societies, or community groups. Trail entries are arranged by state. Each entry gives the location, type, and topography of the trail. Details regarding registration and awards are provided. There is a separate section listing interstate trails.

Both serious and recreational hikers will find this a useful guide. Theme travelers too will enjoy exploring the possibilities of including a relevant hike as part of their itinerary. Recommended for public libraries.

Antarctica: An Encyclopedia from Abbott Ice Shelf to Zooplankton. Ed. by Mary Trewby. 2002. 208p. bibliog. illus. index. maps. Firefly, $35 (1-55297-590-8). 919.8.

Antarctica could be called the largest natural research station in the world. The variations of Earth's weather for millions of years are recorded in the 12.5 million cubic miles of ice that cover more than 97 percent of the continent. The Southern Ocean contains a myriad of unique animals, including fish with antifreeze in their veins, and scientists are studying the mitochondrial DNA of Adelie penguins to learn about the rate of evolutionary change within a species. Before sending probes to Mars and Venus, NASA tested them in Antarctica's Dry Valleys. Antarctica is also unique politically. Owned by no country, it is jointly shared by 44 countries that adhere to the 1959 Antarctic Treaty.

Yet for all of its scientific and environmental importance, few people really know much about Antarctica. This encyclopedia will help remedy that. With nearly 1,000 entries and a wealth of stunning photographs and illustrative maps, this resource will be frequently used to answer both simple and complex questions. Entries range from several lines to nearly two pages, with several topics (*Antarctic Treaty*, *Dry Valleys*, *Exploration*, *Icebergs*, *Penguins*, and *South Pole*) covered in two-page special entries. Items that have their own entries are shown in all caps within other entries, and there are numerous cross-references to related topics. Entries are preceded by physical and political maps of Antarctica. The book concludes with a selected bibliography, a list of 34 Web sites of interest, and a comprehensive index.

On the whole, the material is presented clearly and completely. This will prove to be a valuable resource for both public and academic libraries. Libraries that already have *Antarctica and the Arctic: The Complete Encyclopedia* (Firefly, 2001) will probably not need to add this title to their collections.

100 Greatest African Americans: A Biographical Encyclopedia. By Molefi Kete Asante. 2002. 345p. bibliog. illus. Prometheus, $49 (1-57392-963-8). 920.

Asante, professor in the African American Studies program at Temple University, has written a volume in which he attempts to distill his work on the history of African Americans into a list of the 100 greatest people in that history—a difficult task to be sure, and one that can lead to arguments over the choices. Whether one feels Barbara Jordan would make a better choice than Shirley Chisholm, or that Matthew Gaines was a stronger educator than John Russwurm, it is hard to disagree with the people who Asante chose to highlight. He explains his choices in the introduction and makes it very clear that he left out numerous current popular people because he feels the hype around the pop persona is not what makes an individual important. He makes no attempt to rank the people he selected because he viewed that as an impossible task, so arrangement is alphabetical. A short bibliography lists material for further research.

The 100 people who are included range from former slaves such as Crispus Attucks and Phillis Wheatley to more contemporary individuals such as Amiri Baraka and Toni Morrison. Among others are sports figures Jesse Owens and Tiger Woods, performers Marian Anderson and Bill Cosby, and political activists Marcus Garvey and Jesse Jackson. Each portrait covers two to four pages that summarize the person's life, work, and importance and is accompanied by a black-and-white photograph or illustration. There is enough variety so that students with assignments will have no trouble focusing on someone in their area of interest.

Most of the 100 are covered in other reference sources, but this volume offers a reasonably priced, easy-to-digest collection of articles. Recommended for school and public library collections.

A to Z of Women in World History. By Erika Kuhlman. 2002. 452p. bibliogs. illus. index. Facts On File, $49.50 (0-8160-4334-5). 920.72.

The 260 women who are profiled here have not only made a mark on their own cultures but have also "influenced other women from diverse cultures and different historical periods pursuing the same goals." The *A to Z* in the title is somewhat misleading, because entries are organized first under 14 areas of accomplishment, from "Adventurers and Athletes" to "Writers." This arrangement is not as accessible as a straight A–Z format, but it does help the reader see links between women from different eras and regions. For example, the chapter "Religious Leaders" has entries for, among others, Mahaprajapati, a Buddhist nun of the sixth or fifth centuries B.C.E.; Hildegard von Bingen, of twelfth-century Germany; and Mary Baker Eddy, founder of Christian Science.

Entries are generally around two pages in length, and each offers suggestions for further reading, which is helpful when interest has been sparked. A concluding bibliography offers further suggestions of books on female accomplishments. Two useful sections are the "Entries by Country of Birth" and "Entries by Year of Birth." The volume is completed by an index to subjects and names.

There are a number of other encyclopedias on women, and several of these index their subjects by occupation or area of accomplishment. Such indexes can be cumbersome to use, so *A to Z of Women in World History* is a good place to start for researchers who are taking a sphere-of-activity approach to women's history. This highly readable volume is recommended for high-school, public, and academic libraries.

Current Biography Illustrated. [Online database]. Wilson, pricing starting at $835 [http://www.hwwilson.com/databases/cbillus.htm]. (Last accessed April 23, 2003).

Current Biography, long a staple in many library collections, has been released on Wilson's new WilsonWeb system. The database offers more than 25,000 articles and obituaries and more than 19,500 images.

Search options include Basic, Advanced, and Browse. We tried several Basic searches: *Clare Boothe Luce*, *Katharine Graham*, and *Supreme Court justices*. We had the best results with the personal names—both came up first on our results lists, even though we misspelled both Clare and Boothe. In the Basic mode, users have the option to choose natural language or Boolean searching, using more than 30 operators.

Advanced Search, which is the default, is a better choice for *Supreme Court justices*. Here, we could refine our search so that, instead of looking for occurrences of the term anywhere in the text, it looked only in the Profession/Activity field. We could refine it further to look for Supreme Court justices who are women. Other choices for refining a search include date of birth, place of origin, and ethnic background. Searches can be combined and limited to images or biographies and obituaries. Results can be displayed by date instead of by relevancy, and customized displays are available. An All-Smart Search is also offered. This is a search based on "Wilson-created search rules" that rank occurrences of terms according to where they are found. In Browse, the researcher can enter terms into an entry box and then select from a list of indexes, such as Awards, Place of Origin, or Date of Birth, from the drop-down menu. Browse is an easy way to find all the entries for, say, newspaper publishers or people born in New York. As of this writing, the Awards index includes only the Nobel Prize for literature.

In the results list, search terms appear in bold black italics (changed from red in response to concerns about users with common types of color blindness). Each result is offered as a brief display that supplies subject's name, birth and death dates, profession, and a link to an image. Selecting a hit opens a fuller display that consists of a thumbnail photograph that can be enlarged, links to additional images (if any), subject's name, dates, links to *Current Biography* articles and obituaries, and a list of the professions or activities assigned to the person. Full-text displays repeat most of this information and are attractively laid out on the screen. They can be printed, e-mailed, and saved.

Current Biography Illustrated takes the user well beyond a simple lookup for information on Hank Aaron or Sally Ride. WilsonWeb is a sophisticated system, and this can be a drawback as well as a strength. It is tailored to accommodate and search across a number of often dissimilar Wilson databases—*Biological and Agricultural Index*, for example, as well as *Current Biography*. Younger and less adept users may be confused by all the available choices and by the generic examples in Help (a better explanation of WilsonWeb searching can be found on the Wilson home page), so librarians should be prepared to offer extra guidance. That said, *Current Biography Illustrated* is an attractive, flexible, and powerful alternative to all the linear feet of the annual print cumulations, especially for libraries that subscribe to other Wilson databases. Wilson also offers a less-expensive version of *Current Biography* without the images.

Encyclopedia of American War Heroes. Ed. by Bruce H. Norton. 2002. 292p. appendix. bibliogs. illus. indexes. Facts On File, $60 (0-8016-4637-9); Checkmark, paper, $19.95 (0-8160-4638-7). 920.073.

This volume includes almost 400 entries featuring men and women who fought and, in most cases, died during military service to the U.S. Many of the individuals profiled were awarded one or more citations for their heroic achievements, for example, the Medal of Honor, the Navy Cross, the Distinguished Service Cross, the Silver Star, and the Bronze Star. An introduction, which describes the criteria the editor used for selecting entrants, is followed by a section explaining the different citations. Coverage is extensive, going back to 1675 and extending to the present.

The entries are arranged alphabetically by the individual's last name and include rank, branch of service, and the circumstances resulting in citations. All branches of the military (the U.S. Army, Navy, Marines, and Air Force) are included, as well as Native Americans and Confederate soldiers. Most of the entries are a few paragraphs in length. Some of the records consist solely of a verbatim quoting of the actual citation. Each entry concludes with a section citing source material and additional reading. A few entries are accompanied by photographs.

The encyclopedia winds up with an appendix of American war statistics, a bibliography of print and online sources, and a general index. An index providing access to entrants by war or battle would have been useful for students. Still, this encyclopedia would be a valuable addition for public, high-school, and academic libraries, as there is nothing else quite so extensive.

The Scribner Encyclopedia of American Lives: The 1960s. 2v. Ed. by William L. O'Neill. 2002. 650p. bibliogs. illus. index. Scribner, $250 (0-684-80666-5). 920.073.

The Scribner Encyclopedia of American Lives: The 1960s (SEAL 1960s) is the second in the SEAL Thematic Series dedicated to a specific topic or chronological period in U.S. history. The two alphabetically arranged volumes in SEAL 1960s contain biographical sketches, usually between 1,000 and 2,000 words, of 647 figures who "defined the decade, or who were influential at the time." Americans from different races, socioeconomic groups, classes, and regions of the U.S. are included, along with the occasional person of another nationality who had long periods of residence in the U.S. and was an influence on American culture.

The signed entries, written by scholars, begin with a brief summary of the person's chronology and important accomplishments. This is followed by a narrative of the subject's life; the focus is specifically on activities during the 1960s, although other key points are also mentioned. In many cases, a black-and-white photograph accompanies the narrative, which concludes with an assessment of the subject's overall contribution and a brief bibliography listing a few key sources. Sample subjects include Patsy Cline, Robert Crumb, Catherine Genovese, Jasper Johns, Jonathan Kozol, and Jerry Rubin. Researchers failing to locate a specific person can turn to more specialized sources with a narrower focus, such as *Leaders from the 1960s: A Biographical Sourcebook of American Activism* (Greenwood, 1994), or broader sources, like *The Sixties in America* (Salem, 1999).

There is little overlap between the coverage here and in other components of SEAL, although someone like Joe Namath or Richard Nixon will appear in more than one volume. In these cases, the entries for SEAL 1960s are newly written. Both an occupations index and an alphabetical list of subjects at the back of volume 2 cover the main SEAL series and thematic subsets. Recommended for all high-school, public, and academic libraries wanting complete SEAL coverage or libraries wanting to supplement their collection of 1960s resources with a purely biographical approach.

The Concise Oxford Dictionary of Archaeology. By Timothy Darvill. 2002. 506p. Oxford, $45 (0-19-211649-5). 930.103.

This is an ambitious work with some flaws. Darvill (professor of archaeology at Bournemouth University, U.K.) has undertaken a survey of the vocabulary of archaeology in "Europe, the Mediterranean, and English-speaking countries in which archaeology has become an established academic and vocational subject." The work is intended for students, journalists, "and other professionals who have cause to dip into the archaeological literature."

More than 4,000 definitions range from a couple of lines to a two-column page, with most being quite short. Famous archaeologists have brief biographies, usually taken from obituaries or autobiographies, which are noted. Sources, including excavation reports, are also provided for entries on sites. The "Quick Reference Section" at the back of the book contains lists of international archaeological conventions and recommendations; charts of stratigraphic subdivisions in Europe and North America; cultural periods in North America, Mesoamerica, and South America; and lists of Egyptian, Roman, and British rulers.

We found a number of small errors. Flavius Aetius, who defeated Attila, is called *Flavours Aetius*. Robert Koldewey, who excavated Babylon, is misspelled *Koldeway*. The Roman poet Martial is listed as *Martial, Marcus Valerius*, when his full name is Marcus Valerius Martialis. An entry on the Marcomanni says that they annexed Bavaria "in the 6th century BC," instead of in the sixth century A.D.

The Oxford Companion to Archaeology (1996) is a good choice for libraries wanting a more comprehensive, encyclopedic approach. Although it is weakened by some careless mistakes, *The Concise Oxford Dictionary of Archaeology* is suitable for larger public and academic libraries that need a dictionary of archaeological terms.

History

Encyclopedia of Ancient Egypt. Rev. ed. By Margaret R. Bunson. 2002. 462p. bibliogs. glossary. illus. index. maps. Facts On File, $70 (0-8160-4563-1). 932.

The first, 1991 edition of this work had more than 1,500 entries and covered the predynastic period from around 3200 B.C.E. to the fall of the New Kingdom in 1070 B.C.E. The revised edition has more than 2,200 alphabetically arranged entries and extends coverage to the suicide of Cleopatra and the beginning of Roman occupation in 30 B.C.E. After a brief introduction there is a chronology of major events in Egypt and the Near East and Mediterranean in parallel columns. After the body of the work are a glossary of Egyptian words, a list of suggested readings, and a detailed index. The addition of the latter remedies a deficiency noted in our review of the first edition.

Articles range from a paragraph to several double-column pages. Many of the longer ones, and a few of the shorter ones, have suggestions for further reading. Cross-references and *see also* references are used liberally. There is a table of deities in the entry *Gods and goddesses*, and of queens in *Queens*, but a list of kings appears not under *Pharaoh* but in *Dynasties*, with no cross-reference. Most of the rulers of Egypt have separate entries, but a table of rulers under *Pharaoh* would have been useful for placing them in time.

The text is accompanied by some 14 black-and-white maps and diagrams of Egypt and major temple complexes. The 80 black-and-white photographs and line drawings should photocopy well. The suggested readings include materials published in 2001, and at least some of the readings should be available in most medium-sized to large pubic libraries.

This title is recommended for high-school and public libraries and for smaller academic libraries needing a quick and current Egyptology reference. Less scholarly than *The Oxford Encyclopedia of Ancient Egypt* (2001), it is a good single-volume introduction to the topic.

Handbook to Life in Ancient Mesopotamia. By Stephen Bertman. 2002. 396p. appendixes. bibliog. illus. index. Facts On File, $50 (0-8160-4346-9). 935.

Bertman, professor emeritus of classics at the University of Windsor, has made a useful contribution to Facts On File's Handbook to Life series. Covering the lives of Assyrians, Babylonians, and Sumerians from around 3500 to 500 B.C.E., the book is arranged topically, with chapters on geography, archaeology, government, religion, language and literature, arts, and daily life, among other subjects. Each chapter has citations to the extensive bibliography. Most of the works in the larger bibliography are technical and specialized, but a "Note to the Reader" lists several popular works that could be found in a larger public library. Bertman's writing is formal but accessible, with touches of dry humor.

Subsections within the chapters deal with more specific topics. In the chapter on government, there are capsule biographies of political leaders, mostly kings. The chapter on archaeology provides a list of archaeologists who have made major discoveries in the region. Gods and goddesses are described in the chapter on religion. There is an interesting concluding chapter about the legacy of Mesopotamia and how it endures. A brief section on Aramaic-speaking Chaldeans who migrated from an ancient village in Iraq to Detroit in the twentieth century suggests that the legacy is more alive than we realize. Bertman notes, too, how many archaeological sites have been put at risk by recent political and military actions in the region.

The book is illustrated with black-and-white photographs and line drawings, which should copy well. Appendixes include a chronological table and a list of museums with major Mesopotamian collections. A useful purchase for medium-sized to large public libraries and academic libraries with undergraduate Middle Eastern ancient history classes.

★Encyclopedia of the Roman Empire. Rev. ed. By Matthew Bunson. 2002. 636p. appendix. bibliog. glossary. illus. index. maps. Facts On File, $75 (0-8160-4562-3). 937.

Like its earlier edition, published in 1994, *Encyclopedia of the Roman Empire* seeks to provide multidisciplinary coverage of 500 years of "the most important personalities, terms, and sites" of this period. Expanded to 636 pages from 494, the encyclopedia includes nearly 2,000 entries, with new ones covering daily life, engineering, science, law, and the role of women in Roman society. There are also new reading lists for the major entries as well as an updated bibliography, which has increased from 56 items of only secondary sources to a list of nearly twice as many, now including primary sources that were not part of the earlier edition.

As in the first edition, entries are arranged alphabetically and range from a short dictionary snippet to longer treatments of 4,000 words or more. Some entries include reading lists, but this convention is not widespread throughout the work. As in the first edition, approximately 60 percent of the entries are biographical. The other entries fall within larger topical categories such as government, society, literature and art, law, trade and commerce, warfare, and religion. Among new entries are *China*; *Clothing*; *Food and drink, Roman*; *Law*; *Transportation*; and *Women, status of*. Expanded entries include *Calendar*, *Christianity*, *Industry*, *Legions*, and *Philosophy*. *Legions* is one of the longest, with eight pages of text, including subheadings for development, training and equipment, organization, camps, auxiliaries, the role of legions in the late empire, and a large table of known imperial legions that includes the dates of their beginnings, founders, and where they were stationed.

Other special features of this resource remain unchanged from the first edition: black-and-white illustrations, maps, a chronology of major events, a list of emperors, genealogical tables of the dynasties, a glossary, and an index.

The encyclopedia has become a standard one-volume source on the Roman Empire and is a recommended purchase for any library that did not purchase the first edition. As an updated edition, it would seem a worthwhile purchase for academic and larger public libraries because of its expansion by 100 entries and 140 pages as well as revisions to various existing entries, especially regarding the role of women in the empire. Most high-school and smaller public libraries would have to weigh the usage of the earlier edition and needs of their patrons.

Absolutism and the Scientific Revolution, 1600–1720: A Biographical Dictionary. Ed. by Christopher Baker. 2002. 450p. appendixes. bibliogs. index. Greenwood, $99.95 (0-313-30827-6). 940.2.

King Louis XIV of France is quoted in the introduction to this volume as saying "L'Etat c'est moi" ("I am the state"). Alexander Pope, also quoted, wrote "God said, Let Newton be! And all was light." Louis and Isaac Newton are the personifications of, respectively, absolutism and scientific revolution. The latter's birth comes close to the beginning of the period covered in this volume of the Great Cultural Eras of the Western World series, while the former's death is at the end. Falling within this chronological range are 400 biographical entries on figures of importance to the "social, artistic, and intellectual milieu of seventeenth-century Europe." Examples include Francis Bacon, John Bunyan, Artemisia Gentileschi, Cotton Mather, Moliere, and Peter the Great

The alphabetically arranged entries vary in length from half of a page to two pages. What makes these profiles worthwhile is the focus on the theme of the seventeenth century as an era of decisive change. For example, the entry on poet John Donne mentions the usual biographical information but also discusses how his work stood out from that of his contemporaries and marked a change from older poetic conventions.

The work is well indexed and cross-referenced. Also included are two appendixes, arranging the entries by subject and by country. Short lists of further readings follow each entry and are augmented by a subject bibliography. Overall, this is a worthy addition to the series and highly recommended in its own right, especially for academic libraries.

Peoples of Europe. 11v. 2002. 648p. bibliogs. glossaries. illus. indexes. maps. Marshall Cavendish, $329.95 (0-7614-7378-5). 940.

Similar to the publisher's *Peoples of the Americas* (1999), this attractively designed set "uses geography and national identity to organize information" on 44 countries. Entries are arranged alphabetically by country. Each contains a short introduction to the country, including its landscape, climate, and history. The bulk of each 5- to 30-page entry deals with the people occupying the nation today. All of the following areas are treated: religion, housing, clothing, language, health and education, food and drink, family and social life, and art and music. Political upheavals, economic turmoil and hardship, war, and ethnic disputes are covered with commendable frankness and clarity. Where ethnic groups cross national boundaries, they are cross-referenced.

Each volume begins with clear pictures of the flags of the countries treated in that volume, followed by a volume table of contents. (Volume 1 also has a set table of contents.) Each volume, as well, ends with a volume glossary, bibliography, and index. Illustrations are copious and eye-catching. The full-color relief maps, inset maps showing the position of the country relative to the rest of Europe, color and black-and-white photographs, and detailed captions help make the layout inviting to browsers and effective for locating information. Boxes for "Facts and Figures" (basic demographic information and quick facts) and climate are color-coded and easy to locate. A time line runs along the bottom of multiple pages of each entry. Special information boxes add facts or formative myths that are unique to each country. In general the text, written by college-and university-affiliated subject experts, is clear and accessible to readers and researchers from the middle-school level on up.

The final volume contains a comprehensive bibliography (print, online, and fictional resources) and index along with a one-page listing of significant music of Europe, a pronunciation guide to foreign words by country, a list of national days by both country and date, and separate indexes for biographical and geographical information, arts, festivals, foods, peoples and cultures, religions and religious ceremonies, and sports and games. Given the wealth of information, excellent indexing, and attractive format, this is a recommended purchase for middle-school, high-school, and public libraries.

Renaissance. 10v. 2002. bibliog. glossary. illus. index. maps. Grolier, $345 (0-7172-5673-1). 940.2.

Each volume in this set designed for students in grades 5 through 10 is 80 pages in length. More than 220 entries are arranged alphabetically by subject and cover the innovative and tumultuous time period from 1375 to 1575. Focus is on Europe, but the set also touches on other parts of the world important to the Renaissance, including Africa, China, India, Japan, and the Americas.

The set covers a broad variety of topics, among them adventurers and scholars, architecture, geographic regions, religion, and the sciences. A sampling of entries includes *Drawing*, *Giotto*, *Navigation*, and *Rome*. The majority of the entries are two or three pages in length. Pages are illustrated with paintings, photographs, drawings, and maps, including many reproductions of world-famous art from the period. Each of the pictures is nicely annotated. Entries conclude with cross-references to other entries in the set. In addition, each volume closes with a comprehensive time line to help students relate events in time as well as a comprehensive index. Each volume also includes a glossary and a page of resources for further reading.

The arrangement and layout are appealing, and coverage is thorough. Students seeking a direct route to specific topics from the Renaissance will be well served by this set, which is recommended for school and public libraries. UXL's five-volume *Renaissance and Reformation Reference Library* [RBB D 15 02], which takes a more thematic approach, offers more detailed biographies and a selection of primary source materials but is not as attractively illustrated.

Renaissance and Reformation. 6v. Ed. by Peggy Saari and Aaron Saari. 2002. bibliogs. illus. indexes. UXL, $215 (0-7876-5467-1). 940.2.

The editors of *Renaissance and Reformation* have strived toward and succeeded in making a time of long ago more accessible to today's middle- and junior-high-school students. Coverage focuses on major events and individuals of European history between the mid-1300s and the early 1600s. Like numerous other UXL sets, this one is divided into *Almanac* (two volumes), *Biographies* (two volumes), and *Primary Sources* (one volume). Each of the three elements is indexed separately, and a separate comprehensive paperback index is also included.

The *Almanac* is organized into topical chapters that include sidebars with additional information and more than 100 black-and-white illustrations. Volume 1 begins with a time line of important events. Following the time line are a 17-page vocabulary list and a research and activity guide. Chapters, which range from 30 to 50 pages in length, deal with topics such as the rise of European monarchies, the Protestant and Catholic Reformations, the scientific revolution, the status of women, and daily life. A concluding bibliography lists books, Web sites, and video recordings and DVDs.

The entries in the biography volumes cover 50 individuals, from Isaac Abrabanel to Huldrych Zwingli, and are five to six pages long. Each biography begins with a reproduction of a painting or drawing, a significant quote, birth and death dates, and occupation. Information on each individual's personal life is included, but the focus is on contributions within the context of the Renaissance and Reformation. *Primary Sources* provides selected specific writings of the time. Introductory information about the original author begins each section, and sidebars list definitions of obscure or antiquated words. Following each document piece is a discussion of the historical effects of the piece along with additional readings.

School and public libraries will find that this resource provides good information on its topic.

Cassell's Companion to Eighteenth Century Britain. By Stephen Brumwell and W. A. Speck. 2001. 455p. bibliog. index. Cassell; dist. by Sterling, $45 (0-304-34796-5). 941.07.

Cassell's Companion to Twentieth Century Britain. By Pat Thane. 2001. 455p. bibliogs. index. Cassell; dist. by Sterling, $45 (0-304-34794-9). 941.082.

In one century Britain built and consolidated most of its empire (with the notable exception of the loss of its North American colonies). In another century, that empire was transformed into the post-colonial Commonwealth. Both centuries, the eighteenth and the twentieth, respectively, were rich in domestic political contests, contributions to Western culture, contentious social issues, and foreign entanglements. These two historical dictionaries identify and explain the most important persons, events, places, and issues in those centuries.

Centuries, as illustrated by the debate about whether the events of September 11, 2001, rather than either December 31 of 1999 or 2000 mark the start of the twenty-first century, do not neatly fit into 100 years. The "Glorious Revolution" of 1688 that brought William and Mary to the throne ushered in the eighteenth century in Britain, and Wellington's victory over Napoleon at Waterloo in 1815 capped it. Between those temporal milestones, Alexander Pope penned his immortal couplets, the grand tour of the Continent was a significant feature of a gentleman's education, the French Revolution alarmed crowned heads throughout Europe, Joseph Priestley discovered oxygen, Samuel Johnson published his dictionary, Edward Jenner developed vaccination, the Seven Years' War confirmed Britain's international status, the American Revolution diminished the empire, and the slave trade flourished until Parliament stopped it in 1807. Lucid, well-researched, and short but substantive essays arranged A–Z explain these phenomena and their importance in the context of the century's events and trends. Along with entries on individuals and events, the dictionary treats such matters as *Commerce*, *Crime and punishment*, *Gothic* style, *Population*, *Textiles*, and *Towns*. An extensive network of *see also* references embedded in the text links related articles. These are more important and more effective than the subject index, in which articles are grouped under some forty broad headings such as "Battles," "Ministries," and "Scholarship." The embedded references also appear in the substantial concluding chronology of events. Some entries conclude with very brief selective bibliographies; a three-page bibliographical appendix complements these.

Identical in structure and spirit to the eighteenth-century dictionary, the twentieth-century volume covers the period from 1899 and the outbreak of the Boer War through the milder events of 2000, the latter represented in the chronology by sedate reports of London-wide authority and general Parliamentary elections. Technology and international events play greater roles in this dictionary as demonstrated by entries on *Aviation*, *Communications*, *Submarines*, and *Titanic* as well as on *Decolonization*, *Ireland*, *League of Nations*, and *Palestine*, to say nothing of constellations of entries on each of the World Wars. A rich array of entries on cultural phenomena, social policy issues, political disputes, politicians, artists, and others round out the contents. A chronology, a subject index as blunt as the other volume's, and a one-page general bibliography conclude the book.

Each of these works provides greater depth of coverage of its century than Kenneth Panton and Keith Cowlard's two-volume *Historical Dictionary of the United Kingdom* (Scarecrow, 1997). They also fill gaps in what through happenstance may become a series of historical dictionaries from various publishers providing comparable treatment to each era of British history. Other titles along this continuum are Ronald Fritze's *Historical Dictionary of Tudor England, 1485–1603* (Greenwood, 1991) and *Historical Dictionary of Stuart England, 1603–1689* (Greenwood, 1996). Three more era-specific volumes from Cassell are forthcoming. Recommended for academic and large public libraries.

Collins Dictionary of Scottish History. By Ian Donnachie and George Hewitt. 2001. 384p. appendixes. maps. Trafalgar Square, $29.95 (0-00-712185-7). 941.1003.

The Oxford Companion to Scottish History. Ed. by Michael Lynch. 2001. 732p. bibliog. glossary. index. maps. Oxford, $45 (0-19-211696-7). 941.1.

Did you buy the *Collins Encyclopedia of Scotland* [RBB N 1 01] within the last year? Does one recent book on Scotland satisfy your collection needs? If you did not buy the *Collins Encyclopedia*, or if you need more than one viewpoint of Scotland, Scottish history, and Scottish influence, read on.

While covering the same topic (Scottish history) in the same format (alphabetical entries in two columns per page), the *Collins Dictionary of Scottish History* and the *Oxford Companion to Scottish History* have very different coverage, styles, and cost. *Oxford* has almost twice as many pages and, with the use of a smaller font, more than twice the words. Interestingly enough, even with the same topic, there is still a large number of subjects covered in one title and not the other. For example, rugby is covered in *Oxford*, not *Collins*; coal has an entry in *Collins* but not *Oxford*.

Two authors share credit for the information in the *Collins Dictionary*, with occasional other sources listed after an entry. Beyond the entries, *Collins* has two maps of Scotland, genealogy charts of Scottish rulers, religious houses at the time of the Reformation, and selected statistics. There are 180 authors for the entries in the *Oxford Companion*. For comprehensive entries such as economy or religious life, multiple authors from multiple disciplines combined their expertise to produce well-rounded coverage. Also included are a section of classified contents or a broad subject listing with references to topics, a list of abbreviations, a glossary, a comprehensive chronology, several topical maps, genealogies, an extensive reading list, and a detailed index.

In general, though there are more individual topics covered in *Collins*, it offers brief details, while *Oxford* provides more in-depth contextual coverage. For example, for the battle of Culloden, *Collins* provides a two-paragraph explanation. *Oxford* does not have a separate entry, but in the index, there are references to the battle in numerous entries, among them *Army*, *Buildings*, *Clans of the Highlands and Islands*, *Jacobitism*, *Rough Wooing*, and *Union of 1707*. The *Oxford* treatment of Robert the Bruce (or Robert I) is more than forty percent longer than that in *Collins* and has numerous cross-references to other related entries.

Unlike *Collins Encyclopedia of Scotland*, both of these works focus on historical events and the impact of these events on modern Scotland, so there are precious few modern statistics or coverage of modern events. Both have information on the reformation of the Scottish Parliament in 1999, but don't look for Dolly the cloned sheep or the Lockerbie air tragedy.

These titles are recommended for academic and public libraries that need coverage of Scotland. Price always has an impact on collection development, and Oxford is twice as expensive as the Collins. But if you can only choose one, Oxford is the better buy.

The Oxford Companion to Twentieth-Century British Politics. Ed. by John Ramsden. 2002. 714p. appendixes. bibliogs. Oxford, $60 (0-19-860134-4). 941.082.

This guide to British politics in our most recently completed century provides 3,000 alphabetically arranged entries. More than 100 contributors represent a broad spectrum of experts including journalists, scholars, and former cabinet secretaries.

Entries cover ideas (*Fascism*, *Imperialism*); issues (*Football hooliganism*, *Welsh language*); economics (*North Sea oil and gas*, *Poll tax*); legislation (*Clean Air Act, 1956*; *Secret ballot*); organizations (*Colonial Office*, *Oxfam*); the media (*BBC World Service*, *Morning Post*); events (*Blitz*, *General Strike*); personalities (*Major, John*; *Orwell, George*); and more. Treatment ranges from short, dictionary-style entries to longer discussions of such topics as *Arts policy*, *Immigration*, and *Liberal Party*. Some of the longest entries are devoted to prime ministers. The detailed "Classified Contents List" allows the reader to browse entry headings in topical categories. For instance, "Political Biographies" is sorted by political party as well as by categories such as "Scottish Nationalists," "Private Secretaries to Royal Family," and "Judges." "Election Manifestos" and "Quotations and Phrases" are interesting categories under which entry headings such as *Britain Belongs to You* and *"Jaw-jaw is better than war-war"* can be found.

Three appendixes provide tabular data, including dates of the ministries (giving the prime minister, date of formation, and party); officeholders of each ministry; and results of the general elections from 1900 to 2001 with the number of candidates of each party, the number of Members of Parliament elected, and the number of votes.

This readable source would be a worthwhile purchase for academic and larger public libraries, particularly those with substantial British collections.

A History of the Third Reich. 4v. By Jeff T. Hay. 2003. bibliog. illus. indexes. Greenhaven, $299.80 (0-7377-1283-X). 943.086.

There have been several recent publications about the Holocaust aimed at secondary-school students. Notable selections include *Learning about the Holocaust: A Student's Guide* (Macmillan, 2000), and *Holocaust* (volume 11 of *History in Dispute*, Gale, 2002). This new offering provides essential background information to help students understand the social and political elements that enabled the Third Reich to come to power and set events into motion.

The first two volumes consist of more than 550 alphabetically arranged articles ranging from a paragraph (*Hitler salute*) to several pages (*Anti-Semitism*) in length. Occasional black-and-white archival photos accompany the text. Entries are detailed and complete and employ straightforward language. Numerous *see also* references and a comprehensive index guide researchers to related articles.

The third volume, *Personalities*, offers approximately 140 brief biographies on not only the Nazi Party elite, world leaders such as Churchill and Mussolini, and those who directed their efforts against the Nazi regime, such as Oskar Schindler, but also individuals who laid the political foundation for the Third Reich (Otto von Bismarck, Karl Lueger) and others who provided supposed theoretical or artistic influence (Friedrich Nietzsche, Richard Wagner). The fourth volume presents primary source materials—official proclamations and political treatises; excerpts from *Mein Kampf*; diary entries, not only from Anne Frank but also from Eva Braun and Joseph Goebbels; and snippets of everyday life—a program from a Hitler Youth campout, letters home from soldiers on the Russian front. Hitler's last will and testament is included, as is testimony from the Nuremburg Trials. The set ends with a chronology and a list of print and electronic sources for further research.

The value of this set is that it provides accessible documented data. Student researchers generally depend on the Web as their main information source, and educators will find it useful to have a comprehensive, reliable resource to refute the sometimes sketchy or even intentionally misleading information that appears on some sites related to the Nazis and the Third Reich. This offering is recommended primarily for high-school collections but should be considered for community college and public libraries as well.

The Dreyfus Affair. By Leslie Derfler. 2002. 167p. bibliog. glossary. illus. index. Greenwood, $44.95 (0-313-31791-7). 944.081.

The War of 1812. By David S. Heidler and Jeanne T. Heidler. 2002. 217p. bibliog. glossary. illus. index. Greenwood, $44.95 (0-313-31687-2). 973.5.

Here are the first titles in Greenwood Guides to Historic Events, 1500–1900, a companion to Greenwood Guides to Historic Events of the Twentieth Century. The series is designed "to serve as resources for student research and to provide clearly written interpretations of topics central to the secondary school and lower-level undergraduate history curriculum."

The authors approach their subjects in slightly different ways, although some elements are standard. Each volume starts off with a chronology of events. Following the chronology is a "Historical Overview" containing several chapters of background and analysis. In the *Dreyfus* volume, these chapters provide context for what is commonly known as the Dreyfus affair, discuss how anti-Semitism and socialism played into and were affected by the affair, and summarize how the affair has been viewed through history. *The War of 1812* outlines the events of the war, setting these against a background of conditions in the U.S. and diplomatic relations between the U.S and Europe. The next section in each volume is an A–Z collection of biographies of almost 20 key individuals. The biographies in the *Dreyfus* volume tend to be longer and are especially valuable for providing information on people not often covered in American reference sources.

Primary documents comprise the next chapter in both volumes, and most documents are accompanied by short explanations. Volumes conclude with brief glossaries, annotated bibliographies, and indexes. The *Dreyfus* bibliography lists selected English-language sources, Internet sources, and films. *The War of 1812* bibliography is more extensive, reflecting greater availability of materials for English readers. It is divided by topic and also includes Internet sites and films.

Both these guides are useful for researchers who need more information than they can find in an encyclopedia but don't know where else to turn. The blend of reference material and essays that provide background and context is particularly helpful when applied to topics that may be unfamiliar or are not heavily covered elsewhere. This new series should be useful in high-school, college, and large public libraries.

Political Leaders of Modern China: A Biographical Dictionary. Ed. by Edwin Pak-Wah Leung. 2002. 278p. appendixes. bibliogs. glossary. index. Greenwood, $89.95 (0-313-30216-2). 951.

Covering leaders from the period of the Opium Wars (1839–1842) to the beginning of the twenty-first century—the late Imperial, Republican, and Communist eras—this volume is a very useful reference for anyone studying modern Chinese history. Some 30 scholars contributed the 100 entries, which are one to four pages in length and provide the reader with basic background information along with detailed accounts of the individuals' political careers. Only a handful of leaders, such as Mao Zedong, Puyi, and Zhou Enlai, will be familiar to general readers and are easy to find in other standard reference sources. The names are given in pinyin in Chinese name order, though other well-known transliterations of names (such as Chiang Kai-shek for Jiang Jieshi) are noted. A glossary provides the Chinese characters for the names. A useful 28-page chronology and a list of leaders sorted by period are also appended. Each entry includes a list of references, many of which are in Chinese. English-language works are listed in the general bibliography.

Though most of those who are profiled had an official government role, there are entries for individuals who influenced politics in other ways. Examples include Chen Baochen, tutor to Puyi, and Yan Xishan, a Republican-era warlord, among others. Some local leaders are also here. Many readers of Chinese history find that the array of unfamiliar names can be daunting. For those readers, this dictionary should be a welcome tool. Recommended for large public and academic libraries, the volume complements two other reference sources by the same editor, *Historical Dictionary of Revolutionary China, 1839–1976* (Greenwood, 1992) and *Historical Dictionary of the Chinese Civil War* (Scarecrow, 2003).

The Columbia Guide to the Vietnam War. By David L. Anderson. 2002. 308p. appendixes. bibliogs. index. maps. Columbia, $45 (0-231-11492-3). 959.704.

This volume follows the same type of format as other titles in the Columbia Guides to American History and Cultures series. The first part of the book contains a historical narrative. The rest consists of a "mini-encyclopedia" listing events, individuals, and military operations; a brief chronology; an annotated bibliography of books, feature films, documentaries, and electronic resources; a collection of mostly excerpted documents; and an appendix of pertinent statistics.

Although it does not provide the depth of coverage found in the three-volume *Encyclopedia of the Vietnam War: A Political, Social, and Military History* (ABC-CLIO, 1998) or as many entries as *Dictionary of the Vietnam War* (Greenwood, 1988), this volume is nevertheless an outstanding ready-reference source. For students and researchers, it offers an excellent starting point to find information, including some surprisingly specific material, such as the precise date when the *Domino theory* was first articulated and the names of the individuals who first suggested the Vietnam War memorial in Washington, D.C. The editor, a scholar of the Vietnam War, should be commended for compiling such an informative, balanced, and unbiased reference source on the most contentious war in American history. Recommended for both public and academic libraries.

Encyclopedia of Twentieth-Century African History. Ed. by Paul Tiyambe Zeleza and Dickson Eyoh. 2002. 652p. bibliogs. index. Routledge, $150 (0-415-23479-4). 960.3.

The focus of this dictionary-style work is the past century of African history, covering decades of tremendous change, including resistance to colonial rule and the reestablishment of African independence. Global forces that had an impact on the continent are also considered. An article, for example, on the cold war details the effect of the conflict between the U.S. and USSR on Africa. Although the emphasis is clearly the twentieth century, entries place their topics in context: the long article on Christianity considers the churches established in Egypt in the first centuries after Christ as well as the nineteenth-century missionary movements before considering modern developments. Articles on Islam, Arabic language, and slavery are similarly contextual. The scope includes North Africa and sub-Saharan Africa.

Articles range from 600 words for briefer treatments of some 58 cities up to 4,000 words on major themes such as *Agrarian change*, *Decolonization*, and *Health and disease*. In the midrange are overviews of regions, countries, and language groups and entries on specific topics such as *Migrant labor* and *Transport*. A useful thematic entry list in the fore matter groups entries into 15 categories so the reader can see related articles. The index is very important because many topics are addressed only within larger articles. There are no biographical entries; even well-known current or historical figures such as Nelson Mandela or Julius Nyerere are mentioned in the text as appropriate to the topic but have no separate entries. One must use the index to find discussions related to women because there is no overview essay. Entries are accompanied by cross-references and suggestions for further reading, including many very recent publications. A map of the continent and perhaps a time line of major events would have been nice additions.

The language is too academic for school libraries, but at the college level, even if a library owns the excellent four-volume *Encyclopedia of Africa South of the Sahara* (Scribner, 1997), this is a worthy addition, especially for the thematic essays. For more detailed biographical and local information, the African Historical Dictionaries series (Scarecrow Press) would be complementary in academic and large public libraries.

Key Events in African History: A Reference Guide. By Toyin Falola. 2002. 347p. bibliogs. illus. index. maps. Greenwood, $64.95 (0-313-31323-7). 960.

Distinguished scholar and Africanist Falola surveys the complicated history of the African continent by focusing on 36 pivotal events that either caused or led to significant changes and developments in African social, political, and cultural life from around 40,000 B.C.E. to the collapse of apartheid in the 1990s. Included are such diverse topics as the growth of the ironworks, the spread of Islam and Christianity, the founding of Liberia, military coups, and refugee problems in the 1980s and 1990s. As the author indicates in his preface, this volume is meant to be used together with a text on African history and is intended for high-school and college students.

Following a detailed time line of historical events, each topic is highlighted in an individual chapter including cross-references, historical and political maps, illustrations, a notes section, and a suggested list for further reading that provides many recent references by international scholars. The chapters are in chronological sequence and divided into ancient and precolonial, nineteenth-century, and twentieth-century periods, and the index is well arranged. Only a cursory mention is made of the AIDS epidemic, which now accounts for more than 70 percent of the number of worldwide cases. Perhaps the impact of this disease can be the subject of a chapter in an updated edition.

In his overview, the author comments about the paucity of interest in African history that existed as recently as 100 years ago, with the resulting lack of historiography. Much research is now being published by both non-African and indigenous scholars; one advantage of this volume for the student is that it spans such a broad time frame, where other references, such as Vogel's *Encyclopedia of Precolonial Africa* (AltaMira, 1997) or Oliver and Atmore's *Medieval Africa, 1250–1800* (Cambridge, 2001), address a specific time period or a single subject area, although in greater detail. High-school and college libraries will find this book a valuable addition to their collections.

This Day in North American Indian History: Important Dates in the History of North America's Native Peoples for Every Calendar Day. By Phil Konstantin. 2002. 456p. appendixes. bibliog. illus. index. Da Capo, $35 (0-306-81170-7). 970.004.

This work contains more than 4,000 entries listing significant events in North American Indian history for each day of the year. Events listed are only those that can be traced to an exact date. When more than one date is recorded for an event, the author, a freelance writer and member of the Cherokee Nation of Oklahoma, has "tried to show which date is most acceptable to the widest number of sources." A fairly successful attempt has been made to avoid bias. The tone taken throughout is straightforward and objective, reporting on what happened on a given date in clear, unemotional prose.

The volume is laid out in columnar form in date order, beginning with January 1 and progressing to December 31. Under each date, events are listed chronologically, starting with the earliest recorded event (e.g., for January 1, dates run from 1756–1975, with a final "Every" entry giving an annual event, a form that is consistent throughout). Entries vary in length from three or four words to half a column, with most coming in at four or five sentences. Frequent black-and-white photographs and reproductions run from a quarter to half a column in size, and are placed adjacent to the passages they illustrate.

Several appendixes (including a list of tribal names and their meanings, alternate tribal names, and North American Indian calendars listing month and moon names) are followed by a three-page bibliography of print works and a lengthy, detailed, and accurate index. The index actually serves as a cross-referencing tool, listing all entries for particular tribes and events.

A useful quick-reference work, this is also an attractive browsing book. Though there is some overlap with books like the *Biographical Dictionary of American Indian History to 1900* (Facts On File, 2001) and the *Chronology of American Indian History: The Trail of the Wind* (Facts On File, 2001), the format and purpose of this work are unique enough to justify purchase for public, college, and high-school libraries.

Encyclopedia of Modern Mexico. By David W. Dent. 2002. 343p. appendixes. bibliogs. illus. index. map. Scarecrow, $49.50 (0-8108-4291-2). 972.08.

Dent, a political science professor, has compiled a "reference tool for anyone seeking a better understanding of contemporary Mexico," and within limits, it provides that. Deepest coverage is given to political history since the presidency of Lazaro Cardenas (1934–40), but Dent also has entries for people (*Fuentes, Carlos*; *Salinas de Gotari, Raul*), the economy (*Automobile industry*, *Maquiladoras*), events (*Olympic Games*, *Zapatista rebellion in Chiapas*), the arts (*Ballet Folklorico de Mexico*, *Cinema*, *Corridos*), culture (*Indigenismo*, *Machismo*), and important social and political issues (*Drug trade/trafficking*, *Emigration*, *Human rights*). The goal is not to be exhaustive but to "draw the reader's attention to aspects of Mexico that are often neglected or not well understood in the United States."

The work is in dictionary format, with 250 entries ranging from a few lines to several double-column pages. Each article has suggested readings, including magazine and newspaper articles. Winding up the volume are a selected bibliography, a list of online resources, two appendixes with data comparing Mexico and the U.S., and a thorough index. A time line at the beginning of the book helps place people and events in context. Illustrations consist of 50 or so black-and-white photographs and a blurry map.

The author's opinions sometimes break through, as when he refers to most of Mexico City's daily newspapers as "obedient courtesans to powerful politicians" in an article on the journalist Alejandro Junco de la Vega. His opinions of economic globalization are generally negative. His view of PRI (Partido Revolucionario Institucional), which ruled Mexico until the 2000 election of Vicente Fox, is more complex—he discusses both its positive (political stability and coherence) and negative (corruption and self-serving conservatism) aspects.

The volume does a good job of explaining some of the key issues that face and define Mexico at this point in its history. Public, community college, and undergraduate collections that need information on modern Mexico will want to consider it.

The African American Years. Ed. by Gabriel Burns Stepto. 2002. 475p. bibliogs. illus. index. Scribner, $125 (0-684-31257-3). 973.

When it was published in 1998, Scribner's *The American Years: A Chronology of United States History* was one of the few chronologies besides the standard *Encyclopedia of American Facts and Dates* (10th ed., HarperCollins, 1997) to focus on the U.S. Gale has recently published a second edition of *The American Years* (2002) and has also expanded it into a series by adding chronologies that are more specific. The first of these deals with the history of African Americans.

Whereas *The American Years* provides detailed year-by-year coverage, the chronological portion of *The African American Years* takes up just 65 pages. It extends from 1444 to 2002, with entries for events grouped by year and ranging from a sentence to a paragraph in length. The entries are heavily cross-referenced to what is actually the major part of the volume, six lengthy sections that cover the periods from "The Colonial Period and the Revolutionary War" to the Civil Rights era and beyond. These sections provide general overviews; discussions of more particular topics, such as "African Americans on the Frontier" and "The African American Literary Experience"; bibliographies; and fairly extensive selections of primary documents. Sidebars and black-and-white illustrations complement the text. The volume concludes with a general index and an index to primary source material.

To describe this volume as a chronology is somewhat misleading, for it offers much more than a strictly "what happened when" perspective. At the same time, the researcher who wants exactly that perspective would be better served by other titles, such as Gale's own *Chronology of African American History* (2d ed., 1997), which provide more year-by-year detail. *The African American Years* is recommended for high-school, public, and academic libraries as a useful guide to black history and a complement to works such as *The African American Encyclopedia* (2d ed., Marshall Cavendish, 2000) and *Encyclopedia of African American Culture and History* (Macmillan, 1996).

American Political Leaders. By Richard L. Wilson. 2002. 444p. bibliogs. illus. index. Facts On File, $65 (0-8160-4536-4). 973.

Part of Facts On File's American Biographies series, *American Political Leaders* concentrates on 250 of the most influential leaders who directed the nation's political life from colonial times to present. Each entry considers the subject's life, presenting both personal details and historical context and discussing the person's importance to U.S. history. Each entry also includes further reading suggestions and, in some cases, Web sites.

The scope encompasses presidents, major party candidates, third-party presidential candidates, Supreme Court justices, Speakers of the U.S. House of Representatives, Congress, cabinet officers, diplomats, and three First Ladies. Among examples are Shirley Chisholm, Henry Clay, John Foster Dulles, Horace Greeley, Newt Gingrich, John McCain, and Earl Warren. Inclusion was based on frequency of mention in secondary and college textbooks in U.S. history and political science. For those recent leaders not yet elevated to the status of the college textbook, the author used newspaper and other media sources, relying on Internet resources only when they were considered authoritative. Colonial and Revolutionary War personages are included as well as leaders of the Confederate States of America.

Of great importance for a reference book such as this one are the indexes. In addition to a general name and subject index, entries are indexed by "Offices Held or Sought" and year of birth. "Offices Held or Sought" has categories such as "Unsuccessful Candidate for President or Vice President," "Subcabinet Official," and "Diplomat." This readable volume is recommended for high-school, public, and undergraduate libraries, especially those that have found other titles in the American Biographies series useful.

Encyclopedia of the JFK Assassination. By Michael Benson. 2002. 348p. appendixes. bibliog. illus. index. Facts On File, $75 (0-8160-4476-7); Checkmark, paper, $21.95 (0-8160-4477-5). 973.922.

With dozens of books available on one of the most famous assassinations in modern history, another one hardly seems needed. That said, this volume provides a listing of people, places, and events related (however slightly) to November 22 to 24, 1963. Following an introduction that describes the events and summarizes conspiracy theories are hundreds of entries, from *Abundant Life Temple* (which figures in theories regarding Oswald's movement following the assassination) to *Zoppi, Tony* (*Dallas Morning News* columnist). These range from a paragraph to identify people and groups (*Cuban Revolutionary Council*; *Garner, Dorothy Ann*), to 4 or 5 pages (*Autopsy of John F. Kennedy*; *Federal Bureau of Investigation*), to the 16-page *Oswald, Lee Harvey*, with most entries about a half page in length.

No sources are listed for individual entries, but a lengthy bibliography of books and articles, with some citations annotated, is at the end. An index and numerous *see* references help a user through the entries. Some photos and maps illustrate people and sites in the text. Four appendixes include JFK organizations (but no Web sites), Jack Ruby's written statement, a list of films and videos on the assassination, and the conclusion of the House Select Committee on Assassinations.

For the most part, this volume is readable and intriguing. The topic holds such interest for so many people that the encyclopedia is sure to be useful for high-school students just learning about the assassination, the general public, and even knowledgeable researchers.

The Hispanic American Almanac: A Reference Work on Hispanics in the United States. 3d ed. Ed. by Sonia G. Benson. 2002. 886p. bibliogs. glossary. illus. index. Gale, $130 (0-7876-2518-3). 973.04.

Hispanics have grown to be the largest minority population in the U.S., surpassing African Americans, so the third edition of *The Hispanic American Almanac* arrives at an opportune time. It is a thorough resource covering people of the U.S. whose ancestors come from Mexico, Cuba, Puerto Rico, and Central America.

The book contains 25 subject chapters (e.g., "Spanish Explorers and Colonizers"; "Law, Government, and Military"; "Art"). The introduction tells us that 24 of the chapters were written by Hispanic studies scholars, although no credentials are listed for the contributors. A chronology offers a year-by-year outline of the migration of Hispanics to this country. Following the chronology, the "Historical Overview" chapter details the evolution of three major Hispanic groups: Mexicans, Puerto Ricans, and Cubans. The "Significant Documents" chapter provides the researcher with documents such as the Treaty of Guadalupe Hidalgo (1948), the NAFTA agreement, and California's Proposition 227. Having the actual documents in the volume is quite valuable to the young researcher.

The final chapter contains more than 500 biographies highlighting Hispanics, including actor Antonio Banderas, writer Oscar Hijuelos, and Congresswoman Nydia Velasquez. Biographies range in length from a short paragraph to more than one-half page in length. Each chapter ends with a list of references for further research, and a general bibliography is found at the end of the volume. The approximately 330 illustrations include black-and-white photographs, drawings, tables, and figures. A glossary of Spanish terms assists the non-Spanish-speaking user with word definitions. A comprehensive keyword index provides easy access to the volume's contents, with biographical articles indicated in bold type.

Well organized and written at a reading level that is easily understood, this volume is an excellent resource for high-school and public libraries for starting research on the Hispanic population.

Historic Events for Students: The Great Depression. 3v. Ed. by Richard C. Hanes and Sharon M. Hanes. 2002. bibliogs. glossary. illus. index. maps. Gale, $225 (0-7876-5701-8). 973.917.

Designed for high-school students, this set presents the Great Depression in terms of 45 key topics arranged alphabetically from "American Indians" to "Tennessee Valley Authority." Among other chapters are "Everyday Life," "Global Impact," "Labor and Industry," "Political Ideologies—Leaning Left," "Public Health," and "Radio."

Chapters are 20 pages or more in length and consist of a standard format. In "Literature," for example, a brief introduction is followed by a chronology of relevant events, from the Nobel Prize for Literature awarded to Sinclair Lewis in 1926 to the publication of James Agee's *Let Us Now Praise Famous Men* in 1941. "Issue Summary" provides an overview of literary trends, such as the proletarian fiction of John Dos Passos and John Steinbeck, and puts them into context. "Contributing Forces" lays out the conditions and events that helped create these trends. "Perspectives" reflects opinions and views of people both inside and outside the New York literary establishment, and "Impact" discusses later literary developments. "Notable People" presents brief profiles of five key writers, while "Primary Sources" provides excerpts from some key documents, including Steinbeck's *The Grapes of Wrath* and Richard Wright's *Uncle Tom's Children*. The chapter winds up with a list of suggested research topics (for example, "What were the benefits of government support for writers enrolled in the Federal Writers' Project?"), a bibliography, and cross-references to other chapters. The text is supported by maps, photographs, and sidebars

At the end of each volume, the student has access to a glossary of terms and phrases and a general bibliography that is subdivided into books, periodicals, novels, and Web sites. Also found in each volume is a detailed cumulative index.

This set examines in great detail an important period in U.S. history, offering social, cultural, and ideological as well as historical perspective. It is recommended for public and high-school libraries.

Jewish Americans and Political Participation: A Reference Handbook. By Rafael Medoff. 2002. 369p. bibliog. index. ABC-CLIO, $55 (1-57607-314-9). 973.

This latest volume in ABC-CLIO's Political Participation in America series provides a historical survey and current analysis of Jews in American political life. Written by a prolific scholar of some important historical works on both American Jews and U.S. foreign policy and also on the Middle East, this volume primarily consists of five essays covering the history of Jewish political involvement since the nation's founding; a discussion on various movements, including labor unions, civil rights, New Left, Soviet Jewry, and Zionism; voting behavior; and Jews in Congress. Each chapter concludes with a list of references, and many of these entries appear later in an annotated bibliography. A useful feature is a collection of primary documents, including Washington's famous letter to the Touro synagogue in Rhode Island. Among other features are an A–Z list of "Key People, Laws, and Terms"; a brief, descriptive list of American Jewish historical and political organizations including their addresses, phone numbers, and Web sites; and a chronology.

This book is well written and provides a compact and easily accessible history of American Jewish political life. *Jews in American Politics* (Rowman & Littlefield, 2001) and *The Congressional Minyan: The Jews of Capitol Hill* (KTAV, 2000) are more comprehensive and useful ready-reference sources. Nevertheless, this book serves as an important complement to some of the previous volumes in the series covering African Americans, Asian Americans, and Native Americans.

The Language of the Civil War. By John D. Wright. 2001. 377p. bibliog. illus. index. Oryx, $62.50 (1-57356-135-5). 973.7.

The language, expressions, oaths, euphemisms, and jargon spoken by both soldiers and civilians during the Civil War provide unique slices of the life of the time. From the various types of coffee made of some unlikely materials (*Cane seed coffee*) to expressions still used today (*Hard row to hoe*), this volume opens up life in the 1860s for casual readers, historians, students, and Civil War enthusiasts.

Most of the approximately 4,000 terms come from diaries, letters, magazines, newspaper articles, and secondary sources. Some of the terms, such as *Borden's milk*, would be familiar to a modern audience, and others, such as *Desecrated vegetables* (a derogatory name for dessicated or dehydrated vegetables), would be obscure. A few terms that meant one thing during the middle 1800s mean something totally different today. For example, *Flunk out* meant retreat, not fail at school. The term so associated with the British—*Keep a stiff upper lip*—is actually American in origin.

Entries are arranged in alphabetical order with some *see also* references to related terms. Length varies from a few sentences to several paragraphs. A small number of photographs and drawings illustrate terms. A "Guide to Related Topics" organizes entry headings under almost 40 categories, including such as "Euphemisms," "Food, Drink, and Cooking," and "Nicknames." A bibliography of works useful for locating terms is followed by an index with main entries in bold type. Some errors escaped the editing process—Mary Boykin Chesnut's name is misspelled as Chestnut in several places.

This fascinating look at language provides a treasure trove of not just words but anecdotes, history, trivia, and lifestyles of the Civil War. It is recommended for public and academic libraries.

The Library of Congress Civil War Desk Reference. Ed. by Margaret E. Wagner and others. 2002. 949p. bibliogs. illus. index. maps. Simon & Schuster, $45 (0-684-86350-2). 973.7.

The Civil War remains a fascinating and controversial event in American history. The fate of the nation and of slavery hung in the balance, and the resolution affects America today. Following the popular desk reference format, this work provides a thematic approach to the war.

Beginning with the antebellum period, the 13 chapters cover topics such as "Wartime Politics," "Battles and Battlefields," "Medical Care and Medicine," "The Home Front," and "The Civil War in Literature and the Arts." Most chapters include a chronology, and these, although somewhat repetitive, help place events in proper order. Although the maps are sometimes a bit hard to read (such as "Seven Days Battles," which is jammed with information), they do help in understanding troop location, topography, and movements. A section on mapmaking illustrates the importance to both armies. The chapters end with bibliographies of sources, and a massive bibliography provides even more resources.

The final chapter, "Studying the War: Research and Preservation," is especially noteworthy in its comprehensive approach. Anyone wanting to find information on books, people, monuments, battlefields, organizations, or reenactments will find a starting point here. Both print and electronic resources are included.

Encyclopedia of the American Civil War: A Political, Social, and Military History (ABC-CLIO, 2000) is more comprehensive. But *Civil War Desk Reference*, with its solid scholarship, informative approach, and broad sweep, is an excellent source for school, academic, and public libraries that cannot afford the five-volume set or need a one-volume supplemental source. Highly recommended for all Civil War collections.

Lifetimes: The Great War to the Stock Market Crash: American History through Biography and Primary Documents. Ed. by Neil A. Hamilton. 2002. 328p. appendixes. bibliog. illus. index. Greenwood, $74.95 (0-313-31799-2). 973.91.

This alphabetically arranged biographical encyclopedia is an especially effective way of presenting history in an immediate and engaging style. Representative personalities are used to illustrate various aspects of American politics, society, and culture from approximately 1917 to 1930. Sixty individuals are profiled in original biographies accompanied by primary source material.

Subjects include writers (Dorothy Parker, Gertrude Stein), entertainers (Charlie Chaplin, Duke Ellington), politicians (Roger Nash Baldwin, Jeannette Rankin), social activists (Emma Goldman, Margaret Sanger), athletes (Knute Rockne, Helen Wills), criminals (Sacco and Vanzetti), and other celebrities (Joseph P. Kennedy, Aimee Semple McPherson). Each profile covers its subject's entire life with particular emphasis on this era and the person's contribution to—or divergence from—general society. Each biographical essay is accompanied by a selection of illustrative contemporary documentation. These primary source materials include vintage photographs, political cartoons, song lyrics, letters, treaties, amendments, excerpts from speeches and writings, and so on. Original language and spellings have been preserved.

Of special interest to student researchers are the explanatory notes that accompany primary source material. These asides appear in outer margins and summarize the significance of each document. Other user-friendly accommodations include a list of documents by type and by subject, a time line, a comprehensive index, entry-specific "For Further Reading" lists, and a thematic bibliography of print materials.

This title is recommended for high-school and public library collections. Though there are numerous other biographical reference sources, the combination of biography and primary source material makes this one particularly interesting for both researchers and browsers.

The Louisiana Purchase: A Historical and Geographical Encyclopedia. Ed. by Junius P. Rodriguez. 2002. 513p. bibliogs. illus. index. maps. ABC-CLIO, $95 (1-57607-188-X). 973.4.

With the two hundredth anniversary of the Louisiana Purchase coming up in 2003, this encyclopedia is a timely addition to the literature on the subject. The Louisiana Purchase was a major event in U.S. history, affecting not just geography and politics but culture, economics, and diplomatic relations with other countries.

This work begins with an essay covering the events leading up to the

Louisiana Purchase, the political and diplomatic maneuverings to bring it about, and the repercussions. The encyclopedic portion consists of lengthy signed articles that cover people (James Bridger, Thomas Jefferson, Sacagawea), Native American tribes (Blackfoot, Cree), places (Fort Jesup, Natchitoches), and other topics (*Black Hawk War, Fur trapping, Newspapers [international] and the Louisiana Purchase*). Each state in the Louisiana Purchase has a substantive article. Many of these articles are accompanied by black-and-white illustrations. The encyclopedia contains a comprehensive chronology beginning in 1497–98 and ending in 2002, when the U.S. Mint announced it would reduce production of the Sacagawea dollar coin. Full-text copies of 49 important documents, such as Jefferson's message to Congress and the Louisiana Purchase Treaty, are provided. The documents are followed by a substantive bibliography and a detailed index.

Some articles, such as *Creoles*, tackle difficult issues. *Textbooks: the Louisiana Purchase in high school textbooks* discusses the Eurocentric perspective offered by many school texts, in which Native American issues are ignored.

The timeliness of this encyclopedia and the breadth of coverage make it an important reference book. Overall, this will be an excellent resource for high-school, public, and academic libraries.

Multicultural Reference Center. [Online database]. Marshall Cavendish, [http://www.marshallcavendish.com/mcc/multi_ref.asp]. (Last accessed February 24, 2003).

This full-text resource, a partnership with EBSCO, draws from the publisher's *African American Encyclopedia, Asian American Encyclopedia, Encyclopedia of Multiculturalism, Latino Encyclopedia,* and *North American Indian Encyclopedia,* supplemented by 35,000 periodical articles from the EBSCO database and 2,500 images.

Users can conduct a basic or advanced keyword search or search within several indexes: Subjects, Publications, Encyclopedia Entries, or People. A Basic search uses standard Boolean operators as well as all words, any words, and exact phrase. Searches can be expanded or limited by, for example, categories (e.g., African Americans, organizations) or reading level or by specifying that only full-text items are wanted. In the Advanced mode, the user can add field codes (e.g., AU for author) and retrieve a search history.

Results lists offer the option of limiting the display to encyclopedia articles, periodical articles, or images. The citation is displayed first, followed by image or text. Encyclopedia articles have links to related items from the Subjects and People indexes. Depending on local settings, an entry can be saved in a folder and printed or e-mailed. In some cases, a PDF option is available.

We did several sample searches. A wide range of articles on Colin Powell was quickly located, including several not primarily about him. A search for Navajo Indian insurance policies also yielded results, as did one on the Hutterites, a communal society. *African Americans and medicines* brought up 10 entries, a mix of encyclopedia and periodical articles, and *African American education* produced 1,951 entries. Articles published in December 2002 are included. Databases that are a conglomeration of resources can have a hit-or-miss quality despite the amount of content that is available, and this one is no exception, especially where periodicals are concerned. The *New York Amsterdam News* is indexed but not other black-owned newspapers.

This is a fine, easy-to-use resource that fills a niche. It will be especially valuable in a secondary-school library where it is tied to curriculum. In a public or academic library, it might be lost among broader electronic resources.

The New Dictionary of Cultural Literacy. By E. D. Hirsch and others. 2002. 647p. illus. index. Houghton, $29.95 (0-618-22647-8). 973.

The New Dictionary of Cultural Literacy is the most recent list of "background knowledge needed to be able to read with understanding." Hirsch published *Cultural Literacy: What Every American Needs to Know* (Houghton) in 1987, the *Dictionary of Cultural Literacy* in 1988 (Houghton), and a revised *Dictionary* in 1993 (Houghton). He believes that "shared information is the foundation of our public discourse . . . that allows us to comprehend our daily newspapers and news reports, to understand our peers and leaders, and even to share our jokes. Cultural literacy is the context of what we say and read." The compilers selected items "likely to be known by a broad majority of literate Americans" and of "lasting significance."

Cultural Literacy was praised as the most important book on education to appear in years but also criticized as being elitist and conservative, with most of the entries in use for at least 100 years and an emphasis on print media. The authors produced the third edition "to keep up with the changes in American culture," adding 500 new entries, 200 in the "Science and Technology" section, and updating 1,000 others. Internet and computer-related terms (FAQ, *laptop, snail mail*) are among the most important additions.

The 7,000 entries are arranged alphabetically within 23 sections, including "The Bible," "Fine Arts," "World and American History," and "Physical, Earth, and Life Sciences." Entries include brief definitions and cultural associations, such as "an olive branch is now regarded as a sign of peace, as is the dove."

The New Dictionary of Cultural Literacy is a tool for assessing cultural literacy, not a first choice for definitions of terms. It should not be compared with other specialized dictionaries, especially popular culture compendia. In it, *Java* is an island in Indonesia, not programming language or Starbucks staple, and *Pluto* is a planet and the god of the underworld, not a cartoon dog. Popular with trivia fans and familiar to educators, this resource will be requested in academic, high-school, and public libraries.

The New Nation. By Anita Vickers. 2002. 296p. bibliog. illus. index. Greenwood, $49.95 (0-313-31264-8). 973.
The 1910s. By David Blanke. 2002. 318p. bibliog. illus. index. Greenwood, $49.95 (0-313-31251-6). 973.91.
Westward Expansion. By Sara E. Quay. 2002. 301p. bibliog. illus. index. Greenwood, $49.95 (0-313-31235-4). 978.

These three titles inaugurate a new series, American Popular Culture through History, that will examine "the specific details of popular culture that reflect and inform the general undercurrents of the time." *The New Nation* covers the years from the end of the American Revolution until about 1816, and *Westward Expansion* covers 1849 (the year of the first gold rush) until approximately 1890. *The 1910s* reflects the decade-by-decade approach that the series will apply to the twentieth century.

Each volume begins with a time line of popular culture events during the period. The time line is followed by chapters arranged in two parts. Part 1 offers an overview of everyday life in general and the "world of youth" in particular. Part 2 examines 12 broad topics, among them "Advertising," "Food," "Travel," and "Visual Arts." Chapters in this section average 20 pages in length. A brief list of typical costs for products (a Conestoga wagon cost $1,500 in 1877) is followed by extensive chapter notes and further reading.

Within this uniform structure, each volume takes a somewhat different approach. For example, while the authors of *The New Nation* and *The 1910s* confine their discussions to the periods in question, the author of *Westward Expansion* refers throughout the volume to the popular culture of today and the ways it has been shaped by the concept of the West. She discusses the enduring appeal of blue jeans in the chapter on "Fashion" and the western on television and in film in "Performing Arts."

This series joins several others that take a chronological approach to the study of American culture. Titles in Gale's American Eras and American Decades series cover many of the same topics but have a more accessible format and more visual appeal. However, the Gale titles cover politics, economics, religion, and more; and their greater range means that some aspects of popular culture are discussed in less detail than in Greenwood's volumes. For readers who are intrigued by the "Cost of Products" section in *The 1910s*, in particular, Grey House's *Working Americans, 1880–1999* provides much more detail on personal finance, compiling decade-by-decade economic data to create profiles of representative but fictional families.

Greenwood's Daily Life through History series has become a staple resource in many high-school, public, and academic libraries. American Popular Culture through History is recommended for the same libraries and should be equally well received.

New York Year by Year: A Chronology of the Great Metropolis. By Jeffrey A. Kroessler. 2002. 367p. illus. index. NYU, $55 (0-8147-4750-7); paper, $19.95 (0-8147-4751-5). 974.7.

Here is a fascinating chronological history of New York City from 1524 to 2001, looking at the people, buildings, institutions, political events, music, and businesses that helped shape the city. The book is arranged by year and then by date within the year. The events from 1524 to 1899 take up the first 95 pages, while events from 1900 to 2001 dominate the last 200 pages. Descriptions range from one sentence to a paragraph in length and give only the basic facts. In picking events, the author does not claim to be definitive but instead tries to give a feel for the events and people that made the city. He also emphasizes cultural and social events over political ones.

The book is particularly strong on listing important buildings, for example, the Voorlezer's House, the oldest schoolhouse, built in 1695; the World Building, built in 1890; and the Bronx County Jail, built in 1937. Societies and institutions such as the New York Urban League (founded in 1911) and the New York Botanical Garden (founded in 1891) are also listed along with the first performances of operas, musicals, and plays. Though the book is fun to read, it is difficult to use for research. There is no bibliography and there are no citations for any of the entries, so the reader has nothing to refer to for more information. The index lists some people, societies, and specific places, but most of the headings are for more general subjects such as *Apartment buildings*; *Music and musicians, classical*; *Newspapers*. To find when *Die Meistersinger* was premiered in New York, one has to check all of the entries indexed under *Opera and opera singers*.

This book would be a good starting point for the casual reader and a valuable tool for students who need to find out what happened in a specific year and for answering quick reference questions about New York. Libraries needing detailed information about New York City will find *The Encyclopedia of New York City* (Yale Univ., 1995) to be a more in-depth and easier-to-use reference source than *New York Year by Year*. Using both books would give the researcher a good handle on New York history.

Chronology of the American West: From 23,000 B.C.E. through the American Century. By Scott C. Zeman. 2002. 381p. bibliog. illus. index. ABC-CLIO, $85 (1-57607-207-X). 978.

By 1893, the untamed American Wild West had all but disappeared. Indian wars were over, Sitting Bull was dead, Geronimo was in captivity, and frontier towns were turning into major cities. Pioneers and gunslingers, prevalent 20 years earlier, were being immortalized in legends and lore by Willa Cather, Zane Grey, and others. The twentieth century was approaching, filled with inventions, modern conveniences, gangsters, Las Vegas, Hollywood, Disneyland, world wars, space exploration, and high technology.

That period is a speck in Zeman's chronology of 25,000 years. *Chronology of the American West* begins at 23,000 B.C.E., when humans arrive on the North American continent, and ends with George W. Bush's election in November 2000. Zeman breaks the time line into four unequal but natural divisions: 23,000 B.C.E.–1502, 1502–1840, 1840–1932, and 1932–2000. The names he gives to these divisions accurately reflect the broad developments: "The Native West" for the original (human and animal) inhabitants and terrain; "The Imperial West" for the European explorers, settlers, and colonists; "The Incorporated West" for expansion and development of the U.S.; and "The Contested West" for the twentieth century. Within this framework, events are listed year by year and briefly annotated. Black-and-white illustrations and full-page sidebars on events, people, or places pepper the chronology and bring the history to life. Sidebar articles have further reading lists attached, and an extensive bibliographic essay follows the main text.

Zeman has produced a balanced, well-rounded chronology. Every effort has been made to capture the vast ethnic and cultural diversity that is so responsible for the region's unique flavor and character. *Chronology of the American West* is intended for everyone interested in the development of the West and is recommended for high-school, public, and academic libraries.

Subject Index

Italics indicate special features. Items that are followed by "Web" in parentheses are sites that were reviewed in Reference on the Web.

ACTIVISM
American Social Leaders and Activists.. 45
Citizen Action Encyclopedia. 50
Rebels and Renegades. 45

ADVERTISING
Advertisements Are Forever (Web). 24
Advertising Age Encyclopedia of Advertising. 73

AFRICA
Encyclopedia of Twentieth-Century African History. 98
Key Events in African History. 98

AFRICAN AMERICANS
100 Greatest African Americans. 93
African American Athletes. 76
African American Autobiographers. 88
African American Recipients of the Medal of Honor. 54
African American Years. 99
African Americans in the Performing Arts. 76
Black Firsts. 90
Harlem Renaissance. 86
Malcolm X Encyclopedia. 49
Zora Neale Hurston Companion. 88

AGING
Encyclopedia of Aging. 20

ALMANACS AND FACTBOOKS
Essential Desk Reference. 39
Financial Times World Desk Reference. 92
Just the Facts: A Look at Almanacs. 11

ANATOMY
Encyclopedia of the Human Body. 69
World of Anatomy and Physiology. 69

ANTARTICA
Antarctica. 93

ARCHAEOLOGY
Concise Oxford Dictionary of Archaeology. 94

ART
Outsider, Self Taught, and Folk Art Annotated Bibliography. 38
Painters & Prices (Web). 33

ARTISTS
African Americans in the Performing Arts. 76
Artists from Latin American Cultures. 73

ASIA
East Asia and the United States. 45
Encyclopedia of Modern Asia. 22

ASIAN AMERICANS
Asian American Playwrights. 87
Asian American Poets. 87

ASSASSINATIONS
Assassinations and Executions. 90
Back and to the Right (Web). 25
Encyclopedia of the JFK Assassination. 99

ASTRONOMY
Astronomy Encyclopedia. 64
Facts On File Space and Astronomy Handbook. 64

ATLASES
Atlas and Dictionary Update, 2003. 6

BIODIVERSITY
Life on Earth. 61
World Atlas of Biodiversity. 52

BIOGRAPHY
Another look at . . . Biography Resource Center. 19
Current Biography Illustrated. 93
Scribner Encyclopedia of American Lives: The 1960s. 94

BIOLOGY
Science of Everyday Things: Volume 3: Real-Life Biology. 61

BOTANY
American Horticultural Society Encyclopedia of Plants and Flowers. 72
Botanical Garden: Volume 1: Trees and Shrubs. 72
Botanical Garden: Volume 2: Perennials and Annuals. 72
Illustrated Encyclopedia of Trees. 67
Magill's Encyclopedia of Science: Plant Life. 67

BRIDGES
Encyclopedia of Bridges and Tunnels. 72

BUSINESS
Business Trailblazers. 7
Business: The Ultimate Resource. 51
Gale E-Commerce Soucebook. 59
World Consumer Lifestyles Databook. 58

CANADA
Canadian Reference Sources. 8
Oh Canada—Desktop Reference (Web). 32

CAREERS
Encyclopedia of Careers and Vocational Guidance. 51

CHEMISTRY
A to Z of Chemists. 65

CHINA
Political Leaders of Modern China. 97

CIVIL WAR
Language of the Civil War. 100
Library of Congress Civil War Desk Reference. 100

COMPUTERS
Computer History (Web). 27
Computer Science and Technology. 37
Computer Sciences. 37

COUNTRIES
Encyclopedia of the World's Nations. 90
Worldmark Encyclopedia of National Economies. 51

CRIME AND CRIMINAL JUSTICE
Encyclopedia of Juvenile Justice. 57
More Sites on Sleuths: Chicago Crime (Web). 31

CRYPTOZOOLOGY
Mysterious Creatures. 37

DEATH
Macmillan Encyclopedia of Death and Dying. 47
The Quick & the Dead (Web). 34

DICTIONARIES
American Heritage Dictionary for Learners of English. 59
American Heritage Student Science Dictionary. 62
Atlas and Dictionary Update, 2003. 6
Firefly Visual Dictionary. 59
McGraw-Hill Children's Dictionary. 60
McGraw-Hill Dictionary of Scientific and Technical Terms. 62
Oxford Dictionary of Word Histories. 60
Shorter Oxford English Dictionary. 60
Works in Progress: Defining a Dictionary. 17

DISASTERS
Floods, Fire, Famine—and Worse (Web). 28
Man-Made Catastrophes. 90

DRUGS
Drugs and Controlled Substances. 69
Drugs, Alcohol, and Tobacco. 70
Encyclopedia of Addictive Drugs. 70

EARTH SCIENCE
A to Z of Earth Scientists. 65
Science of Everyday Things: Volume 4: Real-Life Earth Science. 61
World of Earth Science. 65

EDUCATION
Encyclopedia of Education. 57
Encyclopedia of Learning Disabilities. 58
Higher Education in the United States. 58
Women in Higher Education. 58

ENCYCLOPEDIAS
Britannica Online School Edition. 40
Compton's Encyclopedia. 1
Encyclopaedia Britannica Online. 1
Encyclopaedia Britannica. 1
Encyclopedia Americana. 2
Encyclopedia Americana Online. 2
Grolier Multimedia Encyclopedia Online. 3
New Book of Knowledge. 3
New Standard Encyclopedia. 4
NewBook of Knowledge Online. 3
Van Nostrand's Concise Encyclopedia of Science. 62
World Book Encyclopedia. 4
World Book Online. 4

ENGLAND
Cassell's Companion to Eighteenth Century Britain. 96
Cassells' Companion to Twentieth Century Britain. 96
Oxford Companion to Twentieth Century British Politics. 97

ENVIRONMENT
Columbia Guide to Environmental History. 46
Environmental Encyclopedia. 57
Famous First Facts about the Environment. 57

EVOLUTION
Encyclopedia of Evolution. 66

EXTREMISM
Encyclopedia of Modern American Extremists and Extremist Groups. 49

FAMILY
International Encyclopedia of Marriage and Family. 47

FASHION
Contemporary Fashion. 74

FICTION
Christian Fiction. 80
Make Mine a Mystery. 84
Mammoth Encyclopedia of Modern Crime Fiction. 88
Reference Guide to Science Fiction, Fantasy and Horror. 38
Scouting for SF (Web). 34
Social Impact of the Novel. 84
Strictly Science Fiction. 39

103

Subject Index

FIRE
Encyclopedia of Fire. 56

FOLKLORE
South Asian Folklore. 59

FOOD AND DRINK
Cocktails in Cyberspace (Web). 26
Reference Sources on Beer. 13
Reference Sources on Wine. 14

FORENSIC SCIENCE
Encyclopedia of Forensic Science. 56

GENETICS
Genetics. 66

GEOGRAPHY
Geo-Data. 92
How Geography Affects the United States. 46

GOVERNMENT AND POLITICS
American Political Leaders. 99
CQ Electronic Library. 48
Dictionary of World Politics. 90
Guide to the Presidency. 53
Jewish Americans and Political Participation. 100
SYBWorld. 49
U.S. Constitution A to Z. 53
Worldmark Encyclopedia of the Nations: World Leaders. 92

GRAPHIC NOVELS
Graphic Novels (Web). 29

GUNS
Guns in American Society. 57

HARLEM RENAISSANCE
Harlem Renaissance. 86

HEALTH AND MEDICINE
American Heritage Stedman's Medical Dictionary. 68
Biographical Dictionary of Women Healers. 68
Biological Hazards. 70
Directory of Independent Ambulatory Care Centers. 56
Diseases. 71
Encyclopedia of Asthma and Respiratory Disorders. 71
Encyclopedia of Blindness and Vision Impairment. 56
Encyclopedia of Diabetes. 71
Encyclopedia of Skin and Skin Disorders. 71
Encyclopedia of the Brain and Brain Disorders. 69
Gale Encyclopedia of Mental Disorders. 71
Health Matters! 70
Patient's Guide to Medical Tests. 72
Women in Medicine. 69

HIKING
Historic Hiking Trails. 92

HISPANIC AMERICANS
Hispanic American Almanac. 99

HISTORY, AMERICAN
Chronological History of U.S. Foreign Relations. 50
Chronology of the American West. 101
Columbia Guide to the Vietnam War. 97
Dictionary of American History. 22
Encyclopedia of American History. 22
Encyclopedia of American War Heroes. 94
Historic Events for Students: The Great Depression. 99
Historical Atlas of the United States. 92
Lifetimes: The Great War to the Stock Market Crash. 100
Louisiana Purchase. 100
War of 1812. 97

HISTORY, ANCIENT
Ancient Rome in Cyberspace (Web). 25
Clay Tablets Go Digital (Web). 26
Encyclopedia of Ancient Egypt. 94
Encyclopedia of the Roman Empire. 95
Handbook to Life in Ancient Mesopotamia. 94
Sports and Games of the Ancients. 79

HISTORY, WORLD
Absolutism and the Scientific Revolution. 95
Dreyfus Affair. 97
Encyclopedia of the Enlightenment. 21
Great Events. 91
Greenwood Encyclopedia of International Relations. 50
Timelines of World History. 89

HOLOCAUST
Encyclopedia of Holocaust Literature. 82
Oryx Holocaust Sourcebook. 38

ISLAM
Islam (Web). 30

JUDAISM
New Encyclopedia of Judaism. 43

LATIN AMERICA
Artists from Latin American Cultures. 73
Encyclopedia of Latin American Politics. 49

LAW
Gale Encyclopedia of Everyday Law. 53
Landmark Decisions of the United States Supreme Court. 53
Legal Systems of the World. 52
Oxford Companion to American Law. 53

LIFE SCIENCE
Facts On File Dictionary of Biochemistry. 65
Facts On File Dictionary of Cell and Molecular Biology. 65
Student's Guide to Biotechnology. 73
World of Microbiology and Immunology. 66

LITERACY
Literacy in America. 44
New Dictionary of Cultural Literacy. 101

LITERARY MOVEMENTS
Literary Movements for Students. 83

LITERATURE, AFRICAN
Encyclopedia of African Literature. 81

LITERATURE, AMERICAN
American Writers Classics. 89
Encyclopedia of American Literature. 84
Great American Writers: Twentieth Century. 85
Zora Neale Hurston Companion. 88

LITERATURE, CHILDREN'S
Favorite Children's Authors and Illustrators. 82
Major Authors and Illustrators for Children and Young Adults. 84

LITERATURE, ENGLISH
British Writers Classics. 89
Thomas Hardy A to Z. 89
Twayne Companion to Contemporary Literature in English. 86

LITERATURE, GAY AND LESBIAN
Gay and Lesbian Literary Heritage. 82

LITERATURE, SPANISH
Feminist Encyclopedia of Spanish Literature. 89

LITERATURE, WORLD
Literature and Its Times. 83
Reference Guide to World Literature. 84

MAPS
Mapping the World. 66

MATHEMATICS
Dictionary of Quotations in Mathematics. 64
Real-Life Math. 64

MEXICO
Encyclopedia of Modern Mexico. 98
Mexico and the United States. 51

MIDDLE AGES
Medieval Jewish Civilization. 91
Sports and Games of Medieval Cultures. 76

MILITARY STUDIES
Air Warfare. 54
AmericanSubmarines. 54
Directory of Military Aircraft of the World. 54
Encyclopedia of the Navy Seals. 55
Ground Warfare. 54
Naval Warfare. 55

MOTION PICTURES
American Film Institute Desk Reference. 76
Baseball Filmography. 76
Biographical Dictionary of Silent Film Western Actors and Actresses. 77
British Film Institute Classics. 77
Edward G. Robinson Encyclopedia. 77
Encyclopedia of Ethnic Groups in Hollywood. 77
Europe of 1500-1815 on Film and Television. 38
Horror Films of the 1970s. 78

MULTICULTURALISM
Multicultural Rererence Center. 101

MUSIC
Chronology of Western Classical Music. 75
Country Music. 75
Encyclopedia of Contemporary Christian Music. 74
Haydn. 75
Oxford Companion to Music. 74
Women and Music in America since 1900. 74

MYTHOLOGY
Handbook of Egyptian Mythology. 44

NATIVE AMERICANS
Distinguished Native American Spiritual Practitioners. 44
This Day in North American Indian History. 98

NEW YORK
New York Year by Year. 101

ONLINE DATABASES
Another look at . . . Biography Resource Center. 19
ARBAonline. 37
Black Drama. 87
Britannica Online School Edition. 40
Columbia Guide to Digital Publishing. 40
Consulta. 41
CQ Electronic Library. 48
Critical Companions to Popular Contemporary Writers. 81
Current Biography Illustrated. 93
E-book Roundup. 10
Encyclopaedia Britannica Online.. 1
Encyclopedia Americana Online. 2
Grolier Multimedia Encyclopedia Online. 3
Lit Finder. 80
Multicultural Rererence Center. 101
NewBook of Knowledge Online. 3
Opposing Viewpoints Resource Center. 55
SYBWorld. 49
The Horn Book Guide Online. 39
Times Digital Archive. 41
World Book Online. 4

PEOPLES
Encyclopedia of the Stateless Nations. 91
People around the World. 46
Peoples of Europe. 95

PETS
Caring for Your Dog. 72
Dogs. 73

PHILANTHROPY
Notable American Philanthropists. 55

PHYSICS
Core Collection: Physics. 9
Facts On File Dictionary of Atomic and Nuclear Physics. 65

POETRY
Asian American Poets. 87
Bits and Bytes of Poetry (Web). 25
Contemporary American Women Poets. 87
Core Collection: Poetry. 10
Critical Survey of Poetry. 81
Thematic Guide to American Poetry. 39

POLITICAL SCIENCE
American Political Scientists. 48

POPULAR CULTURE
1910s. 101
Bowling, Beatniks, and Bell-Bottoms. 46
New Nation. 101
The Greenwood Guide to American Popular Culture. 47
Westward Expansion. 101

PROVERBS
Facts On File Dictionary of Proverbs. 41

PSYCHOLOGY
Magill's Encyclopedia of Social Science: Psychology. 42
Psychology. 42

PUBLISHING
Columbia Guide to Digital Publishing. 40
World Press Encyclopedia. 40

QUOTATIONS
Another look at . . . Bartlett's Familiar Quotations. 18
Dictionary of Quotations in Mathematics. 64

RELIGION
American Religious Leaders. 42
Great Popes through History. 42
Pilgrimage. 43
Religions of the World. 43

RENAISSANCE
Renaissance. 95
Renaissance and Reformation. 96

SCIENCE HISTORY
Chronology of Science. 61
History of Science. 63
Science in Everyday Life in America. 63
Science, Technology, and Society. 63

SCIENTISTS
A to Z of Chemists. 65
A to Z of Earth Scientists. 65
Nobel Scientists. 63
World Book Biographical Encyclopedia of Scientists. 64

SCOTLAND
Collins Dictionary of Scottish History. 96
Oxford Companion to Scottish History. 96

SHAKESPEARE
All Things Shakespeare. 88
Shakespeare's Words. 89

SOCCER
The Other Football (Web). 33
World Soccer Yearbook. 80

SOCIAL ISSUES
Current Issues. 47
Encyclopedia of Abortion in the United States. 56
Exploring Animal Rights and Animal Welfare. 41
Minority Rights in America. 50

SOCIAL SCIENCES
Dictionary of the Social Sciences. 44
Social Sciences: A Cross-Disciplinary Guide to Selected Sources. 39

SPACE SCIENCE
Facts On File Space and Astronomy Handbook. 64
Space Sciences. 61

SPANISH LANGUAGE MATERIALS
Consulta. 41
Reference Books in Spanish for Adolescents and Adults. 12

SPORTS
A to Z of Women in Sports. 78
African American Athletes. 76
Encyclopedia of North American Sports History. 78
Lives of Champions. 12
Olympic Century. 79
Scribner Encyclopedia of American Lives: Sports Figures. 79
Sports and Games of Medieval Cultures. 76
Sports and Games of the Ancients. 79
Sports Nicknames. 79
Women in Sports (Web). 35

TELEVISION
D'oh! Springfield on the Web (Web). 28
Encyclopedia of American Television. 77
Sitcom Factfinder. 78

TERRORISM
Encyclopedia of Terrorism. 45
Encyclopedia of World Terrorism. 45
Terrorism, 1996-2001. 91

THEATER
Asian American Playwrights. 87
Chronology of American Musical Theater. 75
Continuum Companion to Twentieth Century Theatre. 78

THESAURUSES
American Heritage Thesaurus for Learners of English. 59
Microsoft Encarta College Thesaurus. 60

THIRD REICH
History of the Third Reich. 97
Nazi Germany (Web). 31

UNITED NATIONS
Encyclopedia of the United Nations. 52
Encyclopedia of the United Nations and International Agreements. 52

URBAN STUDIES
Encyclopedia of Urban Cultures. 48

WEATHER
Oryx Resource Guide to El Nino and La Nina. 66

WOMEN
A to Z of Women in Sports. 78
A to Z of Women in World History. 93
Biographical Dictionary of Women Healers. 68
Contemporary American Women Fiction Writers. 87
Contemporary American Women Poets. 87
Women and Music in America since 1900. 74
Women in Higher Education. 58
Women in Medicine. 69
Women in Sports (Web). 35
Working Women. 16

WRITERS
Contemporary American Women Fiction Writers. 87
Encyclopedia of Pulp Fiction Writers. 88
Supernatural Fiction Writers. 84

ZOOLOGY
Firefly Encyclopedia of Insects and Spiders. 67
Firefly Encyclopedia of Reptiles and Amphibians. 67
Grzimek's Animal Life Encyclopedia: Birds. 21
Insects and Spiders of the World. 67
Reptiles and Amphibians. 68
World of Animal: Mammals. 68

Title Index

100 Greatest African Americans. 93
1910s. 101
A to Z of Chemists. 65
A to Z of Earth Scientists. 65
A to Z of Women in Sports. 78
A to Z of Women in World History. 93
Absolutism and the Scientific Revolution. 95
Advertisements Are Forever (Web). 24
Advertising Age Encyclopedia of Advertising. 73
African American Athletes. 76
African American Autobiographers. 88
African American Recipients of the Medal of Honor. 54
African American Years. 99
African Americans in the Performing Arts. 76
Air Warfare. 54
All Things Shakespeare. 88
American Film Institute Desk Reference. 76
American Heritage Dictionary for Learners of English. 59
American Heritage Stedman's Medical Dictionary. 68
American Heritage Student Science Dictionary. 62
American Heritage Thesaurus for Learners of English. 59
American Horticultural Society Encyclopedia of Plants and Flowers. 72
American Political Leaders. 99
American Political Scientists. 48
American Religious Leaders. 42
American Social Leaders and Activists. 45
American Writers Classics. 89
American Submarines. 54
Ancient Rome in Cyberspace (Web). 25
Another look at . . . Bartlett's Familiar Quotations. 18
Another look at. . .Biography Resource Center. 19
Antarctica. 93
ARBAonline. 37
Artists from Latin American Cultures. 73
Asian American Playwrights. 87
Asian American Poets. 87
Assassinations and Executions. 90
Astronomy Encyclopedia. 64
Atlas and Dictionary Update, 2003. 6
Back and to the Right (Web). 25
Baseball Filmography. 76
Biographical Dictionary of Silent Film Western Actors and Actresses. 77
Biographical Dictionary of Women Healers. 68
Biological Hazards. 70
Bits and Bytes of Poetry (Web). 25
Black Drama. 87
Black Firsts. 90
Botanical Garden: Volume 1: Trees and Shrubs. 72
Botanical Garden: Volume 2: Perennials and Annuals. 72

Bowling, Beatniks, and Bell-Bottoms. 46
Britannica Online School Edition. 40
British Film Institute Classics. 77
British Writers Classics. 89
Business Trailblazers. 7
Business: The Ultimate Resource. 51
Canadian Reference Sources. 8
Caring for Your Dog. 72
Cassell's Companion to Eighteenth Century Britain. 96
Cassells' Companion to Twentieth Century Britain. 96
Christian Fiction. 80
Chronological History of U.S. Foreign Relations. 50
Chronology of American Musical Theater. 75
Chronology of Science. 61
Chronology of the American West. 101
Chronology of Western Classical Music. 75
Citizen Action Encyclopedia. 50
Clay Tablets Go Digital (Web). 26
Cocktails in Cyberspace (Web). 26
Collins Dictionary of Scottish History. 96
Columbia Guide to Digital Publishing. 40
Columbia Guide to Environmental History. 46
Columbia Guide to the Vietnam War. 97
Compton's Encyclopedia. 1
Computer History (Web). 27
Computer Science and Technology. 37
Computer Sciences. 37
Concise Oxford Dictionary of Archaeology. 94
Consulta. 41
Contemporary American Women Fiction Writers. 87
Contemporary American Women Poets. 87
Contemporary Fashion. 74
Continuum Companion to Twentieth Century Theatre. 78
Core Collection: Physics. 9
Core Collection: Poetry. 10
Country Music. 75
CQ Electronic Library. 48
Critical Companions to Popular Contemporary Writers. 81
Critical Survey of Poetry. 81
Current Biography Illustrated. 93
Current Issues. 47
Cyclopedia of Literary Places. 81
Dictionary of American History. 22
Dictionary of Quotations in Mathematics. 64
Dictionary of the Social Sciences. 44
Dictionary of World Politics. 90
Directory of Independent Ambulatory Care Centers. 56
Directory of Military Aircraft of the World. 54
Diseases. 71
Distinguished Native American Spiritual Practitioners. 44

Dogs. 73
D'oh! Springfield on the Web (Web). 28
Dreyfus Affair. 97
Drugs and Controlled Substances. 69
Drugs, Alcohol, and Tobacco. 70
East Asia and the United States. 45
E-book Roundup. 10
Edward G. Robinson Encyclopedia. 77
Encyclopaedia Britannica Online. 1
Encyclopaedia Britannica. 1
Encyclopedia Americana. 2
Encyclopedia Americana Online. 2
Encyclopedia of Abortion in the United States. 56
Encyclopedia of Addictive Drugs. 70
Encyclopedia of African Literature. 81
Encyclopedia of Aging. 20
Encyclopedia of American History. 22
Encyclopedia of American Literature. 84
Encyclopedia of American Television. 77
Encyclopedia of American War Heroes. 94
Encyclopedia of Ancient Egypt. 94
Encyclopedia of Asthma and Respiratory Disorders. 71
Encyclopedia of Blindness and Vision Impairment. 56
Encyclopedia of Bridges and Tunnels. 72
Encyclopedia of Careers and Vocational Guidance. 51
Encyclopedia of Contemporary Christian Music. 74
Encyclopedia of Diabetes. 71
Encyclopedia of Education. 57
Encyclopedia of Ethnic Groups in Hollywood. 77
Encyclopedia of Evolution. 66
Encyclopedia of Fire. 56
Encyclopedia of Forensic Science. 56
Encyclopedia of Holocaust Literature. 82
Encyclopedia of Juvenile Justice. 57
Encyclopedia of Latin American Politics. 49
Encyclopedia of Learning Disabilities. 58
Encyclopedia of Literature and Science. 82
Encyclopedia of Modern American Extremists and Extremist Groups. 49
Encyclopedia of Modern Asia. 22
Encyclopedia of Modern Mexico. 98
Encyclopedia of North American Sports History. 78
Encyclopedia of Pulp Fiction Writers. 88
Encyclopedia of Skin and Skin Disorders. 71
Encyclopedia of Terrorism. 45
Encyclopedia of the Brain and Brain Disorders. 69
Encyclopedia of the Enlightenment. 21

Encyclopedia of the Human Body. 69
Encyclopedia of the JFK Assassination. 99
Encyclopedia of the Navy Seals. 55
Encyclopedia of the Roman Empire. 95
Encyclopedia of the Stateless Nations. 91
Encyclopedia of the United Nations. 52
Encyclopedia of the United Nations and International Agreements. 52
Encyclopedia of the World's Nations. 90
Encyclopedia of Twentieth-Century African History. 98
Encyclopedia of Urban Cultures. 48
Encyclopedia of World Terrorism. 45
Environmental Encyclopedia. 57
Essential Desk Reference. 39
Europe of 1500-1815 on Film and Television. 38
Exploring Animal Rights and Animal Welfare. 41
Facts On File Dictionary of Atomic and Nuclear Physics. 65
Facts On File Dictionary of Biochemistry. 65
Facts On File Dictionary of Cell and Molecular Biology. 65
Facts On File Dictionary of Proverbs. 41
Facts On File Space and Astronomy Handbook. 64
Famous First Facts about the Environment. 57
Favorite Children's Authors and Illustrators. 82
Feminist Encyclopedia of Spanish Literature. 89
Financial Times World Desk Reference. 92
Firefly Encyclopedia of Insects and Spiders. 67
Firefly Encyclopedia of Reptiles and Amphibians. 67
Firefly Visual Dictionary. 59
Floods, Fire, Famine—and Worse (Web). 28
Gale E-Commerce Soucebook. 59
Gale Encyclopedia of Everyday Law. 53
Gale Encyclopedia of Mental Disorders. 71
Gay and Lesbian Literary Heritage. 82
Genetics. 66
Geo-Data. 92
Graphic Novels (Web). 29
Great American Writers: Twentieth Century. 85
Great Events. 91
Great Popes through History. 42
Greenwood Encyclopedia of International Relations. 50
Grolier Multimedia Encyclopedia Online. 3
Ground Warfare. 54
Grzimek's Animal Life Encyclopedia: Birds. 21

Title Index

Guide to the Presidency. 53
Guns in American Society. 57
Handbook of Egyptian Mythology. 44
Handbook to Life in Ancient Mesopotamia. 94
Harlem Renaissance. 86
Haydn. 75
Health Matters! 70
Higher Education in the United States. 58
Hispanic American Almanac. 99
Historic Events for Students: The Great Depression. 99
Historic Hiking Trails. 92
Historical Atlas of the United States. 92
History of Science. 63
History of the Third Reich. 97
Horror Films of the 1970s. 78
How Geography Affects the United States. 46
Illustrated Encyclopedia of Trees. 67
Insects and Spiders of the World. 67
International Encyclopedia of Marriage and Family. 47
Islam (Web). 30
Jewish Americans and Political Participation. 100
Just the Facts: A Look at Almanacs. 11
Key Events in African History. 98
Landmark Decisions of the United States Supreme Court. 53
Language of the Civil War. 100
Legal Systems of the World. 52
Library of Congress Civil War Desk Reference. 100
Life on Earth. 61
Lifetimes: The Great War to the Stock Market Crash. 100
Lit Finder. 80
Literacy in America. 44
Literary Movements for Students. 83
Literature and Its Times. 83
Lives of Champions. 12
Louisiana Purchase. 100
Macmillan Encyclopedia of Death and Dying. 47
Magill's Encyclopedia of Science: Plant Life. 67
Magill's Encyclopedia of Social Science: Psychology. 42

Major Authors and Illustrators for Children and Young Adults. 84
Make Mine a Mystery. 84
Malcolm X Encyclopedia. 49
Mammoth Encyclopedia of Modern Crime Fiction. 88
Man-Made Catastrophes. 90
Mapping the World. 66
McGraw-Hill Children's Dictionary. 60
McGraw-Hill Dictionary of Scientific and Technical Terms. 62
Medieval Jewish Civilization. 91
Mexico and the United States. 51
Microsoft Encarta College Thesaurus. 60
Minority Rights in America. 50
More Sites on Sleuths: Chicago Crime (Web). 31
Multicultural Rererence Center. 101
Mysterious Creatures. 37
Naval Warfare. 55
Nazi Germany (Web). 31
New Book of Knowledge. 3
New Dictionary of Cultural Literacy. 101
New Encyclopedia of Judaism. 43
New Nation. 101
New Standard Encyclopedia. 4
New York Year by Year. 101
NewBook of Knowledge Online. 3
Nobel Scientists. 63
Notable American Philanthropists. 55
Oh Canada—Desktop Reference (Web). 32
Olympic Century. 79
Opposing Viewpoints Resource Center. 55
Oryx Holocaust Sourcebook. 38
Oryx Resource Guide to El Nino and La Nina. 66
Outsider, Self Taught, and Folk Art Annotated Bibliography. 38
Oxford Companion to Scottish History. 96
Oxford Companion to Twentieth Century British Politics. 97
Oxford Companion to American Law. 53
Oxford Companion to Music. 74
Oxford Dictionary of Word Histories. 60

Painters & Prices (Web). 33
Patient's Guide to Medical Tests. 72
People around the World. 46
Peoples of Europe. 95
Pilgrimage. 43
Political Leaders of Modern China. 97
Psychology. 42
Real-Life Math. 64
Rebels and Renegades. 45
Reference Books in Spanish for Adolescents and Adults. 12
Reference Guide to Science Fiction. Fantasy and Horror. 38
Reference Guide to World Literature. 84
Reference Sources on Beer. 13
Reference Sources on Wine. 14
Religions of the World. 43
Renaissance. 95
Renaissance and Reformation. 96
Reptiles and Amphibians. 68
Science in Everyday Life in America. 63
Science of Everyday Things: Volume 3: Real-Life Biology. 61
Science of Everyday Things: Volume 4: Real-Life Earth Science. 61
Science, Technology, and Society. 63
Scouting for SF (Web). 34
Scribner Encyclopedia of American Lives: Sports Figures. 79
Scribner Encyclopedia of American Lives: The 1960s. 94
Shakespeare's Words. 89
Shorter Oxford English Dictionary. 60
Sitcom Factfinder. 78
Social Impact of the Novel. 84
Social Sciences: A Cross-Disciplinary Guide to Selected Sources. 39
South Asian Folklore. 59
Space Sciences. 61
Sports and Games of Medieval Cultures. 76
Sports and Games of the Ancients. 79
Sports Nicknames. 79
Strictly Science Fiction. 39

Student's Guide to Biotechnology. 73
Supernatural Fiction Writers. 84
SYBWorld. 49
Terrorism, 1996-2001. 91
The Greenwood Guide to American Popular Culture. 47
The Horn Book Guide Online. 39
The Other Football (Web). 33
The Quick & the Dead (Web). 34
Thematic Guide to American Poetry. 39
This Day in North American Indian History. 98
Thomas Hardy A to Z. 89
Timelines of World History. 89
Times Digital Archive. 41
Twayne Companion to Contemporary Literature in English. 86
U.S. Constitution A to Z. 53
Van Nostrand's Concise Encyclopedia of Science. 62
War of 1812. 97
Westward Expansion. 101
Women and Music in America since 1900. 74
Women in Higher Education. 58
Women in Medicine. 69
Women in Sports (Web). 35
Working Women. 16
Works in Progress: Defining a Dictionary. 17
World Atlas of Biodiversity. 52
World Book Biographical Encyclopedia of Scientists. 64
World Book Encyclopedia. 4
World Book Online. 4
World Consumer Lifestyles Databook. 58
World of Anatomy and Physiology. 69
World of Animal: Mammals. 68
World of Earth Science. 65
World of Microbiology and Immunology. 66
World Press Encyclopedia. 40
World Soccer Yearbook. 80
Worldmark Encyclopedia of National Economies. 51
Worldmark Encyclopedia of the Nations: World Leaders. 92
Zora Neale Hurston Companion. 88